On the **Duty** and **Power** of Architectural Criticism

On the Duty and Power of Architectural Criticism

Kenneth Frampton Philippa Tumubweinee
Ruth Verde Zein Zheng Shiling

Elias Constantopoulos Manuel Cuadra
Fernando Diez Hélène Jannière Li Xiangning
Robert McCarter Valerio Paolo Mosco
Louise Noelle Gras Şengül Öymen Gür
Xing Ruan Paolo Scrivano Ana Tostões

Carolina Chaves Błażej Ciarkowski
Carlos Eduardo Comas Marcos Almeida
paolo conrad-bercah Cláudia Costa Cabral
Özlem Erdoğdu Erkarslan Murat Burak Altınışık
Mustafa Batu Kepekçioğlu Jasna Galjer
Christophe van Gerrewey Berna Göl
Kristen Harrison Martin Hartung
Morten Birk Jørgensen Kevin Low
Konstantinos Petrakos Jaime Solares
Alexandra Staub Horacio Torrent
Konstantinos Tsiambaos Caroline Voet
Lynnette Widder Seda Zafer

Editor Wilfried Wang

Credits

This book is published following the International Conference on Architectural Criticism held online on October 9, 10, 16, and 17, 2021.

Scientific Committee	Elias Constantopoulos, University of Patras
	Manuel Cuadra, Director of CICA, Universidad Nacional de Ingenieria, Lima
	Fernando Diez, Chief Editor of Summa+, Universidad de Palermo, Buenos Aires
	Hélène Jannière, Université Rennes 2
	Li Xiangning, Tongji University, Shanghai
	Robert McCarter, Washington University, St. Louis
	Valerio Paolo Mosco, Istituto Universitario die Architettura di Venezia
	Louise Noelle Gras, Universidad Nacional Autónoma de México
	Şengül Öymen Gür, Beykent Üniversitesi, Istanbul
	Xing Ruan, Shanghai Jiao Tong University
	Paolo Scrivano, Politecnico di Milano
	Ana Tostões, Instituto Superior Técnico, Lisboa
	Ruth Verde Zein, Universidade Presbiteriana Mackenzie, São Paulo
Supporting Institutions	CICA International Committee of Architectural Critics; Hellenic Institute of Architecture, Athens
Sponsorship	O'Neil Ford Centennial Chair in Architecture, The University of Texas at Austin
	CICA International Committee of Architectural Critics
	Beykent Üniversitesi, Istanbul Hellenic Institute of Architecture, Athens
	Instituto Superior Técnico, Lisboa
	Istituto Universitario Architettura Venezia Shanghai Jiao Tong University
	Tongji University, Shanghai
	Universidade Presbiteriana Mackenzie, São Paulo
	Universidad Nacional Autónoma de México
	Universidad Nacional de Ingeniería, Lima
	University of Patras
	Washington University, St. Louis
Editor	Wilfried Wang
Co-editors	Trenton A. Sexton, João Navarrete
Copy Editors	Dean Drake, Lisa Schons, Trenton A. Sexton, João Navarrete, Wilfried Wang
Proofreader:	Colette Forder
Graphic Design	Sabine Hahn, www.sh-gd.de
Typeface	Neue Haas Grotesk, Christian Schwartz
Paper	GalaxiArt Samt
Image Processing, Printing, and Binding:	DZA Druckerei zu Altenburg GmbH, Thuringia
© 2022	The University of Texas at Austin, the editor and Park Books AG, Zurich
© 2022	For the essays, the authors
© 2022	For the images, the photographers/copyright owners, see image captions

All rights reserved; no part of this book may be reproduced, stored in a retrieval system or transmitted in any form of by any means, digital, electronic, mechanical, photocopying, recording or otherwise, without the prior written consent of the publisher.

Park Books is being supported by the Federal Office of Culture with a general subsidy for the years 2021–2024.

Park Books
Niederdorfstrasse 54
8001 Zurich
Switzerland
www.park-books.com

ISBN 978-3-03860-271-2

Table of Contents

Introduction

On the Duty and Power of Architectural Criticism	*Wilfried Wang*	10
An Outline of Architectural Criticism	*Wilfried Wang*	13
The Power to Behold	*Louise Noelle Gras*	18
For a Historiography of Architectural Criticism	*Hélène Jannière, Paolo Scrivano*	22
The Architect as Critic	*Elias Constantopoulos*	30
Architectural Curation: A Practice of Architectural Criticism	*Li Xiangning, Mo Wanli, Zhang Ziyue*	38
Translating Scale from Models to Buildings	*Fernando Diez*	46
In the Absence of Appropriateness: On the Need to Respect and Sustain Existing Places in Making Additions	*Robert McCarter*	58
In Praise of Urban Continuity: Siza's Re-creation of the Chiado	*Ana Tostões*	68

1 Origins and Approaches

Architectural Criticism and the Politics of Architecture	*Kenneth Frampton*	80
A Critique of Building Construction: Tactics of "Resistance" in Pikionis's Acropolis Works	*Kostas Tsiambaos*	84
Paradigms of Design and Deep Readings: The Creative Emancipation of Critical Building Analysis	*Caroline Voet*	94
The Dominant Paradigm We Call Design	*Kevin Low*	106
Truth Content: SANAA's Rolex Learning Center	*Christophe van Gerrewey*	116

2 High Culture in Conflict

The End of Architectural Criticism?	*Zheng Shiling*	126
Niemeyer Do(o)med: Remembrances of Planes Past	*Carlos Eduardo Comas, Marcos Almeida*	132
"The New MoMA": Architectural Criticism, 1979–2019	*Martin Hartung*	142
On Lina Bo Bardi's Iconography: Three Drawings	*Cláudia Costa Cabral*	152
Imported Starchitect in a Local Market	*Seda Zafer*	162

3 Criticism and Its Effects

The Role of Architectural Criticism in the Design
of Twenty-first-century History Surveys
Ruth Verde Zein — 172

Architectural Criticism in the Space
for the Unexpected
Jasna Galjer — 180

Aphaeresis and Urban Policies
Konstantinos Petrakos — 192

Nineteen Verdicts on the Viking Ship Hall
Morten Birk Jørgensen — 200

Architectural Criticism on Post-World War II
Collective Housing:
    Complicity in a Historical Prejudice?
Carolina Chaves — 212

4 Explicit Criticism

Architectural Criticism in the Emergent
Urbanscapes of the Global South
Philippa Tumubweinee — 224

"The Lightest Parliament in the World":
    Hans Schwippert's Bundeshaus (1949)
Lynnette Widder — 234

Whose Architecture? Whose Criticism?:
    Applying Stakeholder Theory to the Process of Criticism
Alexandra Staub — 244

The Lost Battle for Memory:
    The European Solidarity Centre in Gdańsk and
    Architectural Criticism in Poland
Błażej Ciarkowski — 254

The New Istanbul Museum of Painting and Sculpture
as a Case for Multi-perspectival Criticism in Contemporary
Turkish Architecture
*Özlem Erdoğdu Erkarslan,
Burak Altınışık, Batu Kepekcioğlu* — 262

5 Critical Reflections

Critical Misfortune, Canonical Narratives,
and the Failure of the Practical Sense:
    The UN-ECLAC Building in Santiago de Chile
    by Emilio Duhart (1960–1966)
Horacio Torrent — 274

Critical Influence:
    The Influence of the Popular Architectural
    Critic on Architectural Decision-making
Kristen Harrison — 284

In Search of the Latent Kairos of Architectural Form
paolo conrad-bercah — 292

The Squatting of Technology:
    A Twofold Continuum
Berna Göl — 302

The Architecture of Redemption:
    A House on the Periphery of the Discipline
Jaime Solares Carmona — 310

Introduction

On the Duty and Power of Architectural Criticism
Introduction

Wilfried Wang

Architectural Criticism in the Twenty-first Century

While the global construction industry has continued to produce new buildings at a high rate, the proportion of them that might be considered by both architectural critics and interested lay observers to be of a high design quality has been considerably lower. Yet, for buildings to contribute to the goal of sustainability, they not only must be well built but also need to be embraced by the communities and users that they purport to serve. Sustainability is not reducible to just a technical question; it must also provide enduring aesthetic delight in order to be organically rooted in a given culture.

Parallel to this continued high rate of production in the building industry, there have been momentous changes in the media. Printed matter, whether in the form of widely available daily newspapers or specifically distributed professional journals, is on the wane. There are fewer full-time architectural critics writing for these media now than there were at the turn of the millennium. The growth of online platforms has, alas, not led to an increase in profound and well-written architectural criticism. On the contrary: given the overwhelming productivity of the construction industry, most websites engaged in the mediation of new projects do not and cannot commission critics to analyze the quality of the published buildings. Instead, they rely on the descriptions provided by the submitting architects. For a requisite fee paid by the architects, a more prominent placement at the top of the home page of an architectural website will increase exposure. These practices are leading to an architect-funded self-promotion. Coupled with the demise of printed media in general, the eclipse of architectural criticism in the online media does not bode well for independent criticism.

In this context, the idea of holding an international conference on the duty and power of architectural criticism—conceived before the effects of the global Covid-19 pandemic—with the endorsement of the Conference of International Architectural Critics (CICA) and numerous universities across the world, was to encourage current and future generations of architectural critics to reflect on the state of architectural criticism. Interested contributors were asked to address central challenges: Should architectural criticism be enlightening? Should it help in the creation of a better built environment? Is there a factual basis to it? Does it have a duty to present evidence in the evaluation of a building? Or should it simply take on what architects say about their designs? Should architectural criticism define best practices? Does it wield the power to dictate who is in and who is out?

Architectural criticism, like all human endeavors, is at a crucial juncture. While serious architecture struggles for recognition, much so-called architectural criticism is merely a poorly paid, decorative legitimation for hyperbolic practice. Incisive criticism is rare, while the definition of criticism itself has become opaque. The conference and this book seek to define the purposes and methods of architectural criticism. What should be the ethical basis of architectural criticism? Can it be objective in the context of paid content? Should it outline ideal practices? Each submitted abstract was to address either the duty or the power of architectural criticism, in either case offering the analysis of one existing building.

One hundred and five submissions were received following the international call for abstracts at the beginning of 2021. In a double-blind peer review conducted by members of the international Scientific Committee, thirty-two abstracts were selected to continue to the second phase, and from these developed versions, sixteen were invited to present short papers to the four-session online conference in October 2021. Each session was opened by a keynote lecture. All presentations and discussions were recorded and placed on YouTube.[1] The timing of each session was set to allow for live online participation across the globe: from Asia to the Americas. In contrast to a conference held in a single physical place, then, the online conference not only saved financial resources but also avoided unnecessary flying around the globe. Of course, as participants we all regret not being able to enjoy the informal encounters that are offered during in-person conferences, but given the pandemic situation, this online format provided a true alternative. Most importantly, the conference was timed in such a way that discussions were comparatively numerous and long. These discussions

[1] **International Conference on Architectural Criticism 2021:**

First Session, October 9, Origins and Approaches: https://www.youtube.com/watch?v=Hc0inZrkJtw;
Second Session, October 10, High Culture in Conflict: https://www.youtube.com/watch?v=d_3d50k4Ga8;
Third Session, October 16, Criticism and Its Effects: https://www.youtube.com/watch?v=r43cmo27lYQ
Fourth Session, October 17, Explicit Criticism: https://www.youtube.com/watch?v=Tgr6z-RNq6o.

are available on YouTube. For this book, a further editorial process was undertaken, and a number of Scientific Committee members were inspired by the conference to contribute essays of their own to this publication.

Following an outline of architectural criticism, there are essays by the CICA cofounder Louise Noelle Gras on the invaluable in-person experience of buildings; by Hélène Jannière and Paolo Scrivano on the recent history of architectural criticism; by Elias Constantopoulos on two prominent cases of architects as writer-critics; by Li Xiangning, Mo Wanli, and Zhang Ziyue on the curation of architectural exhibitions as a critical activity; by Fernando Diez on the skills required to translate scales from architectural model to reality; by Robert McCarter on the loss of the sense of appropriateness in some recent prominent architectural projects; and by Ana Tostões on Alvaro Siza's respect for history as a prerequisite for ensuring the continuity of the urban fabric.

The subsequent four sections are edited versions of the conference contributions: **1.** "Origins and Approaches" gathers presentations on core questions of design, construction, and architectural language; **2.** "High Culture in Conflict" assembles reviews of museum designs; **3.** "Criticism and Its Effects" discusses the power of public criticism in deciding the fate of buildings; and **4.** The section "Explicit Criticism" provides paradigmatic evaluations of puplic buildings in three continents. Section **5**, titled "Critical Reflections," complements the spectrum of the four previous sections with additional penetrating analyses.

On behalf of the organizers, I would like to thank the many colleagues who have participated in the realization of the conference and this publication. My thanks go to the O'Neil Ford Endowment for financing these enterprises; Nadja Otto and Josette Lehman at the School of Architecture, The University of Texas at Austin, for their administrative help; Trenton A. Sexton and João Navarrete for their assistance in the conference organization and their extensive editorial collaboration; the members of the Scientific Committee for their intense scrutiny of the submitted abstracts and their active participation in chairing the conference sessions; the associated universities that supported the conference in distributing the call for abstracts; Louise Noelle Gras and Manuel Cuadra from the board of CICA for their support and guidance; Thomas Kramer and Lisa Schons from Park Books for their personal involvement; Dean Drake for the meticulous copyediting; Sabine Hahn for the careful graphic design; and the keynote lecturers, conference speakers, and authors of this collective effort. All of us hope that the readers of this book will find answers to the questions that the conference raised at the outset.

Biography

Wilfried Wang
Born in Hamburg, studied architecture in London; with Barbara Hoidn, founder of Hoidn Wang Partner in Berlin. Taught at the PNL, UCL, ETH Zürich, Harvard University, UT Austin, and Universidad de Navarra. Foreign member of Kungliga Konstakademien, Stockholm; member of the Akademie der Künste, Berlin; honorary doctorate from the KTH Stockholm; honorary member of the Ordem dos Arquitectos, Portugal.

An Outline of Architectural Criticism

Wilfried Wang

Criticism: the Obverse of Design

Architectural criticism is as much an act of creation as is architectural design. In a way, it reverses the design process by viewing the designed project, analyzing its parts, and deducing the underlying intentions. The latter is necessary especially in cases in which there is little communication from the designers with regard to their underlying intentions. By "underlying intentions" is meant all intentions, including social and cultural ones. Frequently, architects express goals regarding cultural and ethical value systems, economic costs, and technological performance, or they speak generally about the design's generating metaphors. Architectural criticism should be able to assess to what extent these aspects of value systems, costs, technological performance, generating metaphors, etc. are factually realized in the designs.

Beyond this comparative assessment, architectural criticism should also uncover the unspoken, suppressed, or even unintentional qualities of a design. Architectural criticism is thus concerned with the context in which intentions are effectively translated into reality or not. As such, architectural criticism is interested in finding the degree of truth present in the realization of conceptions, intentions, propositions, or theses into objectively analyzable, factual, physical materialization. Thus, while the individual act of architectural criticism concerns itself with a singular instance of design from conception to realization, a collection of architectural criticisms reveals the ethical stance that this body of built work constitutes as well as represents.

Architectural criticism is essential in enabling architects and the general public to evaluate architectural designs, preferably ahead of their realization. In the context of the broader debate on sustainability, buildings need to achieve a long-lasting overall design quality that includes the broadest level of public acceptance as a means by which interest, care, and maintenance become cultivated. Architectural criticism thus requires both a comprehensive approach to the political and physical context, design conception, and material realization of a built phenomenon and a precise, concise, incisive analysis of these issues themselves. The following is an outline of a method that encompasses description, analysis, and evaluation. Architectural criticism, at its best, should be neither exhaustive nor exhausting, but rather an act of synthesis, thus paralleling the act of design.

The Need to Understand and Judge Buildings

As the era of rapid and conspicuous consumption comes to an end, and civilization faces the challenges of adapting its lifestyles to mitigate the effects of the climate crisis, the opportunities to construct new buildings should be taken with the requisite earnestness. It is no longer acceptable to compromise the quality of a building by following the conventional shortcut toward immediate gratification and ignoring the core Vitruvian tenets that a building should exhibit the qualities of *firmitas*, *utilitas*, and *venustas*, or when translated into contemporary terms: sustainability, adaptability, and aesthetic delight.

We need to understand how buildings succeed or fail to be sustainable, adaptable, and appreciated. While all buildings are superficially the same—they are all made of matter, they stand up, provide shelter, have facades, contain spaces on the inside—some buildings last longer than others, some are more flexible and adaptable than others, and some are more carefully designed and assembled than others and are therefore more appreciated by users and observers.

Before buildings come into existence, it is possible to evaluate their constitutive qualities, their likely overall design quality (as defined above), and their impact on society and the environment. Some of a building's aspects can be objectively assessed (e.g., life-cycle analysis), others relatively compared, and others still subjectively gauged. The person undertaking this analysis of a design on paper needs to be practiced in the reading of written and drawn documents, and to possess a well-developed sense of spatial and material imagination to compensate for the absence of real space and form.

Once realized, buildings are incontrovertible physical evidence, leading an existence distinct from spoken or written words, drawings or photographs. Therefore, regardless of what critics, politicians, clients, architects, and others might claim about buildings, their real presence in a specific physical and cultural context can be analyzed and evaluated independently from such statements. Conscientious architectural research is therefore publicly transparent, scientifically analytical, and independently verifiable—in short: forensic, according to the Latin origin of the word.

However, rather than investigating buildings in their pathological or criminal dimensions—some buildings indeed possess these; for example, mass housing schemes in conjunction with their occupational regimes—the goal of any research into buildings is to identify their sociocultural ambitions, their contribution to the architectural discourse, and their architectural achievements. Research should uncover a building's character of reality.[2] What is meant by this is the identification of the embodied intentions: How would the world be constituted and represented if only all buildings were designed and built along the same lines as the building under investigation? Every building expresses a worldview, whether consciously or not.

At a basic, quotidian level, we need to understand buildings because we need to ensure that buildings reach an overall minimum design quality. In simple technical terms, most societies have planning regulations and building codes. At the most ambitious level, we should expect that buildings constitute and represent our social and cultural aspirations. We should strive for buildings to be appropriate for their tasks and to accommodate normal needs, while some should rise above this to celebrate communal values; some buildings need only be comfortably modest, others should inspire and become symbols of a period and a society.

However, the sad reality is that few people are concerned with questions of architectural quality. Neither politicians nor clients, nor even the majority of so-called architects, are interested in this issue. If they were, there would be better buildings in the world.

We need to understand buildings, because we need to design and build better buildings. We need a differentiated understanding of buildings, because we need to know when, where, and how to apply our knowledge. As diverse as society is, as varied as our needs are, and as specialized as the activities in our settlements are, we need to design buildings appropriately in response to each of these conditions. That means not every building should be an icon. We want to learn from buildings, so that we can instill in those interested in designing and building an awareness of what is appropriate, a sense of quality as well as an idea of the scope of what has been achieved and what might be possible.

Built Reality

Buildings create reality; they create facts. This reality is not only spatial and physical but also bears intentions and meanings. Buildings can consist of symbols; they can also be symbols themselves.

[2] Dagobert Frey, "Zur Wissenschaftlichen Lage der Kunstgeschichte," in *Kunstwissenschaftliche Grundfragen: Prolegomena zu einer Kunstphilosophie* (Vienna: Rudolf M. Rohrer Verlag, 1946), 96–101.

Buildings are objects in a context, they are "figures" against a "ground." They differentiate themselves from the context and from other buildings. The act of differentiation is spatial and physical and can be read in terms of the underlying intentions and meanings.

At the level of a building's components, a wall differentiates between two sides; further, an enclosure defines an interior and an exterior. The factual clarity of such spatial and formal divisions establishes social and cultural values. A wall between two groups of people can be used to separate these two groups. An enclosure around a group of people can protect as well as control, even incarcerate, them.

The way such walls or enclosures are constructed and the way that such constructions appear—whether the walls are made of massive materials or of different layers with an outer, visibly decorative surface—can be analyzed and evaluated in relation to their actual intentions and perceived meanings.

The way that a given building constitutes intentions and meanings can be compared to the way it actually represents these intentions and meanings. However, just as in any other form of human expression, what is truly intended in a built expression is not necessarily what can be observed on its surface. For example, some architects like to describe their designs with metaphors. The terms *rue corridor* or *streets in the air* were used by architects to evoke richer associations than the reality they were able to create. The phrases were coined to blur what was built rather than to precisely describe how the designed spaces really perform. A *rue corridor* inside an apartment building is not a street, since it is not a public space nor is it connected to a network of streets. The mismatch between an intention, stated in a phrase such as *rue corridor*, when analyzed, reveals the rhetorical device.[3] In this case the phrase is a hyperbolic metaphor.

So, the rhetorical devices themselves, by which buildings mediate between the constitution of a physical and spatial presence and the representation of a sociocultural context or value system, are subject to analysis. Any building analysis can be both exhaustive and subject to selective examination at junctures where indicative or characteristic revelations provide the key to the comprehensive understanding of the whole.

[3] Rhetorical figures of composition and of conception.

Buildings as Primary Evidence

In the way that buildings create facts, they offer themselves to be analyzed and evaluated through their prima facie composition. Understanding buildings relies on observers looking at the physical evidence before them. Built reality supersedes spoken or written discourse. Built reality is primary evidence.

Describing and Analyzing Buildings

Facts require description before they can be analyzed. The focus of this method is the description and evaluation of the connections between the physical manifestation of a built edifice on the one hand and its sociocultural significance, as well as its spatial and formal qualities, on the other hand. Any building can therefore be described in terms of its formal and spatial components and overall composition. In acquiring information on the building's context, both physical and sociocultural, it becomes possible to deduce the building's significance, its impact on the sociocultural context, and the contribution it makes to the wider architectural discourse.[4]

[4] In the development of this descriptive and analytical method, the greatest impact was made by Paul Frankl's *Das System der Kunstwissenschaft* (Brünn and Leipzig: Rudolf M. Rohrer Verlag, 1938), given its structural clarity and its comprehensive definition of art theoretical terms. The morphological variables were derived from Frankl.

Differentiation: Figure Against Ground

The factual basis of any phenomenon resides within the difference it establishes in contrast to a context. Its recognizability depends on its degree of differentiation from its context or background. Similarly, the joint between two objects or the abrupt change in direction on a surface permits a distinction to be made. In other words, articulations permit parts to be identified. Buildings are assemblies of parts and each articulation can be recognized for the syntactic and semantic meaning it contributes toward the overall statement.

Basic Relationships: Parts to Wholes

Buildings consist of parts that are composed into wholes, which in turn can become elements of even larger wholes. For example, a wall could consist of blocks, a group of walls could enclose a space. Buildings are understood by examining the material and spatial composition of parts to wholes.

Architectural Relationships: Morphological Categories of Building Components

The activity of building has structured the way all societies think about its components and the resultant wholes. There are five morphological categories to the composition of buildings that are logically related by way of a hierarchical, telescopic concatenation:

1. Constructional
2. Tectonic
3. Compartmental
4. Configurational
5. Contextual

Assembling elements of the constructional category renders wholes, which in turn become elements of the tectonic category, and so on.

Buildings Constituting the World

On the basis of understanding buildings as primary evidence, the aim of any building analysis and evaluation is to further understand the building's implicit or explicit intentions and effective contributions to the making or shaping of the world. Which elements of a building adhere to convention and which intend to reform or advance contemporary practice? How do buildings support or contradict the status quo? To what extent does a building or its parts change common practice, conventional patterns of use, or entire lifestyles? Is the designer's claim of being innovative justified or is it simply just another bold but unsubstantiated assertion, if not a downright item of fake news?

Architecture as a Conscious Act of Building

The goal of understanding buildings is to identify their ambitions and their contributions to the discourse, their achievements as part of the culture of building. Insofar as buildings are recognizably making a conscious contribution to building culture, they can be considered pieces of architecture.

Qualities of a Building

Qualities are compared against criteria. For example, if the life expectancy of a building material is known, its interplay with other elements, when properly detailed, can ensure that a building component meets that maximum life expectancy. The long-term endurance—*firmitas*—of a building material and a building component can be considered a desirable, positive quality. The durable quality of a material or component can be measured objectively: it is an *immanent* quality. The designer's choice for a specific period of endurance can be assessed by an external observer in terms of both immanent requirements and subjective preferences.

To give another example, the different uses that a building can accommodate over its existence are limited, but could nevertheless be relatively large in range. *Utilitas*, the way that spaces in a building can ideally, comfortably, or merely adequately accommodate use patterns, is a *relative* quality. Further, buildings possess different degrees of flexibility based on the constructional system's adaptability and the spatial typology. A building's flexibility is a quality that is also objective, inherently defined by the building's morphological constitution as well as by its designers' ability to imagine change.

Similarly, the way that people feel protected in a space, to the way that a building is seen to harmonize with its context, go beyond functional fitness and touch on psychological and atmospheric sensations. While the shapes of spaces and forms, even resultant atmospheres, can be described objectively, their evocation of beauty—*venustas*—is *subjective* and varies from individual to individual.

Design Quality

Given that buildings consist of different components and intentions, it is possible to evaluate the quality of each component and intention in relation to the contribution a building makes both toward the whole and toward the cultural context. A building has a high level of design quality if on the one hand the compositional and intentional relationships of the parts to the components and to the whole are logically coherent, mutually reinforcing, and spatially and formally integrated, and if on the other hand the building fulfills the designers' stated or implied intentions. Such intentions can be as abstract or theoretical as designers might like; no building is exempt from being analyzed on its own as a built fact. The quality of a design, of a building, as a singular term is a synthetic judgment.

Outlook

In the context of climate change, the 2003 essay "Sustainability is a Cultural Problem"[5] makes the case that measures against climate change will need to begin with redefining cultural ideals, and that sole reliance on innovative technology will lead to failure. Subsequently, the 2020 essay "Site-Specificity, Skilled Labor, and Culture: Architectural Principles in the Age of Climate Change"[6] argues that for architecture to become sustainable, it needs to embrace principles that ensure an immediate connectedness between regional resources and craft construction techniques to contribute toward a lasting and stable regional culture. It is a summary reckoning with the failures of technocratic modernism, and a plea for an architecture in the coming age of climate change that acknowledges the unique qualities of place, the creative role of skilled labor, and the need for the presencing of physically constructed culture—as opposed to placeless virtuality—as the matrix for our existence.

[5] Wilfried Wang, "Sustainability is a Cultural Problem," *Harvard Design Magazine*, no. 18, spring/summer 2003, 1–3.

[6] Wilfried Wang, "Site-Specificity, Skilled Labor, and Culture: Architectural Principles in the Age of Climate Change," in *Modern Architecture and the Lifeworld: Essays in Honor of Kenneth Frampton*, ed. Karla Cavarra Briton and Robert McCarter (London: Thames & Hudson, 2020), 53–63.

The Power to Behold

Louise Noelle Gras

fig. 1
Kandariya Mahadeva Hindu Temple, 1003–1035, Khajuraho, India.
General view in the archaeological site. Photo: Louise Noelle Gras.

"Criticism must be one-sided, passionate, political, that is, made from an exclusive point of view, but from the point of view which opens up the most horizons."[1]

Charles Baudelaire

The French poets and literati of the second half of the nineteenth century established a new approach to art through the critique of the works of the artists of their time. Not only did they fight for those who pushed the boundaries of visual expression, they also knew how to assess the quality of their contributions and placed them at the center of the debate. We are talking about the combative lucidity of Charles Baudelaire and Émile Zola, as well as the committed proposals of Stéphane Mallarmé, among others. They were the witnesses of their time, seeing firsthand the works that many disqualified and writing about them in order to redeem their slighted creators. In short, they were the spectators of the moment, teaching us that analysis always comes from being a direct observer of the creative act.

At that time too, photography, as an instrument in support of the visual, was laying its foundations; it was both a recording tool and a new form of artistic expression in its own right. However, it is essential to point out that, as a mechanism of examination, photography should neither displace nor be a substitute for direct observation of the work of art. It goes without saying that the same must be true when the analysis concerns an architectural work. Given that the photographer creates a new visual re-creation of the reality they are facing, and if the architectural critique is based on their images, the authenticity of the architectural work is in danger of being lost.

For this reason, it is necessary to emphasize that a visit to a building is indispensable when conducting a responsible and profound analysis. Let us remember that one of the leading architecture critics of the last century, Bruno Zevi, affirmed the importance of this approach, which was present in the very title of his best-known book, *Architecture as Space. How to Look at Architecture*.[2] It is logical that this historian's proposals for approaching the architecture of the modern movement and its spatial concepts have an intrinsic relationship with the gaze.

Between 1984 and 1986, in collaboration with Carmine Benincasa, Zevi published three volumes in the collection *Comunicare l'Architettura*, which are named: *1. Venti Monumenti Italiani*; *2. Venti Complessi Edilize Italiani*; and *3. Venti Spazi Aperti Italiani*.[3] In this case, the significance is not only in the works selected or in the undoubted quality of the edition, but in the interest of the editors of the series to effectively "communicate architecture." To achieve this, they indicate in the preface that architecture, unlike the visual arts, requires a "bio-psychic" participation—which is why it is essential to make a journey through the edifices in question with a pre-established reading and a substantial set of questions. Thus, the architectural critic is faced with the problem of finding a method or a system as a way of profoundly and intimately understanding an edifice, not just an approximation.

Unlike with music or literature, there is as yet no modern means of reliably conveying architecture; that is why communication through critical writing is essential, and photographs, plans, and other documents can help in this task. While this information will never be as enriching as a personal visit, it is of unquestionable assistance for those who wish to "read" a work of architecture.

[1] Charles Baudelaire, "À quoi bon la critique?," Salon 1846, Paris, 1846. "La critique doit être partiale, passionnée, politique, c'est-à-dire faite à un point de vue exclusif, mais au point de vue qui ouvre le plus d'horizons."

[2] Bruno Zevi, *Architecture as Space. How to Look at Architecture* (New York: Horizon Press, 1957). Published originally as *Saper vedere l'architettura* (Torino: Einaudi, 1948).

[3] Published yearly by Edizioni SEAT, Societa Elenchi Ufficiali Abbonati al Telefono, in Torino.

fig. 2
Kandariya Mahadeva Hindu Temple, 1003–1035, Khajuraho, India. Detail. Photo: Louise Noelle Gras.

Initially, anyone seeking to convey their opinions or criticism of a building or landscape should prepare a series of questions to which they will seek to respond in their text. It is clear that a critic must have documents on the object in question to support the research undertaken. The direct confrontation with the work, a "bio-psychic" journey, an analysis in situ alone provides direct contact with the architecture set in its physical and cultural environment; in this sense, it is understood that the site and the moment of the work in question must play a fundamental role in the interested party's keen gaze.

Once in the presence of the edifice, its appearance and function will further arouse the curiosity of the analyst; this curiosity will uncover novel elements that are at the very basis of the selection of the building. Such a close reading challenges the systems of transmission and knowledge of architecture, going well beyond a beautiful photograph or a mechanical opinion.

In a certain way, following Baudelaire's revealing opening words, we can add from him that "the best critique is funny and poetic, not cold and algebraic, which, under the pretext of explaining everything, has neither hatred nor love, and voluntarily sheds all kind of temperament."[4] A fundamental task, the one pointed out by the poet, where criticism will be nothing other than the reflection of the work it deals with.

Throughout time, those who have been interested in culture and art have taken to visiting the masterpieces in situ; the lessons of a Grand Tour or the much coveted residence of the Prix de Rome attest to these travails. However, if it is not possible to visit in person, then images and publications, videos, or virtual tours may serve as a substitute for the real experience. These are approximations of the object in question, in which the passionate narration of those who have studied and visited it will be of much assistance.

Undoubtedly, architectural critics should go beyond the barrier of available information, selecting with care the foundations for their evaluations, but most importantly they should engage with the object of their concern. The commitment to carefully see architecture in context and detail brings about the energy provided by a visit, the richness acquired through a sensible observation and wealth of the power to behold. No amount of photos can replicate the emotion felt when entering the Pantheon, how the spatial sensation isolates the visitor from the multitude. In Angkor Wat, it is the overwhelming impression felt when approaching the site that will accompany the exploration of its richly decorated corridors. The marvel of overpowering detail in the temples of Khajuraho, the gardens and the warm weather, cannot be captured in an image. A visit to Luis Barragán's house will endow you with silent sensations, a personal immersion in serenity and beauty. The daring command of the addition to the Morgan Library by Renzo Piano provides an irreplicable lesson of respect and creativity. The power and energy of Le Corbusier's Chapel at Ronchamp cannot be enclosed in a sketch

[4] Charles Baudelaire, "À quoi bon la critique?" "La meilleure critique est celle qui est amusante et poétique ; non pas celle-ci, froide et algébrique, qui, sous prétexte de tout expliquer, n'a ni haine ni amour, et se dépouille volontairement de toute espèce de tempérament."

or an illustration. These visual memories will be present in and accompany countless critics and researchers, as they become observers and witnesses of the might and the seduction of architecture.

In sum, architectural critics, in addition to providing theoretical support and a conscientious study of their project, must necessarily visit the object of their criticism. The analysis of the structure and its materials provides an essential constitutive angle that is accompanied by the sensation of space and the tactility of the finishes and is enriched by the observation of the environment and its relationship with the interior. Thus nuances, subtle differences, and gradations arise in the appreciation of the architectural object, where perceptions and concepts are refined and integrated into the analysis. The wealth of knowledge thus acquired by the critical observer will be added to their research to provide a text that, by being enriched, will radiate to whoever receives it.

fig. 3
Luis Barragán, roof terrace of the Barragán House, Mexico City.
Photo: Louise Noelle Gras.

fig. 4
Le Corbusier, south entrance, Chapelle Nôtre Dame du Haut, Ronchamp.
Photo: Louise Noelle Gras.

fig. 5
Interior of the Pantheon, Rome.
Photo: Louise Noelle Gras.

fig. 6
Detail of the dome of the Pantheon, Rome. Photo: Louise Noelle Gras.

fig. 7
Bruno Zevi, *Venti monumenti italiani*, vol. 1, Edizioni SEAT, Rome, 1984.

Biography

Louise Noelle Gras is a professor at the Instituto de Investigaciones Estéticas of the Universidad Nacional Autónoma de México. Involved in many aspects of architectural history and criticism as co-founder and director of the Comité International des Critiques d'Architecture, CICA, member of the Arts Academy, and honorary academician of the Sociedad de Arquitectos Mexicanos. Contributor to numerous architectural journals, and author of various books on Mexican and Latin American twentieth-century architecture.

For a Historiography of Architectural Criticism

Hélène Jannière and Paolo Scrivano

Introduction

Since the 1980s, art historians have succeeded in giving a solid structure to the history of art criticism as a research field. Their studies on the protagonists of art criticism, on the relations of criticism to the art market, and on the vectors of criticism have consolidated methodological approaches and historical interpretations. Before then, from the 1960s onward, art criticism had been a subject of research for sociologists[1] and social historians.[2] More recently, cultural history has also begun to tackle the issue of art criticism and its actors. Conversely, the scholarship on architectural criticism and its history seems not to have developed in the same manner, nor as deeply. In striking contrast, and perhaps even paradoxically, the discourse on architectural criticism has been centered on the idea of its supposed "crisis."

Whether authored by architects, by critics, or by specialists and scholars, many of the recent contributions to architectural criticism seem to complain about its apparent demise.[3] Such a negative assessment of criticism's condition may stem from a sense of weakness and lack of efficacy, as well as from a perceived distance from the architectural discipline and from the specific tools of design. This widespread perception about the presumed "poor" quality of current criticism, or about its inadequacy with regard to the needs of architectural design and practice, constitutes a significant part of the recent abundance of texts on architectural criticism.[4] This phenomenon is not completely original. From the beginning of the twentieth century onward, on the one hand specialized journals had denounced the "weakness" of architectural criticism, its ineffectiveness with respect to improving the quality of the built environment, and its failure to reach a broader audience (in contrast with art, theater, or film criticism in the general press); on the other hand, they have underlined the lack of a theoretical basis in relation to architecture considered as a discipline. But interest in architectural criticism has dramatically increased since the 1990s. During the past three decades, roundtables and symposia, special issues of journals, editorials, and blog posts have revealed a growing concern for criticism and its current state. In parallel, some scholars began to explore the "conundrums of architectural criticism."[5] However, before becoming the subject of scholarly studies, criticism was mostly an object of polemics and controversies, focusing on, for example, the interference of criticism with communication campaigns, its dependence on architects or on contracting authorities, and—last but not least—the loss of its values and the fading of its aesthetic and political commitments. This recent attention on criticism often reveals a nostalgia for a "golden age" of architectural criticism, when the "heroic" critic or the *critique engagé* were committed to avant-garde groups or architects. In this regard, many commentators have emphasized that the passing of eminent "historian-critics" belonging to the generation of the 1960s to the 1980s (including individuals such as Peter Collins, Reyner Banham, Giulio Carlo Argan, and Manfredo Tafuri) has not led to them being adequately replaced. The absence, or at least the rarity, of clear-cut theoretical positions in the contemporary architectural debate is sometimes invoked as both a reason for and a consequence of this "crisis" of criticism.

Thus, finding a path to build a history of criticism entails taking into account the peculiarity of this "difficult" object, which reveals rather blurred boundaries with other forms of writing on architecture, mainly history and theory, and which may equally have close ties with disciplines such as aesthetics and philosophy. A review of the state of the discipline demonstrates that the history of architectural criticism—considered as a specific field—has so far experienced relatively little development:[6] as German historian Klaus Jan Philipp has put it, writing the history of architectural criticism "in the very sense of the term" is almost equal to a "Herculean work."[7] One reason for this might be that since architectural criticism appears to be a sort of elusive object, writing its history should first and foremost depart from a clear definition of the object itself. As a matter of fact, most of the "histories of architectural criticism" consist of histories of architectural theories, where the word "criticism" is associated with large corpora of texts. In Italy, for example, studies of art criticism have initially descended from a long tradition established by scholars such as Lionello Venturi (who in 1936 dedicated a marginal part of his *History of Art Criticism* to contemporary architecture) and, in more recent times,

[1] Raymonde Moulin, *The French Art Market: A Sociological View* (New Brunswick and London: Rutgers University Press, 1987). Originally published as *Le marché de la peinture en France* (Paris: Minuit, 1967).

[2] Cynthia A. White and Harrison C. White, *Canvases and Careers: Institutional Change in the French Painting World* (London and New York: Wiley, 1965).

[3] Numerous special issues of journals testify to this sense of crisis; for example, the dossier by Catherine Slessor, "Who Needs Architecture Critics?," *Architectural Review*, no. 1408 (June 9, 2014); Stephen Games, "Where are All the Critics?," *Architects' Journal* 237, no. 11 (March 18, 2013), 51–54; and, among many other posts in the electronic press and blogs, Vanessa Quirk, "The Architect Critic Is Dead (Just Not for the Reason You Think)," *ArchDaily*, April 6, 2012, https://www.archdaily.com/223714/the-architect-critic-is-dead-just-not-for-the-reason-you-think.
The Strange Death of Architectural Criticism by Martin Pawley is one of the numerous examples of such complaints about the "current state" and the so-called "crisis" of architectural criticism. See Martin Pawley, *The Strange Death of Architectural Criticism: Martin Pawley Collected Writings* (London: Blackdog Publishing, 2007).

[4] For an extensive survey and analysis of these texts, see Hélène Jannière, *Critique et architecture: un état des lieux contemporain* (Paris, Éditions de la Villette: 2019).

[5] Trevor Boddy, "The Conundrums of Architectural Criticism," in *Critical Juncture: Joseph Rykwert Royal Gold Medal and CICA 2014 International Committee of Architectural Critics*, eds. Louise Noelle and Sara Topelson de Grinberg (Mexico City: CICA – Docomomo, 2014), first published in Mohammad Al-Asad and Majd Musa, eds., *Architectural Criticism and Journalism: Global Perspectives*. Aga Khan Award for Architecture (Turin: Allemandi, 2006) and then in Trevor Boddy, "The Conundrums of Architectural Criticism" and "Op Arch Continued," in "Criticism in Architecture," special issue, *Journal of Architectural Education* 62, no. 3 (February 2009): 8–9, 94–100.

[6] Jannière, *Critique et architecture*.

[7] Klaus Jan Philipp, *Architekturtheorie und Architekturkritik in Deutschland zwischen 1790 und 1810* (Stuttgart and London: Menges, 1997), 63.

Gianni Carlo Sciolla.[8] According to this tradition, the history of art criticism was the history of theories permitting the evaluation of art. This conception of criticism encompassing a historical approach partially shaped the discourse on architectural criticism until the 1980s. Thus, in the Italian debate, "criticism" came to include a broad array of definitions. Despite their titles openly evoking criticism (like in the case of Renato De Fusco's *Storia della critica da Viollet-le-Duc a Persico* and Renato De Fusco and Cettina Lenza's *La critica da Rogers a Jencks*[9]), writings belonging to this stream focused more on the history of architectural theories or, more precisely, on a history of ideas about architecture rather than on criticism both as a practice and as a genre of text.

In the context of North American historiography, Peter Collins has been among the first authors to try to define criticism and to advance a possible typology of it.[10] Attributing a central role to judgment and its criteria, in *Changing Ideals in Modern Architecture* (1965) and then in *Architectural Judgement* (1971) Collins advocated for a criticism rooted in the discipline, and not descending from art or literary criticism—for him, the influence of the art criticism of the salons and of the literature on architectural criticism produced during the late eighteenth and the nineteenth centuries was one of the factors behind the decline of architectural criticism and judgments.[11] Interestingly, Collins's conceptions of criticism did not really influence mainstream North American architectural criticism, which on the one hand concentrated on the "public" or "lay" criticism of newspapers and magazines and, on the other, on academic or "learned" criticism developed in theoretical magazines. Following the latter tendency, in many "History, Theory, and Criticism" departments in American universities the term "criticism" has been given the meaning of critical theory.

In light of such a variety of diverging conceptions of criticism, one can realize how difficult the writing of its history can prove. It was for these reasons that the research project and international network of scholars, Mapping Architectural Criticism, was founded in 2015 at the University of Rennes.[12] One of Mapping Architectural Criticism's goals has been to chart the variety of discourses on architectural criticism, and the various definitions given to it in different cultural and intellectual contexts. Such a "cartography" is a crucial step in constructing the history of criticism, since upon the definition of criticism depends also the construction of the narratives of its history. The project's ambition has been to write a history of criticism that is neither a history of architectural theories, as in the case of the Anglo-American histories of criticism, nor a history of ideas or of judgments about architecture, as has been the case in the Italian historiographical tradition since the times of Lionello Venturi.

The task of architectural historians is hardly to express observations on the current state of criticism. From the standpoint of history, criticism should be the object of scholarly investigation, taking into account its multiple intersections with several fields of research more or less close to mainstream architectural history, such as the history of professional journals, the historiography of architecture, and the intellectual biographies of historians and critics.

Architectural Criticism as a Subject of Research

As a starting point, solid scholarship of architectural criticism should choose to analyze the elements that facilitate its circulation and consolidation, what one could call the actors and the vehicles of criticism. These terms can be used to refer to both the agents of criticism—such as the critics, the architects, the historians, the book publishers, the photographers, and the institutions dealing with architecture—and the media through which criticism is disseminated—for example, the press, photography, and exhibitions. Historical research should aim at expanding knowledge about the specific functions of these actors and their networks, outlining at the same time their mutual relationships, and highlighting the links between the actors, the media of criticism, the historical contexts within which they are materialized, and the cultural, intellectual, and institutional milieus from which they originate.

The notion of "actor" of architectural criticism not only encompasses critics or authors (the notion of "authorship" in criticism might be subject to question) but also includes

[8] Lionello Venturi, *History of Art Criticism* (New York: Dutton, 1936); Gianni Carlo Sciolla, *La critica d'arte del Novecento* (Turin: UTET, 1995).
[9] Renato De Fusco, *L'idea di architettura. Storia della critica da Viollet-le-Duc a Persico* (Milan: Edizioni di Comunità, 1964); Renato De Fusco and Cettina Lenza, *Nuove idee di architettura. La critica da Rogers a Jencks* (Milan: Etas, 1991).
[10] Peter Collins, "The Philosophy of Architectural Criticism," *AIA Journal* 49, no. 1 (January 1968): 46–49.
[11] Peter Collins, *Changing Ideals in Modern Architecture, 1750–1950* (Montreal: McGill University Press, 1965); idem, *Architectural Judgement* (Montreal: McGill-Queen's University Press, 1971).
[12] Mapping Architectural Criticism is both an international research project and an international network of architectural and art historians, founded and coordinated by Hélène Jannière and Paolo Scrivano. It aims to investigate the history of architectural criticism along several axes of research, according to different definitions of the subject, and utilizing a variety of methodological approaches. Additional information can be found at: https://mac.hypotheses.org/about-the-project.

professional and academic institutions and the various specialists who are involved in the actual production of professional outlets that deal with the architectural subject. The historian's aim should be to scrutinize the profile and the "professional" specificity of the critic, who is neither a historian nor a theorist necessarily, since defining such a profile on the basis of a corpus restricted to architectural historians and theorists appears in many ways too narrow an approach. Instead, a productive approach should promote the investigation of a broader range of critics, whose writings are sometimes limited to newspapers or architectural magazines and who have been until now largely overlooked by architectural historiography. The goal should be twofold: on the one hand, to cast light on more "ordinary" criticism; on the other hand, to question the role of the critic, delineating the often-overlapping boundaries between their activity and status and those of other "architectural writers." The history of architectural criticism should indeed cast light on the kind of competencies that the critic shares with other "writers" (such as the historians, the theorists, the social scientists), the specificities of the critic's practice, and the extent to which this practice might earn the definition of "profession." In this sense, historical research should not only be limited to the analysis of works by critics as "authors" but also include studies dealing with the activities of publishers, owners of journals, and, perhaps to a lesser extent, photographers and graphic designers. A history of criticism should also take into consideration the actors and the practices of other forms of criticism, such as radio broadcasts or television programs, in their interactions with architectural criticism. Last but not least, research should consider the role played by the editorial boards of architectural publications and the scientific committees in patronizing specific forms and contents of criticism and in influencing editorial choices.

Additionally, proper attention should be given to the role played by institutional actors. Several professional associations (such as the American Institute of Architects in the US or the Royal Institute of British Architects in the UK) and academic institutions have over time played a significant role in supporting, controlling, or publishing architectural journals. The extent to which these institutions have fostered criticism or, in some specific cases, have even hindered it is open to question. Nevertheless, the influence on the forms, discourses, and contents of criticism on the part of specific types of journals, from daily newspapers to cultural magazines and building construction periodicals, remains unquestionable. Such an approach would help to reanalyze the binaries that recurrently describe the so-called typologies of criticism, such as learned versus popular, professional versus layman, formalist versus technical, and so forth. In this way, one would arrive at properly delineating the relation linking types of publication (daily newspapers, cultural magazines, political magazines, or professional periodicals) to the statuses of the critical discourse—and at understanding the extent to which publications and target readerships influence or create specific forms of criticism.

Equally important would be to stress the role played by the "new media," from online magazines to blogs and social media, in shaping the panorama of contemporary architectural criticism. By modifying the status of the discourse on architecture, and by influencing the circulation or reproduction of texts and images, these new media go beyond being simple vehicles of criticism since they also contribute to producing and fostering specific forms of it: in this respect, their role remains to be deciphered. In fact, numerous aspects characterizing the working operations of these emerging media are largely ignored, such as the extent and size of their audiences; specifically, whether these media reach a broader or different public than the one to which traditional newspapers and magazines are geared or whether they offer to this public a better access to professional or specialized debates. At the same time, the kind of interrelation they have with the sphere of public debate is still to be adequately determined. It is worth noting that these emerging media highlight once again the recurrent opposition of learned criticism versus popular criticism, whatever the conceptual limits of these two notions might be.

Similar considerations can be extended to the image as a possible medium for criticism. Photography and, more generally, all other types of visual *apparati* are just a different vehicle of architectural criticism. Since the 1980s, the history of architectural photography has been largely developed by historians of photography as well as by architectural historians, with a peculiar emphasis on the aestheticizing of architecture through these media.[13] Drawing on the notions of publication and "publicity," conceptualized by Hélène Lipstadt and by Beatriz Colomina respectively, some scholars have then focused on the role played by photography in the mediation of architecture.[14] More recently, the material and visual characters of architectural books and periodicals have begun to be analyzed using approaches borrowed from visual studies.[15] It is from this corpus of studies that a possible definition of "vehicle" of architectural criticism can be drawn. Beyond the pure "indexical" value exploited by operative criticism of the avant-garde movements, photography can be considered a specific form of architectural criticism.[16] However, architectural "visual criticism" still deserves a proper definition. Not limiting their investigations to professional periodicals, architectural historians should additionally focus on the role played by photography and other visual components of the production of specialized publications (from graphic design to typographic setting) in the construction of a critical reading of architecture.

Architectural Criticism and Public Debate

Two additional aspects on which architectural history should concentrate are, firstly, the relationship existing between architectural criticism and the notion of "public opinion"—the "public realm"—and, secondly, criticism conceived as an autonomous discourse, internal to architectural theories and history. This entails considering criticism not merely as a body of historical, theoretical, or philosophical texts on architecture, but rather as a discipline encompassing diverse protagonists, media, and international exchanges. It also implies challenging an existing tendency to see the reception of architecture in the specialized or public debate as a mere passive "reflection" of the building or project.

Addressing the theme of architectural criticism and public debate proves crucial if one wants to clarify the definitions of criticism and better understand the overlapping boundaries between criticism per se and other types of writings and discourses on architecture and the built environment. Criticism came to be historically defined as a literary genre and as a form of judgment in parallel to the emergence during the eighteenth century of a space for public discussion, as Reinhart Koselleck's 1959 publication *Kritik und Krise* made evident.[17] Since the 1980s, art historians or specialists in aesthetics have noted the coincidence between the development of art criticism and the presence of spaces for public debate, the latter conceived in Habermasian terms.[18] Similarly, Richard Wittman has grounded his analysis of the formation of a "public discourse on architecture" precisely in the concept of the public sphere.[19] Several other scholars have discussed the interactions between art discourse and the public sphere.[20] The questions on the table are whether a similar debate can be transposed to the realm of architecture, and whether the intersection with the public sphere gradually disappears once criticism is intended as a disciplinary discourse, mostly relying on architectural history and theories.

A number of questions concerning what could be called the frontiers of architectural criticism follow from these assumptions. The first is whether architectural criticism shares themes, protagonists, and media with the public debate or whether it maintains an almost exclusive relation to the professional and academic spheres. If the latter is the case, it would become necessary to ascertain if architectural criticism pertains to an autonomous disciplinary discourse or if it refers to extra-disciplinary concepts. Given the changeable nature of its autonomy, one should reflect on the extent to which architectural criticism remains separated from social uses, architectural design practices, and economic production. The second question concerns the relation between architectural criticism and its public, and whether an architectural criticism that is aimed at general audiences can be separated

[13] Andreas Haus, "Photogenic Architecture," *Daidalos*, no. 66 (December 1997): 82–91.

[14] Beatriz Colomina, *Privacy and Publicity: Modern Architecture as a Mass Media* (Cambridge and London: MIT Press: 1994); Hélène Lipstadt, "Architectural Publications, Competitions and Exhibitions," in *Architecture and Its Image: Four Centuries of Architectural Representation*, ed. Eve Blau and Edward Kaufman (Montreal: Canadian Centre for Architecture, 1989), 109–37.

[15] Anne Hultzsch and Catalina Meija Moreno, "Introduction: Building Word Image, a New Arena for Architectural History," *Architectural Histories* 4, no. 1 (2016): 13, http://doi.org/10.5334/ah.220.

[16] Andrew Higgott and Timothy Wray, eds., *Camera Constructs: Photography, Architecture and the Modern City* (Farnham and Burlington, VT: Ashgate, 2012).

[17] Reinhart Koselleck, *Kritik und Krise. Eine Studie zur Pathogenese des bürgerlichen Welt* (Freiburg and Munich: Karl Albert, 1959).

[18] Jürgen Habermas, *Strukturwandel der Öffentlichkeit. Untersuchungen zu einer Kategorie der bürgerlichen Gesellschaft* (Neuwied: Luchterhand, 1962), trans. as *The Structural Transformation of the Public Sphere: An Inquiry into a Category of Bourgeois Society* (Cambridge, MA: MIT Press, 1989).

[19] Richard Wittman, *Architecture, Print Culture, and the Public Sphere in Eighteenth-Century France* (Abingdon and New York: Routledge, 2007).

[20] Thomas Crow, *Painting and Public Life in Eighteenth-Century Paris* (New Haven, CT: Yale University Press, 1984); Sylvia Lavin, "Re-reading the Encyclopedia: Architectural Theory and the Formation of the Public in Late-Eighteenth-Century France," *Journal of the Society of Architectural Historians* 53, no. 2 (1994): 184–92, https://doi.org/10.2307/990891.

from criticism geared toward a specialized public. This question relates to the possibility of identifying a relation between types of publication (daily newspapers, cultural magazines, political journals, professional periodicals, etc.) and statuses of the critical discourse, and to the capacity on the part of publications and target readerships to influence or create specific forms of criticism. The relation between architectural criticism and public opinion can be variously discussed; for example, through its connection to the judgment and to the criteria of evaluation of architecture, and through its association to the supposed "crisis" of criticism. Investigating the means by which critics intend to reach various layers of the public and how they connect their discourse to those layers, as well as examining the discourse on "architectural judgment" in the debates on architectural criticism, should be one of the historian's main tasks.

Committed Criticism and Its Place in History

In a 1995 article on the renewal of architectural criticism, French architect and critic Bernard Huet referred to Charles Baudelaire's definition of art criticism as necessarily being—in the poet's words—"partial, impassionate, political."[21] During the 1990s, perhaps as a reaction to the 1980s, when in many specialized publications architectural criticism was identified as "communication" or even as a form of promotion of architects and architectures, a widespread nostalgia for a notion of criticism associated to the historical avant-gardes emerged. Through this "committed" criticism, or through a "politicized" one, it was possible to emphasize the critic's influential and active role in discovering, promoting, and intellectually supporting groups of artists or architects. This resulted in the spread of the idea of an idyllic past time for criticism, occasionally being associated with the end of the nineteenth century, the 1920s, and the 1960s and 1970s.

On the one hand, the figure of a "committed" critic might be linked to the art and architecture avant-gardes from the end of the nineteenth century onward, hence defining a privileged relationship between the critic, artist, and architect; on the other hand, "politicized" criticism can be characterized as understanding architectural and city phenomena in political terms. The historian should also address a series of key questions in relation to these themes. One relates to the way definitions of "committed" and "politicized" criticism converge toward or differ from the notion of "operative" criticism, in the various meanings that have been attributed to it since Manfredo Tafuri's use of the term in the fourth chapter of his *Teorie e storia dell'architettura*.[22] Other questions concern the theoretical tools, the rhetorical constructions, and the intellectual and political references of "committed" and "politicized" criticism and whether the latter should necessarily be bound to the author's proximity to a party or political group. Historical scholarship on architectural criticism should unveil the main modes of circulation of this type of criticism (specialized periodicals, journals, targeted actions), clarify the degree to which "politicized" criticism influences architecture's historical narrative, and highlight the nature of the interlacements and convergences of criticism's intellectual and artistic engagement and its political commitment.

The Intellectual Territories of Architectural Criticism and "Other" Forms of Criticism

Another important issue to be addressed by historians is the "geography" of architectural criticism; that is, the boundaries and territories that the latter has shared with other disciplines since the last decades of the nineteenth century. Here, the overlap with different kinds of architectural writing, in particular with that pertaining to architectural history and theory, but also with texts stemming from disciplines as diverse as sociology, anthropology, and philosophy, is at stake. Such an approach should help highlight the relationships, the terrains, and the conceptual tools that architectural criticism has in common with other genres of criticism, such as art, music, film, and literary criticism. The term "boundary" is used here to denote the zones of exchange and confrontation between criticism, history, theory, and

[21] Bernard Huet, "Les enjeux de la critique," *Le Visiteur* 1 (fall 1995): 88–97.

[22] Manfredo Tafuri, *Teorie e storia dell'architettura* (Bari: Laterza, 1968), 161–93, trans. as *Theories and History of Architecture* (London: Granada, 1980). In this work, Tafuri put forward the concept of "operative criticism," attempting to seize the relations between criticism and design. He defined—and implicitly condemned—operative criticism as "analysis of architecture" intended to "design" a precise poetical aim. In spite of the degree of miscomprehension that characterized their circulation, Tafuri's views soon emerged as the definitive guide to the role and the duties of architectural criticism; they would later be rejected by a new generation of historians and critics.

other types of writing on architecture, as well as between architectural criticism and other forms of criticism, while the term "territory" primarily refers to the various disciplinary fields on which criticism relies and from which it borrows its concepts and patterns of interpretation, as well as its intellectual tools.

Defining the nature of criticism—that is, outlining its boundaries, designating its tasks, and determining its object (the techniques, programs, forms, constructive solutions, or social uses of architecture)—has been variously attempted, in past and recent times. Many of those who have tried to give a clearer definition of criticism seem to have often failed to get past the preliminary question concerning its disciplinary frontiers and its perimeter, thus illustrating the semantic uncertainty that surrounds the term.[23] This uncertainty does not simply concern the question of where criticism ends and parallel disciplines begin: the definition of "architectural criticism," in fact, indicates at once a profession (if one refers to the critics and their activity), a set of social practices, or a discourse on architecture within academic institutions—with a wide range of disciplinary orientations (history, aesthetics, sociology, anthropology, to name only a few fields). Moreover, architectural criticism encompasses multiple registers of discourse, from manifestoes to aesthetic analyses, architectural descriptions, and technical specifications. Architects and architectural critics, for example, put forward the specific nature of architecture—a multifaceted endeavor involved in economic, technological, social, and urban practices—to explain the difficulty of setting the boundaries of architectural criticism and itemizing its modes of writing. Indeed, defining the frontiers and delineating what criticism includes largely depends on the adopted disciplinary standpoints. Moreover, the frontiers and the perimeter of criticism vary from one cultural context to another. Charting these orientations, registers of discourse, and sets of activities might thus constitute a way to provide a first overview of architectural criticism's disciplinary territories. For example, one could determine whether criticism borrows parts of its concepts and patterns of interpretation, modes of description, and schemes of narration from other better-defined or more "canonical" types of architectural writing (like architectural history and theory), or whether it intersects with precise domains of knowledge (like sociology or anthropology). The abovementioned term "territory" equally relates to the boundaries and frontiers that criticism shares with other fields of knowledge and artistic expression. For instance, it might be worth questioning the opposition between two distinct conceptions of architectural criticism, one as "a type of criticism" and the other as an autonomous or disciplinary discourse. Peter Collins emphasized this opposition by stating that architectural criticism is ". . . an activity which must be considered *sui generis*" and exclusively linked to architecture rather than "a species or aspect of a general activity called 'criticism.'"[24]

Architectural critics have already underlined the possible links between architectural criticism and literary criticism—"the source and mold of all other forms of criticism," in the words of Yorgos Simeoforidis.[25] Espousing a parallel with literary criticism, though, came with the rejection of any possible analogy with art criticism, a rejection based on a truism: architecture cannot be reduced to a form of visual art, given the multiple frameworks (aesthetic, technical, social, economic) it encompasses. On the other hand, architects and architectural critics often emphasized the similarities between the fields of architecture and music, or architecture and cinema. Starting from this assumption, they were more willing to compare architectural criticism with music or film criticism. The extent to which such parallelisms are based on shared notions and rhetorical or theoretical tools remains open to debate, since the commonalities between fields need to be adequately assessed. From a historical perspective, similarities and overlaps deserve proper scrutiny and this might be possible only through the interaction with specialists of criticism of art, music, film, and literature, in order to delineate possible relationships.

All in all, the goal of historians should be to interrogate the multiple definitions of architectural criticism, without giving any prescriptive or normative definition of what "good" or "real" criticism might or should be. This objective can be reached by starting from different

[23] Among others: Deborah K. Dietsch, "Architectural Criticism: How the Media Mediates," *CRIT, The Architectural Student Journal*, no. 9 (spring 1981): 13; Frédéric Pousin, "Aperçus sur la critique architecturale," *Espaces et sociétés*, no. 60/61 (March 1992): 61–72; Agnès Deboulet, Rainier Hoddé, and André Sauvage, *La Critique architecturale. Questions – frontières – dessins* (Paris: Éditions de La Villette, 2008); Alexandra Lange, *Writing about Architecture: Mastering the Language of Buildings and Cities* (New York: Princeton Architectural Press, 2012). For an extensive review of these tentative typologies, see Jannière, *Critique et architecture.*

[24] Collins, "The Philosophy of Architectural Criticism."

[25] Yorgos Simeoforidis, "Adrift," *Lotus*, no. 92 (May 1992): 137–38.

cultural and geographical standpoints, in an attempt to sketch a vast set of definitions of criticism, closely related to various cultural and intellectual traditions. Considering this and the conditions outlined above is just one of the passages necessary to construct a cultural history of criticism in architecture.

Biographies

Hélène Jannière is professor of history of contemporary architecture at Rennes 2 University. After several publications on the architecture periodicals of the twentieth century (*Politiques éditoriales et Architecture moderne*, 1923–1939, Paris, 2002 and *Architectural Periodicals in the 1960s and 1970s*, CCA, IRHA, Montreal, 2008, co-edited with France Vanlaethem and Alexis Sornin), her current research focuses on architectural and urban criticism in France in the 1950s to 1980s. Among her main publications on this topic: *Critique et architecture: un état des lieux contemporain* (*Criticism and Architecture: a Contemporary State of Affairs* Paris, 2019); in 2009, with Kenneth Frampton, the special issue of *Les Cahiers de la recherche architecturale et urbaine,* "La critique en temps et lieux." With Paolo Scrivano, she recently co-edited a special number of *CLARA / Architecture + Recherche,* devoted to "Architectural Criticism and Public Debate," as well as an issue of the journal *Histories of Postwar Architecture* entitled: "Committed, Politicized, or Operative: Figures of Engagement in Criticism from 1945 to Today". She is currently the scientific coordinator, together with Paolo Scrivano, of the international research program and network *Mapping Architectural Criticism,* http://mac.hypotheses.org/.

Paolo Scrivano is associate professor of history of architecture at the Politecnico di Milano. He holds a PhD degree in architectural and planning history from the Politecnico di Torino and has held teaching positions at the University of Toronto, Boston University, and Xi'an Jiaotong-Liverpool University. He has been a visiting scholar at the Massachusetts Institute of Technology and at the Canadian Centre for Architecture, as well as the recipient of several grants and fellowships from institutions such as the Center for Advanced Studies in the Visual Arts at Washington, DC's National Gallery of Art, the Social Sciences and Humanities Research Council of Canada, the Australian Research Council, and the French National Research Agency. A specialist of twentieth-century architecture, he has authored numerous publications on history, historiography, and criticism, including the volumes *Storia di un'idea di architettura moderna. Henry-Russell Hitchcock e l'International Style* (2001), *Olivetti Builds: Modern Architecture in Ivrea* (2001, as a co-author), and *Building Transatlantic Italy: Architectural Dialogues with Postwar America : Farnham – Burlington, Vt.* (2013). With Hélène Jannière he is one of the scientific coordinators of the research network Mapping Architectural Criticism, based at the Université Rennes 2.

The Architect as Critic

Elias Constantopoulos

fig. 1
Adolf Loos, *Das Andere*, magazine front cover;
Aris Konstantinidis, *Elements for Self-knowledge*, Greek book cover.

Words and Buildings: The Architect and the Critic

In his opening lecture at the international conference "On the Duty and Power of Architectural Criticism,"[1] Kenneth Frampton expressed his doubts as to whether he could be regarded as a critic, in the sense of not belonging to a time-honored tradition of architectural critics, from Bruno Zevi to Lewis Mumford and Ada Louise Huxtable, to mention but a few.

Manfredo Tafuri, whose concept of operative criticism Kenneth Frampton reminded us of in his lecture, was clearly apprehensive as to whether an architect could perform both roles effectively. As the primary goal of being an architect is to build, Tafuri suggests that therefore he cannot give just voice to his protest, regarding the conditions within which he works. Criticism, according to Tafuri, "has a duty to increase the unease to make precise and operative the 'dissent' of the architect, to exasperate his objective situation."[2]

In this sense, while an architectural critic would use words in order to expose the antinomies within the practice of architecture as Tafuri suggests, an architect could presumably be silent, speaking only through their designs and buildings. In the more recent history of architecture, there have been architects, such as Mies and Aalto, who were men of few words, and when they did speak, they were laconic—their legacy being their buildings, not theoretical treatises. Other architects, such as Le Corbusier and Koolhaas, were very much men of many words, and for some even a philosopher like Derrida would wonder, "Why Peter Eisenman Writes Such Good Books."[3]

Using words to talk about architecture, though, is not the prerogative of architectural critics only, but of all those interested in the built environment, specialists and amateurs alike, though their interests and knowledge of the subject differ. Are we to think that architects' critiques are purely technical and compositional? Do they not consider the larger social, cultural, environmental, and economic issues, the context of legal and manufacturing processes of production, which determine the realization of their designs and on which they depend? And if they do take these factors into account, does this hinder them from practicing as well as they should, as Tafuri suggests?

Architects are familiarized with criticism from their early student days through frequent reviews of their work known as "crits," especially in project-based studios, in front of faculty "juries." Criticism is also part and parcel of the creative process in architectural practice, as each project develops through continuous revisions, and unavoidably through stages of trial and error. Architectural criticism is architectural thinking per se, about its essence, about the appropriateness and articulation of designs on many different levels, and it requires a reflective stance, continually taking a few steps back, as a painter does, in order to grasp the complexity of a project and all its ramifications.

However, as criticism employs language to address design issues, whereas making employs drawing and manufacturing techniques in order to produce built space, there always seems to be a gap, a chasm between "those who make"—practicing architects—and "those who talk" about—historians, critics, and theoreticians—architecture.[4] Assuming this reasoning to be sound, of what use is criticism today?

Frampton, in the same lecture, also wondered: "In his collection of essays entitled *Building, Dwelling, Thinking*, Martin Heidegger cites the German poet Friedrich Hölderlin for his bitter question 'what are poets for in a destitute time?' And in this vein, one may equally ask, what are architects for, in our particular destitute time? Or for that matter, what are critics for in our destitute time?"

If there is need for an architectural critic, it is so that one may first describe through words what one thinks about architecture, and then, if conditions permit it, to demonstrate it by example, through building. In times of crisis, this need is even more pronounced. Such was the state of architecture over a century ago. Critique of the existing architecture came primarily from architects in Europe, leading to what became known as the modern movement.

keywords:

criticism, interpretation, contemporary architecture, learning environments

[1] International Conference on Architectural Criticism, October 9–10 and October 16–17, 2021, hosted by the School of Architecture, The University of Texas at Austin, organized by Wilfried Wang.

[2] Manfredo Tafuri, *Theories and History of Architecture*, trans. Giorgio Verrecchia (London: Granada 1980), 235. Originally published as *Teorie e storia dell' architettura* (Roma and Bari: Laterza 1968).

[3] Jacques Derrida, "Why Peter Eisenman Writes Such Good Books," in *Eisenmanamnesie* (Tokyo: A+U Publishing, 1988), 133–34.

[4] Exemplified by Tafuri's advice to his friend Aldo Rossi, that he should not even teach, "not out of a hysterical and conformist desire to ostracize him, but rather to help him to be more consistent in his fascinating, albeit superfluous, silence." Manfredo Tafuri, *The Sphere and the Labyrinth* (Cambridge, MA: The MIT Press, 1987), 359. Originally published as *La sfera e il labirinto* (Turin: Einaudi, 1980).

What It Means to Be Modern

To be of our own times, to be contemporary, seems self-evident; we are children of our age and, even if subconsciously, we act accordingly.

More than a century ago, however, this self-evident renewal of human endeavor became problematic, due to the discordance between a persistent historicism and the new social landscape created by the Industrial Revolution, which resulted in the establishment of the bourgeoisie and the rise of the working class. A century ago, Le Corbusier's last words in *Towards a New Architecture*, "Architecture or Revolution. Revolution can be avoided,"[5] summed up this tension. Once detected, the solution to the problem of how to move toward this new architecture was to name it, clearly and unambiguously, modern.

Since the nineteenth century, the search for modernity in all creative areas that we call culture became the holy grail of the contemporary world. "Modernity," according to Baudelaire, "is the transient, the fleeting, the contingent; it is one half of art, the other being the eternal and the immovable."[6] Whether it be poetry, music, painting, or architecture, directives were issued as *manifestos*, aimed at fostering the coming of a new age in the fields of arts and letters. The names assumed by artistic movements were characteristic of their purpose: art had to be *Nouveau*, *Jugend*, it had to *Secede*, in order to be free, in *Liberty* style, in *de Stijl*, and eventually, through the confluence of all the movements that followed, expressing a new *Constructivist* ethos, to become an *International Style*, as the exported European modern movement was to be baptized in the United States of America.

Despite the many revisions, oppositions, and attempts at renaming it after World War II, modernity absorbed, not without some scars, postmodernism, critical regionalism, deconstructivism, and other trends, and remained a dominant tendency by reinventing itself, as much as capitalism, always aided by emergent technologies.

A question of truth to the nature of materials and construction, to function and society, seems to run through the whole discourse of modernity, apparently sincere, even if of late its rhetoric becomes evident. With his characteristic bravado, Le Corbusier's opening sentence of the first chapter in *Towards a New Architecture,* "The Engineer's Aesthetic and Architecture," posits a "Question of morality: lack of truth is intolerable, we perish in untruth,"[7] echoing concerns that had already been voiced by architects before him, such as John Ruskin in *The Seven Lamps of Architecture*.[8]

In a landscape of endless transformations that affect the built environment locally and globally, as we have entered the third decade of the twenty-first century, what does it mean today to be of our own times? How are we to think critically of architecture—how are we to judge and how are we to build? If we were to ask for clarity of concepts, we would be much confused, like the figures in Plato's "Allegory of the Cave,"[9] who received a distorted view of truth (*alētheia*) of the real world. In 2017, the Oxford Dictionaries declared "post-truth" Word of the Year, denoting "circumstances in which objective facts are less influential in shaping public opinion than appeals to emotion and personal belief,"[10] after Donald Trump emerged as the winner of the 2016 United States presidential election. More recently, after losing the 2021 election, his media platform is about to be inaugurated, appropriating "Truth (Social)" exclusively.

As the meaning of words has become so profoundly muddled in the public realm, how can architectural criticism retain its composure? Critical discourse today operates in a virtual landscape, fluctuating between unverifiable subjective appraisal and objective fact, in a semi-descriptive, semi-advertising idiom, where it is hard to distinguish any one thing from its representation, from its image.

Wondering whether an architect as a person of action, who is also a critic, may perhaps shed some light on this, I intend to juxtapose the attitudes of two architects who both wrote passionately polemical texts and also built, to give material expression to their ideas.

[5] Le Corbusier, *Towards a New Architecture* (London: The Architectural Press, 1927), 269. Originally published as *Vers Une Architecture* (Paris: Editions Crès, 1923).

[6] Charles Baudelaire, "Baudelaire: Selected Writings on Art and Artists" (Cambridge: CUP Archive, 1981), 403, https://www.azquotes.com/quote/20657.

[7] Le Corbusier, *Towards a New Architecture*, 17.

[8] John Ruskin, "Second Lamp of Truth," in *The Seven Lamps of Architecture* (London: Smith, Elder & Co., 1849), 34. See also Jeff Malpas, "Truth in Architecture," in *The Significance of Philosophy in Architectural Education*, ed. Elias Constantopoulos (Athens: P.& E. Michelis Foundation, 2012), 78–90.

[9] Plato, "Allegory of the Cave," *Republic*, 375 BC, 514a–520a.

[10] "Post-truth is an adjective defined as 'relating to or denoting circumstances in which objective facts are less influential in shaping public opinion than appeals to emotion and personal belief,'" https://languages.oup.com/word-of-the-year/2016/.

Loos and Konstantinidis: The Architect as Critic

Adolf Loos (1870–1933), before designing his beautifully crafted small shops, suburban villas, and workers' housing, wrote some of the seminal essays on architecture at the turn of the twentieth century. In the context of the fin-de-siècle Vienna Sezession, the publication of "Ornament and Crime"[11] was guaranteed to send shivers through the artistic avant-garde, while his short essays such as "Architecture,"[12] and the publication of critical reviews in his short-lived magazine *Das Andere*,[13] consolidated his fame as a fierce critic of Viennese architecture and culture, alongside his friend and mentor, Karl Kraus.

As a student at the Bartlett, I came across Loos[14] by first reading Aris Konstantinidis's texts, who in his relentless search for truth in architecture[15] often quoted whole passages from the Austrian's essays. Intoxicated by their feverish style of writing, and their common concerns about an architecture being appropriate to place and time (genius loci/Zeitgeist), I gradually became acquainted with their architecture, which seemed to physically embody their ideas.

Konstantinidis's (1913–1993) position within postwar Greek architecture, beyond his official posts as head of the Technical Sector of the Greek National Tourism Organisation, and of the Workers Housing Organisation, was consolidated also through his fierce writings, from his early studies on the vernacular (*Old Athenian Houses*[16] and *Two Villages in Mykonos*[17]) to his uncompromising stance regarding the ethos of building practice, exemplified in his *Contemporary True Architecture*.[18] A generation apart, they were born at the southern and eastern fringes of Europe in tumultuous times: Loos in Brno, then part of the newly established Austro-Hungarian Empire, Konstantinidis in Athens at the end of the Balkan wars, in the same year Loos's "Ornament and Crime" was published.

Loos's and Konstantinidis's writings reveal not only a common grounding that takes architecture back to its origins but also their different, distinct conceptions of architecture in relation to culture and nature.

If their writings spoke to the hearts of architects in their time, they both resurfaced in the second half of the twentieth century, Loos's work being reappraised by many scholars as well as by architects such as Aldo Rossi, and Konstantinidis's, who was influential mainly to the generation of postwar Greek architects,[19] within the context of critical regionalism,[20] due to his early consideration of the concepts of "topos" and the "tectonic."

Though both architects aspired to be of their time, to be modern in essence, both opposed the dominant contemporary practices, be they art nouveau and the Sezession or International Style and postmodernism, for their emphasis on ornamentation.

Style and Ornament

If to be modern means to be of its time, then that was already the motto of the Sezession, inscribed above the entrance of the exhibition building in Vienna: "To every age its art, to every art its freedom."[21] The Sezession motto that marked the vivid fin-de-siècle stylistic movement was based on the development of a new style by a collective of artists (Wiener Werkstätte)—in the spirit of the Arts and Crafts movement, which relied heavily on stylized ornamentation—a distinctively Viennese version of art nouveau. Adolf Loos considered such ornamentation superfluous and said as much in his vitriolic essays against artists and professors, stigmatizing them in cultural terms as criminals. In "Ornament and Crime," Loos castigates the practice of decoration by his contemporaries, because he links contemporary culture to an overriding idea of human progress, in both an ethical and an aesthetic sense: "The Critique of Pure Reason could not have been created by a man wearing five ostrich feathers on his hat, the Ninth Symphony did not spring from one wearing a ring around his neck the size of a dish."[22]

Konstantinidis similarly rallies against what he perceives as the empty formalism not only of his own but of past times too, mentioning Le Corbusier's description of eclecticism being "like a feather on a ladies' hat,"[23] and especially of the Renaissance, which he describes as an architecture of scenography, concerned only with buildings' external appearance.[24]

---

[11] Adolf Loos, "Ornament und Verbrechen" ["Ornament and Crime"], 1908, in *Sämtliche Schriften*, Adolf Loos, vol. 1 (Vienna and Munich: Verlag Herold, 1962), 276–88.

[12] Adolf Loos, "Architektur" [Architecture], 1910, in *Sämtliche Schriften*, 302–18.

[13] Adolf Loos, "Ein Blatt zur Einführung abendländischer Kultur in Österreich," *Das Andere* (1903).

[14] For two consecutive years (1976/77 and 1978/79) I borrowed Heinrich Kulka's and Münz and Künstler's only existing German monographs on Loos from the Bartlett School library, and nobody recalled them. This interest in Loos, who was not discussed at the time, was one of the things that brought us together with Wilfried Wang, who in 1980 published texts on Loos in *9H* no. 2. Since the 1980s, there has been a surge of interest and a proliferation of studies and publications on his work.

[15] An embittered open letter (1972) by Konstantinidis to Orestis Doumanis, editor of *Architecture in Greece* (which I was later to become a consultant editor of), was handed to me by Martin Goalen, my tutor at the Bartlett, who had worked in Greece. Konstantinidis's letter aroused my interest and in searching for his work I came across his *Contemporary True Architecture*, where I first read about Loos.

[16] Aris Konstantinidis, *Old Athenian Houses*, 1947 (orig. in Greek).

[17] Aris Konstantinidis, *Two Villages in Mykonos*, 1950 (orig. in Greek).

[18] Aris Konstantinidis, *Contemporary True Architecture*, 1978 (orig. in Greek).

[19] Konstantinidis's work had also been published in German architectural magazines. Kenneth Frampton published "The Work of Aris Konstantinidis" in *Architectural Design* XXXIV (May 1964): 5.

[20] Alexander Tzonis and Liane Lefaivre, "The Grid and the Pathway. An Introduction to the Work of Dimitris and Suzana Antonakakis," in *Architecture in Greece* (Athens: Architecture in Greece 1981): 15; Kenneth Frampton, "Towards a Critical Regionalism: Six Points for an Architecture of Resistance," in *Anti-Aesthetic. Essays on Postmodern Culture* (Seattle: Bay Press, 1983).

[21] "Der Zeit ihre Kunst. Der Kunst ihre Freiheit." The Secession building (1887–1888) was designed by Joseph Maria Olbrich and financed by Karl Wittgenstein. Its interior is dominated by Gustav Klimt's Beethoven frieze. It is an emblematic icon of fin-de-siècle Vienna and today it features on the 50 cent Austrian euro.

[22] Adolf Loos, "Die überflüssigen," 1908, in *Sämtliche Schriften*, 267.

[23] Konstantinidis, *Contemporary True Architecture*, 21–22. He also suggests that compared to the West "only the East, Asia, China and India still holds steadfast."

[24] Ibid., 18–19.

Konstantinidis also feels betrayed by the erstwhile worthy "modern" architecture of the Bauhaus, a liberating model of his youth, which had degenerated into an "International Style," and is further exasperated in later years by what he considers the pointless formal exercises of postmodernism.

Loos and Konstantinidis both reproach ornament in architecture for the same reasons: it is functionally and economically, as well as conceptually, unnecessary. "Style we have," contends Loos, "but no ornamentation,"[25] as the "architect has turned building into graphic art" instead of "building in the style of its own times."[26]

Once the matter of ornamentation has thus been settled, even for a brief period of time, as Louis Sullivan had suggested,[27] then the question of what is modern can be discussed.[28] Through the publication of polemical essays and manifestos, a handful of maxims, such as *ornament and crime*, became the guiding lights of the avant-garde, wishing to be liberated from the past: *less is more, form follows function, the plan is the generator, in the nature of materials*.

Architecture Without Architects: Craftsmanship and the Vernacular

For both Loos and Konstantinidis the answer lies in an architecture that allows them to distance themselves critically from in-vogue currents; that is, those to be found in the vernacular, and in the still unspoiled practice of craftsmen.[29] Loos claims that he learned about joinery from carpenters in their workshops, and from other craftsmen such as tailors and shoemakers who produced "many objects which show the style of the twentieth century in its pure form."[30]

Loos's tale of "The saddle maker,"[31] invited to a competition by a professor, is translated into Greek verbatim by Konstantinidis: "Once upon a time there was a saddler. He was a skilful artisan and used to make very good saddles different from those of the past centuries.... So, the saddles were modern but he was not aware of it. He just knew he is doing his best. One day he heard there is a new movement called Secession that recommends only the modern objects. The saddle master took one of his best saddles and went to the leading representative of the movement and asked him: 'Professor is my saddle modern?' The professor examined the saddles and told the master 'no! This is not modern, but I can help you find a modern design for your saddles.' The day after the professor gave the saddle master several designs for a modern saddle.... The master craftsman looked at the drawings for a long time and then said: 'Professor! If I understood as little about riding, horses, leather and work as you do, then I would share your imagination.' Now the saddle master lives in complete contentment making saddles. Modern ones? He does not know. Just saddles."[32]

Konstantinidis uses the moral of this fable to further condemn the undue overdesign of everyday objects and especially overelaborate chair designs, which he considers tortuously anti-functional,[33] a subject first taken up by Loos.[34]

According to both architects the vernacular is based on the continuous evolution and improvement of techniques, not the slavish adherence to past forms. Loos's aim is not to be different for the sake of difference; he believes that in order to improve our methods while working on a problem, we come upon new solutions, like craftsmen do, thus renewing tradition in the process.

In his important essay "Architecture,"[35] Loos takes us to a lake spoiled by a house designed by an architect, because it disturbs the "tranquility" of the place. The house is incongruous, unlike the farmer's house, which is discreet because it merges with its surroundings. Loos points out that the reason that the architect's (good or bad, regardless) house does not harmonize with the environment is because he has no culture, he is an "upstart."

Loos's idea of the vernacular as an antidote to the designs of his contemporaries seems to be vindicated in the second half of the twentieth century, when anonymous architecture attracts the attention of not only architects and historians[36] but also anthropologists,[37] who shed new light on the artifices and practices of non-Western peoples. But what is the actual lesson of an *Architecture without Architects*[38] to us, then and now?

[25] Loos, "Architektur," 79.

[26] Ibid., 76.

[27] "I should say that it would be greatly for the aesthetic good if we should refrain entirely from the use of ornament for a period of years, in order that our thoughts might concentrate acutely upon the production of building well-formed and comely in the nude. We should thus perforce eschew many undesirable things, and learn by contrast how effective it is to think in a natural, vigorous and wholesome way. This step taken, we might safely inquire to what extent, a decorative application of ornament would enhance the beauty of our structures—what new charm it would give them." Louis H. Sullivan, *Kindergarten Chats* (revised 1918) *and Other Writings*, 1st ed., The Documents of Modern Art, vol. 4 (New York City: Wittenborn, 1947), 187.

[28] Konstantinidis, though always sympathetic to Sullivan, years later stated: "True architecture does not need to be defined as new or modern—it has forgotten the common aspect that architecture arises from a social content and ethos ... and that a house is built to be lived in, not to be looked at from the outside." Konstantinidis, *Contemporary True Architecture*, 23–24.

[29] The craftsman in modernist discourse is followed by the engineer and the plumber, whose primary concern is functional, not aesthetic. It is interesting to relate this to Claude Lévi-Strauss's discussion of the "Bricoleur and Engineer," in *The Savage Mind* (Illinois: University of Chicago Press, 1966). Originally published as *La Pensée sauvage* (Paris: Librairie Plon, 1962). See also Richard Sennett, *The Craftsman* (New Haven: Yale University Press, 2008).

[30] Loos, "Architektur."

[31] Adolf Loos, "Es war einmal ein sattlermeister ...," *Das Andere* (October 15, 1903), 1–2.

[32] Konstantinidis, *Contemporary True Architecture*, 43.

[33] Konstantinidis, *Contemporary True Architecture*, 25.

[34] Adolf Loos, "Sitzmöbel," *Neue Freie Presse*, June 19, 1898, trans. as "Furniture for Sitting," in *Spoken into the Void, Collected Essays 1897–1900* (Cambridge, MA: Oppositions Books, The MIT Press, 1982), 29. See also Karl Arnold's caricature "From the Werkbund exhibition": "van de Velde created the individual chair—Muthesius the chair type—and master carpenter Heese the chair for sitting." *Simplicissimus* (1914/1915).

[35] "May I take you to the shores of a mountain lake? The sky is blue, the water green. And everywhere is profound tranquility ... But what is this? A discordant note in the tranquility. Like an unnecessary screech. Among the locals' houses that were not built by them, but by God, stands a villa. The creation of an architect. Whether a good or bad architect, I don't know. All I know is that the tranquility, peace and beauty have vanished ... And therefore, I ask, why is it that any architect, good or bad, desecrates the lake ... The farmer doesn't. Nor does the engineer who builds a railway along the shore or scores deep furrows in its clear surface

fig. 2
Aris Konstantinidis, Summer Residence, Anavyssos, Attics, 1962.
Photo: Elias Constantopoulos, 1989.

Konstantinidis, in quoting Loos, shares his concern for the essential role of the craftsman as being an "authentic" part of his context, the genius loci; building in every epoch with techniques and materials of its time, which are relevant to a specific place (topos).[39] This German-trained student returns to Greece from Munich, sketches and photographs many such images of indigenous vernacular structures, which he publishes in his "Contemporary Architecture and Anonymous Vernacular" in *Elements for Self-knowledge*[40] and in *God-Built*,[41] recalling Loos's own reference to houses that look as if they were built by God in the landscape.[42] For Konstantinidis, these archetypal, elementary shelters—huts, paddocks, pergolas—which differentiate loadbearing post-and-beam structures from non-loadbearing elements, not only tell the "truth" about construction but also merge into the landscape "as if they had always belonged there." He finds more precedents in the old Athenian houses and self-built refugee dwellings,[43] remnants of a tectonic still present in the landscape, built with whatever humble materials come to hand, for protection from the sun in the Greek climate.[44] These he tries to emulate and reinterpret through metal, stone, and concrete in his residential projects.

Culture Versus Nature: The Urn, the Chamber Pot, and the God-Built

But this is the point where Konstantinidis's and Loos's paths diverge. Konstantinidis regards architecture primarily as an act of natural growth, springing from the earth, where the architect is simply an agent, a midwife assisting in its birth. Loos, on the other hand, regards architecture primarily as a conscious act of being appropriate to its cultural context, its meaning, and its purpose.

Though they share the same principles in regard to their contemporary architectures, there is a rupture between them, which becomes evident in Konstantinidis's only criticism toward Loos, for his entry to the *Chicago Tribune* competition.[45] Because of his unassailable need to be as one with the land, Konstantinidis does not share Loos's equally stern belief that architecture remains primarily a praxis of culture. For Konstantinidis, architecture is, in Elytis's words, the imprint of "the soul of a people on the landscape,"[46] defined by location, climate, and geography: "I build means I am and I exist. And as I build, thus I will be and exist,"[47] and elsewhere: "Let architecture do what nature cannot do. That is, for architecture, to build houses, which nature did not wish to (or did not even think to) build."[48] Frequently referring to Frank Lloyd Wright, according to whom architecture has to be "at one with the spirit, the form and the quality of the landscape,"[49] Konstantinidis's answer to his own rhetorical question "what is Renaissance anyway?" is: "There is only naissance." This total identification between

with his ship. They go about things in a different way. His intention was to erect a house for himself and his family … Is the house beautiful? Yes, just as beautiful as a rose or a thistle, as a horse or a cow." Trans. from Loos, "Architektur," 302.
[36] Sibyl Moholy-Nagy, *Native Genius in Anonymous Architecture* (New York: Horizon Press, 1957); Amos Rapoport, *House Form and Culture* (Englewood Cliffs, N.J., Prentice-Hall, 1969). Trans. into Greek by D. Phillipides (1976; 2nd ed. Melissa, 2010).
[37] Claude Lévi-Strauss, *Tristes Tropiques* (Paris: Librairie Plon, 1955), *La Pensée sauvage*.
[38] Bernard Rudofsky, *Architecture Without Architects* (New York City: The Museum of Modern Art, 1964).
[39] Konstantinidis, *Contemporary True Architecture*, 17.
[40] Aris Konstantinidis, "Heutige Architektur und Anonymes Bauen," *Baumeister* 4 (1965); Aris Konstantinidis, *Elements for Self-knowledge* (Athens: Aris Konstantinidis, 1975). In the 1960s and 1970s many studies on anonymous Greek architecture and on unauthorized settlements were published in *Architecture in Greece* and in Orestis Doumanis and Paul Oliver, *Shelter in Greece* (Athens: Architecture in Greece, 1974).
[41] Aris Konstantinidis, *God-Built: Landscapes and Houses of Modern Greece* (Athens: Crete University Press, 1994). See also Giorgos Triantafyllou, *Archetypes* From Huts and Sheepfolds to Contemporary Art and Architecture* (Athens: K. Adam, 2010).
[42] "They do not look as if they were fashioned by man, it is as if they came straight from God's workshop, like the mountains and trees, the clouds and the blue sky." Loos, "Architektur."
[43] Konstantinidis, *Old Athenian Houses*.
[44] Konstantinidis, *Contemporary True Architecture*, 29. Konstantinidis, as does D. Pikionis, refers frequently to

making-building and being-existence is ontological and existential, reminiscent of Martin Heidegger's *Building, Dwelling, Thinking,*[50] though Konstantinidis makes no mention of him.

We only need to look at the way the two architects conceive of interior space, which both consider to be of primary importance, to clearly understand their different objectives. Loos's story of the "Poor Little Rich Man,"[51] essentially a critique of the stifling total design (*gesamtkunstwerk*) in our residential settings, is also shared by Konstantinidis, who further theorizes on the importance of being able to freely arrange furnishings and objects in interiors as we deem best.

The ways in which the two architects give form to this concept, however, are distinctly different. In the case of Konstantinidis, flexibility of interior arrangement is made possible primarily through the use of the independent structural frame, thus emphasizing once more its necessity. In the case of Loos, through his concept of the *Raumplan,* he constructs intricate interior microcosms, complex spatial arrangements, providing a variety of different settings for our daily habitation. This idea could also be connected to Loos's assertion that "Architecture arouses moods in people, so the task of the architect is to give these moods concrete expression. A room must look cosy. A house comfortable to live in. To secret vice the law courts must seem to make a threatening gesture. A bank must say, 'Here is your money safe in the hands of honest people.'"[52]

Konstantinidis's uncompromising stance rests on his desire to be at one with nature, his modernity manifesting itself in the building of a contemporary primitive hut, making use of any materials available, a tectonic continuation of the vernacular in a specific location. "Architecture is always local," Konstantinidis contends; it "cannot be international, because it responds to the needs of a topos, to the climate, light, habits, history and society, and only then will be recognized as truly universal,"[53] where the natural and the man-made ideally coincide: "Yes, ma'am, this is the miracle here in Greece; when you stand in front of any architectural work; you cannot distinguish what is the work done by man and what is the work done by nature."[54]

For Loos, though, an architect is an educated builder: "Our education is based on classical culture. An architect is a bricklayer who has learned Latin."[55] His position is that of a cosmopolitan urbanite: "If nothing were left of an extinct race but a single button, I would be able to infer, from the shape of that button, how these people dressed, built their houses, how they lived, what was their religion, their art, their mentality."[56]

For Loos, the tale of the house by the lake is but a means to jolt the "upstart," the city folk, the urban denizens who have no culture of their own, in order for them to become aware of the culture to which they belong.[57] The craftsman belongs to an artisan culture and even when he decorates, he is committed to his creative work, gaining pleasure from the process of making things. The bourgeois is not, hence the need for *Das Andere,*[58] their interest in "The Other," and their need to introduce the modern way of life to their compatriots in all its facets, from everyday objects to the most appropriate way to appear in public, to dress so as to be part of civil society, in the most discreet manner. And as far as architecture is part of this civitas, Loos makes his statement with the exemplary building on Michaelerplatz, as Karl Kraus points out: "There, he built them an idea."[59]

In Conclusion: Criticism and Building

Konstantinidis's model seaside house in Anavyssos[60] is quite unlike the current vogue of underground dwellings hiding away so as not to "disturb" nature. A rough but pristine orthogonal prism, while standing proudly in contrast upon the rocky landscape, is best imprinted in our minds through its black-and-white photographs, apparently merging with it, wishing to disappear—to not be Loos's house by the lake! This is Konstantinidis's dream of building an idea, of the heart and the soul, at one with the topos. In its black-and-white images, its tragic, unresolved, potency comes forcefully to the fore, of how to be in a modern mechanized world while remaining a noble savage at heart.

the verses of the national Greek poet Solomos: "me logismo kai m'oneiro," meaning a matter of both the heart and the mind, of the rational and the poetic sensibility. Dionysios Solomos, *The Free Besieged* (1828–1851).

45 Aris Konstantinidis, *Amartoloi kai Kleftes* (Athens: Agra, 1987), 108–9.

46 "A landscape is not, as some perceive it, just a set of land, plants, and water. It is the projection of the people's soul over the material world." Odysseas Elytis, *The Public and Private* (Athens: Ikaros, 1990).

47 Aris Konstantinidis, *I architectoniki tis architechtoniki* (Athens: Agra, 1992), 275.

48 Konstantinidis, *I architectoniki,* 145.

49 See also Wright's comment about his Taliesin East house (1911): "I knew well that no house should ever be on a hill or on anything. It should be of the hill. Belonging to it. Hill and house should live together each the happier for the other." Frank Lloyd Wright, *An Autobiography* (Duell, Sloan and Pearce, 1943; Petaluma: Pomegranate Communications, 2005), 168. Citations refer to the Pomegranate Communications edition.

50 Martin Heidegger, "BAUEN WOHNEN DENKEN," in *Darmstädter Gespräch: Mensch und Raum,* vol. 2, ed. Otto Bartning (Darmstadt: Neue Darmstädter Verlagsanstalt GmbH, 1952), 73 et seq., trans. by Albert Hofstadter as "Building Dwelling Thinking" in *Martin Heidegger: Poetry, language, thought,* (New York: Harper & Row, 1971).

51 Adolf Loos, "Von einem armen reichen manne," *Neues Wiener Tagblatt* 34 (April 26, 1900), trans. as "Poor Little Rich Man," in *Spoken into the Void,* 125–27.

52 Loos, "Architektur."

53 Konstantinidis, *Contemporary True Architecture,* 27.

54 Aris Konstantinidis, "The Problem for a True Greek Architecture," *Architecture in Greece* 6 (1972), in Aris Konstantinidis, *Gia tin architectoniki* (Athens: Agra 1987), 245.

55 Adolf Loos, "Ornament und erziehung," in *wohnungskultur,* eds. Adolf Loos, B. Markalous, Joh. Vaněk, Ernst Wiesner (Brno: wohnungskultur, 1924/25; Wien: Herold, 1962); trans. by Michael Mitchell as "Ornament and Education," in *Ornament and Crime: Selected Essays* (Riverside, Calif.: Ariadne Press, 1998), 187.

56 Quoted in Berel Lang, "Style as Instrument, Style as Person," *Critical Inquiry* 4, no. 4 (summer 1978): 715–39, https://en.wikiquote.org/wiki/Adolf_ Loos.

57 "And I repeat my question, why is it that the architect, no matter whether good or bad, desecrates the lake? Like almost all city dwellers, the architect lacks culture. He lacks the sure touch of the farmer who does possess culture. The city dweller is rootless. What I call culture is that balance between our physical, mental and spiritual being, which alone can guarantee sensible thought and action." Trans. from Loos, "Architektur," 74

58 Loos, *Das Andere.*

Loos's Michaelerplatz urban building, on the other hand, wishes to distinguish in its exterior form the interior contents as a precise "presentation of self in everyday life."[61] The contradictory identity of this "Looshaus," corresponding to its diverse program and meaning, clearly differentiated on its facades, comes most forcefully through in color photography, the stark, white-plastered upper walls contrasting sharply with the classicistic opulence of the green Evian marble of the ground floor.

Criticism, defined as an act of "*krisis*," a "separating, power of distinguishing, decision, choice, election, judgment, dispute,"[62] readily relates to Kraus's formulation, expressing a crucial act of discernment: "Adolf Loos and I—he, literally and I, grammatically—have done nothing more than show that there is a distinction between an urn and a chamber pot, and that it is this distinction above all that provides culture with elbow room. The others, those who fail to make this distinction, are divided into those who use the urn as a chamber pot and those who use the chamber pot as an urn."[63]

Both architects, in their very different ways, created such furors in their time, acquiring dedicated followers as often as they did enemies, and expressed through words and buildings the unresolved contradictions of their societies in times of crisis. If we are correct in our reading, the approaches followed by the two architects demonstrate the innate ambiguities of a modern sensibility, wishing to move from criticism through to instruction, by means of built and printed matter alike. In Loos's case, this is expressed as a disbelief in the possibility of formal unity (in Michaelerplatz par excellence) and the rejection of ornament, which he considered can only be supplemented by that which has acquired historical meaning, that is, classicism. In Konstantinidis's case, it is expressed as a disbelief in the possibility of adopting any type of building system other than that of framed construction, which he considered diachronic and transhistorical.

If twenty-first-century technical and aesthetic concerns, which seem to adopt epidermal routes,[64] be they body tattoos or building enclosures, make the two architects' concerns seem outdated, we should consider that, within their contexts, they both intended for architects' voices to be heard first as critics of culture and society. It was through such a conceptual framework that they formulated their perception of what architecture means and how it should be practiced. These architects' critical desire to stand before their contemporaries and to have a considerable appeal, through their words as much as through their buildings, perhaps challenges Tafuri's notion that an architect had better be silent. All the more so, given that, as their complexities and contradictions are gradually understood in time, they better serve to throw light on architecture in different epochs.

fig. 3
Adolf Loos, Goldman & Salatsch Building, Michaelerplatz, Vienna, 1910. Photo: Elias Constantopoulos, 2009.

[59] "Er hat Ihnen dort einen Gedanken gebaut." Karl Kraus, in *Die Fackel*, no. 313/314 (December 31, 1910): 5.
[60] Konstantinidis's larger urban buildings, workers' housing, and many hotels adopt the concrete domino type of structure that has been used in Greece for nearly a century.
[61] Erving Goffman, *The Presentation of Self in Everyday Life* (New York: Doubleday & Company, 1959).
[62] https://en.wiktionary.org/wiki/crisis
[63] "Adolf Loos und ich, er wörtlich, ich sprachlich, haben nichts weiter getan als gezeigt, daß zwischen einer Urne und einem Nachttopf ein Unterschied ist, und daß in diesem Unterschied erst die Kultur Spielraum hat. Die andern aber, die Positiven, teilen sich in solche, die die Urne als Nachttopf und die den Nachttopf als Urne gebrauchen." Karl Kraus, in *Die Fackel*, no. 389/90 (December 15, 1913): 37. Trans. in Allan Janik, Stephen Toulmin, *Wittgenstein's Vienna*, (New York; London: Simon & Schuster, 1973), 89.
[64] As witnessed by the plethora of publications since Gilles Deleuze's *Le Pli*, from Greg Lynn's *Blob Tectonics, or Why Tectonics is Square and Topology is Groovy*, to "bioinspired" *Skin In Architecture* facades, and the widespread *Ink & Skin* practice of tattooing.

Biography

Elias Constantopoulos is Professor of Architecture, University of Patras. "Hellenic Institute of Architecture" President, "Hellenic Society for Aesthetics" Secretary, DoCoMoMo member. Greek Curator, 10th Venice Architecture Biennale, EU-Japan exhibition Tokyo, Patras Conference "The Role of Philosophy in Architectural Education". Co-editor 9H, NTIZAÏN. Publications: Atelier 66, K. Krokos, N. Valsamakis.

Architectural Curation: A Practice of Architectural Criticism

Li Xiangning, Mo Wanli, Zhang Ziyue

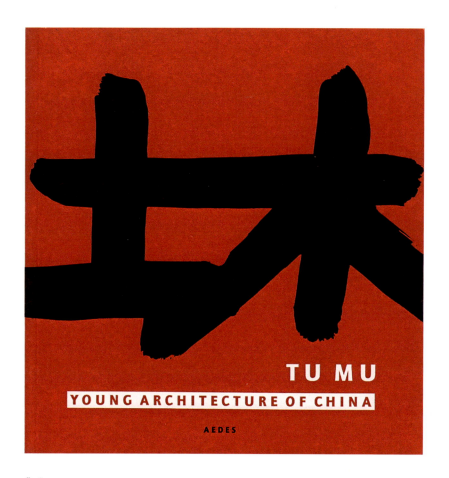

fig. 1
Catalog cover for the exhibition "Tu Mu: Young Architecture of China."

Starting from the entangled relationship between architectural curation, the production of theoretical discourse, and the writing of history in the development of modern architecture, the paper contends for the important role played by architectural exhibitions in history, theory, and criticism, and further discusses the rise of architectural curation in China and its role in promoting the development of contemporary Chinese architecture. The paper argues that architectural curation is a form of architectural criticism that can precisely break through the limitations of textual criticism through its site-specific and public nature, and establish a multidirectional and open criticism between curators, exhibitors, and audiences.

Since the beginning of the twentieth century, the practice, production, and circulation of art has undergone tremendous changes. During this time, exhibitions as a form of artistic practice have also gradually entered the disciplinary horizon of architecture, while the task of curating has often overlapped with the work of critics and theorists. Over the course of the disciplinary evolution of architecture in the twentieth century, the intellectual approach and practical system of architectural curation undoubtedly had a profound influence on the direction of architectural criticism and the discipline as a whole.

In *The Curator's Handbook*, Adrian George defines the work of a curator as follows: "The curator must explain and then rationalize their curatorial practice in layman's terms, challenge new trends in the visual arts, and place them in a historical context. In our current age of rapidly expanding cultural production, the curator must also act as a filter or gatekeeper—an arbiter of taste. In short, they need to be able to assess and explain what constitutes 'good' art."[1] Thus, it seems that the work of the curator and of curation itself encompasses and even centers on the selection, interpretation, and assessment of works of art, architecture, or ideas. This may also explain why most of the important architecture curators of the twentieth century were either architecture critics or theorists.

If Manfredo Tafuri's critique of so-called "Operative Criticism"—perhaps best represented by architecture critics like Sigfried Giedion—is more or less motivated by his own frustration with the inability of the capitalist system to support the ideal of an architectural utopia, then what is the meaning and role of contemporary architectural criticism? Can it be practiced in a more direct, visible, and easily accessible form—such as in an exhibition—that goes beyond the traditional written word? In this paper, we try to respond to these questions and combine our practice as critics and curators to generate a preliminary overview and discussion of the methods of curating and its critical value.

Curation and Architectural Criticism in Modern Architecture History

According to Barry Bergdoll, the former curator in the Department of Architecture and Design at the Museum of Modern Art (MoMA) in New York, 1760 was the year that architecture exhibitions first came about[2]. Nowadays, architecture exhibitions have already become an important part of testing, dissemination, and consensus building in the field of architecture. Without the 1932 MoMA exhibition *International Style*, which was curated by Philip Johnson

keywords:

architectural curation;
architectural criticism;
discourse; site; publicness

[1] Adrian George, *The Curator's Handbook: Museums, Galleries, Independent Spaces* (London: Thames & Hudson, 2015), 24.
[2] Barry Bergdoll, "Out of Site in Plain View: On the Origins and Actuality of Architecture Exhibition" in *Exhibiting Architecture: A Paradox?* (New Haven: Yale School of Architecture, 2015), 13.

and Henry-Russell Hitchcock, it is unlikely that the historical narrative of modernism could have become dominant so quickly and that its formal language could have been so widely disseminated. Similarly, postmodernism owes its formation to the Venice Architecture Biennale of 1980, entitled *The Presence of the Past* and curated by the Italian architect Paolo Portoghesi. It is evident that although exhibitions have existed in the field of architecture for a long time, it was not until critics and theorists began to take on the role of curator that exhibitions emerged as an effective mechanism for the production of critical discourse on architectural theory, while also influencing the direction of architectural practice and the writing of architectural history.

In 1932, MoMA set up the world's first curatorial department dedicated to architecture exhibitions. The establishment of a curatorial mechanism enabled architecture exhibitions to integrate collection, education, research, archives, and publications to establish an institutionalized system—just as art exhibitions did. It is only through the combination of exhibitions as a format with reflections on the developmental state of architecture that the act of curating is able to become critical in nature, which means it not only inspires discussions on a single building or a group of works but also generates a broader "echo." Through the conscious selection of a curatorial theme, exhibition structure, and exhibited works, architecture exhibitions both critically reflect on current architectural practice and provide a guideline for future developments, while becoming an important part of architecture history in the long run. In 1975, MoMA's curator of architecture, Arthur Drexler, opened the exhibition *The Architecture of the École des Beaux-Arts*. Holding this exhibition at MoMA, an institution that had been dedicated to modern art and architecture since its inception, and revisiting the architecture of the École des Beaux-Arts in the context of the overall triumph of postwar modernist architecture, was undoubtedly a reevaluation of both the modernist architecture movement and the position of MoMA. From this perspective, the exhibition amounted to a criticism not only of the discipline but also of the institution itself, while simultaneously being somewhat oriented toward the future. Therefore, the exhibition and the discussions it caused are seen as a precursor to the postmodernist architecture movement that emerged in the 1980s. Furthermore, in contemporary studies on the culture of postmodern architecture, this exhibition is also considered an important archival source, reexamined and appreciated within a historical context. Although the boundary between exhibition, criticism, and historical research is very delicate in this case, it becomes clear that this exhibition was a vehicle of criticism, thus marking a turning point in the flow of history and becoming part of the historical archives itself.

As Terry Smith points out in his discussion of art curation, curators—unlike critics or historians—do not pursue "more definite statements about the nature and significance of the art they study," but rather "do everything necessary to bring works up to the point where they may become subject to critical and historical judgment."[3] Therefore, the significance of the curator's work more often resides in creating a space for critical discourse rather than in passing final judgment on the works themselves. In this realm, the curator not only plays the role of critic but, due to the nature of the exhibition as a medium, also often becomes the object of criticism and discussion themself.

The Rise of Architecture Curation in China

Architecture exhibitions as a form of cultural exchange began to appear in China in the 1980s. The *Environnement Quotidien en Chine* exhibition held at the Centre Pompidou in France in 1982 was one of the first of its kind to showcase the state of contemporary Chinese architecture to a European audience. By the mid-1990s, the first independent architects slowly started to appear in China. In January 1998, Wang Mingxian and Shi Jian published their article "Chinese Experimental Architecture in the 1990s," which astutely identified the new trends that were developing within commercial architectural practice during the 1990s and for the first time proposed the name "Experimental Architecture" for the phenomenon.

[3] Terry Smith, *Thinking Contemporary Curating* (New York: Independent Curators International, 2012), 44.

As a form of textual criticism of contemporary Chinese architectural practice, this article identified an experimental branch of local architecture circles pioneered by a few young architects. Wang Mingxian then curated the exhibition *Experimental Architecture by Eight Young Chinese Architects* in Beijing in 1999, which was an example of an exhibition with a critical perspective. When it finally emerged in the public sphere in a visual and spatial way, it caused ripples in the media. *Sanlian Life Week* magazine commented: "Judging from the exhibition on *50 Years of Architecture Achievements* presented during the architects' conference, as well as the exhibition on *Experimental Architecture by Young Chinese Architects* that failed to pass censorship the day before its planned opening and that was subsequently displayed in a separate exhibition gallery at the International Convention Center, we get the impression that there is a division between mainstream and experimental architecture in China, in which various conflicting architectural ideas are intertwined."[4] Moreover, perhaps even to the curator's surprise, one of the visitors to the exhibition included Eduard Kögel, a German architect and scholar who was working in China at the time. Kögel saw the work of this group of young architects and felt "the potential of an emerging design force. A new chapter is about to unfold,"[5] which led to the first collective presentation of contemporary Chinese architecture in Europe, titled *TU MU: Young Architecture of China*.

Whereas architectural criticism in the written form creates a rather unidirectional relationship between author and reader, curating architecture establishes a space for discourse in which multiple actors can participate. In this space, members of the audience may also become critics, or even future curators. Just like the exhibition *Experimental Architecture by Eight Young Chinese Architects*, the curatorial exhibition of architecture as critical practice is not an endpoint to summarize and present architecture, but on the contrary, it constitutes a starting point for discussions.

Architectural Curation as Critical Practice

As Foucault points out in his description of museums as heterotopias, a museum space often creates an alternative, imaginary space and time through the narrative that emerges based on the selection of works and their display.[6] Whereas art exhibitions generally present the works directly, architecture exhibitions normally require an intermediary medium to present buildings, amounting to the addition of another dimension to the act of selection: not only are the works selected, but also the media through which they are reproduced. Moreover, when these buildings are removed from their original contexts and rearranged and reproduced in a new space, what new contextual connections are created between them, and in what way will they affect the production of architecture in the present and in the future? These questions construct a tug of war between history, theory, and practice. When an architecture exhibition addresses these questions, its curation moves beyond a simple working method and becomes a problem-conscious way of thinking, thus forming the practice of architectural criticism.

Curating as critical practice does not summarize, present, and reflect current reality, but tries to question, challenge, and transcend it. In this sense, the 2016 Venice Architecture Biennale *Reporting from the Front*, curated by Chilean architect Alejandro Aravena—which aimed to respond to the social issues faced by the "front lines" of practice in different countries and regions around the world and to present their respective solutions—ended up being mostly a summary and enumeration. The 2000 Venice Architecture Biennale *Less Aesthetics, More Ethics*, curated by the Italian architect Massimiliano Fuksas, also responded to the ideological and sociopolitical imperatives of globalization, yet it more explicitly showed the perspective that architects facing these issues ought to have. Additionally, it also broke with the tradition of using buildings as exhibits at architecture exhibitions through the introduction of the concept of the "twenty-first-century megalopolis." In the 300-meter-long Arsenale exhibition space, a set of giant screens showed nearly twenty contemporary cities, including Paris, New Delhi, Mexico City, São Paulo, and Montreal, outlining the problems of globalization,

4 Mingxian Wang, "Fragments of Spatial History: An Exhibition of Experimental Works by Young Chinese Architects," in *AVANT-GARDE TODAY: Experimental Architecture* (Tianjin: Tianjin Academy of Social Sciences Press, 2000), 2–14.

5 Eduard Kögel, "The Perception of Chinese Architecture in the West: TU MU—an Exhibition at the Aedes Gallery in Berlin and its Context," trans. Hang Su, *Time + Architecture 2* (2018): 26–30.

6 Michel Foucault, "Of Other Spaces: Utopias and Heterotopias," in *Rethinking Architecture: A Reader in Cultural Theory*, ed. Neil Leach (New York: Routledge,1997), 330–36.

such as the overdevelopment of tourism, the decline of old towns, urban expansion, and environmental pollution. This urban context is both the background and the footnote of contemporary architectural practice. Furthermore, it provides strong backing for the curator's view that architecture should not only focus on aesthetics; it needs to reflect on its ethical dimension too. In the curatorial work for the exhibition *Building a Future Countryside*, as part of the Chinese Pavilion for the 2018 Venice Architecture Biennale, we also attempted to present not only a panoramic overview of contemporary Chinese rural practice but also a future-oriented perspective: when the internet and robotic construction technologies become available in the countryside, what opportunities can they provide to solve the many contemporary problems that villages face? In fact, the title of the exhibition, *Building a Future Countryside*, already hints at this attempt. Similarly, the 2013 Bi-City Biennale of Urbanism/Architecture in Hong Kong and Shenzhen titled *Urban Border* not only showcases global and local phenomena, theoretical discussions, and practical cases of "urban borders," but also proposes how to move "Beyond the Urban Edge" and explore the potential for positive interaction and transformation between "edge and center."

Just as the identities of curators and critics often overlap, curating as a critical practice does not happen overnight, but arises from investing considerable amounts of time and requiring curators to continuously work and immerse themselves in the ecosystem of architectural practice and theoretical discourse. In order to be able to open a space for critical discourse, a critical exhibition has to be based on several years of thinking and preparation. Looking back at the exhibitions on contemporary Chinese architecture that have taken place since the 1990s, the depth and breadth of communication between the curators themselves and the architects has often largely determined the direction of the exhibition and the intended message. Often, these exhibitions are not onetime events, but are perhaps preceded by written critiques—as in the case of the aforementioned exhibition *Experimental Architecture by Eight Young Chinese Architects*—or maybe critical essays on the exhibition will later open up the possibility for other curatorial displays. Whatever the case, curating as a critical practice is a long-term activity.

Currently, the development of architecture and mass media allows for the massive transfer of information through the internet, media, and high-speed communication tools, thus transcending boundaries of time and space. However, we believe that precisely because of this information overload, the act of curating as a critical practice becomes all the more valuable. It is the critical consciousness generated through long-term observation, accumulation, and work that differentiates curating as critical practice from the "curation" of exhibitions that merely lists and displays exhibits. The curator should visit architects' studios and construction sites to obtain first-hand information and timely updates on project dynamics; the curator should understand architects' lives and educational backgrounds; they should learn about their mentors and their references in the design language of different architects; and they should experience ongoing projects, this being more important than commenting on completed works. Additionally, curators need to engage in extended discussions and interactions with architects and other scholars, whether in the form of various critiques on a project or by exchanging ideas at various academic events. The 2016 exhibition *Towards a Critical Pragmatism: Contemporary Architecture in China* at Harvard University marked an important appearance of contemporary Chinese architecture on the international stage, bringing together sixty of the most representative contemporary Chinese practices. For us, this exhibition was not only a collective exposure of current Chinese architectural practice but also an advancement of critical and curatorial work. The 2016 theme of "critical pragmatism" stands in line with the article "Makeshift Architecture: Young Architects and Chinese Tactics" published in 2005 and the exhibition *24 Key Words: Mapping the Situation, Discourse and Strategies of Contemporary Young Chinese Architects* presented at the 2013 West Bund Biennial of Architecture and Contemporary Art. Over the course of this period of more than ten years, some works have joined the ranks of the classics, while other new works and

fig. 2
The Chinese Pavilion at the 2018 Venice Architecture Biennale. © Gao Changjun.

fig. 3
"Taobao Village, Smallacre City" by Drawing Architecture Studio at the Chinese Pavilion. © Gao Changjun.

fig. 4
"Cloud Village" by Philip F. Yuan at the Chinese Pavilion. © Gao Changjun.

young architects have emerged. This curatorial progression has not only refined and changed the theoretical discourse from "makeshift architecture" to "critical pragmatism," but also revealed, to some extent, the development of contemporary Chinese architectural practice, the maturation of a group of Chinese architects, and the growth of young architects. Some of the featured architects were once part of a controversial and radical young group who participated in the *TU MU: Young Architecture of China* exhibition in 2001, yet some fifteen years later, they had become representative figures in contemporary Chinese architecture circles, and the subtle changes in their design strategies and practices can be observed through these progressing exhibitions. Further, through this long-term observation and interaction, curators can also gain increasing support from architects and practitioners in other disciplines. In a way, this creates an interdependent, progressive relationship between practice and criticism.

Art historian Robert Storr's criteria for what constitutes a good exhibition can also be applied to the field of architecture.[7] A good exhibition offers a clear, but not deterministic, point of view, one that not only welcomes debate about the works on display but also stimulates analysis of and discussions about the ways in which curators present and evaluate them. In fact, this kind of exposition, as a tangible open space for discourse created by the curator, invites exhibitors, architects, critics, and scholars from other disciplines to enter and engage in some kind of re-creation of the exhibition. Thus, for the curator, the exhibition is not only a static display but also a dynamic process. In the course of curating it, the preparatory work

[7] Robert Storr, "Show and Tell," in *What Makes a Great Exhibition?*, ed. Paula Marincola (Chicago: The University of Chicago Press, 2007), 20.

fig. 5
Towards a Critical Pragmatism: Contemporary Architecture in China at Harvard University. © Gao Changjun.

fig. 6
Poster of *Towards a Critical Pragmatism: Contemporary Architecture in China*. © Gao Changjun.

fig. 7
2017 Shanghai Urban Space Art Season. © Gao Changjun.

of setting the theme and of selecting the exhibitors and works is just as important as the preparation of public events—such as forums, lectures, seminars, workshops, and public education activities—that take place during the exhibition. The 2017 Shanghai Urban Space Art Season, titled "This CONNECTION: Sharing a Future Public Space," featured courses in the form of twenty-six academic events, twenty-three children's events, photography competitions, art festival performances, riverfront walks, and other public events, all as part of the main exhibition. As an urban biennial, these activities may not be entirely academic, but they do resonate with the exhibition's theme of "connections" on another level by encouraging the participation of architects, planners, scholars, and the general public.

The many different practices of design, research, history, theory, and curation can all be seen as forms of architectural criticism. All that matters is that we have an eye for the truth and a critical mind. Columbia University's Graduate School of Architecture, Planning and Preservation (GSAPP) opened a new program a few years ago called "Critical, Curatorial, and Conceptual Practices in Architecture." This program suggests the possibility of freely engaging in critical intellectual discourse around architecture across different modes of practice. Looking ahead, architectural curation as a form of architectural criticism may emerge as a more active practice that engages with broader social and cultural realities. Michael Sorkin, a prominent New York architect and architectural critic, who sadly died from Covid-19 in 2021, was described in an article in *The Architectural Review* as a warrior who fought on both the design and the criticism fronts. For Sorkin, design and criticism were "simply different registers of the same expression." As a critic, he constantly reminded himself of the need to analyze and expose the truths about social relations and not limit himself to tectonic matters. The same article also stated that *Architectural Review*'s ambition is "to publish stories that resonate beyond buildings' walls and extend outside architects' control," and that "rather than disseminating outwards, the role of *AR* is to digest a deluge of information and critically filter, curate and edit, carefully framing and telling the story the instant press release doesn't." This is also the goal of problem-conscious and critically aware curatorial work. Perhaps in the title of the *AR* article, "Selecting, Visiting, and Publishing Buildings," we might also add "Exhibiting." The essence of the specific work of curating is to vote with the hand, the brain, and the pen, when producing publications and exhibitions. It is a form of careful screening, selection, and critical practice across different media in the face of architecture works, architects, and architecture ideas.

Biographies

Li Xiangning is dean and professor at the College of Architecture and Urban Planning, Tongji University. He was a visiting scholar at MIT, and also a visiting professor in architecture at Harvard GSD. His research focuses on the history, theory, and criticism of architecture. He has published widely on the architecture and urbanism of contemporary China in books such as *Contemporary Architecture in China: Towards a Critical Pragmatism*, and has been published in *The Architectural Review, Architecture + Urbanism, Time + Architecture*, etc.. Li Xiangning has been working with international museums and institutes, curating exhibitions on Chinese architecture. He was the curator of the Chinese Pavilion at the 2018 Venice Architecture Biennale.

Mo Wanli
PhD candidate, College of Architecture and Urban Planning, Tongji University.

Zhang Ziyue
PhD candidate, College of Architecture and Urban Planning, Tongji University.

Translating Scale from Models to Buildings

Fernando Diez

fig. 1
Redevelopment of Plaza de la Encarnación, Seville, Spain / 2011.

The dominance of spectacular architecture in highly visible public commissions and its repetitive failure in understanding building and urban scale can be linked to the prevalent use of models as the primary tool for design and judgment.
A comparative criticism of four high-profile buildings in Europe from 2011 illustrates how misunderstanding scale threatens public interest in terms of architectural and urban qualities, environmental responsibilities, and the waste of public money.

keywords:

architecture, criticism, model, scale, Metropol Parasol, Rolex Learning Center, City of Culture of Galicia, Riverside Museum

Criticism consists of understanding. Even failure must be understood, because without understanding, there is no chance of improvement. Of course, criticism can disagree with something to the extent of its complete rejection. Unfortunately, that is becoming more and more frequent. When criticism takes the form of absolute rejection, it inevitably equates itself with religious condemnation, pointing to the sinner to be expelled from the paradise of what the critic considers true architecture. The religious analogy is appropriate because of the moral tone that is so frequent in what could be called a *criticism of rejection*, which exercises simultaneous condemnation on the way a building was designed, the author's intentions and priorities, the building's purpose, and even on the system that all these three seem to serve: whether it is commercial greed, corporate arrogance, nationalistic rhetoric, or what has been called the *architecture of spectacle*.

Clearly, the ends and the general ideological context can be the object of criticism, but that evaluation does not need to exclude consideration of the many other concrete and particular aspects of a building.

The inability to consider a building's strengths and weaknesses separately turns the critic into a priest, ready to excommunicate the sinful and to praise the virtuous; quite frequently, this ends in the celebration of what Colin Rowe called *the architecture of good intentions*, where some works are condemned despite evident talent being displayed while others are praised even if they are mediocre because they are concerned with moral issues or are presented as such. *Purpose* and *quality* are different aspects and, regardless of purpose, under the same circumstances, a building can be of better or worse quality.

So, criticism needs to understand limitations and possibilities, but it also needs to *discern* between the different aspects of architecture. A fair judgment can only be made when both are considered.

This marks the turning point when criticism can be directed to a higher level of evaluation, not only discerning the different qualities, accomplishments, and failures of a building, but also advancing into *diagnosis*: understanding which procedures, misconceptions, or flawed assumptions lead to failure in one or many aspects of a piece of architecture.

This kind of *diagnosis* can be applied to a single building, but when repetitive failure is visible to the naked eye in works by different architects, then practice itself must be subject to insightful scrutiny.

These initial considerations are necessary for three reasons. First, because I will consider buildings whose purpose I do not approve of, at least not in the terms of what has been called architecture of spectacle. Second, because I will present the case of a specific repetitive failure in high-profile buildings made by high-profile architects: the misunderstanding of scale. Third, because I have a diagnosis for this specific failure: it is related to how these kind of high-exposure public buildings are conceived, judged, and only afterwards, fully designed.

This repetitive failure has to do with scale and can be simply described as *misunderstanding scale*. The title already anticipates my thesis: watch the model. This brings us to the old idea that the analogical design tools, those used to anticipate the final constructed building, condition the outcome of the project itself in specific ways.[1] Alfonso Corona Martínez underlines the determining role of representation in architecture, tracing this relationship from the Renaissance to modern times. He shows how perspective preludes Renaissance's regulated space and how projective precision allowed for Durand's compositional tools to develop.[2] We are also aware of how the axonometric projection, such as in Hannes Meyer's or Le Corbusier's projects for the League of Nations in Geneva of 1927, was the medium for the additive, volumetric expressionism of modern monumentality that matured in what I have previously called *the congress palace*, the modern type that firstly materialized in Lúcio Costa et al.'s seminal Education and Health Ministry in Rio de Janeiro of 1936.[3] The same connection exists between computer-aided design and architectural projects, an argument that has been well amplified and which has given rise to a wide range of *isms*, in superficial celebration of digital's liberating powers, while seemingly unable to notice less obvious limitations.

In the specific case of high-profile public architecture, known as *architecture of the spectacle*, the influence of the analogical model extends itself to the judging process.

One of the deceiving properties of the model is its literal analogical appearance. It looks as if it were the real building, making it easy to forget that it is only a simulation of the future. It presents itself to our intuitive perception as if the miniature and the gigantic could belong to the same world. They do not. That is why insects can walk the walls or why it is so easy to build a cardboard skyscraper model. Quoting Corona Martinez: "... physical models (maquettes) are analogical as they intuitively bear characteristics similar to objects, they show 'aspects' similar to their visible form, geometric relations, scale dimensions. This similarity is at the same time intuitive and conventional, and opens a discussion on the 'iconic sign' as it has been called by semiologists (see *La struttura assente* by Umberto Eco)."[4]

The Cost of Spectacular Architecture

Spectacular architecture may constitute a very small percentage of what is being built around the world, but it represents a very high percentage of architecture being published and discussed. These two percentages are inverse, the first being a one-digit number. Ideally, avant-garde, experimental architecture should produce new and better exemplary cases to inform and enhance the broader production of generic buildings. I argued previously in favor of a wider "production architecture" being informed by a "proposition architecture." That ideal relation, however, is no longer in the minds of the leading or most visible architectural players.[5]

What has been referred to by Iñaki Abalos as "the iconic pulse" of contemporary architecture can be described as a race to produce buildings as pure objects, eager to catch the attention of the international media. Unfortunately, this seems to be the unchallenged visual priority for both high-profile developers and the so-called "star architects."

From the end of the 1990s, suspicion arose that such high-exposure buildings are no longer designed considering cost, rational construction, common sense, or service, but the globally distributed photographs they would be able to generate.

The paradigm for this form of image production was established by the so-called Bilbao Effect: the worldwide media phenomenon unleashed by the combination of franchising the Guggenheim brand and hiring Frank Gehry to produce an iconic building. Its communication

[1] Alfonso Corona Martínez, *El proyecto: la influencia de los medios analógicos en arquitectura* (Buenos Aires: Mac Gaul, 1976).

[2] Alfonso Corona Martínez, *Ensayo sobre el Proyecto* (Buenos Aires: Editorial CP67, 1990). Trans. as *The Architectural Project* (Texas A & M University Press, 2003).

[3] Fernando Diez, "El Palacio de Congresos: um tipo del siglo XX," in *O Modeno Já Passado o Passado no Moderno. Reciclagem, Recualificaçao, Rearquitetura*, eds. Carlos Eduardo Comas, Marta Peixoto, and Sergio M. Marques, DOCOMOMO Brasil (Porto Alegre: Ediciones UniRitter, 2009); also "El Palacio de Congresos, un tipo del siglo XX," in Summa+ 86 (Buenos Aires: Donn, 2007), 58–63, http://www.revistasummamas.com.ar/revista_pdf/86/30#visor

[4] Corona Martínez, *Ensayo sobre el Proyecto*, 14.

success gave world attention to the city of Bilbao and guaranteed large numbers of tourists for several years. After that triumphant outcome, attracting global attention became an implicit but dominant condition in the program requirements of similar institutional buildings, an accomplishment to be achieved by the combined effect of a well-known, even controversial architect, and the spectacular appearance of the design. Appearance as the dominant criterion has led to the fatal consequence that construction and cost are no longer considered when selecting design proposals, and, thus, spectacular architecture is usually no less than twice as expensive. As in the following examples, in many cases these institutional buildings are publicly financed and, as they often are integral to personal and political promotion, taxes are irresponsibly spent regardless of so many other considerations, leaving social and environmental issues waiting to be addressed.

Even if we reject spectacular architecture in principle, echoing the early warnings of Guy Debord,[6] we should acknowledge that it represents a good part of what is being built, discussed, and made visible to the general public of architecture's interests and goals. We should also admit there are urban and social issues arising from the repetitive failure of this kind of architecture. It therefore makes sense to address these problems and to try to understand their common roots. In the course of this review, we shall acknowledge that spectacular iconic buildings are not all the same, that even in this controversial category there are better and worse buildings.

I am presenting four buildings from the year 2011, all of which I have visited in the following years, in which the unwritten but most important part of the program was to produce an idiosyncratic, charismatic, iconic object that would put the respective clients, institutions, and cities on the front pages of newspapers. The prosaic requirements of ordinary buildings were only secondary considerations: economy, solidity, ease of use, sober but beautiful aesthetics, context-friendly, energy-efficient, low maintenance, reasonably sustainable. Not surprisingly, all of them were absurdly expensive.

The Metropol Parasol in Seville by Jürgen Mayer H., the Rolex Learning Center in Lausanne by SANAA, and the City of Culture of Galicia in Santiago de Compostela by Peter Eisenman have all failed dramatically in terms of addressing scale in different ways. A fourth project, Zaha Hadid Architects' Riverside Museum in Glasgow, gives a counterexample, a building in which the requirements of space and scale have been masterfully achieved, even if construction rationality, economy, and sustainability have been put aside in favor of a spectacular and iconic shape.

I believe that the recurrent misunderstanding of scale originates in the way the model has come to dominate both the project and the selection processes. As the jury concentrates on what models can say, it is obvious that the bird's-eye view gains in importance, as do the object-like qualities of the proposed building. The dominance of the scale model in design and judging has led to construction issues being postponed in favor of the desired spectacular, idiosyncratic appearance. But models have proved to be especially deceiving in terms of scale.

Imagining the proper scale of spaces is not easy, even for experienced architects. The same can happen in terms of material strength and section, which is not as difficult to predict, but architects competing in the field of spectacular architecture tend to postpone construction issues or not consider them seriously enough in the design process.

The first three projects illustrate different kinds of failures in terms of scale: in the relation between material strength and form, as happened in Seville; in the insensitive consideration of the ratio between usable area and the overall surface envelope produced by a continuous shape to achieve an iconic identity, as happened in Lausanne; or in the overall dimensional relation between building and landscape, as happened in Santiago de Compostela, where the scale of the external configuration necessary to achieve the landscape metaphor fatally diverged from the size of the inner spaces resulting from reasonable program requirements.

The extent to which models became the centerpiece of the design process in architecture schools has helped to naturalize them as the single legitimating device of a project. That

[5] This kind of idealism was still present in the first modern manifestos, such as Le Corbusier's *Vers une Architecture*.

[6] Guy Debord, *La Société du spectacle* (Paris: Ed. Gallimard, 1967).

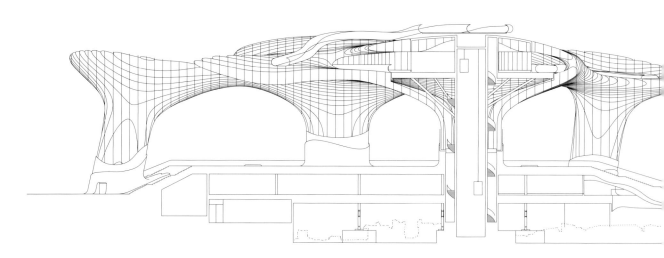

fig. 2
Redevelopment of Plaza de la Encarnación.
Program: urban space, covered market, ruins conservation, bars and restaurants.
Architect: Jürgen Mayer H., Andre Santer, Marta Ramírez Iglesias.
Seville, Spain / 2011.

was followed by a similar shift in how projects are chosen in competitions, in part because of the excluding importance that is now given to the image, but also because models appear to be easily read and compared. This also leads to a customary bias in favor of the aerial view, even though there are no high points from where the buildings in question could be contemplated. I am not arguing against the use of the model as a valid means in designing and judging a project, but against the complete displacement of all the other instruments that provide a comprehensive understanding of the different qualities of a project.

Misunderstanding the Strength of Materials at Different Scales

Jürgen Mayer H.'s project concentrated its efforts on the design and construction of an urban-scale canopy that places the rest of the program below in unlit, uninteresting, second-class spaces. The Parasol consists of a very large, apparently wooden structure that covers part of the plaza, and an elevated upper public space that can be accessed by means of very long escalators. In fact, this is the roof of the covered market, restaurants, cafés, and, below them, some Roman ruins. The huge canopy casts shadows on a sizable but limited part of the lower plaza, except at midday, when it is most needed. Because of its high elevation, the obvious problem of the upper plaza is that it lacks a fluid transition with the urban space of the Plaza de la Encarnación. Furthermore, the project sacrifices the importance of the former covered market, as it now has little natural light and no spatial interest at all, thereby ignoring the magnificent tradition of nineteenth-century covered markets that has been particularly powerful in Spain.

The main feature of the project, the one that catches the visitor's attention, is the canopy. The promenade across the roof offers a truly spectacular view of the canopy itself and of the city. The observatory and café at that level can only be reached by taking elevators that are hidden inside the pillars of the canopy, thus completely separating this experience from the urban space and the covered market.

It is clear that jurors for this competition were fascinated by the promise of the wooden canopy without paying attention to the distance between model and reality, between form and construction. Following the jury's decision, the internationally renowned engineering firm Arup declared that the first version was impossible to build. The simple constructive logic of the wooden sheets in the model proved to be almost impossible to translate into reality. Its suggestive shapes resulted from the intersection of openwork plywood sheets, but the strength of wood diminishes proportionally in real scale. Wood fibers do not grow

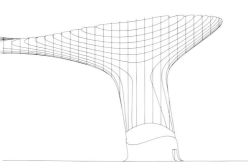

stronger with size, they retain the same structural properties. It is known that avant-garde engineering firms working in highly publicized projects enjoy solving the most irrational challenges as long as budgets allow unrestricted research. This is the fatal outcome of a competition system that is interested neither in determining what the constructive solutions should be, nor in the cost and time that its completion will require. The result is a trip into the unknown. In the case of the Parasol this trip culminated in political scandal. When a solution was finally detailed, it involved birch wood from Finland, the only material light enough to allow for the large cantilevers, but only after extensive and complex steel reinforcements and joints were devised that replaced the simple interlacing wooden sheets of the model; not to mention the enormous reinforced concrete cores and steel structures that remain intentionally hidden so as to present a seemingly all-wooden structure.

    This disproportionate effort pays off in the picturesque views that are offered both from below and from the upper promenade and panorama restaurant above the city. However, the construction cost was exactly twice the original budget, thereby delaying the project and raising legal claims and fierce criticism on the misuse of public funds. Summarizing the failures of the project, it is evident how both architects and jurors misunderstood the material scale, deceived by the visual quality of the model and its constructive suggestions that laid claim to an unrealistic constructional analogy. It was the seductive effect of the perspectives of the canopy that justified the poor spatial interiors for the covered market.

It is an indictment of the poverty of contemporary criticism that the Parasol won numerous industry awards thanks to its photogenic and spectacular appearance, despite being unmistakably weak in all other aspects as an urban space intervention. Unfortunately, real trees were not considered. They would have been a cheaper, simpler, more sustainable way of providing shade, having the additional advantages of shedding their leaves in winter, and producing, instead of consuming wood.

Misunderstanding the Scale between Configuration and Usable Area

Again, in the case of the Rolex Center, the model is the key means of communication for the project. The parti relies on the allusion of a pliable sheet with holes, like a thin slice of Emmental cheese, a formal quality that is clearly visible in the photographs of the model presented by the architects. The model assumes this suggestive role, producing a pregnant and synthetic image of an iconic, sculptural object that could have been appreciated when seen from above, if only there were sufficiently elevated viewpoints around the building.

This decision produced two radical effects. Although the inclined interior surfaces seem playful, suggesting freedom and a continuous flow of space, in most cases they are too steep, and therefore too uncomfortable either to walk across or to use in another way.

fig. 3
Rolex Learning Center of the Federal Polytechnic School of Lausanne.
Program: education, learning center, library, office workspace, café, meeting spaces.
Architect: SANAA – Kazuyo Sejima, Ryūe Nishizawa.
Lausanne, Switzerland / 2011.

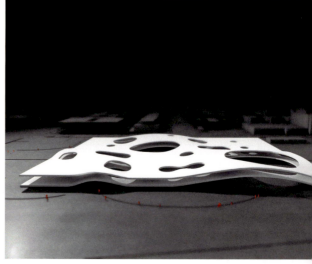

With mystifying informality, they suggest the naive idea that casual lying on the floor can enhance learning or creativity, but their ultimate reason is undeniably formal. The fatal consequence of this assumption is that only half of the interior space is really useful, and in most cases only after installing horizontal platforms, as is clearly seen in the library, enclosed offices, and glass boxes. The larger room that serves as the auditorium surprisingly has a flat floor and a uniformly low ceiling so as to make it a completely soulless space. An opportunity has been lost to use the sloping floor theme, perhaps because it should also serve as an exhibition space.

The competition model consisted of a curved, perforated sheet that suggested flexibility, contrasting flaccid deformation with the known rigidity of construction materials, in an unavoidable evocation of Dalí's surreal soft clocks—a plastic, visual priority that subordinated most construction considerations. Its materialization required constructive efforts at odds with common sense and with the principle of sustainability that was already expected from university buildings even in those days.

The construction company proudly explained that the concrete slab, which in the end had to be one-meter thick, required 50-mm-diameter reinforcement bars, and that it had to be poured in a continuous session lasting several days and nights.[7] All this extraordinary engineering effort meant that CO_2 emissions were several times higher just to fulfill a strictly aesthetic metaphor. The thickness of the slab may not have been properly anticipated, as the competition model suggests. Nevertheless, this unconscionable waste is presented by the client as an extraordinary accomplishment, as a proof of its commitment to the cause of education, a corrupted logic that has become standard for spectacular architecture: to present as a virtue something that is actually unnecessarily complex and exorbitantly expensive.

The building's rather lax program, suggesting a social condenser for the campus, allowed more precise functional specification to be avoided, proving that clients and sponsors were more interested in the spectacular nature of the proposal than in the building's usefulness. In stunning contrast with more calibrated projects by the same architects (Grace Farms in the US, for example), the project fails to establish any connection with the surrounding gardens. Due to the wavy section, it also fails to connect the inner spaces with the exterior vaulted covered spaces. This shape restricted the ability of the interior space to connect to the exterior, quite in opposition to the flexibility that should be expected from any continuous open plan. In conclusion, in terms of sustainability and economical use of materials, it can be said that, except for military bunkers, the Rolex Center is one of the heaviest one-floor buildings ever built.[8]

Misunderstanding the Scale between Configuration and Inner Space

Located on the southern outskirts of Santiago de Compostela, the mimetic geographical ambition of this project is quite obvious, not only from the architect's use of artificial hills but also from the scale itself. The built mass required to achieve this landscape metaphor largely exceeds the volumetric needs of the program spaces. The resulting rolling hills covered in rustic stone produce a disconcerting effect, looking like neither topography nor building.

Peter Eisenman won the competition with a suggestive wooden model, in which the new City of Culture resembled low hills, showing a similar dimension to that of the historic center. Narrow creeks were to echo the scale of the narrow streets of old Santiago. The model emphasized the old city and the new citadel in thin plywood, producing an irresistible image that seduced most of the jury, except Wilfried Wang, who noticed the scalar trap contained in the model.

After winning the competition, Eisenman wanted to take the model to New York, insisting that he needed it to reliably document the project. But the client refused, because he understood that the model represented the "contract" between the city and the architect and, therefore, should remain in Santiago;[9] a symptomatic episode revealing that the model itself was the only available register of the winning project, and that the author himself did not have any further detailed information of the design.

[7] Agnes Weilandt, Manfred Grohmann, Klaus Bollinger, and Michael Wagner, "Rolex Learning Center in Lausanne: From Conceptual Design to Execution," in *Proceedings of the International Association for Shell and Spatial Structures (IASS) Symposium 2009*, eds. Alberto Domingo and Carlos Lázaro (Valencia: Universidad Politécnica de Valencia, 2009).

[8] The famous critical question asked by Buckminster Fuller about The Sainsbury Centre can be recalled here: "How much does your building weigh, Mr. Foster?" See Deyan Sudjic, "How Much Does Your Building Weigh?" in *AV Monographs*, no. 143 (Madrid, 2010).

[9] Lecture by Eric Goldemberg at the University of Buenos Aires Architectural School, September 1, 2003.

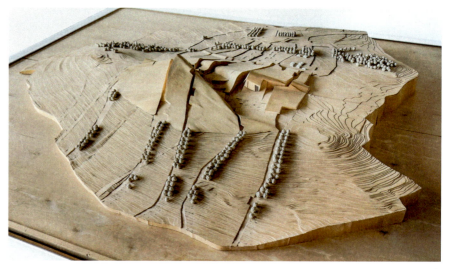

Eisenman was given no choice but to scan the wooden model and to take the digital data to New York to produce precise orthographic plans for the entire project that until competition stage had existed only as vague documents, not to even mention detailed construction plans. For this reason, Eisenman's project contained huge voids between the outer envelope and the usable inner spaces. This immense poché was reserved for the engineers, enabling them to integrate the structural frame and services. It was also a design resource that allowed for the independent design of exterior and interior surfaces, in a process by which the architect could completely ignore practical issues to concentrate exclusively on plastic and expressive aspects.[10] Eisenman delegated all practical issues like structure and services to Eurostudios International, an engineering firm, whose mission was to turn the architect's design into something buildable and operable without altering the appearance of the exterior and interior expressive surfaces.

fig. 4
City of Culture of Galicia.
Program: National Library, National Archive, Heritage Research Center, Galician History Museum, International Art Center with Children's Museum, Cultural Liaison Center and Workshop Stage.
Architect: Peter Eisenman Architects. Santiago de Compostela, Galicia, Spain / 2006–2011.

[10] Eric Goldemberg, "Entrevista a Peter Eisenman," in *Summa+ 63* (Buenos Aires: Donn, January 2004), 62–71.

Eisenman enjoyed this total split between appearance and construction. Despite this freedom and the elaborated fragmentation of the ceilings, most of the realized inner spaces lack a sense of scale or any proportional grace, as can be seen in the library and the outer galleries. On the outside, the shapes of the artificial hills do not engage in any perceivable way with the surroundings.

The stone slabs covering the hill-like shapes presented so many problems that they had to be retrieved and remounted, exposing the artificiality and constructional difficulties of the chosen solution. All these construction setbacks only added to the inherent scalar problems of the originally oversized scheme, to the point that it became financially impossible to finish. While the Junta de Galicia should take blame for the oversized program, the acceptance of the model's promise of a geographical allegory necessarily pushed to add more program surface. Anyway, for all of the project's intentions to produce a parallel landscape, it lacks both physical and visual connections to the immediate natural and urban surroundings.

Counterexample

Although Zaha Hadid's Glasgow Museum was also born from a model, and even a quite sculptural metallic one, she managed to define the appropriate scale for the gigantic interior space, twisting it so as to suggest dynamic movement and, at the same time, avoiding the presentation of a complete view of the whole exhibition space, in such a way that the colossal window at the back cannot be seen from the front of the building and neither can the equally enormous front window be seen from the rear part of the single nave. The simplicity of its continuous, bright, and optimistic interior generously frames the heterogeneous contents of this museum dedicated to transport.

It is ironic that the mighty machines of the nineteenth and twentieth centuries, those objects of superb mechanic rationality that inspired the first modern movement in architecture, the *machine age* in Banham's terms, now lie meekly like harmless toys in this fantastic twenty-first-century container, whose shapes are pure emotion, where construction goes against all the rational rules that made the factories in which those same cars and locomotives were produced.

From the outside, the most visible aspect of the building is the deliberately cartoonish gesture of a factory roofscape that is projected on the main facades, reminiscent of pop art, sources rarely seen in Hadid's work. All the same, the almost comical stylization of the factory roofscape is presented as a tribute to Glasgow's industrial history.[11] At first glance, the Riverside Museum could not look simpler: a huge factory shed with sloping tin roofs, whose rectilinear plan is curved twice. But a second look reveals exactly the contrary, a building of extreme constructive complexity conceived against the typology of the conventional industrial building with long trusses supported on two parallel load-bearing walls, producing generous spans. In the so-called sawtooth or shed roof, the inclined roofs connect the top of one truss with the bottom of the next, fulfilling the double function of draining rainwater and taking advantage of the height of the truss to admit generous daylight. The rational logic that generated the sawtooth profile was widely identified with the nineteenth-century factory.[12]

Defying this logic, Zaha Hadid breaks with the very nature of the traditional factory roof. Its graceful lightness is replaced by a complex and sophisticated tubular structure of uniform thickness that follows the folds of the roof. All these efforts are bound to remain hidden, just as is the mysterious journey that rainwater must follow to drain from the valleys of the roof. The goal was to produce iconic, memorable, playful forms that would evoke factory roofs in the facades. But the apparent innocence of the playful and cheerful outside forms is only made possible by difficult constructive solutions and the discretional use of steel in quantities beyond any practical thinking, arriving at a structural scheme whose technical complexity and cost defies common sense.

Even if we were justified to condemn the building in terms of its constructional irrationality, wasteful economy, and unsustainability, it is a success in terms of its exhibition program.

[11] Malca Mizrahi, "La mujer artificial," *Summa+ 164* (Buenos Aires: Donn, June 2018), 50–51; Fernando Diez, "FFF (Form Follows Fiction)," *Summa+ 164* (Buenos Aires: June 2018), 52–63.

[12] A fine example is the Parque Móvil del Estado of Madrid, built by José Fonseca in 1944.

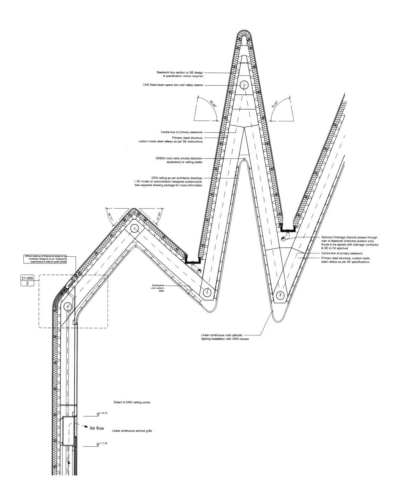

In terms of scale, it fulfilled the goal of containing in a cheerful, optimistic space the most nostalgic and gigantic machines of the past. It is also an obvious success in terms of exhibition space, public acceptance, and image memorability. Especially in terms of scale, it is a contrasting example with the three previous buildings.

In summary, the impressive, colorful interior spaces succeed in the scalar integration of both the visitors and the giant machines, and the external appearance provides a pregnant and playful image that gets the approval of visitors, especially the very young, but—and this is a big but—the irrationality of the structure makes it an inexcusably expensive, unsustainable construction.

Comparative Criticism

Contrary to the apparent ease in the process of enlarging a model, the translation from an architectural model to a real building could prove even more challenging than "Translations from Drawing to Building," which Robin Evans critically analyzed in his memorable essay of that title.[13]

These four cases of spectacular architecture, conceived by star architects, all originated in the bold and sheer expression of a model. Three architects succumbed to the hypnotic power of the model, misunderstanding scale in one way or another. Zaha Hadid did not. So the first question can be answered: design based only on a model provides a dangerous path to understanding scale, something that is frequently happening in the case of spectacular architecture judgment processes.

[13] Robin Evans, *Translations from Drawings to Buildings and Other Essays* (Cambridge, Massachusetts: The MIT Press, 1997).

fig. 5
Riverside Museum.
Program: transportation museum.
Architect: Zaha Hadid Architects.
Glasgow, Scotland / 2011.

Yet another important question remains to be answered in relation to the Glasgow Riverside Museum: could equivalent spectacular results be achieved with a rational structure, economy of means, and sustainable construction?

As a final exercise in the implicit method herein developed that can be called *comparative criticism,* I would like to answer that question by recalling the way Stirling and Gowan reshaped the factory sawtooth roof to produce a fantastic, yet light and luminous, volumetric form in their Leicester School of Engineering of 1963.

Biography

Fernando Diez (Buenos Aires, 1953)
Architect (1979) received his doctorate at UFRGS, Brazil, in 2005. Professor at Palermo and Torcuato DiTella universities and editorial director of *Summa+*. He holds a chair at the Argentine Academy of Environmental Sciences, the National Fine Arts Academy, and the Architecture and Urbanism Academy.

In the Absence of Appropriateness: On the Need to Respect and Sustain Existing Places in Making Additions

Robert McCarter

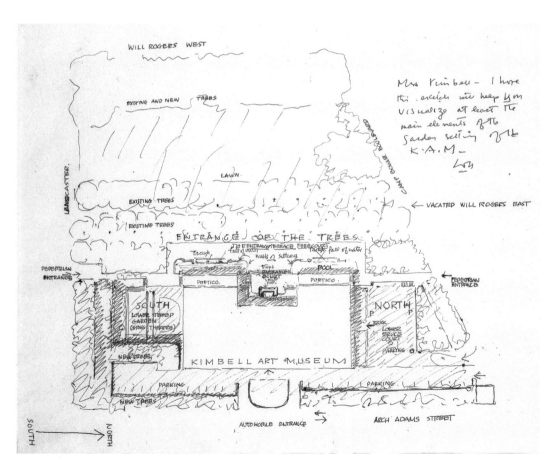

fig. 1
Sketch by Louis Kahn of site plan concept for Kimbell Art Museum, with the building opening and fronting on the existing double rows of elm trees, which Kahn calls the "Entrance of the Trees." Letter, Louis I. Kahn to Mrs. Velma Kimbell, June 25, 1969; Kimbell Art Museum Archives.

"I teach appropriateness. I don't teach anything else."[1]

Louis Kahn

Louis Kahn's significance as an architect is most powerfully present to those who inhabit his built works. Kahn's statements of principle, compelling though they may be as conceptual insights, remain abstract to us until we experience them embodied in his buildings. Thus, it can be argued that damage to Kahn's relatively few existing buildings, whether through outright demolition or, more insidiously, through inappropriate additions, is a loss of Kahn's legacy for us all and for all time. While there have been the notable exceptions of respectful renovations, since Kahn's passing in 1974, and with increasing frequency in recent years, a number of his most important buildings have been afflicted with additions that have damaged them in deeply disturbing ways—ways that have too often been insufficiently recognized and acknowledged. The most egregious of these additions have revealed the almost total lack of value the contemporary architectural profession places on the landscape, as opposed to the built form, by effectively erasing for all future inhabitants of the buildings both the experience of approach and entry through the landscape and the fundamental, complementary, and interdependent relationship of the building and the landscape that Kahn had worked so hard to achieve. These inappropriate and damaging additions and renovations also raise the troubling question of why, in undertaking such commissions, some contemporary architects, including the most celebrated, have been unwilling to treat Kahn's works and their contexts with the same deep respect that he invariably exhibited towards the places made by all the generations of architects who came before him.

As an example, this essay will undertake a critical evaluation of the recent addition to the Kimbell Museum, built to the designs of Renzo Piano in 2013. The Kimbell Art Museum (1966–1972), in Fort Worth, Texas, is rightly considered Kahn's greatest built work, in that it fully integrates and brings to the highest level of resolution all the elements comprising Kahn's conception of architecture: immeasurable and measurable, archaic and modern, mass and structure, light and shadow, room and garden, poetics of action and poetics of construction. Due to its significance among Kahn's works, and the fact that it is thought by many to be the greatest art museum of the twentieth century, the Kimbell Museum has been the most widely published of all Kahn's works and has been the subject of more scholarly studies than all his other works combined.[2] Furthermore, the Kimbell was the last building designed by Kahn that he lived to see completed.

The site selected for the Kimbell Museum in 1966 consisted of nine acres (3.6 hectares) in western Fort Worth, across the Clear Fork Trinity River from downtown. The

[1] Kahn, quoted in "Kahn on Beaux-Arts Training," ed. William Jordy, *Architectural Review* 155, June 1974, 332.

[2] Among the books are Michael Brawne, *Kimbell Art Museum: Louis I. Kahn* (London: Phaidon Press, 1992); Nell E. Johnson, *Light is the Theme: Louis I. Kahn and the Kimbell Art Museum* (Fort Worth, TX: Kimbell Art Foundation, 1975); Luca Bellinelli, ed., *Louis I. Kahn: The Construction of the Kimbell Art Museum* (Milan: Skira, 1997); and Michael Benedikt, *Deconstructing the Kimbell* (New York: Lumen Books, 1991). Kahn's three museums are examined in the excellent Patricia Cummings Loud, *The Art Museums of Louis I. Kahn* (Durham, NC: Duke University Press, 1989).

site was on the eastern edge of Will Rogers Park, to the north of the Will Rogers Auditorium, Coliseum, and Tower, and at the bottom of a gentle tree-covered slope at the top of which stood Philip Johnson's Amon Carter Museum, completed in 1960. Together with the future modern art museum, these buildings were intended to transform the public park into a kind of campus of art museums.[3] Kahn found the sprawling commercial development that surrounded the site uninspiring, and in response he focused his designs from the beginning on anchoring the new museum to the majestic double row of mature elm trees—originally planted as street trees in the city-owned right-of-way, aligning with the Will Rogers Coliseum and now centering the park—that were adjacent to the west edge of the site.[4]

Kahn arrived at what would be the final scheme for the Kimbell Museum in September 1968: a double-square overall massing divided into three equal volumes to form a C-shape in plan, the central volume recessed on the west, or park, side to form an entry court, flanked by open porticos, which together anchored the building to the double row of elm trees. The five sets of north–south vaults that form the roof and light-source of the museum were set parallel to the double row of elm trees, so that the lines of trees may be said to have given the "grain" of the building.[5] It is the existing public park with its double row of mature elm trees, not the streets and parking lots, that was to be shared by the cultural institutions making up the arts campus, and that Kahn believed his building should open onto and be entered from: notably, Kahn called this the "entrance of the trees." The landscape of the museum, in which the existing park and elm trees are an integral part, was accomplished with the assistance of the landscape architects George Patton and Harriet Pattison, and is recognized as Kahn's most elegant and convincing design of what he called "land architecture."[6]

Following the stated desires of the museum's original director, Richard Brown, and the trustees, Kahn designed the three open vaults of what he considered the primary or front facade of the museum to face the broad public park to the west, with its majestic double rows of elm trees. Kahn designed the museum to be entered, on foot, from the park and parallel to the elm trees to the west, where one arrives at the main gallery level. This is the result of his fundamental opposition to public buildings being oriented to arrival by automobile, rather than any "flagrant miscalculation of suburban habits," as it has been characterized.[7] In presenting this preference for the pedestrian over the automobile approach, the dramatic difference between the museum's front facade—the open, fully glazed wall, sheltered under an open vault at the upper (gallery) level, facing the park and the trees to the west—and the museum's back facade—the closed, solid concrete wall, recessed into the lower (service) level, facing the parking lot to the east—could hardly be more clear.

[3] Tadao Ando's Museum of Modern Art, designed for the southwest quadrant of the Will Rogers Park and which opened in December 2002, completes this impressive grouping of art museum buildings. The "campus" description comes from Brawne, *Kimbell Art Museum*, 7.

[4] This relation of the museum to the existing double row of trees to the west is clear in the letters Kahn wrote to Harriet Pattison, which included sketches of Kahn's ideas of opening the museum only to the trees as a way of anchoring the building to its site and landscape. Letters from Kahn to Pattison shared with the author during the efforts to stop or change the addition to the Kimbell Museum in 2010–13, some of which are published in Harriet Pattison, *Our Days are Like Full Years: A Memoir with Letters from Louis Kahn* (New Haven, CT: Yale University Press, 2020).

[5] Michael Merrill, *Louis Kahn: The Importance of a Drawing* (Zurich: Lars Müller, 2021), 180.

[6] Kahn, quoted in Richard Saul Wurman, *What Will Be Has Always Been: The Words of Louis I. Kahn* (New York: Rizzoli, 1986), 74. Kahn designed the landscape plan with Harriet Pattison, who, after serving an apprenticeship with Dan Kiley and receiving a landscape architecture degree from the University of Pennsylvania, was working in the office of the landscape architect of record, George Patton, who had been with Kahn at the American Academy in Rome.

[7] Doug Suisman, "The Design of the Kimbell: Variations on a Sublime Archetype," *Design Book Review* 11 (Winter 1987), 38. Suisman orientates his analysis to the tourist-architect, flying into the airport and driving to the Kimbell Museum, rather than to the experience of those who live in the Fort Worth area.

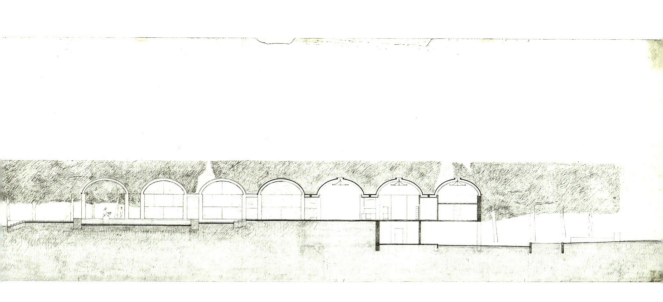

fig. 2
Drawing by Louis Kahn of the east–west section of the Kimbell Art Museum and its site, with existing elm trees in the park shown left and the roof vaults of the Kimbell Art Museum on the right; note the continuous shading canopy formed by the existing trees and building roof vaults. The Louis I. Kahn Collection, University of Pennsylvania and Pennsylvania Historical and Museum Commission.

The approach Kahn designed to the upper, gallery-level front doors on the museum's west side is very carefully articulated, involving a lateral approach on long, gently rising walks from north and south, one's passage framed between the building to the east and the double row of elm trees to the west that parallel the open vaults. One first passes sunken sculpture courts, walking under vaults closed to the museum to the east and open to the large trees and broad park to the west, beside sheets of cascading water, stepping down into a gravel court with a gridded bosque of small holly trees, and then, quietly, passing beneath an open vault and into the very heart of the gallery itself. After entering the museum beneath the central vault, the *only* view one is given outwards from within is through the one-hundred-foot-wide, ten-foot-tall glass wall of the entry foyer, which opens to the park and elm trees to the west.

As is evidenced in Kahn's correspondence with Harriet Pattison,[8] in Kahn's own words and drawings, and in appropriate criticism of the building since its construction, the relationship of the Kimbell Museum to the existing double row of elm trees to the west was absolutely critical to Kahn's conception of the museum as a building in dialogue with the landscape—as a set of vaulted rooms in a park, approached parallel to its tree rows so as to inextricably bind interior and exterior space together in what Kahn called the "entrance of the trees." Pattison noted that the three vaulted porches "were places of arrival and gathering that belong equally to the park and the museum. In them you are both inside and outside; they gather in the park—which owed so much of its character to the avenue of elm trees … That means the experience of the museum actually begins the moment you enter the park."[9]

Kahn intended that the architecture's three open porch vaults join with the natural canopy of the elm trees to provide the entire site with a continuous layer of cover and shading from the intense Texas sunlight—a possible reference to architecture's origins in the arboreal primitive hut.[10] This fusion of building, park, and trees is perhaps best shown in the remarkable east–west section through the Kimbell Museum and its site, a twelve-and-a-half-foot-long drawing (among the largest to be found in the archives) that indicates Kahn's desire to unify the vaults of the building with the elm trees and the landscape of the park. The section drawing, cut through the entrance and vaulted porch, shows Kahn pulling both the topography and the shading tree canopy of the park into the interior of the museum. In this drawing, "it is tempting to speak of the trees as architecture and the museum as landscape," as Michael Merrill has noted. "This drawing makes Kahn's *intent* clear: the reciprocity of building and park. Museum, trees, and topography are equal parts of a whole. If there is a single drawing that can be read as an indictment of the later addition to the Kimbell, then this is the one."[11]

[8] Harriet Pattison, *Our Days are Like Full Years*.
[9] Harriet Pattison, "Land Architecture, a Great Conversation," in Michael Merrill, *Louis Kahn: The Importance of a Drawing*, 310.
[10] I am indebted to Wilfried Wang for this suggestion.
[11] Michael Merrill, *Louis Kahn: The Importance of a Drawing*, 181.

Despite the ample evidence of the importance of the park to Kahn's design seen in the way the building closes itself off on three sides and only opens to and embraces the existing elm trees, the entirely inappropriate addition to the Kimbell Museum, completed in 2013 to the designs of Renzo Piano, has resulted in the destruction and removal of the existing elm trees (to make way for a two-story underground parking garage) and the obliteration of Kahn's intended intimate relationship between the museum and the park landscape, replacing it with an axial relationship between the original museum and the addition that now sits directly across from its entrance. Yet, as will be made clear in the following pages, Piano was originally commissioned in 2007 to design the addition to be built on the Kimbell-owned site to the southeast (behind and to the side) of the Kimbell, across from Tadao Ando's Modern Art Museum, and not in the public park to the west. Thus, there was never a need to choose between the new addition and the park and its existing mature elm trees to which Kahn intentionally and effectively anchored and opened the Kimbell Museum.

Before turning to the 2013 addition, a brief review of the history of efforts to make an addition to the Kimbell Museum since its completion in 1972 is in order. Less than ten years after its opening, it had become clear that the museum needed additional spaces for its growing collection of large-scale contemporary artworks, and the increasingly common temporary exhibitions (often requiring daylight control not possible in Kahn's top-lit galleries). In retrospect, Richard Brown's decision in early 1968 to cut the museum's program area in half and remove the temporary exhibition spaces, included in Kahn's earlier designs, proved to have been shortsighted.

By the late 1980s, the need for an addition had become urgent, and the Kimbell Museum's director, Edmund Pillsbury, commissioned a design for the addition from Romaldo Giurgola, a colleague of Kahn's at the University of Pennsylvania who was at the time teaching at Columbia University in New York. Giurgola proposed adding matching sets of vaulted rooms to the south and north ends of the museum, extending over and filling the sunken landscape courts, and thereby doubling the size of the galleries and the lower-level service and support spaces. Giurgola's design for the addition was met with an international protest, led by his fellow Columbia faculty members, among others, and Pillsbury decided to abandon the plans for the addition in February 1990. Following this decision, members of Kahn's family came to an agreement with the Kimbell director and trustees that any future addition would "not touch the original Kahn building."[12] Nothing was said about the building's relation to the landscape and existing elm trees, which were so critical to Kahn's anchoring of his building to the site and to his intentions regarding the entry sequence.

The need for an addition remained a pressing issue for the Kimbell Museum, however, and in the mid-2000s a decision was made to develop a new proposal. The site for the addition was the large rectangular block purchased by the museum in 1998 for this express purpose, which sits across Van Cliburn Way to the southeast of the Kimbell, bounded by West Lancaster, University Drive, and Darnell Street, and across from Tadao Ando's Modern Art Museum, which opened in 2002. In late fall 2006, I was asked by the Kimbell's curator of architecture, Patricia Cummings Loud (a leading authority on Kahn's museums), representing the Kimbell Museum staff, to conduct a studio for an addition to be built on the Kimbell-owned site to the southeast of the museum, with the understanding that the studio results would be used either to organize an architectural competition or to structure the hiring of an architect for the addition. I gave this as a graduate studio at Washington University in spring 2007, titled "Light is the Theme: An Addition to Kahn's Kimbell Art Museum." The program of spaces we generated with the Kimbell staff for the studio—which included temporary exhibition galleries, a bookshop, a larger auditorium, and additional service spaces, among others—was a close match for that later used in commissioning the addition.

Due to the fact that the Kimbell-owned land is at the highest elevation of the lower section of the park, and is not visible from within the Kimbell Museum, the students were able to explore partially burying and top-lighting the larger temporary exhibition galleries in

[12] As related to the author by Sue Ann Kahn and Nathaniel Kahn on several occasions since 2005.

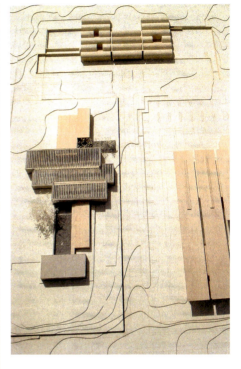

order to remain at or below the height of the Kimbell (as Ando had done with the much larger program of the Modern Art Museum), as well as to explore designs that were higher than the Kimbell and employed widely varying volumes, structural bays, and materials. Patricia Cummings Loud participated in the final jury, and a book documenting the twelve student designs was presented to the director of the Kimbell Museum, Timothy Potts. Just before the conclusion of the studio, the Kimbell announced on April 5, 2007 that Renzo Piano had been selected to be the architect for the addition. In keeping with the agreement with the Kahn family, the announcement stated, "The addition will comprise a separate building located across the street from the current Museum, on land acquired in 1998." Loud told me that Piano was given a copy of the booklet we prepared of the twelve Washington University student projects.

It is my understanding that, from receiving the commission in April 2007 until Potts stepped down as the Kimbell director, Piano developed schemes for various sites to the east of the Kimbell Museum, including the southeast site owned by the Kimbell, but also explored closing portions of the private roads (Darnell and Van Cliburn) to the east of the Kimbell. However, very shortly after Potts left and Eric Lee became director, rumors began to circulate that Piano was designing the addition on a different site—in the park to the west of the Kimbell. I visited the museum with the Dutch architect Wiel Arets in early May 2010, and during this visit we became aware of the proposed park site for the addition and its parking garage, which would result in the destruction of the double row of mature elm trees. Arets and I met with Lee, and argued that this was an egregious mistake, one that would destroy the Kimbell's relation to the land-

fig. 3
Site model photograph, Kimbell Art Museum addition design by graduate student Jessica Pfeffer, spring 2007, McCarter studio, Washington University in St. Louis.

fig. 4
Site model photograph, Kimbell Art Museum addition design by graduate student Kyle Thiel, spring 2007, McCarter studio, Washington University in St. Louis.

fig. 5
Site model photograph, Kimbell Art Museum addition design by graduate student Katie Meredith, spring 2007, McCarter studio, Washington University in St. Louis.

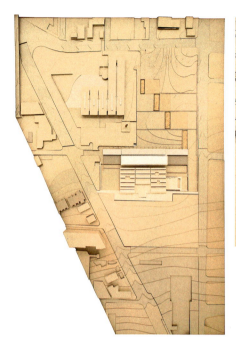 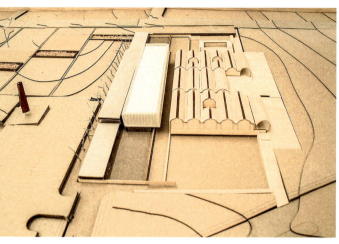

scape of its site and the critical qualities of the approach and entry sequence as envisioned by Kahn. Lee indicated to us that the architect had maintained that the sites to the east of the Kimbell could not be made to work, and that the site in the public right-of-way park to the west, directly in front of and on an axis with the Kimbell, was the only one that would work. I pointed out that the results of my 2007 graduate studio had shown that the Kimbell-owned site could in fact be made to work.

After it became clear in late 2010 that, instead of the Kimbell-owned site to the southeast, the public right-of-way park site to the west was where the addition was to be built—as a kind of "productive protest" as well as an "architectural offering" (in the spirit of Kahn), I taught a second graduate studio, titled "Alternate Reality: An Appropriate Addition to Kahn's Kimbell Art Museum," which ran in spring 2011. The students were allowed to propose their additions on *any* site around the Kimbell with the sole exception of the park site employed by Piano, which they were not to touch. The studio group visited the site in early February 2011, at which point the entire public park to the west of the Kimbell had been dug out to a depth of twenty-five feet, with the double row of mature elm trees destroyed. It was one of the most shocking and depressing events of my forty-five years of practicing architecture and thirty-five years as a teacher of architecture, and it highlighted the fact that the contemporary architectural profession often seems either unwilling or unable to make new buildings that are appropriate additions and that do not irreparably damage their contexts and landscape settings.

The premises of *appropriateness* that structured the spring 2011 studio were:
First, that architectural projects should be conceived not as freestanding, self-referential objects, but as appropriate and respectful additions to preexisting contexts. Kahn himself said that the only thing he felt he could teach his own students was to always consider "what was the appropriate thing to do" in any situation. **Second,** that the building and the landscape cannot be considered separate things, and must be designed, and added to, together. Kahn designed the Kimbell Museum to be a set of vaulted rooms in a garden, entered through the garden and its trees in an experience that inextricably binds interior and exterior space together. **Third,** that the primary ethical im-

fig. 6
Site model photograph, Kimbell Art Museum addition design by graduate student Guannan Chen, spring 2011, McCarter studio, Washington University in St. Louis.

fig. 7
Site model photograph, Kimbell Art Museum addition design by graduate student Guannan Chen, spring 2011, McCarter studio, Washington University in St. Louis.

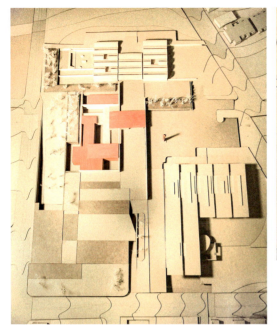

perative of any architectural project should be to never make the place in which one builds worse, and ideally to make it better, than it was before one intervened—this is the definition of appropriateness in action. **Fourth,** due to the canonical stature of the Kimbell Museum as the greatest art museum of the twentieth century, any proposed addition to it should be subjected to the most intense scrutiny, questioning, and criticism *before* it is built.

The results of the spring 2011 studio indicated, even more than the 2007 studio, that the sites to the south and southeast, being at the solid-walled "back" of the Kimbell, and in dialogue with the Modern Art Museum of Ando across the street to the north, allowed the addition designs considerable freedom in ordering geometry, position and scale, and could easily accommodate the building and the required underground parking garage without the removal of even one mature tree. The sites in the footprints of the private roads running north–south (Van Cliburn), parallel to the Kimbell vaults, and east–west (Darnell), on an axis with the rear entry of the Kimbell, proved particularly convincing as establishing a formal and spatial relationship with the closed back facade of the Kimbell without being visible from any place inside the museum. One could imagine a gifted architect making a true masterpiece of their own on these eastern sites, without having to build in the "front yard" of the Kimbell, and thus confront the Kahn building, as is necessitated by the formal, symmetrical, axial relation that inevitably occurs on the western, park site. Piano was repeatedly asked by the students and me to attend the final jury of this studio, but he did not accept our invitation.

The new addition designed by Piano has irreparably damaged Kahn's intended entry sequence (for those still stubborn enough to insist on taking it), so that one walks not between the Kimbell vaults and the park and trees, as Kahn intended, but between the vaults of Kahn and the addition of Piano. Upon entering the Kimbell and turning to look out the one-hundred-foot-long glass wall, one now sees a building, not the park and trees as in Kahn's design. Even worse, one now emerges from the new underground parking garage, which required removal of the double row of mature elms (and on top of which no large trees will ever be able to grow, despite any statements to the contrary by the architect[13]), and walks axially across the grass towards the Kimbell to the east, so that the west facade of Kahn's Kimbell, which was designed to be seen in parallel or tangentially to the approach, from within the vaults,

fig. 8
Site model photograph, Kimbell Art Museum addition design by graduate student Uros Stanajec, spring 2011, McCarter studio, Washington University in St. Louis.

fig. 9
Site model photograph, Kimbell Art Museum addition design by graduate student Uros Stanajec, spring 2011, McCarter studio, Washington University in St. Louis.

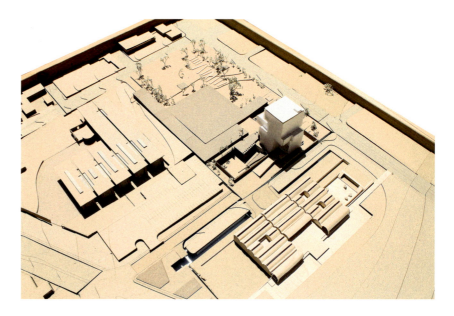

fig. 10
Site model photograph, Kimbell Art Museum addition design by graduate student Lynette Salas, spring 2011, McCarter studio, Washington University in St. Louis.

is now presented as a *frontal* facade—this drastically changes Kahn's original design and intention, and profoundly damages the experience he intended the visitor to have.

What has been lost is Kahn's intended relation of the museum and its approach to the park and trees, a change for the worse that is the direct result of the architect's insistence on putting the addition in the city-owned right-of-way park to the west, rather than on the sites to the east, owned by the Kimbell, that were given in the original commission. This western site for the addition necessitates a frontal, symmetrical "confrontation" between the new addition and the original Kimbell. As a result, the experience of the Kimbell Museum, in which Kahn's approach sequence and the view to the park from the interior play the most critically important part, is now irreparably damaged. We are now forced to approach the museum from the west, not from the north or south as Kahn intended. It has been suggested that the new approach from the garage to the west helps reinforce Kahn's reading of the Kimbell "front" being on the west side, but this is simply not true. Kahn never intended people to approach from the west, and certainly not from another building. Nothing whatsoever has been gained by the placement of the addition in the park to the west and the parallel destruction of the park and trees that Kahn designed as an integral part of the experience of both entering and being inside the museum. Kahn's idealized entry sequence to the Kimbell, and its relation to the landscape, park, and trees, all of which is now lost forever, will continue to exist in my and other earlier visitors' memories, for it was a very powerful and moving experience. But for those who never visited the Kimbell before the addition, what Kahn intended them to discover on approaching and entering the building is something they will never be able to experience.

Throughout this process, from the initial commissioning of the Kimbell Museum addition in 2007 to the completion of the Piano-designed addition in 2013, the silence of architectural critics and historians on the issue of the inappropriateness of Piano's siting of the building and the concomitant destruction of the landscape has been deafening. With the exceptions of Charles Birnbaum of the Cultural Landscape Foundation and myself (both of us being in contact with Harriet Pattison), no US-based critics or historians went on record in opposition to, or with any substantive criticism of, Piano's refusal to employ the Kimbell-owned site to the east given in the commission and the resulting destruction of the museum's essential relationship to the existing elm trees and park. Publications of the Kimbell addition after its opening focused exclusively on Piano's building and completely ignored the devastating effects of his site strategy on Kahn's intended experience of the Kimbell. Yet the architectural qualities of the

[13] In trying to convince the Kahn family to support the addition, Piano told them that the trees planted on top of the parking garage, replacing the nearly one-hundred-year-old elm trees he destroyed to make way for his addition, would match the original trees in size "within a few years"—a blatant falsehood; discussion between Kahn family members and the author in 2013.

addition's new galleries are entirely beside the point, as the fact remains that those galleries, and the addition they are housed in, could have been built on the Kimbell-owned sites to the east of the Kahn building, and thus coexisted with the Kimbell's intended relationship with the park and mature elm trees.

The addition to the Kimbell Museum exemplifies the absence of *appropriateness* in its design, and the concomitant lack of respect for the larger context of the landscape, which characterizes far too many contemporary additions and renovations. Yet in this case the situation has been compounded by Piano using the commission for the Kimbell addition to attempt the *appropriation* of Kahn's legacy. Since the start of his career, Piano has been obsessed with the legacies of Kahn and Le Corbusier,[14] and having been given the commissions to make additions to both architects' works, has used them as opportunities to attempt to appropriate their legacies for himself. More than any other building, Piano has throughout his career been mesmerized by Kahn's Kimbell Museum, on which his first major museum, the Menil Collection in Houston, Texas, is almost entirely based, and to which all his later museums may be directly related. But rather than engaging Kahn's Kimbell Museum as an inspiration for his own designs, Piano has been obsessed with appropriating Kahn's legacy as a museum designer.

In his attempt to appropriate the "mantle" of Kahn by the most inappropriate means, Piano destroyed the landscape which the Kimbell Museum embraced and employed to frame the entrance sequence, replacing it with the confrontation of the addition to the original building, thereby constructing a self-serving and fictitious "equal" relationship between Kahn and Piano through their respective buildings and forcing Kahn's Kimbell to face and front onto Piano's addition, rather than the now-destroyed landscape and elm trees that Kahn had so carefully integrated into his building.

In making the addition to the Kimbell Museum there was never a need to choose between the park and its trees and the new building—this was a "problem" entirely invented by the addition's architect. This is the opposite of what I would argue architects must do, which is to find a way to do the right thing and to do what is appropriate, however difficult that proves to be and however long it takes. The discipline of architecture must recognize that all architectural projects, in both urban and rural contexts, must be conceived as *additions* to preexisting places. In the making of additions, *appropriateness*, which Kahn believed was all that he could teach his students, resides in caring for, respecting, and sustaining those existing places.

[14] A separate essay would be required to discuss the equally egregious and damaging additions Piano has made to the Ronchamp Chapel and the Carpenter Center, both of which involve the destruction of the Le Corbusier-designed entry sequences and their being replaced by entry sequences that require one to confront the new buildings of Piano before arriving at the original buildings.

Biography

Robert McCarter is a practicing architect, author, and Ruth and Norman Moore Professor of Architecture at Washington University in St. Louis. He is the author of twenty-four books; he has had twenty-five architectural commissions realized; he has taught at eight institutions; and he has been named one of the "Ten Best Architecture Teachers in the US."

In Praise of Urban Continuity: Siza's Re-creation of the Chiado

Ana Tostões

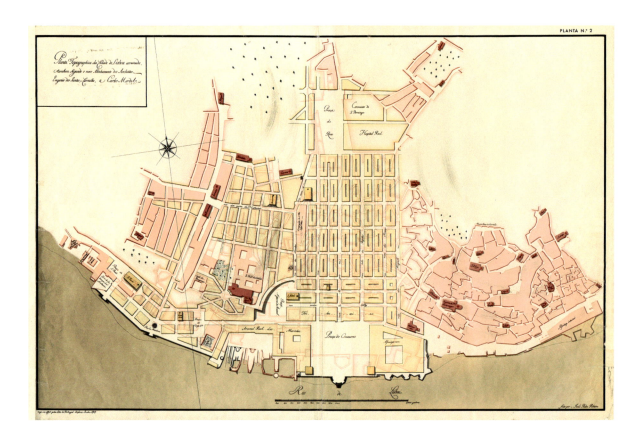

fig. 1
Eugénio dos Santos e Carvalho and Carlos Mardel, Baixa Reconstruction Plan, Lisbon, 1758.
Topographic plan showing the area in ruins (red) and the new street alignments. © Câmara Municipal de Lisboa, in Ana Tostões, Walter Rossa (ed.), *The Baixa Plan Today. Lisboa 1758* (Lisbon: CML, 2008).

"In the city of today, in an insensitive way, or almost, for many, slowly but continuously and in an accelerating process, the environment with which we identify is destroyed, as if that would be the condition for its transformation.

The transformation of the city is a natural phenomenon and proof of vitality, providing it takes place in accordance with the city's needs, which is, with the collective needs of the citizens.

And one of the collective needs is the daily experience of preserving the history of which the city is made, a fundamental contribution to the consciousness of history and becoming."[1]

Álvaro Siza

Looking at the architectural discipline as a civic art, architectural criticism requires us to consider how to respond to social demands, users, and the public in the creation of a better environment. Unlike architecture, city design has not been the subject of intense critical analysis in recent years. Indeed, the complex problems faced by large cities around the world, combined with changes in climate, global health crises, and demands for social equity, have led to an emphasis on the large interdisciplinary realm of urbanism at the metropolitan scale.[2] Nevertheless, some other refreshing approaches to the subject should be mentioned, namely the curatorial research *Demo:Polis* conducted by Barbara Hoidn and Wilfried Wang,[3] and Ricky Burdett's theme for the 10th Venice Architecture Biennale. The topic of public space has been identified as a crucial one for contemporary society, involving interactions between architecture and citizens, its real users.[4] More specifically, "much attention was paid to the role of architects when it comes to designing democratic and sustainable urban landscapes, as well as their links to policies of intervention, government statements and social cohesion."[5]

Kenneth Frampton, in his keynote lecture at the International Conference on Architectural Criticism, challengingly declared that "we [architects] are not designing cities anymore."[6] The difficulties of addressing the problems of the city are well-known, as they are linked to politics and the demands of a dominant market economy, which constantly foment urban chaos. In fact, there is an urgent need not for a city design that is "based on a modernist *tabula rasa*, but one that uses the existing fabric and structures to reinterpret and transform the city of today in a vibrant, yet sustainable and socially equitable—even beautiful—model of modern civilization."[7]

Continuity with the Existing City

In Lisbon, the reconstruction of the Baixa-Chiado area after it was destroyed by the fire of August 25, 1988, is a beautiful story that emerged from lively critical discussions on the preservation of historic city centers worldwide.

Álvaro Siza received his first commission in Lisbon to carry out the Plano de Reconstrução da Baixa-Chiado (Baixa-Chiado Reconstruction Plan, 1988–2015). He sought to restore the dignity and character of the area, originally determined by the 1758 Pombaline Plan of Eugénio dos Santos and Manuel da Maia, following the earthquake of 1755.[8] This led Siza to recognize the modernity of the typological principles underlying the plan, and their

keywords:

city reconstruction, urban continuity, public space, Siza, Lisbon, preexistences

[1] Álvaro Siza, "A cidade que temos," in *01 Textos por Álvaro Siza* (Porto: Civilização Editora, 2009), 19–20.

[2] Barbara Hoidn and Wilfried Wang, *21BB—Model Region Berlin-Brandenburg* (Zurich: Park Books, 2020).

[3] Barbara Hoidn and Wilfried Wang, *Demo:Polis: The Right to Public Space* (Zurich: Park Books, 2016).

[4] Hoidn and Wang, *21BB*.

[5] The importance of cities and their significance to society was identified in 2006 by Richard Burdett in his approach at the 10th Venice Architecture Biennale to the topic "Centered on Cities. Architecture and Society" that focused on the theme of "global cities," they being cities where more than three or four million people permanently live and which face various problems, from immigration to growth complications, from the evolution of mobility to sustainable development research. The exhibition takes into account some crucial questions of contemporary society, trying to delve into the possible interactions between architecture and its real users. More specifically, much attention was paid to the role of architects when it comes to designing democratic and sustainable urban landscapes, as well as to their links to policies of intervention, government statements, and social cohesion.

[6] "On the Duty and Power of Architectural Criticism," ICAC International Conference on Architectural Criticism, online conference, October 9–10 and October 16–17, 2021, hosted by the School of Architecture, The University of Texas at Austin, organized by Wilfried Wang.

[7] Hoidn and Wang, *21BB*.

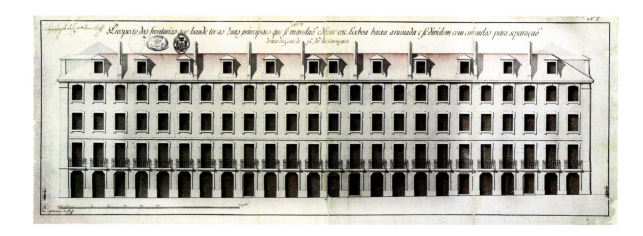

fig. 2
Eugénio dos Santos e Carvalho, Baixa Reconstruction Plan, Lisbon, 1758. Project for the facades of the main streets. © Câmara Municipal de Lisboa, in Ana Tostões, Walter Rossa (ed.), *The Baixa Plan Today. Lisboa 1758* (Lisbon: CML, 2008).

unique and underappreciated place in the history of global urban planning, and the innovative and remarkable example of the Enlightenment city they produced.[9] The fundamental unit that determined the character, flexibility, and capacity for transformation and resilience of the Baixa-Chiado was an urban typology with uniform facades, incorporating residential and church buildings in a single block.

Notwithstanding the strongly postmodernist leanings in Lisbon in 1987, when Siza was invited, he proved himself capable of dealing with the complex situation and the strong feelings it stirred among architects. In this, he was fully supported by the project's commissioner, Mayor Nuno Abecasis, with the wise backing of the president of the Order of Architects, Nuno Teotónio Pereira, who deemed that the nature of the project did not warrant an architectural competition.[10]

Siza had long been familiar with Fernando Távora's 1969 urban renewal project for the Barredo neighborhood, which became a landmark for urban renewal in Porto and for historic city centers in general. Following Távora's acknowledgment of heritage considering the importance of what already exists, remained a twofold concept that has characterized the most erudite architectural culture in Portugal. In fact, the idea of preexistence was key for Siza's practice, not just in his early work but also in the SAAL projects from the 1970s,[11] the design of the Malagueira Plan in Évora, and his designs to renew the Giudecca neighborhood in Venice (1985), just to mention projects on a city scale.

When, in 1966, Aldo Rossi published *L'Architettura della Città*,[12] he initiated a powerful redirection that had a profound impact on architectural culture and helped reestablish the discipline of urbanism. The search for the continuity of the historic city was one of the fundamental strands of his work.

In line with the teaching of Ernesto N. Rogers,[13] three key themes for the construction of architectural culture were explored: firstly, the importance of context; secondly, the fundamental role of the history of architecture, and the consequent duty to continue expounding the teachings of the masters, ancient and modern; and lastly, the centrality of discussion about tradition in the European city and the idea of the monument.[14] The emblematic role and influence of *L'Architettura della Città* was immense, comparable in its time to the treatises of the classical period. To understand architecture in relation to the city—in terms of political management, memory, rules, layout, and housing—it seized on urban morphology and constructive typology as the scientific basis for analysis and action, and identified two basic elements of the Aristotelian city: the public sphere and the private sphere. Consequently, both the monument (a building or public space that appears exceptionally in the city as a result of uncommon collective efforts) and residential areas (the housing that forms the basic fabric of the city conceived from a logic of repetition) were considered to be of equal importance

[8] On the morning of November 1, 1755, an earthquake—known as the Great Earthquake—succeeded by a tsunami and several fires shattered into ashes a large area of Lisbon city center. For the reconstruction of this area a legal charter by Eugénio dos Santos and Manuel da Maia was published in 1758 constituting the basic law governing this reconstruction plan. This event drew international attention, leading, for example, Voltaire to write about it and Telemann to compose an ode. See Ana Tostões and Walter Rossa, eds., *The Baixa Plan Today: Lisboa 1758* (Lisbon: CML, 2008).

[9] The plan for the reconstruction of Lisbon city center has to be placed between the creation of Saint Petersburg and Washington in order to fully understand its international importance. Pombaline Lisbon is an example of the Enlightenment philosophical approach to urban design between these two events: in 1703 Peter the Great ordered the construction of the city of Saint Petersburg, in a place where there was nothing—raising it from mud of the Neva River; in 1791, along the Potomac River, Washington was established as the symbolic city of a new country, the United States of America, representative hereby of the new world freed from colonial power. And exactly in the middle of the eighteenth century, a new Lisbon was designed within the ruins of an old city, as a radical redefining plan, which was approved on the same day that Louis XV approved the plan of the Place de la Concorde in Paris. In Lisbon a magnificent square was designed too, but Pombaline Lisbon is more than just the fantastic Praça do Comércio: it is a whole system that reflects a global idea of the city, an ideology at the service of a

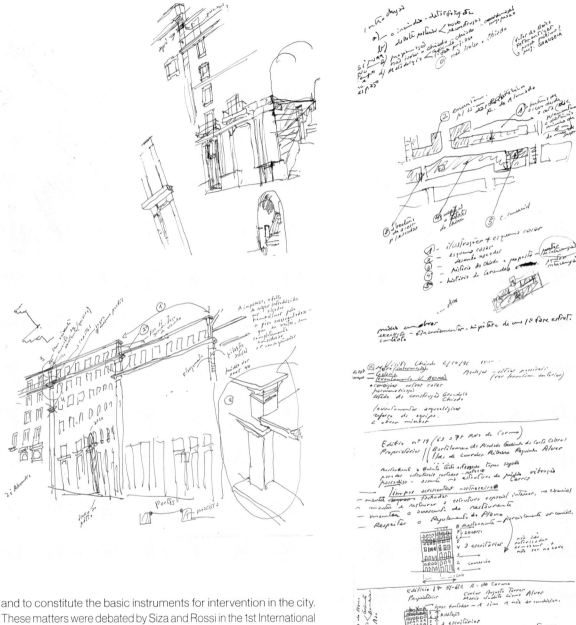

and to constitute the basic instruments for intervention in the city. These matters were debated by Siza and Rossi in the 1st International Seminar on Contemporary Architecture (SIAC), held in Santiago de Compostela in 1976.[15] During these years there were diverse inputs. Fernando Távora was working on preserving the historic center of Guimarães, there was an ascendant Italian contribution to typology by Gregotti, Grassi, and Giancarlo De Carlo, while important exchanges with Spanish practitioners, such as the Barcelona architects Oriol Bohigas, Rafael Moneo, and the young Carlos Martí Aris, were fundamental for reconsidering a contextual approach to intervention in the city.

At the end of the 1980s, Álvaro Siza surprised everyone with his Baixa-Chiado Reconstruction Plan, by choosing to enhance the existing built heritage, recognizing the validity and modernity of the Pombaline Plan, and restoring the typical urban blocks and facades.

fig. 3 a–d
Álvaro Siza, Baixa-Chiado Reconstruction Plan, Lisbon, 1988–2015. Sketch. © Álvaro Siza Archive/CCA.

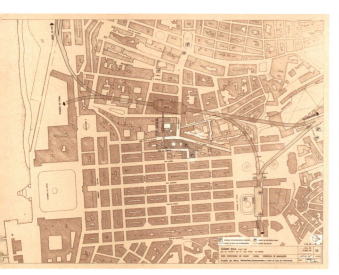
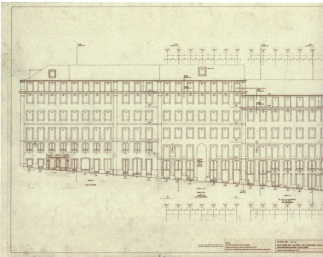

An Unprecedented Rationality: The Enlightenment and Portuguese Plain Architecture

Usually known as the Pombaline Plan (in reference to its instigator, the Marquês de Pombal), the 1758 "pilot plan" of Baixa-Chiado was the first planning tool to dictate the form of an area that was crucial for the city and for the image of the country itself. Besides this immediate contribution, the plan represents an innovative part in the larger global mosaic of urban planning, and a fine example of the "Enlightenment City" whose importance had never previously been adequately considered. The Baixa, as we know it today, is the result of combining different building typologies (those of apartments and churches) into a unified whole. Eminent military engineers in the field of designing and constructing buildings worked pragmatically to produce a plan whose architectural features were dominated by the urban scale defined by the block.[16] This was the most avant-garde aspect of the plan, which expressed an unprecedented, dry, severe, and systemic rationalism, forcefully characterized by the uniformity and urban scale of its facades. This uniformity—which determined the character of the Baixa and gave it its ductile capacity for transformation and resilience—was not always appreciated and, during the nineteenth century, a series of attempts were made to gradually transform its system, described as being "insipid uniformity and boring austerity."[17]

A similar approach to that of Siza can be seen in the winning proposal for the Belém Cultural Center (CCB, 1988–1993) competition. Employing a rational and enduring architecture, directly integrated into the design of the city, Gregotti and Salgado's solution was based on a mixed hybrid megastructure that, taking the form of city blocks and a large building, assumed an undeniably urban vocation. The CCB asserted itself with a monumentality on an urban scale, rooted in the history of the city. In other words, the architectural design was a response to the desire to make a city that rejected abstract, non-contextual desires and the object-based fantasies of postmodern architecture.[18] The chosen course was to design a section of the city using contemporary architecture that was as neutral as it was erudite. It took its inspiration from the city of Lisbon, and also recognized the modernity of the 1758 Pombaline Plan for the Baixa. The architects of the CCB shared Siza's belief that a continuously produced city was key to retaining the meaning, character, and unique beauty of the city of Lisbon.

It is a city whose architecture has withstood the prevailing context of a market economy that views the city as a great spectacle and insists on the idea of novelty at all costs. However, when the art of building cities is primarily seen as a service, it is understood that individual, unrestrained, and isolated gestures tend to undermine various aspects of normality on which

fig. 4
Álvaro Siza, Baixa-Chiado Reconstruction Plan, Lisbon, 1988–2015. Plan of Baixa with the intervention area marked and indication of the subway line and station and parking garages, 1989. © Álvaro Siza Archive/CCA.

fig. 5
Álvaro Siza, Baixa-Chiado Reconstruction Plan, Lisbon, 1988–2015. Elevation of Rua do Carmo, west side, 1993. © Álvaro Siza Archive/CCA.

rationalist pragmatism. It is a global plan that manifests design and thought in an integrated and consequent way, also taking into consideration legislation and financial engineering: Pombaline Lisbon has not singular buildings, it has blocks that synthesize the whole. It proposes a new, rigorous, and rational urban order of an unprecedented modernity. See Ana Tostões, "O Iluminismo Segundo José-Augusto França," in *Lisboa Pombalina e o Iluminismo*, ed. José Augusto França (Lisbon: Imprensa Nacional/Casa da Moeda, 2022).

[10] Siza reported the invitation in a peculiar way, disclosing some of the political details: "'Hello? Is it architect Siza? This is Nuno Abecasis. I am inviting you to direct the reconstruction of Chiado.' This was my first contact with Mayor Abecasis. So, with total conviction, almost as an order. I explained to him that it was an absolutely unexpected proposal for me, that I had to think about it. 'Fine. Think and then tell me yes.' (He had already referred to me as 'you,' and soon as 'kid'). At that time there was a controversy about 'what to do.' The Order of Architects argued for the holding of a competition, some declared it was an opportunity to modernize the Chiado (thinking about shapes?)." He continued further, stating that "at my request, the President organized a municipal office under his direct influence, appointing Engineer Pessanha Viegas, a highly

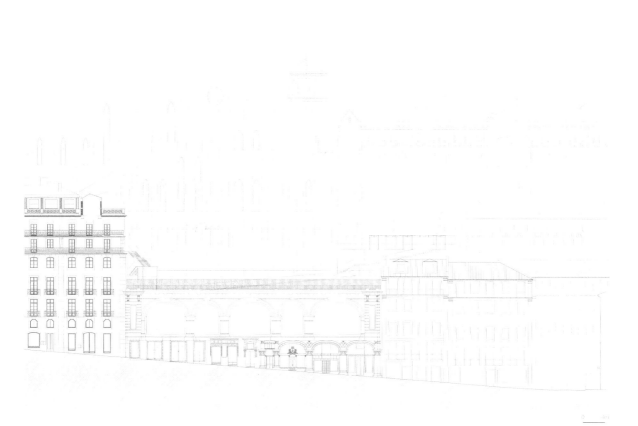

fig. 6
Álvaro Siza, Baixa-Chiado Reconstruction Plan, Lisbon, 1988–2015. Section, showing the surrounding area. © Álvaro Siza Archive/CCA.

the city's viability and the quality of urban life depend. The strategy adopted by Siza for the Baixa-Chiado Reconstruction Plan reflects this understanding.

Siza focused on the interaction between urban design and architectural scale, keeping existing elements and proposing new elements in continuity with them. As was his habit, he revisited the original methodology of the eighteenth-century post-earthquake reconstruction plan and, in so doing, confirmed the value of researching historical urban documents for devising strategies for building the city of the future.

Siza understood that, with the exception of the special typology of the Chiado and Grandella buildings, the typology of all the buildings within the plan area, despite their varying construction dates, was "Pombaline," and recognized the importance of successive changes to their facades. He distinguished the Chiado building (or Palácio Barcelinhos) as a unique case with a complex history, and interpreted the specificity and persistence of its condition as a monument, built by geography and time. He also highlighted that the Grandella building introduced a new typology and a new technique, and that, like the Armazéns do Chiado building, it formed a connecting piece between the Baixa and Chiado levels.

Siza's reconstruction plan became a reference work because it was based on the courageous choice to remake the city in continuity with its permanencies. With great insight, Siza placed the discourse of architectural language secondary to the the discourse of the city.

After the fire that dramatically exposed the deterioration and loss of housing in this area, the reconstruction plan focused precisely on improving public space. It did so in two ways: firstly, by designing the whole as a neighborhood and creating new urban paths through interstitial patios in the courtyards; and secondly, by using a repetitive modular facade design that adopted the eighteenth-century Pombaline typology as a central unifying element of the urban space. Furthermore, Siza's plan sought to programmatically improve this important civic and commercial space of the old city by reinforcing its housing component. Thus, the reconstruction rescued the memory of the site by restoring the typological principles of the

competent technician with recent experience in the rehabilitation of Angra do Heroísmo, as director. My work was thus surrounded by all the support possible, not least the support of Abecasis's unwavering optimism—a rare and almost inexplicable kind of serenity surrounding a feverish activity. Nuno Abecasis's action at Lisbon City Council provoked many critics, great controversy, and great passion. Since the beginning of my work, all these 'things that are too agitated' have become secondary for me, due to the evidence of one thing that does not have to be agitated: authenticity." In Álvaro Siza, "Abecasis," in 01 Textos por Álvaro Siza, 221–22.

[11] Started after the 1974 Revolution by Nuno Portas, then secretary of the state for housing, the Serviço de Apoio Ambulatório Local (Local Ambulatory Support Service, SAAL) process was an architectural and political experiment where architects collaborated with city-dwellers, intended to address extreme housing shortages and poor living conditions in Portuguese cities by creating decent, affordable homes. See Delfim Sardo, ed., O Processo SAAL: Arquitectura e Participação 1974–1976 (Porto: Fundação Serralves, 2014).

[12] Aldo Rossi, L'Architettura della Città (Padova: Marsilio editori, 1966).

eighteenth-century Pombaline Plan. At a time when the works of prominent architects seemed destined only to affirm their creator's idiosyncrasies, based on an aesthetic of rupture with the urban fabric and a personal reading of the city, the choice to make a new city in continuity with the existing one provided a countervailing example for the future. In fact, in the 1990s, it was an unequivocal symbol, bearing the authority of the Portuguese architect who was most famous internationally, that it was possible to remake the city without resorting to rupture.

City, Memory, and Transformation

Two decades later, in the Pombaline Baixa, but outside the area covered by Siza's plan, Gonçalo Byrne and João Pedro Falcão de Campos rebuilt a Pombaline block in their design for the headquarters of the Bank of Portugal, and reinvented the *Fábrica Pombalina* (the typical block of the Baixa). They revealed a deep understanding of this dynamic by restoring three key elements of the plan: the block; the hierarchization of the facades shaping the public space; and the typological relevance of the "*saguão*" (a longitudinal light well) and its role in the articulation of the whole.

Allied to the wisdom of Byrne's long experience was Falcão de Campos's trained Loosian rigor, applied with irreprehensible logic in their utilization of existing things as tools for new architectural creation. The intervention restored the memory and the identity of the Baixa, and reaffirmed its institutional, representative, and cultural centrality.[19]

fig. 7a
Baixa-Chiado, Lisbon, Rua de São Julião. © Ana Tostões/José Manuel Espada.

fig. 7b
Baixa-Chiado, Lisbon, Rua Garrett. © Ana Tostões/José Manuel Espada.

fig. 8
Baixa-Chiado, Lisbon, Calçada de São Francisco. © Ana Tostões/José Manuel Espada.

fig. 9
Baixa-Chiado, Lisbon, window and door detail at Rua Nova do Almada. © Ana Tostões/José Manuel Espada.

It was the Lisbon Master Plan of 1968 that consummated the political strategy of transferring the central business district from the Baixa to the Avenidas Novas quarter, and condemned the city's former business area to decline, thus hastening the process by which the exceptional architectural ensemble resulting from the Pombaline Plan became increasingly disfigured.

However, with the renovation of the headquarters of the Bank of Portugal, the institutional, representative, and cultural centrality of the Baixa was once again revived, and the *Fábrica Pombalina* reinvented through reconsideration of the three key elements of the plan. Byrne and Falcão de Campos reestablished the planimetric matrix of the block, articulating the church and the adjacent buildings according to the hierarchical principles of the Pombaline program.

fig. 10
Baixa-Chiado, Lisbon, patio. © Ana Tostões/José Manuel Espada.

In an erudite work of architecture, which followed the principles Siza had developed in the Chiado, Byrne and Falcão de Campos then reconciled extremely demanding regulatory and constructional requirements. Envisaged as an ongoing process of knowledge and clarification, they interpreted the historical context of the place, and responded to technical infrastructure and energy needs, and to problems of access and security. They combined the lengthy time spans of archaeological research and faithful restoration of stone elements with a discussion of the functional program and technical solutions.

The revitalization process was clearly spurred by a new element in the form of the Baixa-Chiado subway line, which had recently been inaugurated and functioned as a link between the lower and upper topographic levels. The future of the Baixa, undoubtedly hinted at in the Detailed Plan for the Devastated Area of the Chiado (Plano de Pormenor para a Zona Sinistrada do Chiado), involves a concerted strategy to embrace progress while ensuring continuity. The structuring projects being launched in the first decades of the new millennium are proof of this desire to continue the "first integrated plan" and confirm the resilience of this exceptional "conceptual plan."

In the 1990s, still within the Chiado plan, Siza designed the housing, services, and commercial complex Terraços de Bragança (1991–2004). Built on the ridge line of the Fernandina wall, it confirmed the course he had previously set, and filled the last void in an otherwise perfectly consolidated area of the city. He worked with this "gap" within the city, situated between two important streets at different levels, by seeking to create a dialogue with its surroundings, and discovering in them, and in the qualities of the site, the determining parameters of the project. A careful reading of the land, its topography, and the traces it had accumulated over time allowed a "natural" meaning to be found for the project. Thus, this topographical, topological, and historical "cleavage" was acknowledged morphologically and programmatically and, thus, continued the sense of the city.

Against an "Adjectivated Architecture"[20]

The award of the Secil Prize in 1997 to the Castro & Melo building, which was rebuilt in an area of the Baixa-Chiado destroyed by fire, recognized the remarkable way in which Siza had responded to a damaged part of the city center by rebuilding it while retaining its identity. The jury praised the fact that "the historical, environmental, literary and political precedents were transferred to specifically architectural, programmatic, typological, and morphological matters."[21] It was the first time the most important Portuguese award for architecture had recognized Siza's work, and specifically acknowledged a rehabilitation project, and also represented a

[13] Ernesto Nathan Rogers, *Esperienza dell'Architettura* (Milano: Skira, 1997 [1958]).

[14] Tostões and Rossa, *The Baixa Plan Today*.

[15] The I Seminario Internacional de Arquitectura Cintemporánea (SIAC), took place in Santiago de Compostela, coordinated by Rossi. This conference was followed by those in Seville (1978), Barcelona (1980), Naples (1982), and Belfort (1984). In each one, the debated theme was centered on the rehabilitation and reconstruction of historic city centers that were greatly impacted by the industrialization process, as happened with Belvis in Santiago, la Cartuja in Seville, and the Poblenou area in Barcelona. The contributions to the I SIAC are compiled in Salvador Tarragó and Justo G. Beramendi, eds., *Proyecto y ciudad histórica: I Seminario Internacional del Arquitectura en Compostela* (Santiago de Compostela: COAG, 1976). See Carolins Garcia Estévez, "Tan cerca tan lejos: Aldo Rossi Y el Grupo 2C. Arquitectura, ideología y disidencias en la Barcelona de los 70," in "arquitecturas en común," special issue, *Proyecto, Progreso, Arquitectura*, no. 11 (November 2014): 104–19.

[16] Tostões and Rossa, *The Baixa Plan Today*.

[17] Cyrillo Volmark Machado, *Collecção de memórias, relativas às vidas dos pintores e escultores, architetos e gravadores portuguezes, e dos estrangeiros que estiverão em Portugal...* (Lisbon: Imprensa de Victorino Rodrigues da Silva, 1823).

[18] "Vittorio Gregotti entrevistado por Nuno Grande e Roberto Cremascoli. 22.11.2017," in *CCB Vinte e Cinco Anos / Twenty Five Years*, ed. Nuno Grande (Lisbon: Fundação Centro Cultural de Belém, 2018); Ana Tostões, *Lisboa Moderna* (Lisbon: Docomomo International/Circo de Ideias, 2021).

[19] Ana Tostões, "Un presente perfetto: città, memoria, e reinvenzione. Il Banco de Portugal di Lisbona," *Casabella*, no. 839/840 (July/August 2014): 46–53.

recognition of architectural criticism at a key moment for the architectural profession, which was still dominated by the will to "make form." As Siza stated: "At that time there was a controversy about 'what to do.' The Order of Architects argued for the holding of a competition, some declared it was an opportunity to modernize the Chiado (thinking about shapes?)."[22]

In this context, the impact of the award, dispelling the controversy and claims from others in the sector that the Chiado intervention was meaningless because it still looked the same, increased Siza's prestige in his own country, and, moreover, reconciled citizens, and the majority of architects, to their city. As he stated: "One way or another, all cities are my city. The fascination of each city—the always different fascination—irresistibly compels us to adopt it, or it adopts us."[23]

That is why it is important to praise a city designed using contemporary architecture that is as neutral as it is erudite, and to address Siza's recognition of the modernity of the earlier 1758 Pombaline Plan as a key for coherently creating the new, in continuity with the history of Lisbon. Based on the realm of the polis, and the primacy of public space over private, the collective over the individual, the Plano de Reconstrução da Baixa-Chiado was inspired by local culture and was able to respect the environment and relate to the place's history. The eighteenth-century plan for the reconstruction of Lisbon carried out by the Pombaline architects was acknowledged as being key to the urban continuity of the modern city, and advantageous in confronting a historic area with a very delicate geography. Realizing that the plan's unity is dependent on the city block reveals the deep understanding that Siza acquired of the city of Lisbon and its history, from the contribution of the military architects of the Casa do Risco to the development of what George Kubler (1912–1996) called "Portuguese Plain Architecture."[24]

Based on a learned, sensitive, and rigorous analysis, Siza undertook a process of rehabilitation, and confirmed his conviction that intervening in historical legacies represents an essential challenge for contemporary architecture and for furthering critical discussion.

Acknowledgments

To Álvaro Siza for generously sharing his memories, and for sparing the time for an inspiring conversation; and to Chiara Porcu for the help provided in the search through Siza's archive and the selection of the drawings.

Biography

Ana Tostões is an architect, critic, and architectural historian; a full professor at IST-University of Lisbon, where she is chair of the Architecture Scientific Board and in charge of the PhD program, and leader of the *Heritage* research line at CiTUA. She is a visiting professor at the University of Tokyo, University of Navarra, University of Porto, and KULeuven. From 2010 to 2021, she was president of Docomomo International and editor-in-chief of the *Docomomo Journal*. During this period, the organization transformed into a global network and the *Docomomo Journal* became the only international periodical providing a broad vision of the modern movement architecture and its reuse. On this topic she has published *Key Papers in Modern Architectural Heritage Conservation* (with Liu Kecheng, 2014) and *Modern Heritage. Reuse, Renovation, Restoration* (Birkhäuser, 2022). Her research field is the critical history and theory of modern movement architecture. Focusing on the colonial and postcolonial condition, she coordinated a research project on sub-Saharan African architecture whose publication *Modern Architecture in Africa* was awarded the Gulbenkian Prize, as well as the "Health and Care" project with the edition of the book *Cure & Care, architecture and health* (2020). She received the Prize of X Bienal Ibero-Americana de Arquitectura y Urbanismo and is a Distinguished Commander of the Order of Infante Dom Henrique.

fig. 11
Gonçalo Byrne and João Pedro Falcão de Campos, Bank of Portugal Headquarters, Lisbon, 2007–2013. Exterior view from Praça do Município. © Ana Tostões/José Manuel Espada.

fig. 12a
Gonçalo Byrne and João Pedro Falcão de Campos, Bank of Portugal Headquarters, 2007–2013. Nave of the Church of São Julião after restoration. © José Manuel Rodrigues.

fig. 12b
Gonçalo Byrne and João Pedro Falcão de Campos, Bank of Portugal Headquarters, 2007–2013. Former presbytery of the church of São Julião with the velarium of Fernanda Fragateiro after restoration. © José Manuel Rodrigues.

[20] On this matter, see Oriol Bohigas, *Contra una arquitectura adjetivada* (Barcelona: Seix Barral, 1969), and Joana Couceiro, Chiado e Estilo. A importância da noção de Estilo na construção do Chiado de Siza, PhD Thesis (Porto, FAUP, 2018).
[21] Secil Award jury declaration, 1997.
[22] Siza, "Abecasis," 221.
[23] Álvaro Siza, "Cidade," in *01 Textos por Álvaro Siza*, 175.
[24] George Kubler, *Portuguese Plain Architecture: Between Spices and Diamonds, 1521–1706* (Middletown, CT: Wesleyan University Press, 1972).

1 Origins and Approaches

Architectural Criticism and the Politics of Architecture

Kenneth Frampton

"The old is dying and the new cannot be born and in this interregnum many morbid symptoms appear."[1]

Antonio Gramsci

I would like to devote this address to tracing the trajectory of my own evolution as an historian/theorist during the last two decades of the twentieth century. For me the year 1980 was momentous because it was the year in which *Modern Architecture: A Critical History* was first published.[2] This account of the modern movement was directly influenced by Reyner Banham's *Theory and Design in the First Machine Age*,[3] which had appeared twenty years before. Apart from covering virtually the same material, perhaps the most fundamental difference between these accounts was the way in which they ended, for where Banham envisaged the future in terms of the techno-idolatry of Buckminster Fuller, I closed my account by advocating the "vernacular modernism" of Alvar Aalto, not only for his capacity to design an organic architecture combining the tactile use of traditional materials with modern structural form but also for his ability to create environments as phenomenologically accessible as his National Pensions Institute (NPI), which was realized on a prominent site in Helsinki in 1953. It was significant that the central interviewing hall of the NPI was top-lit by a monumental crystalline skylight, symbolizing the social security provisions of the Finnish welfare state, to which the institute was directly dedicated.

The year 1980 was also seminal in terms of "post-68" intellectual reflection, since it saw the assimilation of two significant texts: Jean-François Lyotard's *La condition postmoderne* of 1977[4] and Guy Debord's *La societé du spectacle* of 1967.[5] Both Lyotard's provocatively postmodern thesis that techno-scientific calculation would ultimately transcend ideological discourse and Debord's comparable insistence that the mediatic was in the process of falsifying all forms of culture found their joint fulfillment in the Venice Biennale of 1980, the first Biennale to be devoted exclusively to architecture. Promulgated under the slogan "the end of prohibition and the presence of the past,"[6] this Biennale was focused around the centerpiece of the so-called *Strada Novissima*, constructed as an enfilade of fictitious shopfronts, designed by a rising generation of largely transatlantic, self-styled "star architects." It is ironic that the curator of this scenographic exhibition, Paolo Portoghesi, would focus on such a theme just at the moment when the traditional main street was being rendered obsolete by the proliferation of suburban supermarkets.

This mediatic reduction of architecture to scenographic imagery provoked my essay "Towards a Critical Regionalism—Six Points for an Architecture of Resistance," which appeared alongside Jürgen Habermas's essay critiquing the same exhibition in Hal Foster's 1983 anthology *The Anti-Aesthetic: Essays on Postmodern Culture*.[7]

Critical regionalism had been first formulated as a concept in a 1981 essay entitled "The Grid and the Pathway" by Alex Tzonis and Liane Lefaivre, in which they justified their coinage of the term through a comparative analysis of the respective works of two prominent Greek architects of the 1950s, Dimitris Pikionis and Aris Konstantinidis.[8] The title of their essay already hinted at the necessity of integrating with the topography in which it is situated. This resistant stratagem had, in fact, already been articulated in Vittorio Gregotti's 1967 thesis "Il territorio di architettura."[9] The essence of this anthropogeographic proposition taken from the work of German geographer Friedrich Ratzel would be summed up by Gregotti himself in a lecture given in New York in 1983, when he insisted that "architecture does not begin with the primitive hut but with the marking of ground . . . that is to say with the placing of a stone on the earth in order to create a cosmos within the chaos of nature."[10]

Accordingly, my six points for a resistant architecture were predicated on the necessity for place creation as a bounded domain within which to resist the late capitalist tendency to commodify the entire environment. My position was categorically opposed to the populism of

---

1. Antonio Gramsci. *Selections from the Prison Notebooks* (New York: International Publishers Co., 1971).
2. Kenneth Frampton, *Modern Architecture: A Critical History* (London: Thames & Hudson, 1980).
3. Reyner Banham, *Theory and Design in the First Machine Age* (London: The Architectural Press, 1960).
4. Jean-François Lyotard, *La condition postmoderne* (Paris: Les Éditions de Minuit, 1979).
5. Guy Debord, *La societé du spectacle* (Paris: Éditions Gallimard, 1967).
6. Paolo Portoghesi and La Biennale de Venezia, *Architecture 1980—The Presence of the Past: Venice Biennale* (New York: Rizzoli, 1980).
7. Kenneth Frampton, "Towards a Critical Regionalism—Six Points for an Architecture of Resistance," in *The Anti-Aesthetic: Essays on Postmodern Culture*, ed. Hal Foster (Port Townsend: Bay Press, 1983).
8. Later published in Alex Tzonis and Liane Lefaivre, *Times of Creative Destruction* (London: Routledge, 2016).
9. Vittorio Gregotti, *Il territorio dell'architettura* (Milan: Giangiacomo Feltrinelli Editore, 1966).
10. Vittorio Gregotti, "Lecture at the New York Architectural League," Section A, no. 1 (Montreal: February/March, 1983).

Robert Venturi; that is, to his idea of the "decorated shed" as elaborated in his essay "Complexity and Contradiction in Architecture," published by the Museum of Modern Art, New York in 1961.[11] My stance, two decades later, was to emphasize the resistant potential of a topographically grounded architecture, as articulated by a building's long-term resistance to the impact of climate, light, and wind acting upon it, according to the season at a particular point on the earth's surface.

Following the lead of Paul Ricoeur's transcultural essay of 1961 entitled "History and Truth,"[12] which I cited at the beginning of my 1983 essay "Towards a critical regionalism," I proposed the potential of revitalizing locally grounded form by the use of cultural tropes lying outside its own tradition. This idea implied the self-conscious creation of a hybrid architecture that could be construed as pertaining to a mythically redeeming "world culture." Thus, the only illustration in my 1983 essay was a section through Jørn Utzon's Bagsvaerd Church of 1976, which I saw as a reinforced concrete construction in which the shell vaults spanning across the nave subtly referred to both the Chinese pagoda and the European Gothic tradition.

The other value implied but never fully articulated in my excursus on Critical Regionalism was the precondition for a decentralized form of social democratic governance; that is, the ideal of participatory democracy as outlined by Hannah Arendt in her 1958 magnum opus, *The Human Condition*.[13] Arendt favored the direct democracy of the city-state, which after World War II was perhaps available most remarkably in, of all European nations, "bombed-out" Germany, where priority was given to the reconstruction of provincial city theaters.

Thirty years later in Spain, following the death of Franco in 1976, the city-state again came into its own, most decisively in Barcelona—the time-honored seat of Catalan independence—where it expressed itself in terms of civic reconstruction under the progressive mayoralty of Pasqual Maragall as Barcelona prepared to host the Olympic Games of 1992 with the assistance of then city architect Oriol Bohigas, who created the master plan for an Olympic village that subsequently became a new residential quarter for the city, accommodating 10,000 people. Similar progressive building programs prevailed in provincial cities throughout Spain, in the wholesale construction of schools, universities, sports stadia, and public housing, as the country engaged in modernization after forty years of stagnation under fascism.

The election of Margaret Thatcher to the premiership of the UK in 1979, like the election of Ronald Reagan to the presidency of the US in the following year, had the effect of inaugurating the still-ongoing neoliberal reaction against the regulating neocapitalist social-democracy. This hastened the all but final eclipse of the long-standing legacy of the Roosevelt New Deal in the US and led to Thatcher's fiscal deconstruction of provincial city governance in the UK, most dramatically evident in the liquidation of the Greater London Council.

In a similar way the neoliberal deregulation of the liberal professions was particularly impactful on architecture, with the elimination of fixed fees for professional services. This was especially the case in Spain, where the powers of the city-based *colegios de arquitectos* were greatly diminished under the auspices of the European Common Market, which sought to standardize the practice and teaching of architecture across the entire continent, reducing Spain's professional architectural education from an average of six to eight years to a standard five-year program.

The implementation of this program across Europe had a dramatic effect on Spanish architectural education, particularly noticeable in the lower quality of the graduating architectural portfolios coming out of the architectural department in the Technical University of Madrid. This was the essence of the critique advanced by the Spanish architect Rafael de la Hoz in his 1992 lecture to the Chicago chapter of the American Institute of Architects (AIA), when he argued that the professional competence of architectural students graduating after the de facto standardization of architectural education throughout Europe was far lower than that which had been obtained prior to this paradoxical regulated deregulation.[14] As de la Hoz argued, this drive to level the playing field and make the liberal professions more competitive would only have the long-term consequence of reducing the quality of the work produced.

[11] Robert Venturi, *Complexity and Contradiction in Architecture* (New York: Museum of Modern Art, 1966).

[12] Paul Ricoeur, *History and Truth* (Evanston: Northwestern University Press, 1965).

[13] Hannah Arendt, *The Human Condition* (Chicago: University of Chicago Press, 1958).

[14] Rafael de la Hoz Arderius, "Delenda est architectura," keynote lecture, AIA/CICA/UIA World Congress, Chicago, June 24, 1993, https://activoarquitectos.files.wordpress.com/2013/01/1301_rafaeldelahoz.pdf

This neoliberalist reduction in the standing and remuneration of the architect may be compensated for by the introduction of the BIM cybernetic system of constructional management, although this system is hardly able to maintain control over the micro-dimensioning of a specific joint, with the result that such joints have finally to be drawn by hand.

This may well account for the remark Rem Koolhaas made early in his career to the effect "that we cannot afford details."

It is unfortunate that this inherent reduction in our capacity to produce and appreciate the design and realization of built form should occur at a moment when we not only are incapable of promulgating new towns but also have lost all sense of what urbanity is, which no doubt accounts for the predicament of such cities that seem bent on destroying the profile and consistency of their established urban fabric by the construction of one ill-conceived, excessively high, freestanding structure after another as the meaningless manifestation of globalized capitalism. This is very much the fruit of the dominant worldwide neoliberal ideology of our time, as we may judge from the current proliferation of megacities with populations of twenty to thirty million, far in excess of many nation states. Such is the dearth of public transportation in these cities that the underclass is condemned to, on average, a five-hour commute each day by car, traveling back and forth between affordable housing on the periphery of the megalopolis and the location of their employment in the high-rise center.

Debord's prophetic reflections on the devastating consequences of the "society of spectacle" find their proof in the phenomenon of branding first typified by Frank Gehry in the "baroque" titanium envelope enclosing the franchised Guggenheim Museum that he designed and realized in 1992 in Bilbao at the behest of Thomas Krens, the then director of the Guggenheim Museum in New York. Gehry provided a spectacular image supposedly capable of transforming an old industrial city into a new tourist consumerist destination. Where does this phenomena leave the architect or, for that matter, the architectural critic? For while we may still criticize and interpret one-off works of quality for an enlightened public, the neoliberal commodification worldwide hardly provides a convincing context in which to expatiate on the poetic substance and sociocultural implications of architectural form. And while we may still evaluate and interpret the finer points of an occasional architectural work of quality, a more pertinent critical discourse may perhaps be found in territorial place creation than in the narcissistic spectacular aesthetics of today's architectural form.

Biography

Kenneth Frampton was the Ware Professor of Architecture at the Graduate School of Architecture, Planning, and Preservation at Columbia University from 1972 until 2020. He practiced in England, Israel, and the US. From 1962 to 1965 he was technical editor of *Architectural Design*, and from 1976 to 1982 editor of *Oppositions*. He is the author of *Modern Architecture: A Critical History* (5th ed. 2020), *Studies in Tectonic Culture* (1995), *Labour, Work & Architecture* (2005). In 2012 he received the Schelling Architectural Theory Award; in 2018 he was awarded the Golden Lion of of the Venice Biennale. He is a member of the American Academy of Arts and Letters.

A Critique of Building Construction: Tactics of "Resistance" in Pikionis's Acropolis Works

Kostas Tsiambaos

fig. 1
The old temple with its new extension, its shed (right), and the gate to the complex (left). Source: G. Sariyannis Archive. © Kostas Tsiambaos.

While many scholars have discussed the unique quality of Dimitris Pikionis's work as a result of its materiality, few scholars have focused on its materialization. Through analysis of unpublished archival material, I will focus on the construction of Pikionis's Acropolis Works in order to advocate a critique of building construction, rather than the usual consideration limited to architectural form. A view of the microhistory of the specific project's construction can make for a factual, transparent, and responsible form of criticism, one that casts light on the broader social, political, and cultural aspects of modernity.

Introduction

In the introduction to his *Studies in Tectonic Culture*, Kenneth Frampton quoted Vittorio Gregotti's argument that "the worst enemy of modern architecture is the idea of space considered solely in terms of its economic and technical exigencies indifferent to the ideas of the site."[1] Gregotti's argument was followed by the discussion of an architectural work that was, according to Frampton, the "most didactic" example of what is the opposite of a sterile techno-economical understanding of architecture. This work was Dimitris Pikionis's (1887–1968) architecture-landscape intervention on the Philopappos Hill, also known as the "Acropolis Works" *(fig. 1)*. While Frampton, and many others, have explained how and why the unique quality of Pikionis's work is a result of its materiality, few scholars have focused on its materialization. And for those who, unlike some historians, are not aware of the work's specificities, the admirable quality of craftsmanship transcending the typical prerequisites of a modern technical construction indicates not a work made following specific laws, rules, and other techno-economical limitations, but one created just by the will of its sage old architect and the labor of its gifted, humble craftsmen—a creation that was more the result of ethical virtue and aesthetic intuition than modern management and technical planning.

Without denying the fact that the specific work's design philosophy and construction particularities deviate from the norm, I will argue that a reconsideration of this work as a work of the Greek public in the political context of the 1950s and a historical "revisit" of its construction site can cast light on modes of intellectual and material "resistance"[2] that are not limited to the authority of its architect but involve a variety of power relations and practices performed by other persons (supervisors, engineers, civil servants, contractors, managers, etc.) who at the same time serve the technocratic Greek state against which the resistance movement is positioned. Such an inquiry can relocate architectural critique in the open "battlefield" of the construction site in which theories and practices arise and erode, rather than in the formal consideration of architectural construction in its finished state.[3]

One thing not often mentioned is the fact that the Acropolis Works was just one of the many ambitious projects of postwar touristic development in Greece.[4] At the very time Pikionis's work was being completed, the Greek government was signing for the construction of the Athens Hilton—one of the first to be built outside the US—just two kilometers away;[5] as traditionalist or anti-modern as it may seem, Pikionis's work of resistance was as important for Athens's entry into the global tourism market as the Athens Hilton was.[6]

keywords:

Dimitris Pikionis, Acropolis Works, construction materials, construction site, political administration, resistance, technocracy, modernization

[1] Kenneth Frampton, *Studies in Tectonic Culture* (Cambridge, MA: The MIT Press, 1995), 8.

[2] Kenneth Frampton, "Towards a Critical Regionalism: Six Points for an Architecture of Resistance" in: *Postmodern Culture* ed. Hal Foster (London: Pluto Press, 1983), 16–30.

[3] My research is based on the archive of Giorgos Sariyannis (henceforth GSA). Sariyannis is Professor Emeritus at the NTU Athens School of Architecture, and is the son of Marinos Sariyannis (1906–1985), the civil engineer working at the Ministry of Public Works responsible for the supervision of Pikionis's Acropolis Works. See also Giorgos Sariyannis, "'The Works around Acropolis': Pikionis and the Greek State," in *Dimitris Pikionis, 100 Years since his Birth* (Athens: NTUA, 1989), 233–50 [in Greek].

[4] On modern Greek architecture and tourism, see Emilia Athanassiou and Stavros Alifragkis, "Educating Greece in Modernity: Post-War Tourism and Western Politics," *The Journal of Architecture* 23, no. 4 (2018): 150–63.

[5] Ibid. Both Konstantinos Karamanlis and Conrad Hilton were present at the opening ceremony.

[6] Kostas Tsiambaos, *From Doxiadis' Theory to Pikionis' Work: Reflections of Antiquity in Modern Architecture* (London and New York: Routledge, 2018), 185–86.

Another underappreciated detail is that Pikionis was not the head of the project from the start. According to Giorgos Sariyannis, the project's construction advanced in two discrete stages: (1) from May 1954 (or September 1955) to March 1957 and (2) from March 1957 to April 1958.[7] On May 12, 1955 Pikionis wrote a letter[8] to Konstantinos Karamanlis (1907–1998) *(fig. 2)*, who was the politician in charge of the project, first as Minister of Public Works (1952–1955) in the government formed by Alexandros Papagos, and then as appointed Prime Minister in October 1955. Since his role in the project was not that well defined, Pikionis decided to write this letter in order to describe the framework for a future collaboration and set his own priorities. Ultimately, the one and only thing Pikionis asked from Karamanlis was for him to guarantee the necessary conditions of "artistic creativity" so that this creativity, "free from every force, urgency or negligence," could be expressed in a "spirit of total freedom."[9] But what did freedom mean in the case of this public work?

As Pikionis wrote to Karamanlis: "You are surely aware that the important thing is not only *what* is to be done, but *how* it is to be done."[10] Pikionis made clear that the procedures followed during the construction of the specific project would not be the usual, and that was because of its particular nature: "We must exercise the greatest caution in carrying out a project which is in reality artistic rather than merely mechanical."[11] Specifically, Pikionis described a kind of involvement that should go beyond the technical account of drawings:

fig. 2
Konstantinos Karamanlis (on the right) with Dimitris Pikionis (second from the left) inspecting the Acropolis Works. © The Konstantinos G. Karamanlis Foundation.

> **What is commonly designated as architectural supervision is a totally inadequate term for this project, which necessitates the extensive exercise on the site itself of free initiative. A kind that cannot be foreseen in any blueprint or described in any contract. Plans and instructions are insufficient here, for the plan is not applicable as it stands, but serves only as a model representing a general idea which requires constant interpretation. As for instructions, the architect himself will have to interpret them, with the help of his assistants.[12]**

Karamanlis became Prime Minister on October 5, 1955, in a government having successively Lambros Eftaxias[13] (1955–1956), Georgios Rallis (1956–1958), and Solon Gkikas (1958–1963) in the role of Minister of Public Works. Alexandros Theodosiadis was the General Secretary of the Ministry of Public Works, Michail Karakatsanis was Inspector and Head of the Office of state engineers of Attica,[14] and Emmanouil Kolliontzis was the financial manager of the project as Inspector of the Public Works of Attica. The hierarchy was clearly structured, but the decisive factor ensuring that the project would stay on track was Karamanlis's personal interest.

The Construction Site as a "Battlefield"

The official reports of the Ministry of Public Works not only provide information on the implementation of the project but also describe the broader network of actors involved *(fig. 3)*, while explaining why the project was never on schedule. One reads, for example, that the two

[7] Sariyannis, "The Works around Acropolis," 235.
[8] Dimitris Pikionis, "Letter to the Minister of Public Works," in *D. Pikionis, Writings*, ed. A. Pikionis and M. Paroussis (Athens: National Bank of Greece Cultural Foundation, 1999), 266–72 [in Greek].
[9] Quoted by Agnes Pikionis and trans. by Kay Cicellis, in: Kenneth Frampton, Dimitris Antonakakis, I halis Argyropoulos, Savas Condaratos, Dimitris Pikionis, Agnes Pikionis, Alison Smithson, and Peter Smithson, *Dimitris Pikionis, Architect (1887-1965): A Sentimental Topography* (London: AA editions, 1989), 76.
[10] Ibid., 75.
[11] Ibid.
[12] Ibid., 76.
[13] Lambros Eftaxias was also an intellectual, a member of the Athenian economic and cultural elite. His vacation house located at West Attica near Eleusis was one of Aris Konstantinidis's first projects (1938).
[14] State engineers (νομομηχανικοί in Greek) were assigned by the Greek state and had the right and authority to interpret and apply the law during the construction of a public work in a specific geographical-administrative area.

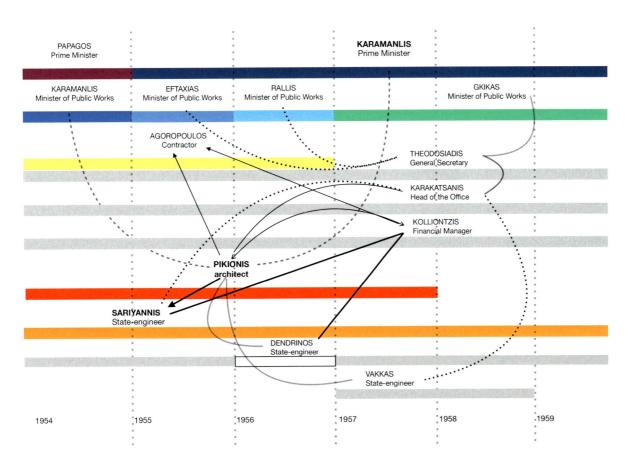

fig. 3
The network of actors in the construction of the Acropolis Works. Diagram by the author.
© Kostas Tsiambaos.

stages of the project refer to two different contracts: since September 1955, if not earlier, the first contractor (named Agoropoulos) had to collaborate with Dimitris Pikionis and architect Eleftherios Dendrinos, the state engineer that the ministry had placed next to Pikionis. The report dated November 25, 1957, explains the circumstances that made Agoropoulos terminate Pikionis's contract in March 1957: Pikionis's complete failure to provide detailed drawings; endless testing of multiple, successive design solutions on-site; and various technical and financial issues, which were impossible to deal with due to the project's unconventional "artistic form."[15] Dendrinos was also replaced after Pikionis insisted (by directly contacting Minister Rallis) the supervision of the project be assigned to Marinos Sariyannis.[16] However, after it became clear that the construction of the project had not advanced any further, Dendrinos was reassigned as supervisor of the project, alongside Sariyannis. It was specified that Dendrinos, in particular, would make the final decisions on construction details whenever exact drawings and directions were not provided by Pikionis; however, Pikionis never allowed Dendrinos to determine anything, claiming that the minister himself had ordered him (Pikionis) to be the only one responsible for every final architectural detail.[17]

What becomes clear is that, despite the delays and the difficulties that both the contractor and the state engineer faced in their collaboration with Pikionis, Pikionis's authority was never questioned. Moreover, the fact that Pikionis got the state engineer he asked for (Sariyannis) is further proof of his control. At the same time, the civil servants at the Ministry of Public Works felt that their work was not facilitated, as it should be, by the choices of their officials. When the principals of the office of state engineers realized that it would not be possible to complete the project as scheduled, they made the suggestion to ignore Pikionis and finish

[15] M. Karakatsanis, *Extremely Urgent*, letter dated November 25, 1957, addressed to the Ministry of Transportation and Public Works and to the Secretary of the Prime Minister (GSA).
[16] Pikionis and Marinos Sariyannis were family friends since the early 1950s.
[17] M. Karakatsanis, *Extremely Urgent* (GSA).

the work by deciding on the final details themselves. In the end Karakatsanis indicated two ways to deal with the problem: either let Pikionis conclude his work without any assistance from the office of state engineers or ask Pikionis to hand over the necessary drawings and instructions so that the office could finish the work without his interfering.[18]

In a report dated November 30, 1957, Karakatsanis confirmed that both civil engineer Sariyannis and architect Dendrinos were responsible for the supervision of the construction.[19] Moreover, another architect, named Vakkas, was assigned as supervisor on behalf of the General Secretariat of Public Works. The letter referring to this assignment followed a previous report where the "unusual" conditions of the work were described in detail.[20] Again, it was emphasized that "the one and only person responsible for the delays in the specifically ordered works, but also since the very start of the project" was the person having general responsibility of the project: "Professor Mr. D. Pikionis, who since the start and until this moment has not handed in the necessary drawings and instructions, and who, despite the recent turmoil . . . shows indifference and does not behave in a proper manner towards our supervisors."[21] In a way, Karakatsanis backed up the two employees (Dendrinos and Sariyannis) that his office had assigned by arguing that the delays were only due to Pikionis.[22]

Stones and Woods

A detailed description of the materials used in the various constructions (mainly masonry and timber) is documented in the official consignment report dated January 27, 1958.[23] The report briefly refers to the renovation of the old temple of St. Demetrius with its new sheds at the eastern and southern sides of the temple *(fig. 4)*, the pavilions' complex[24] *(fig. 5)*, the gate to the courtyard *(fig. 6)*, the "ancient temple"[25] found during the excavation for the toilet and storage building, and the toilet and storage building itself.[26] The report also informs us that sometimes Pikionis himself was signing the orders for materials, but more often it was Pikionis together with Sariyannis, or Pikionis, Sariyannis, and Kolliontzis asking for three different quotes (from three different suppliers) before approving the lowest one.[27] As an example, the main order of stones refers to thirty cubic meters of light gray marble from Mount Dionysos used in two forms: (1) as irregular stones for the paving of the courtyard and the floors of the buildings and (2) as marble roof tiles for the church, its extension, and the two pavilions.[28] Pikionis, Sariyannis, and Kolliontzis checked the three quotes and went for the lowest one by Dionysos-Penteli Marbles S.A.[29]

The courtyard is described as a composition made of marble plates, raw rocks, marble benches, and small stone columns.[30] However, there is no mention of the layout of the courtyard, which was designed and constructed according to Constantinos Doxiadis's system of harmonic regulating traces[31] that Pikionis used in his successive efforts to reach the ideal visual "balance" of the various constructions. Setting the exact angles and distances with the use of sticks and threads *(fig. 7)* was a time-consuming task resulting in much trial and error, various improvisations, and prolonged ponderings on-site; at the time, very few could understand why such an investment of mental and manual labor was needed for such a simple construction. Similarly, the agreement mentions the renovation of the old temple "with the use of 'byzantine' bricks and rich ornament,"[32] but there is no reference to the recycled materials used. These *spolia* (mainly architectural elements and ornament from demolished nineteenth-century houses and marble pavements) were not documented, although their meticulous application was one of the main reasons for the delays *(fig. 8)*. The extensive use of *spolia* was also one of the primary reasons Pikionis could not provide exact drawings since he had to personally supervise every detail until it acquired its proper "artistic" expression. This "handmade" materiality was, obviously, not compatible with the typical standards of modern construction and, as such, it is not mentioned in the official delivery agreement report.

Various kinds of timber were also used for the construction of the pavilions and the sheds: spruce and pine wood from Sweden, teak wood, chestnut wood, oak wood, elm

---

fig. 4
View from the eastern shed of St. Demetrius temple to pavilion A. Source: G. Sariyannis Archive. © Kostas Tsiambaos.

fig. 5
View towards pavilion A. Source: G. Sariyannis Archive. © Kostas Tsiambaos.

fig. 6
The "Japanese" gate to the courtyard (right) and St. Demetrius temple (left). Source: G. Sariyannis Archive. © Kostas Tsiambaos.

fig. 7
Doxiadis's system of visual angles and arcs on the floor of the courtyard. Collage by the author. © Kostas Tsiambaos.

---

18 Ibid.

19 Following the order no. A60060/2378 of the General Secretariat of Public Works, A1/1 administration (GSA).

20 The letter is addressed to the Ministry of Public Works, General Secretariat of Public works.

21 M. Karakatsanis, *Extremely Urgent* (GSA).

22 Ibid. Regarding the absence of M. Sariyannis from the construction site on the morning of November 14, his colleagues claimed that it was not possible for him to be on the site since he had to meet contractors, inspect building materials, etc. Dendrinos was also responsible for other works in Athens like the renovation of the old parliament building, the inspection of the construction of social housing apartment buildings, etc.

23 *Protocol for the consignment of the works realized at the courtyard of the byzantine temple of St. Demetrius Loumpardiaris as supervised by the Office of state engineers*, January 27, 1958. (GSA). The protocol was signed by Petros Vakkas, Marinos Sariyannis, and Eleftherios Dendrinos on behalf of the Office of Public Works, and Andreas Iatridis, Dionysios Theodosis, and Evmenis Mavropoulos on behalf of the Greek Tourist Organization (EOT).

24 There were two pavilions: the canteen pavilion (building A) with its main hall, shed, and kitchenette; the seating pavilion (building C); and the shed connecting the two pavilions. See: *Protocol for the consignment* (GSA).

25 This was a small temple dedicated to Ajax and Hercules. One can still see, just a few meters from St. Demetrius, the remains of the main gate of the 900-meter long-internal walls dating from the fourth century BC.

26 The toilet and storage building was built with thick stone walls supporting a flat concrete slab and had wooden doors and window frames.

27 Contract dated July 7, 1957 (GSA).

28 The use of marble roof tiles was possibly in reference to the marble roof tiles of the Periclean buildings on the Acropolis.

29 For a cost of 150 drachmas per cubic meter, which seems to be a rather low price (about 47.9 USD per cubic meter at current values). See: *Report on the tendering process for the supply of natural slate marble plates*, July 1, 1957 (GSA).

30 The marble was sourced from the areas of Liopesi, Charvati, Dionysos, and Varkiza, all being areas near Athens.

31 Tsiambaos, *From Doxiadis' Theory*, Chapter 5.

32 *Protocol for the consignment* (GSA).

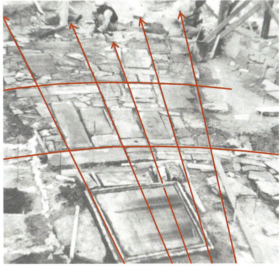

wood, old cypress wood trunks, even raw branches including their full foliage.[33] The southern shed of the temple was made out of oiled European oak wood, including its wooden floor, fences, and steps.[34] Oiled oak wood was also used for the doors and windows of the temple of St. Demetrius[35] after Pikionis, Sariyannis, and Kolliontzis approved the lowest of the three quotes. Interestingly, teak wood was used in large quantities, particularly for the beams and columns of the pavilions.[37] The decision to choose such an exotic, expensive wood rather than an indigenous one like cypress or pine was possibly the result of Pikionis's search for a "Japanese" aesthetic expressed in the form of the two pavilions with their elevated wooden frames, white plastered walls, and cane matt ceilings[38] *(fig. 9)*. However, the most characteristically "Japanese" form in the complex, that of the wooden gate to the courtyard sitting on four raw rocks, was made out of oiled oak wood and not teak, pine, or cypress.[39] This fact may allow us to infer that some decisions were based on the available resources and the desired profiles of the bearing elements rather than on a strictly theoretical assessment. In any case, the use of so many different woods, and in different dimensions, cuts, and finishes *(fig. 10)*, was another reason for the delays, since each piece had to be formed into something that was neither predetermined nor exact but rather highly specific and unique.

[33] *Table of materials and tools*, January 20, 1958 (GSA). Raw trunks were used for the roof of the shed connecting the two pavilions.
[34] *Protocol for the consignment* (GSA).
[35] In total the order was for four exterior doors, four interior doors, seven windows for the church's extension, one window for the old church, and one window for the kitchenette of the pavilion. See: *Report on the tendering process for the construction of wooden frames*, May 27, 1957 (GSA).
[36] Each contractor gave two quotes, one for four-centimeter-thick wood and one for five-centimeter-thick wood. Stylianos Danezis's quote was the best (42.300–43.910 drachmas, or 13.507–14.021 USD at current values). See: *Report on the tendering process*, May 27, 1957 (GSA).
[37] According to the invoice no. 2584 (May 13, 1957), Kolliontzis signed the order of 1.0139 cubic meters (in six pieces) of best quality teak wood. The cost was 10.403 drachmas (or 346.7 USD, equal to 3.322 USD at current values), and the chosen supplier was the Mouratoglou company in Piraeus. The wood arrived

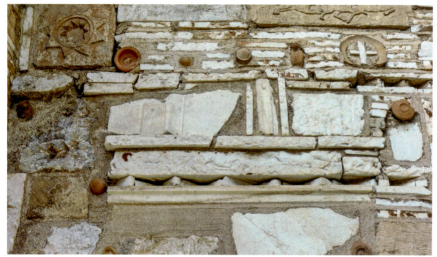

fig. 8
View from the eastern shed of St. Demetrius temple to pavilion A. Source: G. Sariyannis Archive. © Kostas Tsiambaos.

fig. 9
View towards pavilion A. Source: G. Sariyannis Archive. © Kostas Tsiambaos.

fig. 10
The "Japanese" gate to the courtyard (right) and St. Demetrius temple (left). Source: G. Sariyannis Archive. © Kostas Tsiambaos.

The Sariyannis Case

Marinos Sariyannis **(fig. 11)** was hired as a state engineer in 1940. Although a leftist since high school, he had to collaborate with various contractors, engineers, local authorities, etc. during the World War II Occupation and the difficult years of the Civil War that followed.[40] And according to various sources (state documents, official papers, etc.) it becomes clear that Sariyannis's role was more that of an undercover saboteur in contact with the Greek Liberation Front (EAM) than that of an engineer facilitating the constructions ordered by the Italian authorities or the officials appointed by the Germans.[41] However, it was not Sariyannis's legacy of resistance that inspired Pikionis to choose him as a right hand, but the integrity and commitment of the person that Pikionis had personally known and trusted since 1951.[42] Their collaboration in such an important and demanding project as the Acropolis Works allowed Sariyannis to apply for a promotion in his office based on this proof of "good service."[43] In support of Sariyannis's application, Pikionis wrote a letter in which he expressed his gratitude to Sariyannis for showing "full respect to the special requirements that the realization of such an artistic work demands, [a work] located in a place that is crucial in aesthetic terms." Pikionis underlined the fact that Sariyannis was eager to support "the artistic interpretation of the

at the construction site on the same day (GSA).

[38] On the Japanese sources of Pikionis's constructions, see Tsiambaos, *From Doxiadis' Theory*, 105, 149, 153, 167, and 183.

[39] The entrance "propylon" was made out of oak wood and covered with wooden roofing, water proofing (asphalt sheet), and canes. See *Protocol for the consignment* (GSA).

[40] According to the *Patris* newspaper, dated May 12, 1929, M. Sariyannis was among those captured as "dangerous communists" during the events of May 1, 1929.

[41] Among the many incidents that attest to his support of the Greek Resistance, the most characteristic was his report suggesting the demolition of a bridge over the Alfeios River, in Peloponnese, in 1944. The authorities at Megalopoli had asked Sariyannis to inspect the bridge on the main Kalamata–Tripoli road that the People's Liberation Army (ELAS) had tried unsuccessfully to blow up in

project, because that was all it was about, and not at all a mechanical and soulless construction," concluding that: "I never had the chance to have a more harmonious and virtuous collaboration."[44] In this way, Pikionis effectively expressed his gratitude to Sariyannis for sharing a responsibility (for the delays) that was not truly his to bear.

Another person that came out in support of Sariyannis's application was the head of his office, Karakatsanis. In his account of Sariyannis's service on the project, Karakatsanis mentioned that Sariyannis had proved his "trust and loyalty to the Country and the National Ideals"; he had shown responsibility, confidentiality, and proper behavior; he was well qualified, careful, meticulous, enthusiastic, etc.; and never did he "express any political views in public."[145] But Karakatsanis's motive for supporting Sariyannis was, actually, his disapproval of Pikionis; the praise of his employee as a very good civil servant who deserved to be promoted aimed in fact at illustrating Pikionis as the only unreliable person involved in the project.

Nevertheless, the Higher Technical Council rejected Sariyannis's application for promotion, citing the delays in the Acropolis Works;[46] Sariyannis would not be promoted "by choice" but only as a "good enough" employee.[47] Responding to the order no. 374, and avoiding naming Pikionis as accountable, Sariyannis referred to the particularities of the project, explaining that "it was not possible to be on the construction site all the time" since he had to visit factories and quarries, "[traveling] long distances" in order to find the "proper woods, raw woods, wild irregular trunks, raw stones, sea stones, etc." needed for the construction.[48] Eventually, Ioannis Fyssas, Director of the General Secretariat of Public Works, signed the allowance Sariyannis asked for.[49] But it was now Karakatsanis who appeared to no longer support Sariyannis's promotion.[50] And even if the reasons behind Karakatsanis's reversal are not clear, it is very probable that the escalating pressure from his officials made him realize that it was no longer worth supporting an employee who did nothing to protect his superiors from Pikionis's disorganized approach. Under these stressful events, Sariyannis asked for a sick leave that was approved after the assessment of the first-degree Health Committee of Athens.[51] And while the Director of the General Secretariat of Public Works, named Vlachos, rejected Sariyannis's appeal (protocol no. A.55319),[52] the Minister of Transportation and Public Works Solon Gkikas signed Sariyannis's promotion, this time "by choice," to the degree of a second-level inspector.[53]

Ultimately, all these difficulties that Sariyannis had to overcome when he asked to be promoted just reflect the obstacles that his leftist political identity raised in a conservative political milieu. Nevertheless, it was exactly his experience of participating in the World War II Resistance movement and his acquired skills of concealment and distraction that he used in order to keep his position at the ministry while giving Pikionis all the time he wanted. Eventually, he managed to prove his loyalty to the civil service without betraying his colleague and to follow the orders of his officials without ignoring his moral principles and social ideals.

Weaving the Network of Resistance

According to Kenneth Frampton: "Only an arrière-garde has the capacity to cultivate a resistant, identity-giving culture while at the same time having discreet recourse to universal technique."[54] But how would someone define arrière-garde in the case of the construction of Pikionis's Acropolis Works?

What I have tried to show is that in this specific project the description of an arrière-garde can be limited neither to the role of the architect nor to the kind of architecture that was built. The arrière-garde emerged as a fluid formation, an unstable network of different

fig. 11
Marinos Sariyannis serving as Captain in the Greek Army during World War II. Source: G. Sariyannis Archive. © Kostas Tsiambaos.

December 1943. Sariyannis suggested the demolition of the bridge as it was already in danger of collapse, although the structure of it was partially intact. See: *On the actions and conduct of state engineer Marinos Sariyannis*, July 9, 1945 (GSA) [in Greek]. The report was signed by twenty citizens of the city of Megalopolis, where Sariyannis was based.

[42] Pikionis never publicly expressed political views but one could claim that he was much closer to a kind of communitarianism, and he certainly was neither Marxist nor liberal. At the same time, he had strong ties not only to Karamanlis (a former radical centrist turned to the right wing) but also to the Palace. His Potamianos house and Pouris house were actually built for two well-settled Athenian families who were either directly or indirectly linked to the Palace.

[43] At that time, there were two ways for a civil servant to ascend in the hierarchy: the first was based on seniority (κατ' αρχαιότητα), the second was by choice (κατ' εκλογήν) and based on proof of "good service" (which, in practice, meant proof of a positive disposition toward the government).

[44] Pikionis's letter to Sariyannis, February 14, 1958 (GSA).

[45] Karakatsanis also noted that it was Sariyannis's commitment to the Acropolis Works that prevented him from investing equal time in the other projects he was responsible for, concluding that Sariyan-

Η ίδια αντίληψη οδηγεί στον εξωραϊσμό των αρχαιολογικών μας χώρων. Με την διαρρύθμιση του χώρου της Ακροπόλεως το μνημείο έγινε λαμπρότερο, ενώ η Αθήνα απέκτησε ένα καινούργιο θαυμάσιο πάρκο.

fig. 12
Leaflet of the Greek Government entitled "The Battle to Prosperity" promoting the Acropolis Works (1961). © The Konstantinos G. Karamanlis Foundation.

nis is "healthy [sic], he is an articulated scientist with advanced understanding, memory, and judgment, he loves truth, he is fair, he shows dignity and solemnity…." See: M. Karakatsanis, *Report on the service capacity of Marinos Sariyannis*, January 11, 1958 (GSA).

[46] See: *On the allowance for good service to state engineer of 3rd degree Marinos Sariyannis*, December 18, 1957, and I. Fyssas, *Non approval of allowance for good service to state engineer of 3rd degree Marinos Sariyannis*, December 21, 1957, protocol no. A.68265 (GSA).

[47] According to the report dated February 11, 1958 (protocol no. 374) and signed by the Director of the General Secretariat of Public Works (A1/1 administration), Ioannis Fyssas (GSA).

[48] He also mentioned Pikionis's letter, the fact that he had to supervise other projects at the same time, and reminded his officials of his hospitalization and the fact that he accepted the supervision of the project although he had to interrupt his sick leave. See: M. Sariyannis, *Application by M. Sariyannis, state engineer of 3rd degree at the Office of state engineers of Attica*, February 20, 1958 (GSA).

[49] I. Fyssas, report dated March 20, 1958, protocol no. A.14662 (GSA).

[50] In two successive reports, Karakatsanis mentioned Sariyannis's irregular time of arrival and departure from the construction site and indicated his absence from the office on June 30, 1958, against order no. 6757. See M. Karakatsanis's reports dated June 30, 1958 (protocol no. 7258) and August 5, 1958 (protocol no. 8598) (GSA).

[51] Stefanos Natsikas, *Granting a one-month sick leave and approval of medical care expense*, September 24, 1958 (GSA). The General Secretary of Public Works (A1/1 administration) approved the one-month sick leave, starting from September 25, 1958, and approved the prescription for "Vionevrin Forte N.10 tablets" and "Danlets Ablot FL N.2 tablets" (probably acebrophylline-acetylcysteine tablets). Sariyannis had been hospitalized in 1945 with tuberculosis at the Sanatorium of Parnitha. He also had a bile infection.

[52] Em. Vlachos, *Rejection of submitted appeal*, October 21, 1958 (GSA).

[53] Report dated November 21, 1958 by the General Secretariat of Public Works, A1/1 administration (protocol no. A.61170). The following year Sariyannis will be promoted again, but only as a "good enough" employee. See also: Em. Vlachos, *Suggestion of seniority-based promotion*, March 6, 1959 (protocol no. A.13346) by General Secretariat of Public Works (A1/1 administration) following the recommendation (protocol number no. 374) by Em. Vlachos (GSA).

actors and agents who defended their common interests as colleagues collaborating on the same project while often competing with each other: Pikionis was adamant from the start that he was not going to "play" by the rules of modern Greek technocracy, and Sariyannis assisted him in this despite officially working for the benefit of the Greek state. Agoropoulos, the first contractor, stepped away from the project as soon as he realized that he would gain no considerable economic benefit from it. Karakatsanis indicated Pikionis as the only one responsible for the delays, and initially supported Sariyannis even if, in the end, he could not tolerate the fact that Sariyannis neither questioned Pikionis's mentality nor objected to those "artistic" practices that were threatening the project's realization. The ministry, knowing that Pikionis had Karamanlis's support, kept delaying Sariyannis's promotion not only as a way of intimidating Sariyannis but also because of his political profile. Finally, Karamanlis, the Prime Minister himself, kept Pikionis in charge of the project until the end despite the fact that the considerable deferrals in the construction of such an important public work were costing him and his government precious political time.

In the end, the established system of modern technocrats and political officials proved to be more open and flexible than its conservative identity prescribed. Although everyone had to follow strict timetables and specific protocols, many actors succeeded in finding means of diversion and distraction. It was the deep respect afforded to Pikionis as a public intellectual and the recognition of his vanguard creation that provided the alibi for the development of various arrière-garde modes and tactics of resistance; these tactics allowed such a delicate design to flourish despite its restraining techno-economical management. It was also modernity's inherent degrees of freedom that allowed a mobilization in defense of a project that was, in principle, against the myth of modern progress itself. It was, finally, the political insight and social commitment shown by an administration whose conservatism had not yet turned into a kind of postmodern neoliberal cynicism—their insight and commitment made them turn an old man's anti-modern dream into a public work symbolizing postwar prosperity and progress *(fig. 12)*.

In 1968 Marinos Sariyannis was one among the thousands of civil servants to be fired by the military junta; his leftist legacy of resistance could not be accepted any longer.[55] Dimitris Pikionis died in the same year. Since then, Pikionis's "handmade" Acropolis Works has been internationally recognized as a composition of high historic and artistic value, a multivalent creation that merges art, architecture, and landscape architecture within the sensitive ecosystem of a distinguished archaeological site. It is time we also recognize, in the calmness and serenity of the place, the signs of the battle that was once fought for it to be realized.

Biography

Kostas Tsiambaos is an architect and Assistant Professor in History & Theory of Architecture at the School of Architecture of the National Technical University in Athens (NTUA). He is chair of do.co.mo.mo. Greece. He studied in Athens (NTUA) and New York (GSAPP Columbia). His research has been published in international journals (*The Journal of Architecture, ARQ, Architectural Histories,* etc.) and collective volumes. His recent books include *From Doxiadis's Theory to Pikionis's Work: Reflections of Antiquity in Modern Architecture* (London and New York: Routledge, 2018). In 2019 he was Stanley J. Seeger Visiting Research Fellow at Princeton University. Currently, he is working on a book on animal references and representations in twentieth-century architecture.

[54] Frampton, *Studies in Tectonic Culture,* 20.

[55] As one reads in the confidential report issued by the Office of the Minister of Public Works on February 21, 1968 (protocol no. 53), Sariyannis is accused for his "anarchist action in 1929," and for collaborating with ELAS and EAM during the Occupation. He is also accused of supporting a specific political party since 1964 (without mentioning which one, probably United Left [EDA], which came third in the 1964 national elections [the last elections before the junta]).

Paradigms of Design and Deep Readings: The Creative Emancipation of Critical Building Analysis

Caroline Voet

fig. 1a
Roosenberg Abbey, Waasmunster, architect Dom Hans van der Laan, 1974.
One of the three stairs towards the cloister cells. Photo: Caroline Voet.

fig. 1b
Arts Centre deSingel, Antwerp, architect Léon Stynen, 1968.
Walk on the roof inbetween the two performance halls. Photo: Caroline Voet.

> **"Wandering is the way in which man tries to break out from the over-increased purposefulness of his existence. . . . It is not actually the joy of departure in search of the endless distance. The wanderer is no longer in such a great hurry for the distance, as soon as he has become captivated by the landscape."[1]**
>
> *Otto Friedrich Bollnow*

In 1993, Bernard Tschumi noted that "current writing in architectural theory, participating in an exchange of ideas between disciplines—the arts, philosophy, literary criticism—differs significantly from the texts produced up to 1968. Most post-war written work yearned towards responsible ways and means to correct the ills of society."[2] This conference brings this issue to the table again, putting forward the question: should architectural criticism help in the creation of a better built environment?[3] It links aesthetics to ethics, as, for example, Reyner Banham did in his definition of New Brutalism.[4] How and where does this tradition have a place in the future? In a series of "deep readings"—critical readings through explorative drawings and photographs—this paper revisits two very different buildings from 1968 and 1974 in Flanders, Belgium **(fig. 1a, b).** Since architectural theory became an autonomous discipline in the 1980s, it has gradually become divorced from practice and (the) building itself. Since then, the close reading of buildings has been deemed mere description or analysis, and not seen as research. This was definitely the case in Flanders, where local buildings of the 1960s and 1970s were not seen as pioneering, as propellers of an architectural culture.[5] If one could identify "Brutalism" in Belgium, it was "an affair of experimentation more than of theoretical formation."[6] Returning to 1968 in Flanders, this paper redefines the design practice as a research field. From the perspective of space and the intentions of the architect, linking ethics with aesthetics, the contextual building is reconstructed and situated in a more universal pattern of thought. Through the emancipation of architectural practice as layered, fluid, illusive, and multiplicious research, it reconstitutes a certain autonomy to the discipline, granting design itself a responsibility.

The Split Personality Between Theory and Practice

Before embarking on the journey of critical reading, it is necessary to establish what constitutes architectural critique and discuss its changing conception since the 1960s. The Flanders case is symptomatic of a general turning away from architecture itself, its intentions or ulterior motives residing within its creation, since the 1960s. The research on architectural production itself was lost in a new intellectual culture.[7] A new generation aimed to adhere to the complexities of the postmodern condition, seeking to address the abstract patterns behind the things (Adorno, Derrida, Deleuze). Architectural history and architectural theory evolved in the direction of architectural criticism, equally defining themselves as autonomous disciplines. The theoretical practice, which not necessarily entailed building, saw the light, and the discipline of critical architectural

keywords:

architectural history, architectural theory, Dom Hans van der Laan, Léon Stynen, architecture, design, spatial systematics, architectonic space

---

[1] Otto Friedrich Bollnow, *Human Space*, trans. Christine Shuttleworth, ed. Joseph Kohlmaier (London: Hyphen Press, 2011), 112–113. Originally published as *Mensch und Raum* (Stuttgart: W. Kohlhammer GmbH, 1963).

[2] Bernard Tschumi, "Foreword," in *Architecture Culture 1943–1968. A Documentary Anthology*, ed. Joan Ockman (New York: Columbia Books of Architecture/Rizzoli, 1993), 11.

[3] This problematization of architectural ethics takes an altogether different form in this Texas conference. Here, it is not the architect's own intentions or approach that are accused of being non-objective, it is architectural criticism itself that is on trial: can it be objective in the context of paid content? The rise of a criticism that entails the divorce of practice from theory is far removed from the critical approach propelled by, for example, Kenneth Frampton or Wilfried Wang, who stay very close to a building as the object of research. Architectural critique then coheres with the formation of an architectural canon of oeuvres and buildings. This has its echoes in this conference, which puts forward the question of whether architectural criticism is still able to define "best practices." It asks if it should outline "ideal practices." (Content taken from the conference brief, International Conference on Architectural Criticism. On the Duty and Power of Architectural Criticism, Online Conference, October 9–10 and October 16–17, 2021).

[4] Reyner Banham, *New Brutalism. Ethic or Aesthetic?* (London: Architectural Press, 1966).

[5] Geert Bekaert, *Hedendaagse architectuur in België* (Tielt: Lannoo, 1995).

[6] Christophe Van Gerrewey, "Farewell to Architecture: Contrasts and Common Grounds in Flanders and Wallonia," *The Architectural Review*, August 16, 2018, 8–13.

theory became ever more divorced from the sphere of production and the world of action, instead defining for itself an autonomous, self-referential intellectual realm. It was Tafuri who in 1980 criticized the split personality of the architect who writes, theorizes, and also practices. He scoffed at the mix of "mystifications and brilliant eversions, historical and ahistorical attitudes, bitter intellectualizations and mild mythologies."[8] He called into action the architectural historian and theoretician as a "critic" with the foremost task to "diagnose exactly, and to avoid moralizing in order to see. The critic is courageous and exempts an honest scrutiny, questioning the legitimacy of a modern movement as a monolithic corpus of ideas, poetics, and linguistic traditions."[9] From this perspective, operative theory as created by the designer is seen as merely subjective, as intentions of the architect cloud judgment and prevent exacting diagnoses and honest scrutiny. This noncritical position would then render the theory useless within the scholarly field. From this perspective, researching design and drawing would have negative connotations, as a focus on the process of conceptualization and its contingencies toward the built form could be labeled as formalism.[10]

The Nonexistence of Objective Criticism

First, I wonder, is there any such thing as an "objective" critical approach? It was Detlef Mertins who unmasked Manfredo Tafuri's own intentions, as well as those of the architectural historian Fritz Neumeyer, when they both analyzed Mies's Barcelona Pavilion.[11] Mertins described how in 1986 Fritz Neumeyer set forward to revivify Mies's own intellectual horizon, starting from the analysis of his personal library, through his own lens of German idealism. Guided especially by Mies's reading of Romano Guardini, Neumeyer aimed to uncover the intentions behind the design, the "objective totality" of the reality of the Barcelona Pavilion, in order to reveal its essence.[12] In 1973, Manfredo Tafuri had followed a different line of interpretation when he described the pavilion's fragmentation and unresolved dualities as an example of Adorno's negative dialectics in architecture.[13] Through this lens, Tafuri recognized the pavilion as "a montage of parts, each speaking a different language."[14] He defined the space as "a place of absence, empty, conscious of the impossibility of restoring 'synthesis' once the 'negative' of the metropolis has been understood."[15] Detlef Mertins's histories of perception position the building without writing about the building itself or about the creative process of a practice behind it. As such, the building is deemed a representation of a critic's intentions.

Is there no responsibility of the building itself? Where lie the ethics of the designer? Back to the conference: What are "best" or "ideal" practices for a better environment? What should be the ethical basis of incisive architectural criticism? As both practicing architect and critic, I will address the concept of "best practice" from an interdisciplinary perspective, aiming to grasp a building both in its physicality and in its meaning.

Two Deep Readings: Revisiting the Comparative Method

In the tradition of Wölfflin, Frankl, Wittkower, Giedion, and Rowe, I compare in order to reveal. What is compared are two houses with a social and cultural relevance: a cloister and a house for the arts, both built by architects who with their buildings aimed to "correct the ills of society." Both relate to humankind in a particular manner. First a scene is set with the building as protagonist, and from this concrete place the story unfolds toward conceptualization and its architectural culture.

The first building is Dom Hans van der Laan's Roosenberg Abbey, realized in 1974 for the Marian Sisters of St. Francis *(figs. 2–4)*. The sisters specifically chose the Benedictine monk Van der Laan (1903–1991) as their architect, longing for his ascetic and elemental spaces, built out of repetitive rhythms around inner gardens. Their abbey was meant as a guesthouse for contemplation, sitting amidst a clearing in the woods of Waasmunster. Although built with rough masonry and concrete, the cloister induces a sense of antiquity. A rigorous proportional system underlying the design of the abbey supported Van der Laan's quest: to create a House,

[7] Paolo Portoghesi, *Postmodern. The Architecture of the Post-Industrial Society* (New York: Rizzoli, 1983).

[8] Manfredo Tafuri, *Theories and History of Architecture* (London: Granada, 1980), 9.

[9] Ibid., 10.

[10] Caroline Voet, "Design Research. The Unresolved Tension between Drawing and Writing," in *Intentions of Reflexive Design*, ed. Margitta Buchert (Berlin: Jovis, 2021), 206–23.

[11] Detlef Mertins, "Barcelona Pavilion: Spiritualizing Technology," in *Mies* (2014; repr., London: Phaidon, 2017), 138–67.

[12] Fritz Neumeyer, *The Artless World: Mies van der Rohe on the Building Art* (Boston: MIT Press, 1991), 197. First published in German in 1986. As quoted in Mertins, "Barcelona Pavilion," 147. Neumeyer described Mies's search for a higher order through the mediation of a classical dialectic: "Thinking through life in its concreteness promised to unlock the 'objective totality' of reality, the omnipresence of the Divine, which remained inaccessible to the abstract theorizing that had become a dominant feature of modernity."

[13] Manfredo Tafuri, *Architecture and Utopia: Design and Capitalist Development*, trans. Barbara La Peta (Cambridge, MA: MIT Press, 1973), 148. Originally published as *Progetto e utopia: Architettura e sviluppo capitalistico* (Bari: Laterza, 1973). As quoted in Mertins, "Barcelona Pavilion," 146. Tafuri drew a connection with the Frankfurt Schule and their critical theory of culture under capitalism, although Mies remained unfamiliar with this.

[14] Manfredo Tafuri and Francesco Dal Co, *Modern Architecture*, trans. Robert Erich Wolf (New York: Harry N. Abrams, 1979), 155. Originally published as *Architettura contemporanea* (Milan: Electa, ca. 1976). As quoted in Mertins, "Barcelona Pavilion," 148.

[15] Manfredo Tafuri, "The Stage as Virtual City," in *The Sphere and the Labyrinth: Avant-Gardes and Architecture from Piranesi to the 1970s* (Cambridge, MA: MIT Press, 1987), 111–12. Originally published as *La sfera e il labirinto: Avanguardie e architettura da Piranesi agli anni '70* (Torino: G Einaudi, 1980). As quoted in Mertins, "Barcelona Pavilion," 148.

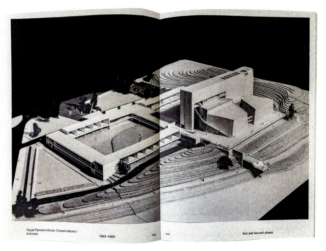

an ordered retreat amidst the mystery of nature that rendered space readable, knowable. The second building, realized in 1968—six years before the abbey and twenty-five kilometers to the west, in Antwerp—is the work of modernist architect Léon Stynen (1899–1990) **(fig. 5)**. This arts school that grew into a public arts center over the years is likewise built around inner gardens, but the wings comprised of wide glass corridors and classrooms are placed on pilotis to let the landscape flow underneath the building. The roof is an equally enjoyable landscape, with many wide terraces and platforms. The entrance and corridors of the arts center are wide, with slow stairs leading the masses upward toward the performance hall **(fig. 6a, b)**. Every building element is there to guide movement in a conscious manner, carefully designed following the regulating principle of the golden ratio (about 5:8). The steps of the stairs are deliberately made too low and deep. It is impossible to move quickly here, as one stumbles over what seems a badly calculated rhythm. This is done deliberately by Stynen, as an invitation to slow down one's pace. To the same ends, the entrance of the abbey follows a proportional system with clearly delineated building elements creating a composition based on Van der Laan's system of the plastic number (about 3:4). A canopy is hung between the walls. A small step comes forward. In between emerges a space with the proportion of 3:4.

fig. 2
Cloister garden of Roosenberg Abbey. Photo: Caroline Voet.

fig. 3
Front facade of Roosenberg Abbey. Photo: Caroline Voet.

fig. 4
Back facade of Roosenberg Abbey. Photo: Caroline Voet.

fig. 5
Arts Centre deSingel. Wooden model. From: *Léon Stynen. A Life of Architecture, 1899–1990.*, ed. Dirk Laureys (Antwerp: Flanders Architecture Institute), 140–41. © Archives Flanders Architecture Institute.

Paradigms of Design and Deep Readings: The Creative Emancipation of Critical Building Analysis *Caroline Voet*

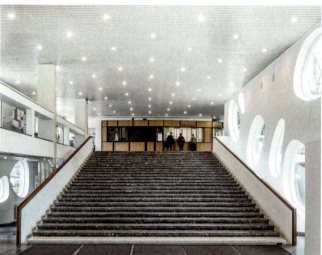

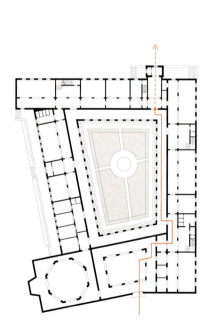

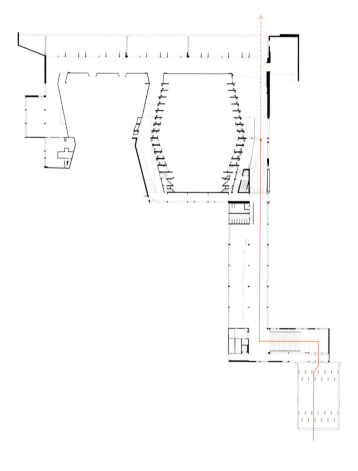

Route in Roosenberg Abbey: 76.5 m

Route in deSingel: 108 m

A wooden gate is 3:4 lower than the opening. One is gradually embraced by the building. Here, it is a column, placed on a 3:4 position within the entryway, that invites one to slow one's pace.

Both buildings are conceptualized as a sequence of spaces leading to a certain interiorization through a winding route *(fig. 7)*. In the case of the abbey, it is a contemplative route of 76.5 meters, gradually leading toward the cloister surrounding its inner garden: again an outside, but an ordered outside through which one is invited to reflect upon one's relation to oneself, and to the other, to God. In the case of the arts center, it is a route of 108 meters toward the art performance. Although the corridors are wider in order to accommodate the passage of a large audience, here the route is also designed in order to prepare the wanderer for an existential experience. Like Van der Laan, Stynen believed that the morphology of a building influenced the experience.[16] Expressive forms were designed with the integrated thought that space, form, and structure were one and that they influenced the experience of the user. Within each building, a decisive perspective on this route has been selected for a closer reading.

The Case Study of Van der Laan's Roosenberg Abbey

Starting with Roosenberg Abbey, we see a cloister with a nearly square section *(fig. 8)*. It is a space without ornamentation, made of many patterns within building forms, materials, and light. It is constructed of thick masonry walls: on the left a classical window series, on the right an opening, all made with concrete lintels. The building components present themselves as fundamental blocks, defined by clear lines between mass and space. Windows are square rhythmical openings with the same dimensions inside and out. The use of simple materials and finishes—roughcast masonry, concrete, and wood—shows how things are made. They are tinted in complementary colors of gray-blue and gray-green, subtracted from the lively slate tiles covering the floor, as such enhancing the sensorial qualities of the space as a whole. Daylight is structured by a series of openings, creating patterns of its own in a pronounced light/dark shadow play. Because of the rough finishing of the spaces, the light plays on the subtle topography of the surfaces, bringing the architecture to life. The tiles have a distinct pattern that changes into a subtle threshold at openings in the walls, and at several places narrower strips of tiles are added. This embodies the position of a room on the other side of the cloister wall. The tile pattern runs throughout the abbey as a matrix, providing keys to understand its spaces.

In order to understand this space, there are different perspectives, one clarifying the other. When studying the work of Dom Hans van der Laan, I did not have to "reinvent" his intentions, as Tafuri or Neumeyer did for Mies. First one has to understand his background as a Benedictine monk, which, since his entry in 1927, guided him in a life of "ora et labora": contemplation and work.[17] As such, he assigned a certain responsibility to earthly things, architecture included, to invite contemplation of the sacred. There is also the possibility of a critical contextualization of Dom Hans van der Laan. For the architectural scene of the Netherlands, Van der Laan was too traditionalist. During his three years at Bouwkunde at TU Delft before his entry into monastic life, Van der Laan openly eschewed the modernism of Mies and Le Corbusier, turning to Berlage and Granpré Molière, the predecessor of the traditionalist Delftse School.[18] His own Benedictine congregation in Oosterhout, however, regarded him as too modern. They mistrusted his working with proportions and his ascetic, elemental architectural language.

fig. 6a
Central entrance stairs at deSingel.
Photo: Jeroen Verrecht.

fig. 6b
Entrance of Roosenberg Abbey.
Photo: Caroline Voet.

fig. 7
Plans of Roosenberg Abbey and arts centre deSingel, showing the route from outside to inside.

fig. 8
Cloister of Roosenberg Abbey.
Photo: Caroline Voet.

[16] Caroline Voet, "Classic Modernism. Léon Stynen's Houses," in *Léon Stynen. A Life of Architecture, 1899–1990*, ed. Dirk Laureys (Antwerp: Flanders Architecture Institute, 2018), 234–45.

[17] This inspired him to reflect on the making and perception of his architecture in the light of Dionysius's "Ima Summis," the highest in reconciliation with the lowest. See Caroline Voet, "Dom Hans van der Laan's Architectonic Space: A Peculiar Blend of Architectural Modernity and Religious Tradition," in *The European Legacy. Towards New Paradigms*, ed. Rajesh Heynickx and Stéphane Symons, MIT Press, 22, no. 3 (March 2017): 318–38.

His biographer, Richard Padovan, appropriately coined him as a "modern primitive."[19] With the undercurrent of Protestant–Catholic tensions, one can follow Van der Laan's struggle for recognition and building assignments. Motivated by a few students, Van der Laan wrote down his theories on how to address space and building, culminating in his book *Architectonic Space: Fifteen Lessons on the Disposition of the Human Habitat*.[20] With this manifesto, Van der Laan summarized a lifelong quest to restore, in all its objectivity, the fundamental and intrinsic architectural laws. Written in 1977, right after the completion of Roosenberg Abbey, which served as a research experiment, it offers us some important keys to understand the building. The book approaches architecture as a formal system and analyzes buildings as compositions from a visual and morphological point of view. Dom van der Laan wanted to identify a logic, just like Vitruvius did with his "logos opticos" in the book *De Architectura*. Spatial experience is central, and the book analyzes the human habitat through philosophical dualities such as inside and outside, mass and space.[21]

What binds the theory and practice together is Van der Laan's concept of "nearness," which he defined as the intrinsic relationship between mass and space. He draws this as an abstract archetypal model: an axonometry of a square cella with two openings, in which the walls are in a 1:7 relation with the enclosed space *(fig. 9)*.[22] The cella is about three to four meters wide, which is the circle of the length of one's body projected outward. As such it borders the thresholds of our intimate experience of space. A second and third drawing, a gallery and a

[18] Caroline Voet, "Between Looking and Making: Unravelling Dom Hans van der Laan's Plastic Number," in *Proportional Systems in the History of Architecture. New Approaches and Considerations*, Architectural Histories, ed. Matthew A. Cohen and Maarten Delbeke (Leiden: Leiden University Press, 2018), 463–92.
[19] Richard Padovan, *Dom Hans van der Laan, Modern Primitive* (Amsterdam: Architectura & Natura, 1994).
[20] Dom Hans van der Laan, *De Architectonische Ruimte. Vijftien Lessen over de Dispositie van het Menselijk Verblijf* (Leiden: Brill, 1977). Trans. as *Architectonic Space, Fifteen Lessons on the Disposition of the Human Habitat* (Leiden: Brill, 1983).
[21] For a detailed analysis on how Dom Hans van der Laan applied his design methodology of the plastic number, see Caroline Voet, "The Poetics of Order. Dom Hans van der Laans' Architectonic Space," in *arq: Architectural Research Quarterly*, Cambridge University Press, 16, no. 2 (June 2012): 137–54.
[22] Dom Hans van der Laan, "XII. Disposition of the House," in *Architectonic Space*, 145–59.

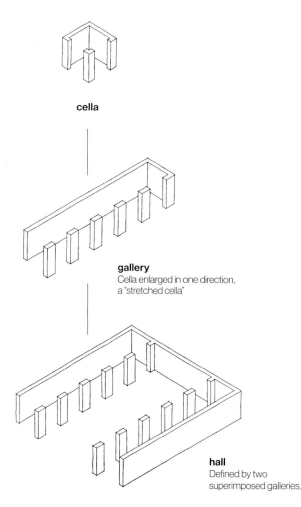

fig. 9
Dom Hans van der Laan. Generic models: continuous superposition of space: cell–gallery–hall (see *Architectonic Space* XII).

hall, explain how larger spaces can grow out of this first cella without losing contact with that first human scale through Van der Laan's second concept, that of "superposition." This first cella and the hierarchical superposition can be found everywhere in Roosenberg Abbey: it is the size of the monastic cells, it is the width of the cloister, and it defines the position of galleries within the larger spaces and gardens. Its walls are half a meter thick, while the defined space is three-and-a-half meters wide.[23]

The cella is the unit for the abbey, offering insights into the abbey's proportion, thresholds, and scale as well as into Van der Laan's design methodology, but these insights still remain fairly abstract. In order to grasp Van der Laan's intended spatiality in relation to the experience of the abbey, so as to come closer to the actual built space, we need to examine Van der Laan's phenomenological concepts of matter and space. The concept of "understood space" enabled Van der Laan to develop his own interpretation of the Neoplatonic idea of *mimesis*. He referenced the phenomenologist Otto Friedrich Bollnow and his theories of the articulation of space and its experience fields that were described in his book *Mensch und Raum*.[24] In his aim to "penetrate more deeply into the relationship with space and thus in the nature of human spatiality," Bollnow differentiated three emerging forms of individual space around a person: the space of one's own body, the space of one's own house, and the enclosing space in general.[25] In *Architectonic Space*, Van der Laan translated these three experience spaces literally into three architectonic spaces: the intimate cella as the workspace; the intermediate court as the walking space, and the larger domain as the visual field **(fig. 10a, b)**. They each exceed each other by seven times.[26] This arrangement can be found in Roosenberg Abbey, where the cella of three-and-a-half meters can be found in the sleeping rooms or the width of the cloister. The scale of the court is that of the building and its wings and courtyards, evolving around twenty-five meters, while the whole terrain, in which the scale of the domain is expressed, is 175 meters. In this domain, the abbey is placed in a peripheral disposition so as to define a front square of twenty-five meters deep; also here an expression of the court.

All of the above readings, established through the study of writings and plans, bring us quite close to understanding the building and the intentions of the designer. Nevertheless, it is through a deep reading of the building itself—that is, through the slow process of experiencing it—that the spatial dynamics can be unfolded, and it is these that draw us inside. We return to the cloister, which we understand now through the concepts of nearness and superposition. Upon entering, there is one element that does not immediately draw one's attention. It is not the cloister itself and its sequence of windows toward the cloister garden; it is a narrow slit at the end—the reveal of an opening disappearing behind the corner **(fig. 11a, b)**. Daylight seeps

fig. 10a
Dom Hans van der Laan. Model showing the three experience spaces around a person: the workspace, the walking space, and the visual field (see: *Architectonic Space* III.4).

fig. 10b
Dom Hans van der Laan. Models showing the experience space translated into architectonic space: cella, court, and domain, and their respective dispositions. Van der Laan's developed a series of nine possibilities, where one became part of the other. The peripheral disposition seemed to be the most interesting condition of superposition: the domain being formed by courts that in turn were formed by cellas.

[23] Caroline Voet, *Dom Hans van der Laan: A House for the Mind—A Design Manual on Roosenberg Abbey* (Antwerp: Flanders Architecture Institute, 2017).
[24] Bollnow, *Human Space*.
[25] Ibid., 267.
[26] Caroline Voet, "Patterns from Wooden Blocks to Woven Scottish Tartans. Dom Hans van der Laan's Rationalist Approach towards Experience Space," in *Architectural Education through Materiality. Pedagogies of 20th-Century Design*, ed. Rajesh Heynickx and Elke Couchez (London: Routledge, 2021 (in print)).

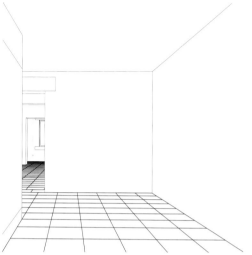
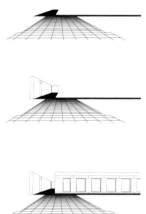

through the crack, as through a succession of porticos a window is framed which looks upon the garden behind the abbey. Moving along the cloister, the slit defines a shifting perspective from inside to outside. From one position in the cloister, one sees a knotted rope hanging from the ceiling; it is one of three, there for the manual ringing of the bells. Advancing nearer to the end of the cloister, one can observe clearly what was experienced from a distance: the opening does not align with the walls of the cloister; neither is it outside its perspective: it overlaps slightly. The floor pattern demonstrates this clearly: there is a shift of fourteen centimeters in the placement of the stones. Also, when walking in the other direction—from the bell tower to the cloister, while taking in the view toward the garden through the window—the space is defined by this slit *(fig. 12)*. Porticos frame the wandering route toward the cloister and the garden, while the slit opens up the perspective ever so slightly, offering a view of the first portico through which one entered the abbey. Although the abbey is the embodiment of a progressive movement from outside to inside, space is never-ending, and it is exactly this that gives the humanizing effect Van der Laan was looking for. Always there is the far away perspective toward the outside, toward wild, immeasurable nature, superimposed on the inward movement. The cloister is not merely conceptualized as an ordered enclosure with measurable cellas and galleries, courts and domains, it is all designed with an emphasis on the spaces that arise, dealing with spatial extension, movement, and outward perspectives. Bollnow refers to Burckhardt's description of a wide view of a mountain peak: "It is the same expanse of the view that is now directed toward temporal space, and it is the same emotional feeling of the immeasurability of space that is also manifest in the immeasurability of the inner world, as the immeasurability of the soul. The emotion of the inner soul is made possible only by the uplifting experience of spatial expanse."[27] The spatial expanse is directly converted into an expanse of the soul itself—in the case of Van der Laan, induced by a very specific small slit in the cloister.

The Case Study of Arts Centre deSingel by Léon Stynen

The small slit in the abbey points us to an equally intense moment in the seemingly very different architecture of the arts center. As within the cloister, a decisive perspective is found within the arts center while slowly moving through it, observing and experiencing it *(fig. 13a, b)*. It is the moment right before one enters the performance hall. The corridor is comprised of washed concrete walls, a ceiling of aluminum slats, and a carpeted floor, all in yellowish grays and browns. The space is quite dark, but just at the point where the floor folds upwards,

fig. 11a
Transgression from cloister to connecting space towards bell tower. Roosenberg Abbey.

fig. 11b
Drawing of the floor pattern showing the 14-cm shift between the opening towards the bell tower and the corner of the cloister. Drawing made by Caroline Voet and Marjolein Geyskens, KU Leuven Department of Architecture.

fig. 12.
Perspectival sequence of the layered porticos. View from the bell tower towards the cloister at Roosenger Abbey. Drawing made by Caroline Voet and Marjolein Geyskens, KU Leuven Department of Architecture.

[27] Bollnow, *Human* Space, 82.

zenithal light illuminates the carpet, after which the ceiling becomes very low. A series of columns leads upward toward a horizontal glass facade, made of thin metal and concrete frames, capturing the blinding daylight. But most crucial is the thin metal railing, which in plan follows the undulating wall of the hall **(fig. 14)**. The two folds, one in section and the other in plan, are both 171 degrees. At this intense spatial moment, the architecture sends out an invitation to mentally prepare for the performance. As an architect who distinctly contributed to society—through his extensive oeuvre from social housing to urban planning, offices, and public buildings, but also through his role as the director of the Academy of Antwerp and later La Cambre in Brussels—Stynen constantly sought a balance between individual freedom and public welfare in his work. Stynen understood "civilité" foremost as architectural unity, as an expression of the collective, following the ideals of Le Corbusier. Modern architects, Stynen argued, should "rediscover the sense of unity as well as the taste for perfection, the collective vision and the delicacy of tact."[28] In 1963, he wrote his manifesto, "Sur la finalité de l'architecture," in which he emphasizes the spirit inspiring a form: "Spirit, not in the sense of an empty abstraction, detached from the earth, but on the contrary, feeding from the air and the water, from the color and essence of all life. I'm worried by the thought that architecture so often lacks this spirit, which belongs to God, that is to say the moral values inherent to mankind. I venture to hope that architecture won't be reduced to a purely technical affair, for its true mission far transcends the merely supporting material and technical laws."[29] He adds: "Architecture is born from the miraculous encounter of spirit and matter." Where the arts center is built upon a decisive grid of regulating lines—a modern, infinite, and floating space—the encounter between the two folds allows for a moment of intimate enclosure immediately reaching outward through the perspectives, a moment where time stops but equally accelerates.

[28] Léon Stynen, 1946, quoted in Karina Van Herck, "Architecture and Civilization," in Laureys, *Léon Stynen*, 246.

[29] Léon Stynen, "Sur la finalité de l'architecture," *La Maison* 6 (1963): 170–72 and 188. As quoted in *Léon Stynen. Een Architect.* Exhibition catalog (Antwerp: Kunstencentrum deSingel, 1990).

fig. 13a
Arts centre deSingel, view from the corridor leading towards the performance hall. Photograph by Laura Vanhoegaerden, student, Studios Structural Contingencies, KU Leuven Department of Architecture.

fig. 13b
Drawing of the perspective in the corridor, emphasizing the two spatial folds: one folded in the plan, the other folded in the section. Arts center deSingel. Drawing made by Caroline Voet and Marjolein Geyskens, KU Leuven Department of Architecture.

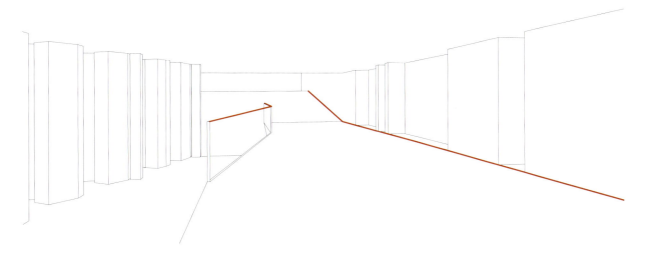

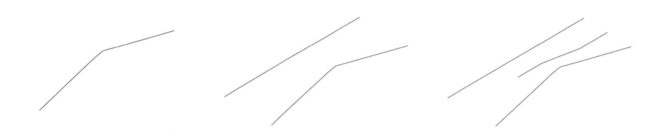

A Return to the Object

Are these deep readings of a building critical reflections? According to Ruth Verde Zein, a description may be considered the near zero point of critique, but without it, the critique may not be able to exist.[30] Analysis is critical reading or a referenced critical recognition of a work of architecture. In order to facilitate substantiated and productive architectural research, she proposes some kind of reference handbook, as a vade mecum.[31] As a teacher in architectural design, but also as a practicing architect, I support this approach. I wrote my book *A House for the Mind* as a design manual on Roosenberg Abbey.[32] This book, receiving the DAM Architectural Book of the Year Award in 2018, found wide international recognition, more than did my academic papers. It reaches teachers and practicing architects searching for guidance in design solutions, for architectural beauty, and for meaning in their profession. The critic remains critical of such a manual, as the work is presented too autonomously, and no critical contextualization is offered. This paper aims to go beyond the manual, starting from a deep reading and from there incorporating different perspectives. In the architectural archives, the communication and lecture materials show that the architects of the 1960s combined thorough structural insights with concepts borrowed from phenomenology, philosophy, and sociology, which led to a hybrid synthetic thinking with the drawing as agent.[33] A deep reading not only provides insights into a play of spatial coherence and perspective, materiality, color, and daylight but also unravels a testimony through processes of analogy and intentions. As such, we move beyond authorship and beyond the canon of exclusion/inclusion, toward methods and tools. The ethics followed in this paper are those of the architects, striving to "correct the ills of society," and as such taking responsibility for their work. The creative descriptions and generated drawings depict aesthetics as the language and expression of

fig. 14
Build-up sequence of the folded regulating lines of the corridor. Arts centre deSingel. Drawing made by Laura Vanhoegaerden, student, Studios Structural Contingencies, KU Leuven Department of Architecture.

[30] As such, Zein links architectural criticism to a critical analysis of buildings or their close reading, in order to bridge the gap between architectural design as a practice and architectural design as a research practice. Ruth Verde Zein, "Back to the Things. Learning from the Buildings," in *Critical Readings* (Sao Paulo and Austin: Romano Gierra Editora, 2019), 14. Originally published as "Ha que se ir as coisas: revendo as obras," in *Leituras em teoria da arquitetura*, eds. Gustavo Rocha-Peixoto, Lais Brostein, Beatriz Santos de Oliveira, and Guilherme Lassance, vol. 3, *objetos* (Rio de Janeiro: Riobooks, 2011), 198–218.
[31] Ibid., 15.
[32] Voet, *Dom Hans van der Laan*.
[33] They set out to control all scales simultaneously, from the architectonic detail to the landscape and connection to the urban fabric, often even to furniture. They used expressive form determined by geometry as a tool to reinvent human shelter and public space. See Caroline Voet, "Research on Space as a Productive Design Tool, Re-introducing Aesthetics into the Design Studio," in *Proceedings Theory by Design Conference—Architectural Research Made Explicit in the Design Teaching Studio*, ed. Els De Vos, Johan De

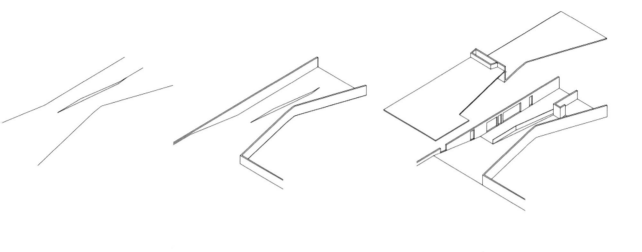

building, granting it a responsibility as well. Combining ethics and aesthetics is put forward as a methodological tool for contemporary architectural practice, one that strives to "correct the ills of society." It provides an attitude to deal with creative densification and sustainable reconversion, where this critical dialogue with a relevant tradition is necessary. Learning from buildings and practice is necessary. Methods do not just describe social realities but also help to create them.[34]

Walsche, Marjan Michels, and Sven Verbruggen (Antwerp: Antwerp University Association: Antwerp University, 2012), 101–09.

[34] Law, John, *After Method: Mess in Social Science Research* (London and New York: Routledge).

Biography

Caroline Voet is a professor at the Faculty of Architecture, KU Leuven, and founder of VOET architectuur. Her focus is on spatial, material and structural systematics within buildings as well as on architectural design processes, searching for new connections between historical–archival research and current practice.

The Dominant Paradigm We Call Design

Kevin Low

fig 1
The shortlisted competition models for the Commerzbank Tower. Left: the proposal from Foster and Associates.
© Richard Davies. Right: the Ingenhoven Overdiek and Partners proposal. © Ingenhoven Overdiek and Partners.

This essay attempts to elucidate the indoctrination of what design is believed to be through discussion of the last great architectural competition in the history of our profession – the seemingly inelegant Commerzbank Headquarters in Frankfurt (1991–1994). Using common and tested methods of analysis that have been largely forgotten, we will examine a variety of issues regarding the relationships of critical content – those between *multiple viewpoints*, rather than those of formal concerns alone – to comprehend the enlightened rejection of a brand of transparency most global banks would have sold their mothers for.

The Commerzbank, Frankfurt, 1991–1997

The design commission for the Commerzbank Headquarters in Frankfurt (1991–1994) was possibly the last great architectural competition in the history of the profession.

A rare moment in architectural history, the event was significant for its competition jury comprising architects, the bank clients themselves, and representatives from the city, with the decision on the winning proposal split straight down the middle: the renowned architect jurists voting in full agreement for one scheme, and the clients and city representatives voting entirely for the other[1] — with the final decision in favor of the proposal that epitomized the profound meaning of critical design, rather than merely engaging primarily with issues of aesthetics.

Founded in 1870 as a consortium of banks, Commerzbank had weathered the Great Depression, World War II, and several financial crises to become one of Germany's leading financial institutions as Commerzbank AG by the early 1990s. The incremental nature of its growth from its established base in Frankfurt resulted in a piecemeal scattering of its locations, precipitating the need for a new, centralized headquarters in Frankfurt am Main, one that was to embody the increasingly popular environmental objectives of the German Green Party in collaboration with the youthful ruling Social Democratic Party.[2] A number of established architectural firms from around the world were invited in a closed competition for idea proposals, out of which two were ultimately shortlisted and their merits passionately debated: that of the office headed by the progressive German architect Christoph Ingenhoven and that of the British firm run by the then Sir Norman Foster. For the purposes of ease and continuity for the remainder of this essay, we will refer to the firms as *Ingenhoven* and *Foster*, respectively.

Apart from incorporating ecological and sustainable initiatives — outlined by the clients in support of the goals of the governing political party — the shortlisted proposals could not have been more fundamentally different in comparison *(fig. 1)*.

Ingenhoven's design, produced together with the engineering firm Buro Happold, was conceptualized around a central core of vertical circulation, services, and primary structural support, with deep floor slabs cantilevered and tapering from this structural core to absolutely minimize the expression of structural depth on the facade of the building *(fig. 3)*. An iconic section from the office of a completed project in Essen (in which the bulk of the ideas that were put into their Commerzbank proposal were realized) suggests

keywords:

form/content, styling/designing, objects/relationships, answers/ questions, solutions/problems

[1] Rüdger Lutz, Tony McLaughlin, Michael Dickson, and Ted Happold, "The Commerzbank, Frankfurt—A Proposal for a Green Headquarters Tower Building," *Patterns* 10 (December 1991): 12. The fact that all the architect jurists were aligned in favor of the Ingenhoven proposal can be read to have lent greater legitimacy to the proposal, or, conversely, to have said more about the culpability of architects themselves in perpetuating regressive paradigms of formal aesthetic bias over relevant critical content.

[2] Steven A. Moore and Ralf Brand, "The Banks of Frankfurt and the Sustainable City," *The Journal of Architecture* (January 2003): 13–14. The objectives of the governing party at the time were preferred and supported rather than mandated, so due credit should be given to the clients and architects involved in upholding such initiatives.

how the structural tapering would have been resolved at the elevation face by way of a sophisticated aluminum extrusion supporting a double-skin glass-walled facade. The bespoke extrusion incorporates multiple functions: open ventilation during summer, closed insulation during winter, the opportunity to have the inner operable glazing open on two different hinge lines for both ventilation and maintenance, and a recess for a built-in, fully adjustable system of venetian blinds *(fig. 3)*.

In order to effect the more powerful machinery of stack ventilation, however, the proposal engaged an additional dimension in a separate "skin," located further inside the envelope, to create a narrow volume that would limit surface stack venting of the building mass to a maximum height of five stories, a limitation necessitated by the powerful forces of updraft that the surface wind pressure would generate.[3] With shallow lenticular gardens cut out of each floor to create a generally cruciform plan, the strategy fit well into the early initiatives from the bank for the competition entries regarding passive environmental controls, sustainability of running maintenance, and social equity: each five-story stack of the cross-shaped plan also helped define the various communities of each floor and the stacks within the entire block of the bank itself[4] *(fig. 3)*.

Apart from shallow lenticular gardens configuring the subtly cruciform plan to limit the depth of internal space for natural daylighting, the building was not organized any differently from most other existing high-rise projects in plan: private offices took precedence, being located along the perimeter of each floor for the best views, with every floor plan of the tower a replication of the one below it *(fig. 4)*. In massing, the building adopted the classic strategy of reducing wind loads and the temperate external envelope to a minimum by way of a circular plan; together with its central core, this resulted in a structural scheme that began with the four primary loadbearing column clusters on the open ground entry level, followed by a denser network of flared bracing on the lower levels of the elevation, reducing to sparse ties as the building rose in height to a facade completely clear of all structural elements on its top floors[5] *(fig. 3)*. Conceptually, it meant that the building, with its energy-efficient and sheer double-walled skin, would be developed as a translucent cylinder rising up from its site by the Kaiserplatz as a gradually dematerialized forty-four-story sculpted column that terminated in sheer transparency at its upper floors *(fig. 2)*. *Transparency.* The very ideal for whose symbolic and marketing rights any modern global bank would have sold its soul.

Well, the "ugly" building won.

Whereas Ingenhoven's tower rose from the head of the Kaiserplatz as a sophisticated cylinder of transparency, Foster's proposal seemed almost naive in its massing: three inarticulate blocks for each side of a triangular floor plan, staggered in height with the tallest facing south. With no bespoke extrusions to disguise structural floor depth and little by way of facade treatment to dignify its presence, the proposal lacked sculptural poise in comparison, and after completion retained its aesthetic anonymity from both near and far—it is not a pretty building from a distance, and it simply grows more weighty and awkward the closer one gets *(fig. 5)*.

But behind the seemingly opaque and faceless curved facades of its triangulated plan, a profound secret of architectural poetry resides, one that delineates with absolute clarity and poise what *design* actually is, and, better yet, could be.

To begin with, enough has been written about the technological feats of passive energy use and structural rigor the Commerzbank Tower achieved that further elaboration by way of numbers, measurements, and citations would be unnecessarily regurgitative. As such, we

fig. 2
Above: the elegant sculpted transparency of the Ingenhoven model.
© Ingenhoven Overdiek and Partners.
Opposite page: elevational diagram showing the external structural bracing filigree as it gradually diminishes to the top of the Ingenhoven proposal. Image from Buro Happold.

[3] Lutz, McLaughlin, Dickson, and Happold, "The Commerzbank, Frankfurt," 13.
[4] Ibid.
[5] Op. cit., 14.

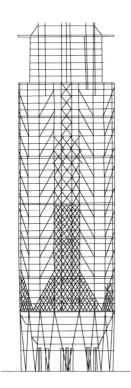

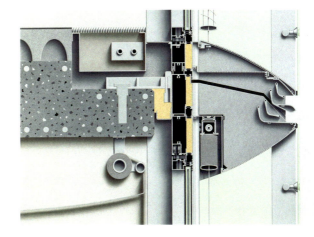

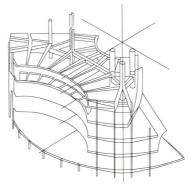

fig. 3
Left: structural axonometric showing the floor slabs and beams cantilevering from the central structural core of eight columns. © Buro Happold.
Above: a section of the iconic extrusion detail from the project at Essen which would arguably have seen implementation in good part or wholly in the earlier Commerzbank proposal, had the office of Ingenhoven Overdiek and Partners been selected instead. © Ingenhoven Overdiek and Partners.

fig. 4
Left: a typical floor plan of the Ingenhoven proposal. © Ingenhoven Overdiek and Partners.
Right: axonometric of the five-story stack. © Ingenhoven Overdiek and Partners.

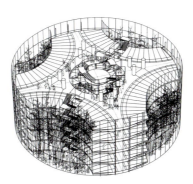

will only touch on those oft-repeated points of note incidentally in the course of the essay before moving on to engage with the more subtly interesting issues of purely architectural merit that have previously gone undiscussed—but first, to the issue of structure.

Whereas Ingenhoven had his consultants, Buro Happold, put great structural effort into conceptually cantilevering floor slabs from a central structural core in the creation of a cruciform plan within an externally transparent cylinder, Foster instead employed the most fundamental structural scheme for construction: the post and beam. The bulk of structural cost went into the lengths of steel beams, spandrels, and girders required to span the column-free plan within, but it still undercut the cost that would have been accrued for the more aesthetically pleasing structural cantilevering and the filigree of subtle bracing by a significant margin.

The clear spans resulted in deep steel perimeter beams externally clad, to the commercially bland horizontal bands that characterize the building elevations. Its exterior appearance, however, belies a very different experience from within—the beams were designed to be aligned mid-depth in relation to the floors they supported, leaving half their depth below the floor line to accommodate service reticulation in the ceiling space below, and only half their depth above each floor level for lower windowsills to increase the daylight entering and to increase ventilation, with the windows able to be opened during the hot summers *(fig. 6)*.

For massing, the proposal turned the tallest block of its triangular plan to face south, the second tallest to face northwest, and its shortest facade to face northeast. The block triangulation left the void of a central chimney running the entire height of the building as a guarantee of morning sun reaching the greatest possible area of space within, while the tallest block to the south maximized total passive heat gain during winter rather than splitting the difference between two separate blocks facing northeast and northwest to reduced effect.

In relation to detail, Foster's office accomplished all the functions of Ingenhoven's bespoke aluminum extrusion by way of products and systems already available for construction application—commercially produced venetian blinds were simply hung between the outer and inner glazing skins; ventilation for the space of the double skin was accommodated in less aesthetically manifest grace, but still functioned similarly; and the inner windows were able to be opened on both vertical and horizontal axes to facilitate natural ventilation and the maintenance of the space between both skins. All of this from commercially manufactured products.

The ground floor plan and its dynamics of urban planning tell an interesting, and subtly different, story: as it was required for the proposals to respond sensitively to the specific historical and social context of the various five-story buildings and pedestrian activity fronting the Kaiserplatz, both proposals set their formal entrances back from the Kaiserplatz instead of elbowing them between existing period elevations, with their ground floor levels filled with amenity and subsequent activity.

Foster had the passage to his set-back tower configured as a formalized skylit corridor, with the existing side wall of rusticated shophouses to the left and a new bank of office space to the right. Three short flights of steps along the passage led up to the main entrance of the building, widening into a glass-roofed food court with other amenities and services on the outer edge. A single continuous space of skylit dining then led one back out through the rear entrance of the building, connecting to the service street behind—in a simple but effective move, the urban gesture was configured as a foodie shortcut from the Kaiserplatz to the back lane *(fig. 7)*.

In this specific instance, it must be noted that Ingenhoven's proposal was considerably more relevant to the existing context than Foster's: instead of Foster's skylit but nonetheless formalized covered corridor, Ingenhoven configured his approach from the Kaiserplatz in what appears to be just another pedestrianized city street—an entrance that made an equally gracious urban gesture to the civic space of the Kaiserplatz *(fig. 8)*. Foster's corridor was designed for

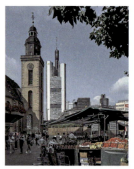

fig. 5
Four external aspects of the built Commerzbank Tower (bottom left).
© Nigel Young / Foster + Partners. Other © Ian Lambot.

semi-enclosed comfort of use only in primary relation to his building; Ingenhoven's design was a street in relation to both building *and* Kaiserplatz. With so many years gone by, research to determine what greater detail of activity was planned for Ingenhoven's "street" has been unsuccessful, but it can be safely assumed that the diversity and density, the pulse, characteristic of the city would have been manifest—together with the cafés and restaurants befitting the gastronomic life of the city. The way it currently functions, the enclosed food court in Foster's Commerzbank caters wholly to the convenience of the employees of the bank rather than the community of the city, evidenced by its location behind securable main entry doors and its being closed when the bank itself is closed.[6]

The architectural acumen of the Foster proposal begins primarily above the ground level with the typical floor plan: a seemingly rounded-edged triangle of a plan at first glance, the typical floor actually has an entire wedge cut out of a side and a further triangular void cut out of the middle—it was, in fact, a plan shaped as a boomerang **(fig. 13)**. The objective was threefold: to reduce the depth of internal office space through the creation of a shared civic courtyard, the central cutout of which would serve as a building-scaled chimney for the purpose of stack ventilation.

But it did not stop there. The architects understood from the very beginning that they did not want a typical commercial tower, a mere symbol of corporate hegemony and hierarchy, but an office environment that exemplified every initiative of the environmentally sensitive Green Party—a tower unlike any that had been designed before, one, above all, that would soften the scale of a high-rise *from within*. From an initial understanding that the upper limit of any environment scaled to be humanizing could not exceed four stories, the boomerang-shaped plan was stacked to create shared courtyards just four stories tall as "community" blocks with a building-scaled window view of the city, with each block then rotated one hundred and twenty degrees from the one below it. This meant that by the time the building-scaled courtyard and its "window" rotated back to the same direction, it was an entirely different view, being twelve stories higher **(fig. 10)**. It was the first time in the history of architecture that orientation was brought to bear in a high-rise, with every four floors of a department or two staking claim to their specific window-view of the city. Some claim that Gordon Bunshaft had accomplished it earlier at his National Commercial Bank in Jeddah (1983), but the differences could not be greater. Bunshaft created vast seven-through-nine-story voids in his project, which dehumanized rather than humanized scale, nor did he do anything in deeper consideration of the orientation and resultant identity of each stack in relation to specific city views, in the way Foster's Commerzbank did.

Where Ingenhoven had mandated sustainable technology as determinant of the five stories required for optimal stack ventilation, and only then came to the byproduct of community-scaled "blocks," Foster mandated social scale and community interaction of four stories, a shared courtyard, and a building-scaled window, which technology was only then called upon to serve.

One scheme emphasized technology; the other, community.

Those three ideas—the chimney void, the stacked boomerang plan, and its rotation—had seen formulation individually in a variety of other prior projects, but superimposed upon each other they were able to transform our understanding of architecture through a series of relationships that have not been witnessed since, bringing us now to the poetic core of the project.

Experiences of a mountain top with a spectacular view are typically memorialized by a panoramic photograph, one that never comes halfway near to recreating the actual experience. Fair comparisons point to the fact that the live experience is a fully sensorial one, but the fact is that the human sense of sight is able to do something

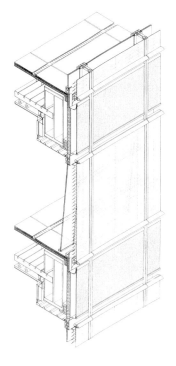

fig. 6
Axonometric of the wall section through a typical spandrel beam for the Commerzbank, showing the details of unremarkable components put together in remarkable assemblage to accomplish a passive energy environmental control system hidden behind the somewhat architecturally bland elevations. Note the depth alignment of the spandrel beam centered in line with the floor level, creating a lower glazing sill height while simultaneously accommodating the ceiling depth required for soffit reticulated services.
© Foster + Partners.

[6] Moore and Brand, "The Banks of Frankfurt," 18.

  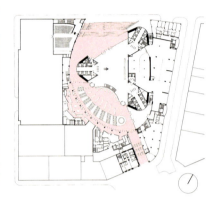

no wide-angle lens could ever do, which is to capture the depth of the borrowed landscape in relation to our contextual foreground. The sense of sight is able to take the measure of the panorama in intimate and powerful relation to scale—the emotional vastness of a panorama is always experienced in relation to the scale of our insignificance within it.

While it is also typical that the most popular offices in any tower are located on the peripheral envelope, preferably at a corner, those of the Commerzbank are not. With a wedge of each floor removed, the offices located along each inner arm of the boomerang plan have the unique position that enables them to afford views first into the space of the courtyard in the foreground and then extending beyond through the building-scaled window of the courtyard to the borrowed landscape of the city—the Commerzbank sites each arm of stacked floors *in relation* to their shared courtyard in underlining the primacy of their personalized community city view. Pressed up against the glazed curtain walls of the typically preferred high-rise office view, the foreground is virtually nonexistent as the view falls away to an equally distant view of the streets immediately below—the subtle absence of scale is the reason why initial visceral reactions to such views quickly fade. The Commerzbank, however, makes a subtle device of its architecture through the creation of a surreal relationship: a foreground of trees, people, and activity in the context of the city hundreds of feet below and miles distant; constantly variable and always in flux—a view of, and possible interaction with, a community in which one could never stop seeing change, and subsequently would never tire of *(fig. 11)*.

And, with the central chimney void in place, a subtle and final relationship comes into play. For possession of the best views along each inner arm of the boomerang plan, sacrifice must be made. Those views come with the understanding and complicity that anyone from any number of windows above and across will have a clear and direct sight line down to little panoramas of corporate malfeasance, internet porn, and all manner of sin being engaged with in those offices below *(fig. 12)*.

In creating profound relationships between passive cooling, community, orientation, and view, Foster turned German corporate privacy entirely on its head: the offices with the best views were also the ones that offered the least privacy to their occupants.

Where Ingenhoven's scheme filled the center of its floor plan with an opaque vertical core in order to make its exterior form appear sculpturally and symbolically transparent, Foster's scheme pulled its opaque core to its three external corners to make its interior relationships functionally and truly transparent.

fig. 7
The Foster entrance from the Kaiserplatz: a semi-enclosed corridor to serve the formalized act of entrance from the city square. © Ian Lambot; ground floor plan drawing © Foster + Partners.

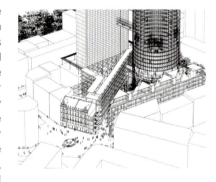

fig. 8
The gracious street entrance in the Ingenhoven proposal is a subtly relevant urban response to both the building and the Kaiserplatz.

fig. 9
Opposite above: the typical boomerang-shaped floor plan of the Commerzbank Tower, plan drawing. © Foster + Partners.

fig. 10
Opposite below: the changing sense of identity and orientation for each community stack of four storys in the Commerzbank Tower, building section. © Foster + Partners.

[7] It is not said often enough that one of the strongest determinants of form and content in a high-rise is its structure, the critical analysis of which inevitably informs what the primary conceptual drivers of its architecture were, be they external expressiveness or lack thereof, or the grace of profound internal relationships.

As accomplished and structurally brilliant as Ingenhoven's proposal was, all evidence indicates that the engineering was begun in support of the conceptual aesthetics of its architecture, as no other explanation could reasonably justify the sheer effort put into the cantilevering and facade bracing in establishing the specific expression of transparency in the presentation model for the competition entry. The deficiency of the Ingenhoven proposal comes not from the stunning effect of its superlative technical and engineering solutions—nor from anything in association with its original intent, in fact—but from comparison to the absolute critical content of architectural design embodied by the proposal that won.

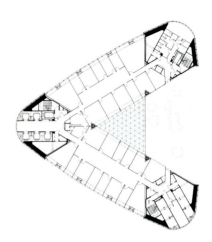

Was Ingenhoven's proposal developed in any other way than that regarding *transparency*, as suggested in this essay? If the highly vaunted *architectural model* is anything to go by in relation to the very first vital impression any jury has of a project, it is highly doubtful. Everything examined thereafter points to heightened attention and effort given to establishing the very aesthetic basis of that model.[7]

Could Foster's proposal have been *designed* any better? Aside from its having fallen terribly short of forming a relevant and inclusive urban connection to the Kaiserplatz in planning, strong argument could be made that considerably greater design development should have gone into the detailing on the glass walls of the circulation corridor centrally located in each arm of every floor—their lack of operability means that an opportunity for the true gold standard of cross-ventilation was neglected. The fact that the Commerzbank Tower is already more energy efficient than almost every other high-rise in the world does not take away from the criticism and, in fact, lends greater impetus to the gravity of such an oversight. The important thing, however, is that the relatively thin arms of each boomerang floor, coupled with the less permanent nature of internal corridor enclosures, suggests that addressing the issue could be easily and somewhat economically accomplished should such decision ever be made. It would activate the mechanism of the central chimney to its fullest effect during the warm summer months.

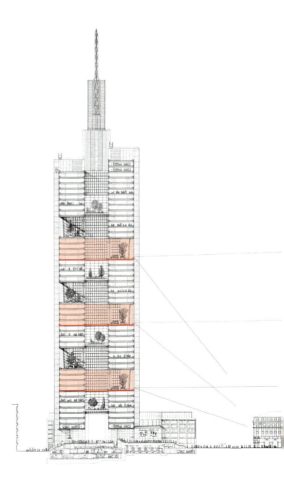

Could Foster's proposal have been *styled* any better? However well it was crafted and technically resolved in form, its lack of external grace and nuance of sculptural architectural expression, in both detail and proportion, could be said to be left wanting. Did how ungainly the building turned out bother the firm? Possibly. However successfully the Commerzbank has performed as a building, and however many technical and sustainable accolades it continues to garner, it is obvious that greater attention to the aesthetics and poetry of form has been paid to every project undertaken by the firm since its triumph in Frankfurt—but none to the same unadulterated poetry of critical content.

More importantly, it could be argued that, despite the fact that no other building completed by the firm has been more technically studied or written about, the Commerzbank is also one of the firm's least recognizable projects among young practitioners and architectural students—at least a dozen other better styled but less critically worthy projects by Foster will be more instantly identifiable and popular than our ugly Commerzbank.

Form and Content

Everything about architecture, and indeed creativity itself, involves a conversation between form and content. The vital issue is how the conversation begins.

Starting with an inspiration of form involves the act of styling, which is all about *how we want things to look*, while content is about design, which is about *how we engage critical relationships*. When architecture begins with form itself, it begins its journey with an answer, a solution which drives everything that comes after—relationships of critical content are obviously still important, but never at the expense of all we want to believe the crafting of tangible aesthetics, space, form, and architecture itself, is about. Styling is a top-down method, which begins as a search for a solution.

Designing, conversely, is a process that begins with a relevant question or a pertinent problem. It is deeply rooted to the specificity of its context and the diversity of critical content that each context involves, since vague and ambiguous characterizations of problems, or none at all, merely breed vague and global solutions that exist of and for themselves. Designing is a process that works from the bottom up.

Styling involves things. Designing engages relationships. The one we choose to begin each conversation determines the path we take, leading to vastly different outcomes. Styling seeks answers of crafting how things are expressed—aesthetically, metaphorically, or symbolically—by way of space and material. Designing asks questions of the relationships that bind or separate things and the understanding of how they are specifically and contextually bound by way of people, function, and time.

The practice of architecture requires both design as a philosophy of process and styling as a method of production in order to find realization, because each aspect of its duality serves very different necessities. The teaching, awarding, and indoctrination of what architecture is believed to be has relentlessly valued method over philosophy and form over content for more than 160 years of modern architectural education.[8]

fig. 11
Typical view from the internally located offices of the boomerang plan of the Commerzbank Tower, with the distant borrowed landscape constantly experienced in relation to its foreground of a constantly changing community square.
© Nigel Young / Foster + Partners.

fig. 12
German corporate privacy turned on its head: the offices with the best views also being the most transparent to views from above.
© Nigel Young / Foster + Partners.

The Dominant Paradigm of Styling We Call Design

The design for the Commerzbank Tower in Frankfurt was the last great architectural competition in history, because no other has put two proposals in such contrast to distinguish the dialectics of styling and design: the styling of beautifully sculpted but somewhat superficial transparency in its architecture, oddly paired with the sublime relationships of urban design for a building entrance in the Ingenhoven proposal; set in contrast to the unfinessed styling of an urban front door for Foster's project, elevated architecturally to touch the most profound considerations of critical content few other works will ever manage.

Things and relationships, form and content—the field of architecture has been egregiously passing off one under the name of the other because neither design nor styling has been given deeper thought or definition in the history of modern architectural education.

This indoctrination of generations of architects, young and old, famous and unknown, teachers and students alike, is the unbalanced ground on which we now stand, all part of the dominant paradigm we unwittingly call design.

[8] The "160 years" being the age of the oldest architectural schools in the US, which could be said to have been one of the primary forces of the modern movement.

Biography

Kevin Mark Low received his bachelor's degree in architecture with a minor in architectural history from the University of Oregon, Eugene (1988) and his master of science degree in architecture from MIT in Cambridge (1991). He has worked with the SRG Partnership, Portland, Oregon (1988); GBD Architects, Portland, Oregon (1989), and joined GDP Architects upon his return to Kuala Lumpur from 1992 to 2002, running the research and design division. In 2002, he founded *smallprojects* with work ranging in scale and function, including dishracks, tapware, lockware and specialist doors, windows and stairs, houses, chapels, office buildings, cemeteries, and fifty-story residential towers. Low began his career in architectural teaching at the Department of Planning and Architecture at MIT in 1990, continuing variously as a visiting and adjunct professor in the US, Europe, Southeast Asia, and Oceania, and principally offering second-year design studios and supervising thesis level students at the University of Malaya for eighteen years. Since 2000, Low has lectured internationally at numerous universities. He has served as technical adviser to the Aga Khan Foundation and has been teaching at CEPT in Ahmedabad since 2019. Low's architectural work and writing has been presented at architectural events and published in design and architectural journals internationally, including the publication of the book *smallprojects* in 2010 (oro/adaptus).

Truth Content: SANAA's Rolex Learning Center

Christophe Van Gerrewey

fig. 1
Jean-Michel Zellweger, *Vaud du ciel. Tome 1.*
(Lausanne: EPFL Press, 2018).

The power of criticism resides in its ability to reveal the "truth content" of a work—a concept introduced by Walter Benjamin in his 1922 essay on Goethe's *Elective Affinities*. The main purpose of architectural criticism is to use a building as a tool to establish knowledge about those topics that are—often invisibly—embedded in that piece of architecture. One building that can be used in such a way is the Rolex Learning Center at the École polytechnique fédérale de Lausanne (EPFL), a project by SANAA completed in 2010. Criticizing this piece of architecture means revealing and developing ideas concerning the evolution of work and leisure, of corporate culture and academic life, of libraries and office spaces in a post-internet world, and of the relationship between Japanese and Western culture. Searching for the "truth content" of this building means articulating what its striking formal characteristics mean.

Introduction

Both the power and the duty of criticism reside in its ability to reveal the "truth content" of a work. This notion was introduced by Walter Benjamin in his 1922 essay on Goethe's novel *Elective Affinities*. Benjamin made a distinction between "critique" and "commentary" and between truth and material content: "Critique seeks the truth content of a work of art; commentary, its material content. The relation between the two is determined by that basic law of literature according to which the more significant the work, the more inconspicuously and intimately its truth content is bound up with its material content. If, therefore, the works that prove enduring are precisely those whose truth is most deeply sunken in their material content, then, in the course of this duration, the concrete realities rise up before the eyes of the beholder all the more distinctly the more they die out in the world."[1]

It is not the main task of the critic to comment or to evaluate, nor to explain intentions or to discern between good and bad. Criticism is the process of trying to gather knowledge while analyzing and investigating a work of art. This knowledge relates not only to the work itself and to its art form but also to general fields of science and cognizance. It shows the proximity of criticism to philosophy, as Theodor W. Adorno has argued. The notion of "truth content" was developed by Adorno in his *Aesthetic Theory*, published posthumously in 1970: "The truth content of artworks is the objective solution of the enigma posed by each and every one. By demanding its solution, the enigma points to its truth content. It can only be achieved by philosophical reflection. This alone is the justification of aesthetics."[2] It is important to indicate how vulnerable criticism becomes because of this—criticism is never a rational or exact science, and its results can never be proven irrefutably. In an essay from 1968 on the life and work of Walter Benjamin, Hannah Arendt grasped this precarity, describing criticism as "the obscure art of transmuting the futile elements of the real into the shining, enduring gold of truth, or rather watching and interpreting the historical process that brings about such magical transformation."[3] Benjamin compared the critic with an alchemist rather than with a chemist, because "the critic enquires into the truth, whose living flame continues to burn over the heavy logs of what is past and the light ashes of what has been experienced."[4]

These statements point in the direction of one question that has to be addressed when reintroducing the notion of "truth content": what has changed since Benjamin defined criticism about a century ago? It's possible to argue that the fragile notion of "truth content" has become

keywords:

criticism, interpretation, contemporary architecture, learning environments

[1] Walter Benjamin, "Goethe's *Elective Affinities*," in *Selected Writings. Volume 1: 1913–1926*, ed. Marcus Bullock and Michael W. Jennings, trans. Stanley Corngold (Cambridge and London: The Belknap Press of Harvard University Press, 1996), 297.

[2] Theodor W. Adorno, *Aesthetic Theory*, trans. Robert Hullot-Kentor (London and New York: Continuum, 2002), 120.

[3] Hannah Arendt, "Walter Benjamin: 1892–1940," trans. Harry Zohn, in *Men in Dark Times* (London: Jonathan Cape, 1970), 155.

[4] Benjamin, "Goethe's *Elective Affinities*," 298.

obsolete: what we need is not so much philosophical reflection or critical speculation on what could be true, but hard, undisputable, numerical proof. Nevertheless, it is also possible to suggest that what is lacking nowadays is exactly the kind of speculative criticism professed by Benjamin. The academic culture of the humanities is increasingly dominated by models and methods from the exact sciences that preclude all-encompassing and unorthodox forms of knowledge, while general culture seems to focus on an endless reproduction of information and data. It is in such a context that criticism's promise of delivering truth content is valuable: to transcend boundaries, and to show that it is possible to think, by means of artworks, independently.

Another question deals not with what has changed, but with the differences between art and architecture: how applicable is the notion of truth content to the art of building? Benjamin's essay from 1922 focused on a novel, and neither he nor Adorno in his *Aesthetic Theory* used architectural examples. But on closer examination, the distinction between truth content and material content, and between criticism and commentary, applies even more to architecture than to art or literature. Two other texts by the same protagonists substantiate that claim. What is Benjamin's statement that "architecture has always offered the prototype of an artwork that is received in a state of distraction and through the collective" other than a suggestion that the truth content of a building is buried deeper than in other, less spatial artworks, in which utilitarian aspects are almost absent, and which offer themselves explicitly, if not for scrutiny then certainly for contemplation?[5] And how can Adorno's appeal to architects in 1966 that architecture "demands constant *aesthetic* reflection" be better understood than as an appeal to cultivate the truth content of architecture too, not only as a critic but also as an architect?[6] In both cases, what is at stake is the duty of criticism to subject architecture to thought, because so much concerning architecture tends to remain unnoticed, hidden by layers of technocratic reasoning and experiential phenomena. The truth content that architecture contains is all the bigger because it is more hidden, and because it requires more effort to be revealed. The purpose of architectural criticism is, therefore, to *use* a building as a tool to establish knowledge about those subjects that are embedded in that piece of architecture.

One building that can be utilized in such a way is the Rolex Learning Center (RLC) at EPFL, a project by SANAA (Kazuyo Sejima and Ryue Nishizawa) completed in 2010.[7] Searching for the truth content of this building means articulating what its striking formal characteristics *mean*, instead of which spatial, sensory, or material experiences they provoke. A phenomenological approach has dominated the reception of this building, and of the architecture of SANAA. When Sejima and Nishizawa received the Pritzker Prize in 2010, shortly after the completion of the RLC, the jury praised them for an "architecture that is simultaneously delicate and powerful, precise and fluid, ingenious but not overly or overtly clever; for the creation of buildings that successfully interact with their contexts and the activities they contain, creating a sense of fullness and experiential richness."[8] Many critics have emphasized the unique spaces of the RLC that call into being feelings of awe, unbelief, and admiration. These effects have been attributed therapeutic powers, for example in the film Wim Wenders made in 2010, entitled *If Buildings Could Talk* and shown at the Venice Architecture Biennale curated by Sejima.

To search for insights and ideas in a building means opposing phenomenology with interpretation and with history. The fact that the RLC is more than a decade old gives it a historical dimension, although this does not imply that a recent building cannot be subjected to criticism. Every building, no matter how new, has a history, although, as Benjamin wrote, "the history of works prepares for their critique, and thus historical distance increases their power."[9] Those aspects of the RLC that can be analyzed on this occasion indeed deal with the histories (and stories) of the building and the knowledge they contain—about the site in a formerly rural landscape and the organization of education in general; about the evolution of the relationship between Japan and the West; about the requirements imposed on buildings in terms of sustainability; and about the entanglement of working, living, and learning.

Until the end of the 1960s, the campus of which the RLC is a part did not exist, and on the same ground corn and grain were cultivated. The operations of the École Spéciale de

[5] Walter Benjamin, "The Work of Art in the Age of Reproducibility (Third Version)," in *Selected Writings. Volume 4: 1938–1940*, ed. Howard Eiland and Michael W. Jennings, trans. Harry Zohn and Edmund Jephcott (Cambridge and London: The Belknap Press of Harvard University Press, 2003), 268.

[6] Theodor W. Adorno, "Functionalism Today," trans. Jane Newman and John Smith, in *Rethinking Architecture: A Reader in Cultural Theory*, ed. Neil Leach (London and New York: Routledge, 1997), 18.

[7] I recently published a short book on the Rolex Learning Center on the occasion of its tenth anniversary: Christophe Van Gerrewey, *Higher Knowledge: SANAA's Rolex Learning Center at EPFL since 2010* (Lausanne: EPFL Press, 2021), also available in a French edition, entitled *Savoir supérieur. Le Rolex Learning Center de SANAA à l'EPFL depuis 2010*, and translated by Thomas Giudicelli. Aimed at a more general audience (and at the EPFL community), it is the fruit of research that is expanded and critically as well as theoretically refined in this article.

[8] Eve Blau, "Inventing New Hierarchies," accessed March 14, 2022, https://www.pritzkerprize.com/sites/default/files/inline-files/2010_Essay_0.pdf.

fig. 2
SANAA, Rolex Learning Center, EPFL Lausanne, construction site, January 31, 2007. © Alain Herzog.

fig. 3
SANAA, Rolex Learning Center, EPFL Lausanne, 2010. © Alain Herzog.

Lausanne, which had taken place in the city since 1853, began moving there in 1969. The democratization and accessibility of higher learning since the 1950s did increase the student numbers and did necessitate a move, but the choice to leave the city was not uncontested. Students wanted to stay connected to city life, while the inhabitants of the surroundings of the new campus were a bit apprehensive about the arrival of so many young people. It was decided that they would eschew the Anglo-Saxon model of fully fledged campuses: students would not live on campus, and housing would not be provided. SANAA won the design competition for the RLC in 2004, with a project that is above all a programmatically undefined "living space," an extension of the campus that enabled students to "reside" while their lodgings remained elsewhere and while research and education took place in numerous other buildings.

Most of the twelve projects submitted to the competition consisted of a large, iconic, and conspicuous building that tried to overpower the campus.[10] The first decade of this century was marked by debates about landmarks that are different from their surroundings, but also different from what architects had produced before. The competition at EPFL in 2004 coincided with the peak of this discussion; not coincidentally, Charles Jencks, who often captured trends that were on the verge of exhaustion, published *The Iconic Building: The Power of Enigma* in 2005.[11] Because the sprawling EPFL campus begged to be dominated—or retroactively structured—it seemed advisable to act accordingly. SANAA presented something else: a project that respected the chaotic campus and acquiesced in being an addition instead of a crowning achievement by concentrating all the programmatic requirements in one big

[9] Benjamin, "Goethe's *Elective Affinities*," 298.

[10] On the competition, see Robert Walker, "Futuristische Lernlandschaft," *Werk, Bauen + Wohnen* 92 (2005): 56–58.

building, but with only one undulating floor. The result was a building that didn't dominate but did fulfill another requirement of the competition: to provide EPFL with an (architectural) logo.

What the competition also explicitly asked for was a "center," although the site that was selected, near the southern border of the campus, couldn't have been more off-center, and neither EPFL's activities nor its seats of power would be concentrated in this building. Another characteristic of SANAA's project is that it seems to ignore this double fact—they made the RLC, in two ways, an *eccentric center*. Although it is located on the edge of the campus closest to Lake Geneva, it is designed to be accessible from all sides. Because of the expanse of space underneath, and because of the sloping floors, it is possible to reach the entrance from every direction. And the reverse is equally true: people can exit the RLC more or less like rays leaving the sun. SANAA has realized both a response to the need for a center (as a public space for the campus) and a questioning of the characteristics of a center.

This achievement can be considered as a critical alternative to a Western emphasis on centrality. Most of the time, in Japanese architecture and culture, a center is of no use. This applies to gastronomy too. In his 1970 book on Japan, *L'Empire des signes*, Roland Barthes suggested how "no Japanese dish is endowed with a center … on the table, on the tray, food is never anything but a collection of fragments, none of which appears privileged by an order of ingestion; to eat is not to respect a menu (an itinerary of dishes), but to select, with a light touch of the chopsticks."[12] SANAA's building not only respects the unordered nature of the campus but also becomes, in itself and in relation to its surroundings, decentered.

It is another unusual thing for a center to be empty. Of course, the RLC is not literally empty—because it is used so intensively, it is often difficult to find a free place—but at least theoretically, the center is *vacant*, certainly in comparison with all the other buildings on campus. Compared to all those spaces and facilities, the hundreds of chairs and tables on the wavy floor of the RLC are undefined: no one has, theoretically, more right to claim them than anyone else. This is reflected in SANAA's predilection for the color white, which has, also in architecture, been mostly discussed in terms of suppression of everything and everyone that's *not* white.

[11] Charles Jencks, *The Iconic Building: The Power of Enigma* (London: Frances Lincoln, 2005).

fig. 4
Wim Wenders, *If Buildings Could Talk*, 2010, still. © Neue Road Movies, Donata Wenders, 2010.

In the RLC, the white homogenizes and attenuates the architecture to such a degree that it becomes a natural presence, not unlike a snow-white mountainside. The space turns into a kind of canvas—an appearance of white that, rather than suppressing everything, tries to form a neutral emptiness, without meaning or symbolization, in which students and people can mill about in all their complexity and unpredictability.

While this is a quality that can indeed be considered Japanese, this does not detract from the fact that the RLC is a creation that can be easily inscribed in the history of Western architecture. Japanese architecture has incorporated modernist and occidental influences with apparent ease, and traditional elements have merged with newer ones (although some of them have simply disappeared forever). Apart from progress or melancholy, this flexibility and openness can not only be reversed (it is well known that Western architecture has learned a lot from Japan) but is also one of its main characteristics. What is truly Japanese about architecture from Japan is that it has succeeded in being more relentlessly modern and Western than Western architecture itself. This can explain why it is not hard to find precedents for the RLC within the history of Western architecture—in the work of Mies van der Rohe, for example, in whose Barcelona Pavilion SANAA intervened in 2008; in the British headquarters of IBM, a building of one floor designed in 1970 by Norman Foster and clad in glass and steel; or in the 1990 design by OMA/Rem Koolhaas for a congress center in Agadir, resembling a hilly landscape, mimicking sand dunes, and supported by a forest of columns.

The difference with this precursor is that the roof in Lausanne no longer needs the support of pillars, while the floor only incidentally touches the earth, opening up a space underneath. The floor height doesn't change; both floor and ceiling remain parallel to each other, like two layers floating up and down in a space without gravity. The biggest problem to solve in order to get the RLC built was the construction of perforated shells: concrete shells have been constructed since antiquity, but generally as one continuous roof, not as a floor interrupted by patios.[13] This building consists of not two but three layers: the ground level, which is also the concrete ceiling of the basement level; the first layer, which is the floor of the actual building but also the vaulted ceiling of the open-air space underneath; and, at the top, the second layer, the upper roof. The middle layer was particularly difficult to construct, because it had to stand on its own: it could not rest on the ground floor (that needed to remain open), and it could not depend on the wooden roof for stabilization (because then the interior of the RLC would become crowded with columns). The strategy adapted by the engineers had more to do with the building of bridges than with architecture: the undulating floor would be connected with the flat ground floor, not by means of vertical (and highly visible) supports, but by means of arches and beams.

Despite all the concrete, according to the regulations and legislations valid during the first decade of the twenty-first century, the RLC can be considered a sustainable building. In terms of energy performance the Swiss Minergie label was obtained thanks to the dominance of natural lightning, the thick insulation, the thermal inertia of the building, the use of underfloor heating, the combination of natural and mechanical ventilation, and the automatically controlled metal shutters. Since 2010, however, criteria have sharpened. Climate change has urged architects to consider not only the energy performance of their buildings following completion but also the energy used during construction and the amount of carbon emitted prior to the opening of a building. Architecture is a "carbon form"—it produces carbon before, during, and after construction, but it can also confirm and strengthen those ways of life that thrive on carbon emissions.[14]

SANAA's architecture, which by now can be found more or less all over the world, has been criticized as an "exercise in global production" in the recent edition of Kenneth Frampton's *Modern Architecture: A Critical History*. Frampton doesn't address the RLC directly—with its wooden roof that looks like concrete, it could be considered a tectonic crime of the worst kind—and he devotes only a few sentences to the work of Sejima and Nishizawa. But concerning the pavilion for the Toledo Museum of Art in Ohio, built in 2006 (and also a singular one-story

[12] Roland Barthes, *Empire of Signs*, trans. Richard Howard (New York: Hill and Wang, 1982), 22.

[13] On the construction of the RLC, see Christian Maillet, "Les coques du Rolex Learning Center," in *L'architrave, le plancher, la plate-forme. Nouvelle Histoire de la construction*, ed. Roberto Gargiani (Lausanne: EPFL Press, 2012), 882–8.

fig. 5
SANAA, Rolex Learning Center, EPFL Lausanne, 2012. © Alain Herzog.

volume penetrated by courtyards), he writes: "Story-height sheets of iron-free plate glass were rolled in Germany, shipped to China where they were laminated, tempered, cut and bent, then transported to the United States where, to add insult to injury, they now enclose the Toledo Glass Museum in a city which, prior to the deskilling of American industry, had been one of the primary centers for glass production in North America."[15]

When constructing the RLC, the Swiss contracting firm Losinger Marazzi worked almost exclusively with local subcontractors. But because no single element in the facade surface of almost 5,000 square meters is identical, it proved necessary to enlist the help of a Spanish firm for the production of energy-efficient curved double glazing, and of a Chinese firm for fabricating flat glazing panels that fit exactly between floor and ceiling. Even if these panels could have been produced nearby, it is clear that the RLC is anything but designed for the careful use of resources—its intentions, aspirations, and predications are on different planes. Whether this means a building like this one, and possibly architecture as we have generally known it, has to become a thing of the past is one of the difficult questions the future has in store—certainly if both petro-consumerism and the worldwide quest for economic growth aren't abandoned.

Many of the construction methods employed for the RLC were necessary to enable the way in which the building organizes work and gathers people—and to let these organizational principles *tell* and reveal something about working and studying today. Rather than a classical library in which to read, to study, and to learn, the RLC is more akin to an open office landscape—a *burolandschaft*, as the genre was coined in the 1950s in Germany. The major difference is that it doesn't have a traditional flat floor surface but a ground level with slopes, hills, and valleys. The result is a space in which hard boundaries may be absent, but in which smaller divisions and more intimate zonings do occur, albeit in ways that are difficult to perceive. What the building is withholding, while one is inside, is an overview—a rational, all-encompassing, panoptic view, available at a glance, on what is happening and what is taking place. That is why, despite all its ostensible transparency, the RLC remains a slightly abstruse and opaque building, because it does not divide people and uses into clear-cut categories and spaces. Differences between studying and socializing; producing and consuming; eating and napping;

[14] The notion of "carbon form" was coined and defined by Eliza Iturbe in a thematic issue of *Log* 47 (2019).
[15] Kenneth Frampton, *Modern Architecture: A Critical History*, 5th ed. (London: Thames & Hudson, 2020), 633.

writing, texting, and reading; relaxing and stressing; watching and listening are all difficult to define. The distinction between work and life has been discontinued, and what opens up is a kind of total space for a total existence, which—depending on one's own poise and sensibility—can be devoid of everything or filled to the brim. The building has been criticized for this—for creating the atmosphere of a lounge in a place where students and staff are advised to be always silent, to work, and to be productive (an admonishment that can be considered as defining for our era).[16]

In more neutral terms, the RLC does not gloss over or nostalgically conceal the way we live and work—or do both at the same time—now. "I concede," Sejima said in an interview early in her career, "that I am indeed living within the present. But that is all the more reason why I don't believe in trying to deny or conceal that fact by creating oppositional architecture. Nor am I simply reiterating contemporary society in its current form.... Instead, I look at architecture as a vehicle that enables us to get a better grasp of society or culture."[17] It is this definition of architecture that can be connected to the power and the duty of architectural criticism: it can reveal the truth content of a building.

[16] See, for example, Pier Vittorio Aureli, "Form and Labor. Toward a History of Abstraction in Architecture," in *The Architect as Worker: Immaterial Labor, the Creative Class, and the Politics of Design*, ed. Peggy Deamer (London: Bloomsbury, 2015), 113; Matthew Allen, "Control Yourself! Lifestyle Curation in the Work of Sejima and Nishizawa," in *Architecture at the Edge of Everything Else*, ed. Marrikka Trotter and Esther Choi (Cambridge and London: MIT Press, 2010), 22–33.

[17] Koji Taki, "Conversation with Kazuyo Sejima," *El Croquis* 77 (1996): 11.

Biography

Christophe Van Gerrewey is assistant professor of architecture theory at EPFL Lausanne. He is a member of the editorial board of *OASE* and *De Witte Raaf*, the author of *Choosing Architecture* (2019) and the editor of *OMA/Rem Koolhaas: A Critical Reader* (2019). He is currently preparing a book on the history of contemporary architecture in Belgium.

2 High Culture in Conflict

The End of Architectural Criticism?

Zheng Shiling

To understand architectural criticism, we shall first have to discuss the nature of architecture and the architect. In doing so, we would find a lot of confusion and contradiction regarding both terms. What architecture, what the architect is today, has greatly changed from traditional meaning. Unsurprisingly, there are therefore many voices that describe both the end of architecture and the death of architectural criticism.

In 1995, at the Vienna Architecture Conference, a group of architects from Austria, the US, England, and Spain posed the question of "The End of Architecture?" They recognized that in reality architecture does not depend on the architect but on authority.[1] It begged the second question: "The End of Experimentation of Grand Designs?" At the roundtable discussion the Austrian architect Wolf Prix stated that architecture, as defined since the nineteenth century, is dead. Thousands of buildings are built by politicians and architects who have no attitude, no faith, no silence, no nothing.[2] This situation is neither unique to Europe nor to North America; it is also the case in China. Conventionally, architecture has been a part of the state's achievements, but architecture is no longer determined by architects or other professionals, but by political authority, capital, builders, and developers. In China, politicians determine what will be built and for which purpose, even giving detailed instruction on the aesthetics of architecture, forbidding "strange buildings," and limiting the height of skyscrapers.

Form follows profit; form follows performance; architecture is turning into statements on social values; it means that architecture is no more about itself, and that architecture is no longer designed by real architects. Iain Bordon, director of the Bartlett School of Architecture, declared the "Death of Architecture" to indicate that architecture, as we have known and conceived it, is dead. As with the death of all institutional forms, the death of architecture is to be invoked in a complete and permanent revolution.[3]

There is a paradox about architecture and art. For the American architecture critic Paul Goldberger, architecture is art and it is not art; it is something more, or less.[4] Architecture is increasingly interplaying between sculpture and building; it has become one of the most intriguing phenomena of twentieth-century art, especially as *archi-installation art* and *archi-sculpture*. Architecture is definitively the most provocative art form of our time. Architects have crossed generic boundaries; modern architecture itself has passed from Modernism, Postmodernism, and Deconstructivism to Parametricism.[5]

1 Coop Himmelblau. "The End of Architecture," in *The End of Architecture?: Documents and Manifestos*, ed. Peter Noever (Munich: Prestel, 1995), 17.
2 Peter Noever, ed. *The End of Architecture?: Documents and Manifestos* (Munich: Prestel, 1995), 99.
3 Iain Borden, "Death of Architecture." *The Berlage Institute Report*, no. 6/7 (2003), 108.
4 Paul Goldberger, *Why Architecture Matters* (London: Yale University Press, 2009), 8.

In 2008, the 11th Venice Architecture Biennale had the theme *"Out There. Architecture Beyond Building."* Some architects presented their work as art installations. In his manifesto for the Biennale Frank Gehry wrote:

> **By definition, a building is a sculpture, because it is a three-dimensional object. But there is a moment of truth that is very similar between art and architecture.**[6]

In his introduction to the exhibition catalogue, the American art and architecture critic Aaron Betsky, director of the 2008 Biennale, presented the idea that architecture must go beyond buildings:

> **Architecture is a way of representing, shaping and offering critical alternatives to the built environment. In a tangible sense, architecture is that which allows us to be at home in the world.**[7]

Elsewhere, Aaron Betsky wrote:

> **Most buildings are not designed by architects. They are the result of economic considerations, they are put together by formulae, and they are final results of endless negotiations. For that reason most buildings are ugly, useless and wasteful.**
> **Yet architecture is beautiful. Architecture can place us in the world in a way no other art can. It can make us at home in modern reality.**[8]

In 2004, Betsky had defined a special domain of architecture:

> **Architecture is not art, nor art architecture, yet the two seem to be approaching each other. I would argue that is not a question of fashion or fatal attraction, but one of responding to the traditional task proper to both fields. It is entirely possible that a third, joint endeavor is coming into being, for which we have no proper name, and which might also give rise to attempts to remake our reality.**[9]

During the Renaissance, an architect was just like a divinity, *"il divino artista,"* or *"l'uomo universale."* According to the definition of the term architect current in the sixteenth century—"Quel nom est architecte?"—in 1567, the French architect Philibert de l'Orme defined the true architect as one who walks on winged feet through a luxurious, private garden, far from all worldly affairs and their immediate exigencies, close to a temple of meditation and an invigorating source of running water. He has four hands, four ears, and three eyes—one to watch God and his works and to fathom history, one to observe and evaluate the current ways of the world, and the other to foresee the future.[10]

Today, unlike superstar architects, an ordinary architect usually does not play a grand role and is no longer the traditional professional. The US architectural critic Paul Goldberger insisted that architecture is just politics, sociology, money, housing, cities, and old buildings both crumbling and revived. Buildings are the products of a peculiar combination of artistic vision, money, political wherewithal, and engineering skill [11]. The French philosopher Michel Foucault thought that architects are no longer the technicians of the three great variables—territory, communication, and speed. Architects could be labelled "social condensers," or "social administrators." In these cases, architects are only managers, team leaders of technicians, defective philosophers, sociologists, and even politicians. Today, architects are also fashion designers and artists; sometimes, architects are employed in every task, from business, commerce, industrial design, development, engineering to management, etc. The architect's practice is organized as a limitless virtual studio, as a laboratory that includes design engineers, financiers, management gurus, process specialists, model makers, and others. Architects produce segregated and essentially small-scale components of the city

[5] Zaha Hadid and Patrik Schumacher. "Parametricist Manifesto," in *Out There. Architecture Beyond Building: 11th International Architecture Exhibition La Biennale de Venezia (vol. 5)* (Venice: Fondazione La Biennale di Venezia, 2008), 62.

[6] Frank Gehry, "Architecture & Process. Manifestos," in *Out There. Architecture Beyond Building: 11th International Architecture Exhibition La Biennale de Venezia (vol. 5)* (Venice: Fondazione La Biennale di Venezia, 2008), 49.

[7] Aaron Betsky, *Out There. Architecture Beyond Building* (Venice: Fondazione La Biennale di Venezia, 2008), 5.

[8] Ibid., 19.

[9] Markus Brüderlin, Gottfried Bohm and eds. Cristoph Brockhaus, Philip Ursprung. *ArchiSculpture* (Berlin and Stuttgart: Hatje Cantz Publishers, 2004), 51.

[10] Geert Beaert, "Quel nom est architecte?," *The Berlage Institute Report*, no. 6/7 (2003), 77.

[11] Paul Goldberger, *Building Up and Tearing Down. Reflections on the Age of Architecture* (New York: The Monacelli Press, 2009), 8.

that are driven by severe market and political constraints. It is society's aesthetics and value system that determine the architects' product. As one Japanese architect said:

> Without question, I think of myself as an architect. But as the virtual world permeates our society, an increasing number of people claim to be architects. However precise computer analysis may be, whatever expanded expressive possibilities the computer offers, the architect is someone who must always think in a comprehensive way and make decisions. At the core of this profession is an engagement with the physical world. Anyone who loses sight of this fact probably shouldn't be called an architect.[12]
>
> The definition of an "architect" has broadened. I find myself involved in a variety of fields—architecture of course—but also in urban master planning, exhibition installation, furniture and product design, as well as writing architectural thought and criticism. Nevertheless, I identify myself as an "architect."[13]

The great changes in the nature of architecture and architects have led to changes in architectural criticism too. In 1998, the British architecture critic Martin Pawley noted "The strange death of architectural criticism."[14] In his article "The Death and Life of Great Architecture Criticism," the US architecture critic Thomas Fisher pointed out that his fellow US critic Nicolai Ouroussoff of *The New York Times* focusses only on the appearance of architecture and that his approach is that of an art critic. That seems to be the most that journalists have done for architectural criticism. The globalization of architectural culture and digital technology has raised the crisis of architectural criticism to a global scale.[15] In this context, the geographic inaccessibility to real buildings prevents critics from covering global architecture with in-depth analysis. Certainly, architectural criticism is in danger of becoming superficial. The US architecture critics Alexandra Lange and Nancy Levinson thought that architectural criticism should be more locally rooted.

The task of architectural criticism is really tough as there are many aspects that cannot be distinguished simply in terms of right or wrong. Becoming an effective architecture critic requires a wide range of qualifications that include vastness of knowledge, years of experience, the power of persuasion, excellent delivery skills, lots of patience, thirst for awareness, the ability to formulate objective comments and logical arguments. Architecture critics not only assist architects in understanding the nature of their projects but also help them in developing a critical point of view. This clarifies the design.

During the design process, architects need constant self-evaluation of their designs. After the building's completion, most architects would like to have some reactions and evaluations from the public. Architectural criticism is certainly a necessity for architects. The British architect Norman Foster said:

> If you are an architect you might think you need a critic like the proverbial hole in the head. Most times you are probably right. This is perhaps a reflection on the level of criticism as much as the architect's vanity or insularity. Fortunately, there are enlightened exceptions. Sometimes a critic emerges whose perception is so sharp, and whose arrow is so swift and accurate, that it stops you in your tracks. It makes you think.[16]

Architecture as a discipline is much more than just a collection of single instances of architecture: it is a metalanguage. The discipline of architecture as metalanguage is thus itself a form of criticism. The Italian theorist and historian Manfredo Tafuri considered architecture and art automatically as acts of criticism.[17] He also cited the argument of the Italian historian Bruno Zevi:

[12] Tadao Ando, "Protecting Life," *The Berlage Institute Report*, no. 6/7 (2003): 250.
[13] Toyo Ito, "To be an architect," *The Berlage Institute Report*, no.6/7 (2003): 250.
[14] Martin Pawley, *The Strange Death of Architectural Criticism* (London: Black Dog Publishing, 2007), 330.
[15] Thomas Fisher, "The Death and Life of Great Architecture Criticism," *Places Journal*, December 2011. Accessed 03 Jul 2021. https://doi.org/10.22269/111201
[16] Norman Foster, *Foreword. The Strange Death of Architectural Criticism* (London: Black Dog Publishing, 2007), 10.

In point of fact, a great many works of art, even very famous works of art, are of critical nature. You can use words to write a poem. Or just to tell a story or criticize an event. It is the same with painting. You can sing and you can speak. Modern art criticism has been able to show that many painters were really not artists but critics, great critics who used the medium of words to express not their feelings but their ideas. And it is the same with architecture.

The challenge for us, in the next few years, will be to find a method by which historical research can be done with the architect's instruments ... Why not express architectural criticism in architectural forms instead of in words?[18]

[17] Manfredo Tafuri, *Teorie e Storia dell' Architettura* (Rome: Laterza, 1976), 120.
[18] Bruno Zevi, "History as a Method of Teaching Architecture," in *Teorie e Storia dell' Architettura*, ed. Manfredo Tafuri (Rome: Laterza, 1976), 122.
[19] Bruno Zevi, "La storia come metodo-logia," in *Teorie e Storia dell' Architettura*, ed. Mafredo Tafuri (Rome: Laterza, 1976), 121.
[20] Dennis Sharp, "Architectural Criticism: History, Context and Roles," *Architectural Criticism and Journalism: Global Perspectives. Proceedings of an International Seminar Organised by the Aga Khan Award for Architecture in Association with the Kuwait Society of Engineers*, vol. 6–7 (December 2005): 33.

While architectural criticism is connected with architectural history and architectural theory, depending on the critic's background, it has varied emphases. Architecture's expressive instruments will be the new subject of critical history ("storico-critica") and no longer only a field of art history.[19] Architectural criticism understands architecture as consisting of structure, material, and logic, thereby implying more dimensions of information than merely the formal architectonic language.

Frank Lloyd Wright presumed that architecture is a form of communication, and therefore architecture as one of the media. The rapidly changing media landscape has had an impact on architectural criticism, shifting both modes of criticism and the media in which it is published. While some large newspapers retain full-time architectural critics, there are now also numerous critics who write for a range of publications on the one hand, and on the other hand, many new online venues have emerged.

In 2005, the Aga Khan Award for Architecture, in association with the Kuwait Society of Engineers, organized an international seminar on the topic of "Architectural Criticism and Journalism: Global Perspectives."

The seminar presented the idea that the purpose of architectural criticism is to bring to a wider reading public—through newspapers, journals, broadcasts, and books—informed, independent, objective, and critical commentaries on buildings and environment issues.[20] The readers of such architectural criticism would be divided into non-professionals such as the public and developers, and professionals such as academics, theorists, historians, architects, architecture students. Given that the readership consists of a variety of backgrounds, so criticism should be written accordingly.

Architecture critics should have multi-disciplinary and professional experience, including the fields of history, theory, philosophy, academia, industrial design, writing, editing, journalism, editorship, and curatorship. In some cases architecture critics are also historians and theorists. Their theories do not only cover architecture, but extend also to urban planning and urban design; in fact, it is difficult to distinguish their careers and work as either architectural theory or architectural criticism. For example, British critic Alan Colquhoun was a historian, an architect, and an academic. His *Collected Essays in Architectural Criticism* cover architectural theory and history, architects, criticism, art, etc. Manfredo Tafuri, too, was an architect, historian, theoretician, critic and academic. US critic Charles Jencks engaged in cultural theory, landscape architecture, and architectural history.

Architectural criticism involves the evaluation, assessment, commentary, classification, analysis, and interpretation of buildings, an extended activity even through history. The assessment may consider the subject from wider perspectives, including planning, social, or aesthetic issues. It may also take a polemical position reflecting the critic's own values. At the most accessible extreme, architectural criticism is a branch of lifestyle journalism, especially in the case of high-end residential projects.

Architectural criticism is a varied activity expressed in a range of media such as— other than architecture itself as mentioned above—architectural journals, newspapers, magazines, exhibitions, conferences, seminars; even appearing in literature, painting, sculpture, photography, film, music, fashion, etc. Architectural criticism is also involved in architectural competitions to select commissions for public buildings. On some occasions, this process has resulted in outstanding architecture.

[21] Noël Carroll, *On Criticism* (London: Routledge, 2009), 7.

Due to the complexities of architectural criticism for real design projects, many disciplines could be involved, potentially requiring a group of critics. A critic is a person who engages in the reasoned evaluation of an object. [21] In China, besides architectural theorists, historians, academics, and practicing architects, architecture critics could be government officials, urban planners, developers, structural engineers, mechanical engineers, traffic experts, accountants, journalists, artists, writers, even lay citizens, etc., all with very different backgrounds; with this breadth of knowledge in mind, there cannot be one single critic who can simultaneously play so many roles and cover so many varied disciplines. For some international design competitions, a number of international architects and critics with different cultural backgrounds will be invited to the jury, certainly resulting in very different views and comments that often lead to differentiated results.

Thus, besides writing reviews and interpretations of buildings for newspapers and professional architectural journals, architectural criticism in the form of jury service for architectural design competitions is playing an increasingly important role. The designs to be judged are in the areas of interior design, architecture, urban design, landscape architecture, preservation and renovation of historic buildings, etc. The design scope extends from single buildings to a complex, the urban regeneration for a neighborhood, and even an urban plan for an entirely new city. Design teams usually consist of multi-disciplinary professionals. Quite often these teams present their projects with elaborate models and spectacular images; however, the jury pays more attention to the design's critical content.

In modern China, the earliest architectural criticism was published in such newspapers as *Shen-pao* (*Chinese Daily News,* from 1872), *Dianshizhai Pictorial* (from 1884), and *Illustrated News* (from 1884). Over the last thirty years, China has probably held more international architectural design competitions than any other country, most of these resulting in realized buildings that are now an important part of Chinese and world architectural history. For architectural competitions, the aim is to select the appropriate design or architectural firm. Typically, before the process gets under way, the jury agrees on a set of criteria or design principles. For each scheme, every juror will not only comment on the advantages and weaknesses, but will also suggest how the presented competition scheme might be developed in order to seek a possible improved resolution, such suggestions being a form of pre-criticism for projects at an early design stage to assist creative architects.

On some occasions, there would be two stage competitions with a mid-term review following which the jury would recommend design developments for the next design phase. For example, in the case of the competition for the Shanghai Pudong Art Gallery of 2016, located on the prestigious site facing towards the Bund of Shanghai, seven international architectural firms participated. The French architect Jean Nouvel proposed a large, bird-like roof. On a nearby site, a bird-like restaurant had only just been demolished, and therefore Nouvel's scheme was not really appropriate. But his concept for the art gallery typology was excellent. So Nouvel, together with three other architectural firms, continued on to the second phase. At the final jury, Nouvel's new proposal for "a fourth space," inspired by Marcel Duchamp's *The Large Glass* (1915–1923), won him the commission. The Pudong Art Gallery was opened in July 2021.

For some important projects, selected jury members would take on the responsibility of consulting throughout the whole design and construction process. For example, the international design competition for the New Development Bank (the Bank of BRICS) was held in 2016 in two phases. The jury suggested modifications to the winning design: the massing of the building was to change from four to five parts, and alternative materials were recommended.

Given that most designs are intended to be realized, there are actually more concept design proposals than architectural competitions. At the very beginning of a project, the criteria for a design proposal might only require an outline concept. The winning design is then usually chosen by an independent panel of professionals and stakeholders, sometimes involving government and local representatives. This procedure is often used to generate new ideas for building designs, to stimulate public debate, to generate publicity for the project, and to allow emerging designers the opportunity to gain exposure.

During 2020 and 2021, building activity in China contracted significantly, in some cases bringing humiliation to some star architects' offices that had participated in competitions or concept design proposals. This development has brought about a divergence in the professional levels between the jury and participating architects, as a juror's understanding of a project is not necessarily as deep as that of the architect. This situation has given rise to some disagreements with jury decisions, especially when the final decision has been taken by a non-professional government representative. However, given that the jury usually consists of experts from different professions, and knowing both the program and environment better than the architects, recommended design modifications and developments tend to improve the ultimate design.

Architectural criticism has helped to promote the international development of architecture, architectural theory and design methodology, thereby helping new relationships to be established between citizens, cities, clients, and architects. As a practicing architectural critic, a juror of an architectural competition would not only participate in the selection of the winning scheme, but would also suggest and recommend developments for a project's design. It is in this way that architectural criticism takes on an active role in laying an important foundation for the creation of good architecture.

Biography

Zheng Shiling is a professor at Tongji University with a PhD in architecture history and theory, Tongji University. He is a member of the Chinese Academy of Sciences, honorary fellow of the American Institute of Architects, a member of l'Academie d'Architecture de France, and Laurea honoris causa of Rome University, La Sapienza.

Niemeyer Do(o)med: Remembrance of Planes Past

Carlos Eduardo Comas / Marcos Almeida

fig. 1
Ibirapuera Park with Palace of the Arts (bottom right), Palace of the Industries (top right), and the curvilinear marquee. Aerial view. Photo: *Manchete* (Rio de Janeiro), special issue, 1954.

fig. 2
The Palace of the Arts seen from beneath the marquee. Photo: *Manchete* (Rio de Janeiro), special issue, 1954.

"The overall view of this building is magnificent. The dome is seventy-six meters in diameter by eighteen meters in height and free from pillars or any columns. Due to the peculiar shape of the building, the large spacing of the pillars, and the floor slabs without exposed beams, there was a great concentration of steel reinforcement bars. The Palace of Exhibitions is covered with small tiles. This building, which is worth around 60 million cruzeiros, including air conditioning equipment and escalators, has its own generator, which operates automatically, to provide lighting sixteen seconds after an eventual blackout."[1]

Acrópole

This remarkable exhibition pavilion is part of a set of four buildings connected by a marquee and a public walkway, which make up the "Ibirapuera Park," designed and built in 1953 by Oscar Niemeyer for the celebrations of the fourth centennial of the foundation of the city of São Paulo. Niemeyer named it the "Palace of the Arts." Another of these four buildings, originally the "Palace of the Industries," has housed the "Fundação Bienal de São Paulo" since the 1960s. Resembling a thin shell resting on the ground, this elegant circular building is one of the most beautiful exhibition spaces in the world. Its interior, which one penetrates through a small gap, reveals an unexpected spatiality, an unexpected volumetry, silent and pleasant. This effect results from the happy arrangement of three clear and independent structural systems, an extremely inventive spatial arrangement. There is delicacy in the envelope of the great dome, whose load is transferred directly to the ground through ribs in diametrical arches. There is surprise as you enter and find out that the ground hangs in the air, because a void reveals the basement, created five meters below the level of the entrance gardens by means of a retaining cylinder. The two additional upper floors have their own structure of columns and floor slabs independent of the other two structures. On the top floor there is no structure. Like a small cloud, the last floor slab floats below the dome that curves away in all directions. It is a wonderful result, due to the technique behind the grace with which the three completely independent structural systems are employed. It is one of Niemeyer's most limpid and simply monumental works. From almost half a century ago! We did everything to keep it intact. As in the architect's original drawing.

Paulo Mendes da Rocha, 2000[2]

I

Sometimes a building we ignored catches our eye and we suddenly see, explore, connect, surrender. This happened to us in the late 1990s vis-à-vis the domed building now called Oca. Known at the time as the Museum of Aeronautics, formerly the Museum of Aeronautics and Folklore, it had been inaugurated as Palace of the Arts, although first designed as a planetarium; biunivocal correspondence between form and function is a myth. Anyway, we ignored it, regardless of its unusual shape, size, and many visits to the neighboring São Paulo Art Biennial pavilion, formerly the Palace of Industries. Both it and Oca were part of the same Ibirapuera Park exhibition complex by Oscar Niemeyer (1907–2012), inaugurated in 1954

keywords:

Niemeyer, Oca, Ibirapuera Park, Mendes da Rocha, remodeling modern architecture

[1] *Acrópole* 16, no. 191 (August 1954): 496.
[2] Translated by Comas from the original in Portuguese, which follows: "Este surpreendente pavilhão de exposições faz parte do conjunto de quatro edifícios ligados por uma marquise, passeio público, que constituem o 'Parque do Ibirapuera,' projetado e construído, todo o conjunto, em 1953, por Oscar Niemeyer para as comemorações do IV centenário da fundação da cidade de São Paulo. Foi chamado por Niemeyer de 'Palácio das Artes.' Um outro destes 4 edifícios, originalmente o 'Palácio das Indústrias,' desde os anos 60, abriga a 'Fundação Bienal de São Paulo.' Este elegante edifício circular, como uma fina casca pousada no chão, é um dos mais belos espaços expositivos do mundo, revelando seu interior, por onde se penetra por uma pequena fresta, uma inesperada espacialidade, uma volumetria imprevista, silenciosa e agradável. Este resultado e efeito se devem ao arranjo feliz de três sistemas estruturais nítidos e independentes, uma disposição espacial extremamente inventiva. Há a grande tênue envoltória da casca, apoiada, através de suas nervuras em arcos diametrais, diretamente no solo. Há a surpresa do chão que se suspende no ar, quando se entra, pois surge um vazio produzido pelo rebaixamento total do piso circular inferior, criado com um cilindro de arrimo 5 m abaixo do nível dos jardins de entrada. E há ainda mais dois pisos superiores com estrutura própria de pilares e lajes independentes das outras duas estruturas. No último piso não existe estrutura alguma. Como uma pequena nuvem, a última laje flutua abaixo da cúpula que foge em todas as direções. É um resultado belíssimo devido à técnica da graça com que são empregados os três sistemas estruturais completamente independentes. É uma das obras mais límpidas e singelamente monumentais de Niemeyer. E já de meio século passado. Fizemos tudo para conservá-la intacta. Como no desenho original do arquiteto." Paulo Mendes da Rocha, accessed July 30, 2021, https://spbr.arq.br/project/restauro-da-oca/.

to celebrate the fourth centennial of the city of São Paulo. When entering the park, greeted by the marquee, Oca stands to the left, rising from the ground. We ignored it, shame on us.

Then one day, flipping through *Modern Architecture in Brazil*, the authoritative 1956 catalog by Henrique Mindlin, there it was: a flying saucer with uncountable portholes and an abrupt rectangular cutout for an entrance, it resembled the landed spaceship from *The Day the Earth Stood Still*, the science fiction movie released in 1951. The plans show a single circular ground-floor slab featuring various cutouts that reveal the basement. In the southwest quadrant, to the left of the entrance and vaguely resembling the curve of a cannon bullet, a large indentation accommodates a horseshoe ramp; a smaller arched cutout opposite the entrance appears bisected by the entrance axis. Above, two floor slabs overlap, each inscribed in the corresponding parallel of the dome, both harmonizing their curves with the arched void. The slab above is a hexagon in plan. The other is a rectangle. Both exhibit concave sides and beveled edges to emphasize their thinness. On paper they look like tense membranes, the lowest pierced by the ramp, the highest tangential to it, a hairline separating them from the dome.

fig. 3
Oca, panoramic photomontage emphasizing the central allée and axial view from the entrance. AC ducts and lighting tracks introduced in the remodeling. Photo: Ruth Verde Zein, 2007.

fig. 4
Palace of the Arts, rendering simulating axial view from the entrance. Render: Rolando Figueiredo, 2021.

The columns fall into three sectors: the transverse rectangular bay prolonging the entrance, the intermediate hexagonal ring, and the irregular peripheral grid. The section is clear. The pyramidal composition is enclosed by the dome, eighty meters wide at the bottom and twenty-five meters high at its apex, with the ring-shaped concrete retaining wall enclosing the basement. José Carlos Figueiredo Ferraz was the structural engineer. We smiled, recognizing the Russian-dolls parti. This was not the first time that Niemeyer had resorted to different types of structure: we were looking at an elaborate version of the choir supported by a pair of columns under the conical vault of the Pampulha Chapel (1941–1945), which rises from the ground too. The voids between the slabs and the dome look outlandish in the photos, vaguely constructivist, whereas the ramp refers to Berthold Lubetkin's London Zoo Pavilion (1935), well known to Niemeyer.[3] The immediate question was that ramp: it might suit penguins, but what about art?[4]

We were intrigued. Time to go visiting. We were met with a surprise: the derelict building welcomes us in 1995 with an allée configured by two rows of cylindrical columns—straight, direct, elementary, and powerful, compressed between two smooth planes. The cutout to the left exposes the thickness of the ground-floor slab. The cantilevered first-floor slab shows off its beveled edges. The conjunction of the concavity of the dome with the concavity of the first-floor slab defines an elliptical clipping, suggesting the pictogram of an eye over the portholes resembling eyeglasses, with the concavity of the dome itself recalling an eyelid. The axial bay extends between voids: the vertical cutout for the entrance door is the counterpart of the horizontal cutout opposite. That vertical cutout frames a suspended airplane. Veiled by the bay's colonnade, another airplane occupies the larger void in front of the ramp. Right in the middle of the allée, it marks the transverse axis. Primordial elements are made alive: the line, the cross, the circle. The centrifugal and the centripetal impulses balance each other. Defined by an independent skeleton with no beams in sight, the archetype of directional space

[3] Henrique Mindlin, *Modern Architecture in Brazil* (Amsterdam: Colibris, 1956).
[4] The building was published in *Revista PDF* IV, no. 16 (May 1935): 401–4.

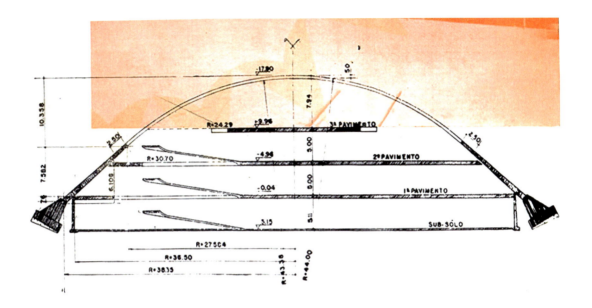

fig. 5
Transversal section through the ramp axis. *Revista Acrópole*, 1954.

is inscribed in the archetype of the focal or radiant space defined by the flattened dome. The echo of the Mediterranean temple (the colonnade) meets the echo of the Mesopotamian ziggurat (the overlapping floor slabs), whose plateaus resemble the hexagons in the baroque chapel of Guarino Guarini[5] and the projection of a pillow with its insinuations of repose. Art is religion, they say.

The allée and the ramp stabilize in the mind the unusual voids, dramatically changing as we move. Constant beacons, as unforgettable as the crevice and tree column of the Biennial Pavilion, they will only disappear upon reaching the top floor. Protected by a nautical guardrail, this floor resembles a *meseta* under the zenith of the dome, now seemingly unsupported. Verticality dominates as we rise, the height of the columns increasing in our memory: the horizontal stratification of space perceived as we descend becomes maximal at the basement. A cellar of cavernous climate, the basement makes the top floor feel like a summit open to the sky. The scheme is tripartite in section, and its middle part is artificial mountain as much as primitive hut in gala attire, an embellishment of the Dom-Ino scheme with which Le Corbusier updated Abbott Laugier.[6] It has architecture as microcosm (or the monumentalized house understood as human body) and architecture as macrocosm (or the monumentalized house understood as man-made nature); one within the other, like the glass balls encasing other objects that are used as paper weights. Confirming Lucio Costa's statement,[7] Niemeyer makes modern architecture an inclusive proposition in terms of origin, sensibility, and types of structure, where a static Mesopotamian-Mediterranean tradition and a dynamic Nordic-Eastern tradition meet and complete each other. It is not just a case of disciplinary foundation, conventionally associated with the sacred monument. After all, in an exhibition pavilion, like in any museum, contemplation does not come separate from the experience of an itinerary. Allusions to vision and to a road are programmatically pertinent.

Allusion to a ziggurat also links Oca with the Corbusian proposal of 1929 for the Mundaneum Museum. Moreover, the São Paulo pavilion was built without walls, and this presupposes that freestanding display panels and cases will be necessary, as in Mies van der Rohe's Museum for a Small City design of 1942. To boot, Niemeyer deploys the constituent elements of the museum type as defined by Karl Friedrich Schinkel in Berlin, modifying their size and articulation. The dome no longer roofs a void flanked by two wings of trabeated structure. Hugely enlarged, the dome becomes the whole building, and the wings condense into

[5] Specifically, the Chapel of the Holy Shroud (Sacra Sindone) in Turin.
[6] Laugier's primitive hut was an argument against the excesses of Rococo. The structural scheme of Maison Dom-Ino (1915) was an argument against the excesses of eclecticism.
[7] The idea of modern architecture as an inclusive proposition appears first in "Universidade do Brasil," published in 1937, involving a Greco-Latin or Mediterranean spirit and a Gothic-Oriental spirit. In "Considerações sobre o ensino de arquitetura," published in 1945, Lucio speaks of an organic-functional concept as in Gothic architecture (in which the plastic expression blossoms like a plant) and a plastic-ideal concept as in classical architecture (in which plastic expression stands sharp like a crystal). In "Considerações sobre arte contemporânea," published in 1952, but dated from the 1940s, he recognizes a Mesopotamian-Mediterranean axis promoting a static spatial concept and crystalline beauty and a Nordic-Oriental axis promoting a dynamic spatial and floral beauty. The baroque is included in the latter category. See Lucio Costa, *Sobre arquitetura* (Porto Alegre: CEUA, 1962).

an interiorized block. The name may change—Palace of the Arts, Museum of Aeronautics, Oca—but the architectural lesson is the same: architecture does not dispense with memory, precedent is the springboard for invention. Like every first-rate artist, Niemeyer is a cannibal, not a noble savage; disciplinary culture is a design tool. And what is good for penguins is also good for featherless bipeds.

II

Oca was a happy choice of name, associating Niemeyer's dome with another type of primitive hut, true and native, for the 2000 reopening with an exhibition celebrating the quincentennial of the Portuguese discovery of Brazil. Paulo Mendes da Rocha (1928–2021), on the road to stardom, was commissioned in 1999 for the restoration and refurbishing project. The executive drawings were contracted to MMBB Architects, at the time including Ângelo Bucci, Fernando de Mello Franco, Marta Moreira, and Milton Braga—among the most talented Brazilian architects of their generation. Ibirapuera Park, its buildings, and the architectural elements built for the fourth centennial had been listed in 1992 by the State of São Paulo Landmarks Commission, CONDEPHAAT;[8] in 1997, by the Municipal Landmarks Commission, CONPRESP;[9] and in 1998 by IPHAN,[10] Brazil's National Heritage, a provisional listing that became effective in 2016.

We could not return until 2005, a decade after that first visit. Our expectations were great. The disappointment, infinite. The magic had vanished, the surprising axiality obliterated. The new front desk prevented access through the central allée. All electrical and hydraulic installations had been deactivated and their exposed elements removed. Recessed lighting built into the floor slabs and the dome had been removed, their sockets filled with acrylic revetment and paint. The same applied to the air-conditioning grilles in the dome. The existing escalator had been removed and its place occupied by utilities comprising lifts, VAC equipment including vertical ducts, and electric cables. The main lighting track ran along the allée ceiling parallel and near to the right colonnade, feeding parallel tracks suspended from the ceiling and perpendicular to the allée axis. The AC plant was built underground, in the park. The primary AC duct ran perpendicular to the allée axis. It fed three ducts of ovular section. The central one ran beneath the main lighting track. The other ducts ran to the left of the other colonnades.

We understood that the use of the building remained the same—a venue for temporary exhibitions—but the context had changed. The building had to conform to more stringent performance norms, codes, and regulations, not only from the side of the city and government preservation agencies at all levels but also from the insurance companies, without which no venue can receive blockbuster international art exhibitions. There were issues of safety, security, comfort, flexibility, access, maintenance, repair, scheduling, logistics, and budget to consider. Restoration and refurbishment on the Oca scale are not minor undertakings. We are really talking remodeling. In medical parlance, we are not discussing noninvasive procedures but surgery.

Despite very much wanting to love the remodeled building, admirers of both Niemeyer and Mendes da Rocha that we are, we cannot: the body image the building brings to our mind is that of someone who, unable to take food by mouth, underwent gastrostomy, exposing

fig. 6
Palace of the Arts. View of the entrance between portholes, showing the inaugural exhibition in the basement. Photo: *Manchete* (Rio de Janeiro), special issue, 1954.

fig. 7
Museum of Aeronautics. Historical airplanes 14BIS, at ground-floor level, and Jahu, at basement level. *Revista Alterosa*, 1961.

fig. 8
Palace of the Arts. View of the upper floor. Dome with built-in lighting and AC system diffusers. Photo: *Manchete* magazine, c.1954.

fig. 9
Palace of the Arts. View toward the entrance, ground-floor longitudinal axis. Photo: *Manchete* magazine, c.1954.

[8] Conselho de Defesa do Patrimônio Histórico, Arqueológico, Artístico e Turístico do Estado de São Paulo.
[9] Conselho Municipal de Preservação do Patrimônio Histórico, Cultural e Ambiental da Cidade de São Paulo.
[10] Instituto do Patrimônio Histórico e Artístico Nacional.

the tubes needed for enteral feeding. For all the evident care in their gridded layout, the lighting tracks disfigure the ceiling plane. The AC ducts are even bigger eyesores, most particularly in the allée, where the clash between the horizontality of the log-like duct and the neighboring columns' verticality is intensified by the main lighting track in the ceiling. The integrity of the allée's original volume is lost, as both the horizontal plane of the ceiling and the vertical plane of the colonnade are now partially obstructed. The dialogue with the Biennial Pavilion is silenced. Niemeyer's original devotion to limpid planarity is forgotten.

Limpid planarity, in this context, means that wiring, cables, and ducts were hidden from view in the original building. They were built in to pass unnoticed, and we had not paid attention to their unobtrusive external finishes—milky glass squares and metallic grilles. As architects, we should have paid attention. For they showed that Niemeyer kept taking into consideration the pressure of service systems upon architectural space, as had already happened in the Ministry of Education building (1936–1945), in which he was first a member of the design team led by Lucio Costa and later the design coordinator. It was a step further from embedding wiring in floor slabs and walls as in the first phase of Le Corbusier's purist architecture, which abhorred poché and only tolerated it as built-in cabinetry. Nevertheless, Oca's Brazilian-branded, post–International Style, late- or post-purist manner still subscribed to a minimalist aesthetic. It was still based on the reduction of the primary elements of architecture to their essential geometry. Floors and walls still aspired to be horizontal and vertical planes, respectively, whereas columns remained cylinders and pillars remained cuboids. Thinness and lightness were still *desiderata*.

Post-purism contrasts with the more sculptural brutalist trend, with which we associate buildings such as Affonso Eduardo Reidy's MAM—the Museum of Modern Art in Rio (1952–1968)—and Lina Bo Bardi's MASP—the Museum of Art of São Paulo (1957–1964). Both cases show that lighting tracks and exposed ducts work very well in columnless spaces featuring ribbed slabs. They appear as industrial *objets trouvés* whose metallic sheen contrasts satisfactorily with the rough texture of raw concrete. Yet both post-purism and brutalism can be seen as vintage modern architecture. We specify "vintage" as the period running from the Roaring Twenties to the Super Seventies (periodization is now frowned upon, but still useful). Another pair of buildings may also be compared to Oca, both classifiable

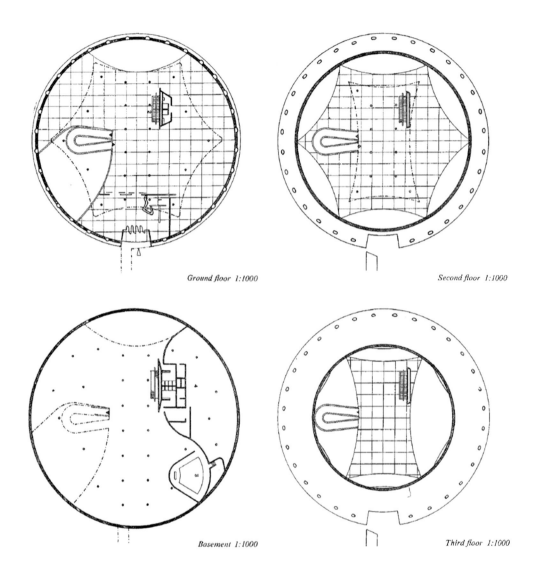

Ground floor 1:1000 Second floor 1:1000
Basement 1:1000 Third floor 1:1000

fig. 9
Palace of the Arts. Plans, Mindlin, *Modern Architecture in Brazil*, 188.

as contemporary modern architecture, still a living tradition. The brutalist attitude informs SESC 24 de maio (2000–2017), the remodeling and expansion of a former department store to fashion a Cultural and Sports Center by Mendes da Rocha and MMBB, a masterpiece in which the denser network of ducts and cables reads as a virtual layer beneath exposed beams and the underside of the floor slab. The whole makes up a materially composite hollowed-out piece that amounts to a virtual thick slab. At the extreme opposite of the SESC 24 de maio strategy stands the neo-purist work of Alvaro Siza in Porto Alegre: the Iberê Camargo Museum (1998–2008), where no lamp or grille is on view. Ducts ran behind gypsum-board walls and dropped ceilings. Luminous ceilings light the galleries, and cove lighting is used in the hall. The result is a superlatively serene ambiance, visually noiseless. The honesty badge is usually applied to MAM, MASP, and SESC (vintage), but not to Siza (contemporary), yet the badge is to be taken with a pinch of salt. After all, at the paradigmatically modern Ministry of Education, of whose design team Affonso Eduardo Reidy was also a member, bracing elements were not exposed but hidden in the blank end walls, and floor slabs had to accommodate an irregular weight distribution. Wiring was concealed in a pioneering attempt at a raised floor (the structural system was of the inverted mushroom variety, in which the underside of the floor slabs was flush with the underside of the mushroom

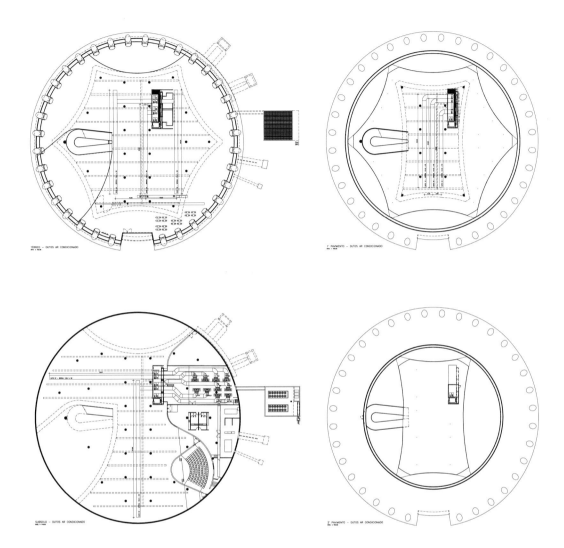

fig. 10
Oca. Plans. Courtesy arch.
Angelo Bucci.

columns' capitals) and in the hollow guardrail in front of and along the glazed walls. Sunlight control and cross-ventilation were used instead of the VAC systems still in their infancy. Nevertheless, another contemporary modern masterpiece one block away, the ABI Building (1936–1939) by Marcelo and Milton Roberto, did feature AC installations—and dropped ceilings that concealed the ducts.

So the particular strategy adopted for Oca's remodeling must have had pragmatic reasons behind it beyond clichéd honesty. On the one hand, the building had to be considered both as a public facility and as a work of art. On the other hand, the architects involved were conscious of their cultural responsibilities, as their irreproachable curricula corroborate. The remodeling was supported by Niemeyer, still alive, and reviewed by the design boards of preservation agencies at the municipal, state, and national levels. All the mantras in the preservation book are respected. The operation is reversible (although it may remain on view for a considerable time). The legibility of different moments in the building's history is not blurred (which is more the historian's problem than the architect's or the public's). And yet, in terms of body image, we kept seeing Oca as a person whose artificial leg could be hidden from public view to preserve decorum (that outmoded word), but needed to be replaced urgently. They do not last long, artificial legs. So, that person got a crutch. A

brand-new, well-designed crutch as crutches go, but still a crutch. Granted, Oca's misfortune was nowhere as great as that of Niemeyer's Dance Hall (1941–1943) at Pampulha, where the restaurant was disfigured by a dropped ceiling and light fixtures worthy of the gaudiest art deco lobby, in a restoration apparently endorsed by Niemeyer himself. We cannot stop thinking about alternatives to keep intact the planarity of Oca's ground-floor ceiling, such as AC ducts hidden in long desks and/or tall cabinets (as in the top floor) combined with metal suspended ceilings on the other floors (as in Mendes da Rocha's Forma Furniture Showroom of 1987). After all, better to lose the saddle than the horse.

fig. 10
Oca. Entrance hall.
Photo: Nelson Kon, 2000.

fig. 11
Oca. Void between first floor and basement.
Photo: Nelson Kon, 2000.

fig. 12
Oca. Exposed electrical tracks and AC ducts below slab.
Photo: Nelson Kon, 2000.

III

A work of architecture exists in time and space. Synonymous with judgment, criticism of a work of architecture in different moments may vary because of the work's changed aspects rather than the critic's changed views—even if criticism always mirrors the critic's cultural baggage. Criticism is based on knowledge—as we cannot and should not judge something we do not know—ideally, firsthand knowledge. Gaining knowledge of a work of architecture includes not only visiting it but also looking for and looking at drawings, photographs, videos, and movies, along with reading and evaluating reports, reviews, interviews, essays, and previous criticisms; to paraphrase Spanish philosopher José Ortega y Gasset, a work of architecture is itself and its circumstances. Architectural criticism implies description before judgment, to better understand the building first, and then to organize rational and emotional experience into words to better communicate the personal experience of it to others and to better compare that personal experience with those of others. Requiring data and taking time, always dated and never the worse for it, imbued with evocative power, criticism has some measure of restorative power, as it may both suggest and guide the renewal of monuments that are also documents and must work as pieces of equipment, not being allowed to be museums in and of themselves.

For if every work of architecture relies upon previous work, every architect is an architecture critic. When looking for previous work that may be relevant to the design problem at hand, an architect remodeling an existing building cannot help evaluating it. And architects in preservation agencies cannot help doing architectural criticism, both when

deciding if a building is worth listing and when approving work on listed buildings. Could our experience of horizontal planes slicing through space like blades have influenced Oca's remodeling were it available to them, the designers as well as the reviewers? Hard to know. Consensus is an elusive goal, all the more so when dealing with modern architecture, whose practitioners and theoreticians had and will have diverse ideas over time, not only about *firmitas* (firmness), *comoditas* (utility), and *venustas* (delight) but also about the weight that should be conferred to each of those domains, not to mention cost/benefit analyses. Even if ever so slightly, judgments are likely to differ from practitioner to practitioner, critic to critic, and practitioner to critic. Yes, good criticism matters. But who said it is easy?

IV

As of May 7, 2021, the São Paulo magazine *Veja* has reported that Oca shows signs of deterioration, but remedial work has not started because the state preservation agency is not approving it.

Biographies

Carlos Eduardo Comas
Architect, UFRGS—Universidade Federal do Rio Grande do Sul, 1966; M. Arch., MCP, University of Pennsylvania, 1977; Professor of Architecture, UFRGS, 1975–2013; Docteur, le Projet Architectural et Urbain, Université de Paris VIII, 2002 (*Architecture moderne brésiliene 1936–1945*); Curator, MoMA New York, 2015 (*Latin America in Construction: Architecture 1955–1980*); Professor emeritus, UFRGS, 2019.

Marcos Almeida
Architect, UFRGS—Universidade Federal do Rio Grande do Sul, 1997; M. Arch., UFRGS, 2005 (*As casas de Oscar Niemeyer*); Professor, Architecture and Urbanism, Centro Universitário Ritter dos Reis, 1999–2018; PhD candidate, UFRGS, since 2019 (Niemeyer, primus inter pares: gênio, educação, ofício).

"The New MoMA": Architectural Criticism, 1979–2019

Martin Hartung

fig 1
The Museum of Modern Art's Abby Aldrich Rockefeller Sculpture Garden (designed by Philip Johnson in 1953). Southwest view including the Garden Hall and Museum Tower (designed by César Pelli & Associates, completed in 1983/1984). Right: The Lillie P. Bliss International Study Center (designed by Philip Johnson, dedicated in 1968). Photographed in 1987. Digital image, The Museum of Modern Art, New York/Scala, Florence. © The Museum of Modern Art, New York/Scala, Florence.

The elaborate expansion projects of the Museum of Modern Art (MoMA) in Midtown Manhattan, which first moved into its own institutional home in 1939, have attracted a variety of critics. The latest expansion by Diller Scofidio + Renfro, completed in 2019 in collaboration with Gensler, was no exception: its smaller neighbor, the American Folk Art Museum, designed by Tod Williams and Billie Tsien, which opened in 2001, was demolished thirteen years later to make room for MoMA—despite the institution's prominent role in the enculturation of architecture. The paper focuses on the role of critics, who protested but could not save an architectural "gem."

keywords:

art museums, commercialism, corporations, culture industry, demolition, developers, expansions, neoliberalism, protest, postmodernism

In 1985, Martin Filler, an American architectural critic with extensive experience writing for professional and popular magazines across disciplines, began an assessment of the state of architectural criticism in the United States in an academic publication by posing the question: "If American architecture is, as many people believe it to be, in a crucial phase of transition—as well as a high level of creativity and world influence—why is this moment not also accompanied by a comparably high level of architectural criticism?"[1] Although the question was not entirely new at this point—it had been publicly debated since the mid-1970s by scholars and preservationists like the Columbia University professor James Marston Fitch and the architect, magazine editor, and former curator in the Department of Architecture at the Museum of Modern Art (MoMA), Peter Blake—Filler summarized the issues related to his field from an insider's perspective, with carefully balanced observations that also took into account the historical moment in which he formulated them.[2] Apart from a general inclination in magazines to promote rather than to criticize architecture—following the basic motto, "if it gets built, it's good for the profession"—Filler distinctly pointed out the driving forces behind publication culture in "a climate in which it is the creator, rather than the critic, who calls the tune."[3] He was not alone in his assessment: shortly after, the *New York Times* critic Herbert Muschamp and magazine editor Suzanne Stephens also critically observed the field.[4] In light of the complex economic and political interests between which an architectural critic is frequently tasked to navigate, Filler's bottom line in 1985 still holds today: "It is the public that is often the loser."[5]

In his polemical talk "On the Failure of [Architectural] Criticism," delivered in 1977 at the Institute for Architecture and Urban Studies in New York, Blake had already come to similar conclusions.[6] Having himself been a frequent victim of censorship, he pointed out that "the architectural profession in the US, individually and collectively, subverts and emasculates an intelligent criticism of architecture, and the certified architectural critics in the US, by and large, do not understand architecture, discuss it as an abstract art, and write not for an intelligent and interested and aware public, but for each other in magazines [and don't] treat architecture as a multifaceted and ever-present human experience."[7] As the root cause for this downright failure of the profession to enable a lay public to comprehend architecture, Blake identified "the tastemakers in America, the museum curators and so on, most of whom work in buildings they would never wish to endorse themselves, [who]

[1] Martin Filler, "American Architecture and Its Criticism: Reflections of the State of the Arts," in *The Critical Edge. Controversy in Recent American Architecture*, ed. Tod Marder (Cambridge, MA: The MIT Press, 1985), 27–32.

[2] See James Marston Fitch, "Architectural Criticism: Trapped in Its Own Metaphysics," *JAE* 29, no. 4 (1976): 2–3; Peter Blake, "On the Failure of [Architectural] Criticism," lecture, Institute of Architecture and Urban Studies, New York, spring 1977. Tape recording housed in the Peter Eisenman Fonds, Canadian Centre for Architecture, Montreal. On October 13, 1976, the 25-year-old *New York Times* critic Paul Goldberger stated in a lecture at Sci-Arc, Los Angeles, that "there seems to be a natural antagonism between architectural criticism and the people involved in the business of getting buildings built," accessed October 28, 2021, https://www.youtube.com/watch?v=h56sqCdlcnl. Goldberger quoted Fitch and the critic Jane Holtz Kay, who stated a year prior that "we relegate our built world to 'Arts and Leisure' and the like when it should be news and politics and part of the business, workaday world—and our environment shows it"; see Jane Holtz Kay, "Architecture and Design—Who Cares? All They Do Is Define the World We Live In," *Columbia Journalism Review* 14, no. 2 (July/August 1975): 30–36, here 36.

[3] Filler, "American Architecture," 28. Filler stated that architects were able to control the publication of their projects by denying certain access to private buildings, background information, and images. On the other hand, the competing publishers, constantly looking for new coverage and for exclusive possibilities to feature the most recent developments in the context of a "notoriously slow-moving" profession, were in desperate need of income from advertisers, the majority of which were building-material manufacturers, who

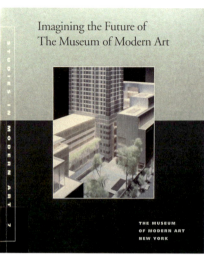

fig 2
The Museum of Modern Art, Garden Hall (designed by César Pelli & Associates, completed in 1984). Photo: Cervin Robinson. Courtesy of Pelli Clarke & Partners.
© Cervin Robinson / Pelli Clarke & Partners.

fig. 3
Cover of *Imagining the Future of The Museum of Modern Art*, Studies in Modern Art 7, ed. by John Elderfield (New York: The Museum of Modern Art, 1998). Frontispiece: Yoshio Taniguchi. Competition Proposal for the Expansion and Renovation of The Museum of Modern Art. Model (detail). 1997.
© The Museum of Modern Art, New York.

fig. 4
Cover of *The New Museum of Modern Art*, ed. by Glenn Lowry (New York: The Museum of Modern Art, 2005). Photo: Timothy Hursley.
© The Museum of Modern Art, New York.

fig. 5
The Museum of Modern Art, expansion designed by Diller Scofidio + Renfro, completed in 2019. Photo: Brett Beyer.
© Brett Beyer.

fuel this conspiracy of silence, this conspiracy of mysterymystery . . . ."[8] Referring to his own curatorial past at MoMA, where he worked between 1948 and 1950 in the Department of Architecture under the directorship of Philip Johnson, Blake understood the museum as being significantly responsible for the aforementioned condition: "As far as the Modern was concerned, architecture was an art. That was that. So that most, if not all, economic, sociological, technological, and political concerns were considered irrelevant."[9]

Assigning this level of impact to MoMA not only showed the, by then long-established, importance the private institution had assumed as a cultural forerunner and tastemaker ever since its foundation in the year of a world financial crisis among an upper-class milieu in 1929—with crucial support of the wealthy Rockefeller family.[10] Based on the "Bauhaus model" of a "synthesis of the arts," the museum was founded at a time when modernism was critically rejected and before the center of Western art was in the process of shifting from Paris to New York in the late 1940s.[11] Blake's "revelations" also pointed to the claim to excellence the museum still upholds as an institution. Consequently, MoMA's high standards became the same as those by which it is judged today.[12] While it established the first Department of Architecture in any museum—spearheaded, first programmed, and funded by Johnson in 1932—MoMA frequently left many critics and the lay public puzzled by the directions its major expansions took after the museum trustees decided against founding director Alfred Barr's endorsement of Ludwig Mies van der Rohe, Walter Gropius, or J.J.P. Oud as architects for the fledgling institution's inaugural building.[13] In 1984, art critic Hilton Kramer observed that "the trustee's decision to settle for a 'safe' solution . . . led to a fundamental split in MoMA's architectural policies—a split that, from the Thirties down to the present day, has separated the ideas put forward in the Museum's architectural exhibition and publications program from those put into practice in the Museum's own building program."[14] Over the course of the second half of the twentieth century, culture-institutional programs were generally informed by fundamental changes in a global leisure economy. In 1978, the modern music patron Paul Fromm observed in *The New York Times*

generally did not appreciate unfavorable reviews. Filler pointed out that architects in the US were not allowed to advertise their services according to the American Institute of Architecture's Code of Ethics until the late 1970s, which made them more dependent on favorable criticism. (Ibid.)

[4] Muschamp ran an architectural criticism course at Parsons School of Design beginning in 1985. See Cynthia Davidson and Matthew Berman, "A Conversation with Herbert Muschamp," *ANY* 21 (1997): 16–17. See also Suzanne Stephens, "Assessing the State of Architectural Criticism in Today's Press," *Architectural Record* 3, 1998, 64–69, 194.

[5] Filler, "American Architecture," 30.
[6] Blake, "Failure of [Architectural] Criticism."
[7] Ibid.
[8] Ibid.
[9] Ibid.
[10] On MoMA's history, see Harriet Schoenholz Bee and Michelle Elligott, eds., *Art in Our Time: A Chronicle of The Museum of Modern Art* (New York: The Museum of Modern Art, 2004). See also David A. Hanks, ed., *Partners in Design: Alfred H. Barr Jr. and Philip Johnson* (New York: The Monacelli Press, 2015).

[11] Felicity Scott, "Underneath Aesthetics and Utility: The Untransposable Fetish of Bernard Rudofsky," *Assemblage* 38, April 1999, 58–89, 63.

[12] The concurrent public expectations of MoMA were lamented by both Richard Oldenburg, then museum director, and Arthur Drexler, head of the Department of Architecture and Design until 1986, in a feature of MoMA's "most ambitious expansion in its history." ("The New MoMA: A New Era?," *Art News*, May 1984, 51–78, 51.)

[13] See Russell Lynes, *Good Old Modern: An Intimate Portrait of the Museum of Modern Art* (New York: Atheneum, 1973). For a general overview of the Department of Architecture and Design's exhibition history, see Barry Bergdoll, "Collecting and Exhibiting Architecture at the Museum of Modern Art," in *Show &*

that "more people than ever before are aware of the arts," and that despite a recession, "the art market continued to inflate."[15] Juxtaposing business, equated with profit, and culture, identified by Fromm with "standards and taste," he made it unmistakably clear to his readers that "in any standoff competition between the two, culture goes down nearly every time."[16] In this context, it was Kramer who noted shifts in both the numbers and the expectations of the museum-going public in the early 1980s—increasingly attuned to "blockbuster exhibitions," he assessed that this "new public [was] anything but confident of its taste" and instead very susceptible to "sheer spectacle" and "media events," which MoMA itself had done much to create.[17]

When Fromm made his assessment under the telling headline "The Cultural Retreat of the 70's," the museum had already embarked on its first major expansion project since Johnson's additions to its inaugural modernist home—designed by MoMA trustee Philip L. Goodwin, who had close ties to the Rockefeller family, and Edward Durell Stone—opened on Fifty-Third Street in a still low-rise Midtown Manhattan neighborhood in 1939.[18] Explicitly tasked with a "real estate development project," César Pelli & Associates were chosen over Johnson in February 1977 and commissioned to significantly expand the museum's gallery spaces. The expansion opened in May 1984, including the addition of a fifty-two-story apartment tower, known as the Museum Tower, which produced income for the private institution through controversial tax benefits[19] **(figs. 1–2)**. The most debated feature of Pelli's museum design materialized in a glass-enclosed structure with escalators, then called the "Garden Hall," that maximized visitor circulation and city views but minimized the space in Johnson's praised Abby Aldrich Rockefeller Sculpture Garden, and was immediately compared by critics to a shopping center and airport terminal.[20] It was again Kramer who noticed that, while the Garden Hall was "in many respects a very beautiful space," it was still "remarkably inhospitable to the exhibition of works of art."[21] The continuous expansional logic to accommodate an ever-growing museum public in a competitive culture industry contrasted the "artistic and intellectual inquiry that is especially true of the Museum of Modern Art," as its director Glenn Lowry formulated in a publication accompanying the largest museum expansion to date: the $858-million project by Japanese architect Yoshio Taniguchi, which became his first realized building in the United States, being executed between 1997 and 2004[22] **(fig. 3)**. Introduced in a headline of the popular *New York* magazine as "Post-MoMA-ism" after a laborious commission process with ten international architects—including Rem Koolhaas, who famously branded the museum as "MoMA, Inc." on this occasion—Taniguchi corrected several aspects of the Pelli expansion and proposed a minimalist design of urbanistic scale by unifying the museum campus in a quasi-monolithic complex[23] **(fig. 4)**. The expansion,

Tell: Collecting Architecture, ed. Andres Lepik (Ostfildern: Hatje Cantz, 2014), 117–47.

[14] Hilton Kramer, "MOMA Reopened: The Museum of Modern Art in the Postmodern Era," *New Criterion*, August 1984, accessed October 28, 2021, https://newcriterion.com/issues/2002/7/moma-kramer-1934.

[15] Paul Fromm, "The Cultural Retreat of the 70's," *The New York Times*, July 23, 1978, D 24.

[16] Fromm, "The Cultural Retreat."

[17] Kramer, "MOMA Reopened." The critic referred to MoMA's hitherto unprecedented Picasso retrospective in 1980, for which new modes of both handling and reaching out to visitors were devised (Kramer mentions 7,000 per day).

[18] On the building's history, which was retold several times in the context of MoMA's most recent expansion, see Suzanne Stephens, "With Yoshio Taniguchi's Design, New York's Museum of Modern Art Finally Becomes What It Wanted to Be All Along," *Architectural Record* 1, 2005, 95–109. See also Peter Reed, "The Space and the Frame: Philip Johnson as the Museum's Architect," in *Philip Johnson and The Museum of Modern Art*, Studies in Modern Art 6, ed. John Elderfield (New York: The Museum of Modern Art, 1998), 71–103.

[19] See Hal Foster, Denis Hollier, Silvia Kolbowski, and Rosalind Krauss, "The MOMA Expansion: A Conversation with Terence Riley," *October* 84 (spring 1998): 3–30. Riley stated: "To be fair to Pelli, when that project was first discussed by the trustees, it was not called the museum extension. It was called the real estate development project" (p. 20). Regarding the complex financial background of the Museum Tower, see Judd Tully, "MOMA's New Monument," *New Art Examiner*, November 1977, 4–5.

[20] See Paul Goldberger, "The New MOMA," *New York Times Magazine*, April 15, 1984, 37–38, 42–43, 46, 49, 68, 72, 74. Written before the museum reopened to the public, Goldberger did not agree it included "the department store interiors that some observers feared." The critic, however, cautiously observed that "Mr. Pelli's building is not as avant-garde by today's standards as the 1939 structure was in its time" (p. 42). Earlier, Goldberger had titled an article about the planned expansion "The New MOMA: Mixing Art with Real Estate," also published in *The New York Times Magazine*, November 4, 1979, 4, 52, 56.

fig 6
The American Folk Art Museum (designed by Tod Williams Billie Tsien Architects | Partners, completed in 2001, demolished in 2014). Photo: Giles Ashford. Courtesy of Tod Williams Billie Tsien Architects | Partners. © Giles Ashford.

fig 7
The American Folk Art Museum (2001–2014), section plans. © Tod Williams Billie Tsien Architects | Partners.

nevertheless, created new issues related to scale, especially with a 110-foot-high atrium that effectively made great artworks appear like "postcard stamps," while the building added to, rather than solved, visitor congestion.[24]

Although the Taniguchi expansion was at first generally welcomed by critics—notwithstanding the fact that the corporate background and commercial spirit of the structure remained a constant point of criticism—the New York-based firm Diller Scofidio + Renfro (DS+R) was hired by the museum in 2013 to solve the problems caused by the growth it had created in increasing visitor capacity to more than three million per year *(fig. 5)*. Known for other museum buildings and successful adaptive reuse projects—such as the High Line, a former railroad converted into a public park in the Chelsea District of Manhattan, and the much-praised renovation of the Lincoln Center in New York, originally designed by Johnson—the firm's productive and subtle institutional criticism as well as its long-standing ties to the art world were welcomed by the museum.[25] However, from the outset, DS+R's selection was closely tied to a large, image-damaging controversy surrounding the demolition of the American Folk Art Museum, designed by fellow architects Tod Williams and Billie Tsien *(fig. 6)*. The narrow, "idiosyncratic" building, forty feet wide and one hundred feet long, had been purchased by MoMA in 2011 to pay off the adjacent museum's debt, which had increased since the Folk Art Museum's completion in spring 2001.[26] In 2013, MoMA faced an outcry of unexpected proportions when it announced the decision to demolish its much smaller neighbor, whose relatively recent building was considered by many to be an architectural "gem," emphasizing its handcrafted bronze facade in relation to the objects on display—standing in stark contrast to MoMA's program and corporate image. With hindsight, the controversy was mainly based on symbolic values: the Folk Art Museum's inauguration was seen as a sign of hope for new beginnings shortly after the 9/11 terror attacks, an image thrown into sharp relief when it was razed for standing in the way

[21] Kramer, "MOMA Reopened."
[22] Glenn D. Lowry, "On the New Museum of Modern Art: Thoughts and Reflections," in *The New Museum of Modern Art*, ed. Glenn Lowry (New York: The Museum of Modern Art, 2005), 7–37, 14. The expansion brought the museum space to a size of 630,000 square feet, compared to the c.109,000 square feet of its original 1939 building. (See Stephens, "Yoshio Taniguchi's Design," 97.)
[23] Mark Stevens, "Post-MoMA-ism," *New York*, December 22–29, 1997, 40–42. See John Elderfield, ed., *Imagining the Future of The Museum of Modern Art*, Studies in Modern Art 7 (New York: The Museum of Modern Art, 1998).
[24] It was later noted by Goldberger and then Kimmelman that by adding highways to solve traffic congestion, it does usually simply lead to more traffic, a phenomenon referred to as "induced demand." See Paul Goldberger, "Friendly Fire on the Culture Front? Why the Museum of Modern Art Is Making a Fatal Mistake," *Vanity Fair*, January 8, 2014, accessed September 2, 2021, https://www.vanityfair.com/culture/architecture/2014/01/american-folk-art-museum-demolition. See also Michael Kimmelman, "With a $450 Million Expansion, MoMA Is Bigger. Is That Better?," *New York Times*, October 9, 2019, accessed September 2, 2021, https://www.nytimes.com/2019/10/09/arts/design/with-a-450-million-expansion-moma-is-bigger-is-that-better.html?searchResultPosition=3.
[25] See Julian Rose, "Machine Age: Elizabeth Diller Talks with Julian Rose about Museum Architecture," *Artforum*, November 2017, accessed September 2, 2021, https://www.artforum.com/print/201709/elizabeth-diller-talks-with-julian-rose-about-museum-architecture-71782.

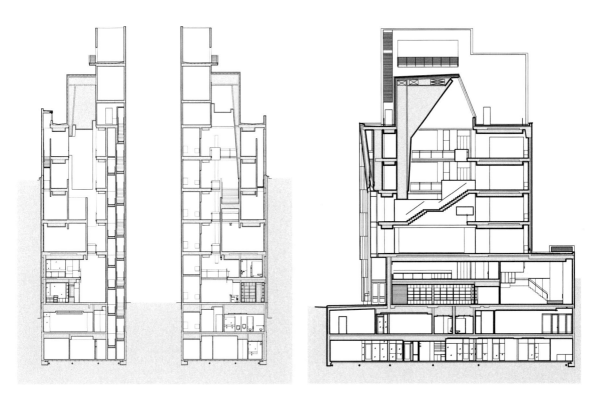

of MoMA's further expansion westward. *The New York Times*' art and architectural critic Michael Kimmelman accordingly likened it to the museum's "Manifest Destiny," referring to the nineteenth-century American ideology of ruthless national expansion.[27] While MoMA defended itself by emphasizing long-term internal efforts to reevaluate and diversify a narrow and exclusive understanding of modernism and contemporary art production—closely tied to a high-priced art market—the idea of a large and powerful institution swallowing a smaller "gem" struck many nerves among architects, scholars, and a variety of critics.[28] Although buildings had been demolished before in the service of MoMA's expansions—as well as in the process of constructing the American Folk Art Museum itself—never before had MoMA spearheaded the destruction of a building of another cultural institution, even though the museum owned it by then.[29] At the time, the prominent architectural critic Paul Goldberger commented: "A city that allows such a work [as the Folk Art Museum] to disappear after barely a dozen years is a city with a flawed architectural heart."[30] To a comment such as Goldberger's that "as art isn't always a rational matter, sometimes architecture isn't either," the MoMA director could, effectively, only reply: "We don't collect buildings."[31] In the process, the institution preserved the Folk Art Museum's facade, which it placed in storage.

Lowry made the statement in an unusual and well-attended public debate, cohosted by the Architectural League and presented at the New York Society for Ethical Culture in late January 2014, where MoMA's director, the chief curator of painting and sculpture, Ann Temkin, and Elizabeth Diller were joined by critics and professionals to come to terms with the ultimate decision to destroy the building. Although Diller explained that the firm had done everything possible to rescue and incorporate it in the design for MoMA, the architect explained they could not find a way to maintain its integrity due to its narrow, horizontal layout and mismatching floorplates, qualities which caused the architect to declare the American Folk Art Museum "obdurate," while, in principle, the building could have been adapted and kept standing

[26] On the complex history of the relationship between MoMA and the American Folk Art Museum since 1979, see Dan Duray, "Negatively 53rd Street: The American Folk Art Museum, in MoMA's Long Shadow," *New York Observer*, May 18, 2011, accessed September 2, 2021, https://observer.com/2011/05/negatively-53rd-street-the-american-folk-art-museum-in-momas-long-shadow.

[27] Kimmelman, "$450 Million Expansion."

[28] Among the many voices that spoke out against the Folk Art Museum's demolition, the journalist Robin Progrebin covered the fate of the institution most extensively for *The New York Times*. In April 2013, architects Richard Meier, Thom Mayne, and Robert A.M. Stern, among others, issued a letter against the demolition. See Robin Progrebin, "Architects Announce Opposition to MoMA Plan for Former Museum Site," *The New York Times*, April 22, 2013, accessed September 2, 2021, https://artsbeat.blogs.nytimes.com/2013/04/22/architects-announce-opposition-to-moma-plan-for-former-museum-site/?searchResultPosition=30. See also Julia Pelta Feldman, "Induced Demand: MoMA Reopens," *Texte zur Kunst*, December 4, 2019, accessed September 2, 2021, https://www.textezurkunst.de/articles/induced-demand-moma-reopens. The latter article stated that MoMA's collection activity had a "fundamental problem: that the museum remains an absolute, unquestionable, and vexing opaque authority."

[29] In the process of the MoMA expansions, altogether six brownstones as well as the former Dorset Hotel were demolished over the last decades to make room for new buildings. In order to build the American Folk Art Museum, in turn, two brownstones were demolished on Fifty-Third Street in Manhattan.

according to the firm's initial proposals to the client.[32] **(figs. 7–8)**. On the one hand, from a legal standpoint, MoMA had the right to tear it down: the much smaller building was essentially considered to stand in the way of connecting MoMA's existing structure with the floors it now occupies in a Jean Nouvel-designed luxury apartment tower, the lot of which was sold by MoMA to the developer Hines in 2007.[33] On the other hand, as the architectural consultant Karen Stein sharply observed at the panel discussion, it was "the basic early assumption [in one of MoMA's main expansion goals that was] problematic, [namely to achieve a] continuous loop of circulation."[34] Stein criticized MoMA, as the client, for being irresponsible by not readjusting its priorities in order to incorporate the Folk Art Museum and further stated that the museum had disappointed "a community that hopes [the museum] would take a building as seriously as it is taking its scholarship about the discipline."[35] The former New York Times architectural critic Nicolai Ouroussoff, also attending the panel, convincingly added that the "cloud hanging over the discussion" was that "the public has generally been pushed out of decisions about New York's architectural future."[36]

fig 8
The Museum of Modern Art, north/south section-perspective, 2017. Courtesy of Diller Scofidio + Renfro. © Diller Scofidio + Renfro.

In the public debate, a general consensus was established that it was not so much DS+R that was to blame for the Folk Art Museum's demolition by failing to come up with a solution to save it—which was not a conclusion reached lightly, as Diller repeatedly stated—but that it was the client that needed to adjust its expectations and ambitions in order to allow its neighboring building to survive.[37] At the same time, veteran art critic Jerry Saltz—who was one of the few writers, maybe the only one, who strongly advocated for the Folk Art Museum's destruction and deemed it "a useless place for the exhibition of art"—likened the related 30 percent added gallery space of 175,000 square meters to "about one Chelsea megagallery."[38] Ever since the Pelli-designed expansion, the loss of intimacy compared to the experience at the earlier museum buildings remains commonly mourned. It is safe to assume that Saltz's and other critics' remarks, which accumulated at the time, will have prompted MoMA officials to attend the public panel. However, making the Folk Art Museum straightaway into an "untouchable masterpiece" further complicated the issue and led to missed opportunities, as architect Stephen Rustow convincingly argued.[39] From this point of view, bold comparisons, such as one by Filler in The New York Review of Books, eventually did little to aid the cause of saving the Folk Art Museum: "Not since the vandalizing of Pennsylvania Station half a century ago has New York City's architectural patrimony been dealt such a low blow."[40] **(figs. 9–10)** Acknowledging that it "was a mixed achievement" with "beautifully crafted moments," but also "cramped and clumsy ones . . . , which briefly fulfilled its original program and then became a kind of lavish ruin," Rustow noted misguided statements and lost conversations about the possibilities of preserving the entire building (or parts of it), the relationship between private properties and civic opportunities, ecological implications related to the destruction and replacement of a building after such a short time, and, lastly, a proper consideration of how "history recycles meanings."[41] After recalling Diller's argument of not preserving only parts of the Folk Art Museum to avoid

[30] See Goldberger, "Friendly Fire on the Culture Front?"
[31] Ibid. Glenn Lowry during "A Conversation on the Museum of Modern Art's Plan for Expansion," lecture, organized by The Architectural League, Municipal Art Society, American Institute for Architects New York Chapter, held at the New York Society for Ethical Culture, New York, January 28, 2014, accessed September 2, 2021, https://archleague.org/article/a-conversation-on-the-museum-of-modern-arts-plan-for-expansion-2/.
[32] See Robert Beauregard, "We Blame the Building! The Architecture of Distributed Responsibility," International Journal of Urban and Regional Research (June 22, 2015), accessed September 2, 2021, https://doi.org/10.1111/1468-2427.12232.
[33] See Martin Filler, "Megalo-MoMA," The New York Review of Books, December 5, 2019, accessed September 6, 2021, https://www.nybooks.com/articles/2019/12/05/megalo-moma. Filler made reference to "a byzantine real estate transaction that involved complicated and costly air-rights transfers from nearby buildings . . . to the museum, and in turn from MoMA to the property developer Hines. (This Houston-based firm realized the 1970s and 1980s corporate skyscrapers of John Burgee and Philip Johnson . . . .") (Ibid.)
[34] Karen Stein during "A Conversation on the Museum of Modern Art's Plan for Expansion." The other participants of the panel discussion, moderated by Reed Kroloff (director Cranbrook Academy), were Cathleen McGuigan (editor Architectural Record), critic Nicolai Ouroussoff, Jorge Otero-Pailos (architect and preservation theorist), and architect Stephen Rustow. While the panel remarked that MoMA had continually preserved its own 1939 institutional building, it came to differing conclusions regarding whether and how to preserve the significantly younger and architecturally still less impactful Folk Art Museum.
[35] Stein, "A Conversation."

"façadism" and dismissing it as "an intellectually shallow response that ignored the reality of how urban spaces change over time," Rustow nevertheless asked: "Were we really expected to believe that MoMA was incapable of turning a museum into … a museum?"[42]

The main question related to the role of the (architectural) critics in this context remains to what extent did they actually influence MoMA's decision to demolish the American Folk Art Museum? Ultimately, revisions were granted by MoMA upon the request of DS+R in 2013 as a condition stated by the firm to accept the commission, and were not due to the critics themselves, who only reacted strongly to the final plan after it was announced by MoMA as a done deal on January 8, 2014. A more poignant question, then, is how much power can an architectural critic have in the first place, if the firm that conceives and oversees the execution of the designs is already so dependent on the client? In 2014, Diller stated that among the major goals of the $450-million project to expand the exhibition space were aims to: create "flexible / multi-disciplinary galleries;" enhance the visitor experience, including improving the circulation; and to "provide a strong interface with the city," which was, among other things, attempted with a large cantilevered canopy that now clearly signifies the museum's main entrance on Fifty-Third Street.[43] In conjunction with a larger lobby, a sunken retail store, more immediate access to artworks, and the reconstructed Bauhaus staircase of 1939, the most visible addition by DS+R was what the firm refers to as the "Blade Stair," a refined construction that connects the Taniguchi building with new gallery spaces in the Nouvel-designed tower.[44] Placed behind a glazed facade on the site of the former American Folk Art Museum, its verticality prompted the contributing editor to *Architect* magazine, Kerrie Jacobs, to describe it as "a subliminal eulogy to the Folk Art Museum, which famously was designed so that its stairway doubled as galleries."[45] However, the transparent facade now stands in stark contrast to the crafted alloyed-bronze panels Muschamp had originally linked to "the 19th-century philosophy of 'truth to materials'," in a building with "an atrium of domestic proportions" and an "intimacy [that was] also an alchemical operation."[46]

DS+R was clearly aware of the issues associated with a MoMA expansion, mentioned by Diller in the 2014 public forum as "the loss of intimacy, irreversible tide of mass tourism, the homogenization of Midtown, whether glass is good or bad …."[47] Kimmelman noted in an article about the new building, written a few weeks before the museum even opened to the public, that while the architects' work was "refined and tactical," the building complex itself was "smart, surgical, sprawling and slightly soulless."[48] Long-term architectural critic Joseph Giovannini concluded in the *Los Angeles Review of Books* that the design was a "success," albeit not a "foregone conclusion," given that MoMA is "conservative architecturally and as budget sensitive as the developers, who have steered its building committees."[49] While Giovannini applauded DS+R's "commendable job refining and expanding MoMA within the scope of their limited brief," he also reminded his readers of "the prevailing standards of New York's commercial architecture" that MoMA had subscribed to in its previous expansions.[50]

Whereas in the context of the Taniguchi expansion several features tackled "MoMA's Big, New, Elegantly Understated Home," with the majority of contributions by either art and architectural critics or scholars, between 2014 and 2020 coverage was provided by a more diverse group of writers in a varied media landscape that generally offered more reviews than substantial architectural criticism. In 2004, Ada Louise Huxtable, who started her career at MoMA and became the first full-time architectural critic for a daily newspaper in the United States (at *The New York Times*) in 1963, noted "an updated MoMA, not a reinvented MoMA" that according to the critic "has never looked so uptight."[51] Stephens agreed. In her view, the new MoMA was "too subtle to be sexy," with an atrium that made a "great party hall," adding: "All it needs is a spa."[52] Goldberger, who wrote favorably about the Taniguchi expansion and had extensively covered "The New MoMA" by Pelli when he still wrote for the *Times*, posited that one "couldn't ask for a clearer symbol of how modernism has moved from the cultural fringe to the mainstream."[53] The writer John Updike observed in the same context of publication that the expensive MoMA building had "the enchantment of a bank after hours

36   Nicolai Ouroussoff during "A Conversation on the Museum of Modern Art's Plan for Expansion."

37   See Suzanne Stephens, "Museum of Modern Art Addition by Diller Scofidio + Renfro in Collaboration with Gensler," *Architectural Record*, December 2, 2019, accessed September 2, 2021, https://www.architectural-review.com/places/united-states/museum-of-modern-art-extension-new-york-by-diller-scofidio-renfro.

38   Jerry Saltz, "To MoMA's Trustees: Please, Reject This Awful Expansion Plan," *Vulture*, January 13, 2014, accessed September 2, 2021, https://www.vulture.com/2014/01/jerry-saltzs-open-letter-to-the-moma-trustees.html. See also the coverage on the most recent expansion by Justin Davidson in the same outlet, as well as Edward Dimendberg, "Bigger and Better: MoMA is Right," *Architectural Review*, February 7, 2014, accessed September 2, 2021, https://www.architectural-review.com/essays/bigger-and-better-moma-is-right.

39   See Stephen Rustow, "Façadism: On the Demolition of the American Folk Art Museum," *Avery Review* 2, October, 2014, accessed September 2, 2021, http://www.averyreview.com/issues/2/facadism-on-the-moma-folk-art-debate. Rustow had worked in the team at the architectural firm Kohn Pederson Fox, which was responsible for cooperating on the designs and implementations of the Taniguchi expansion. In his summary of the debate about the demolition of the Folk Art Museum, Rustow stated that "this 'masterpiece' argument insisted on peerless artistic value as the threshold for public concern about the built environment, an impossibly high standard that ultimately debases our sense of what architectural value is." (Ibid.)

40   Martin Filler, "MoMA Loses Face," *The New York Review of Books*, January 14, 2014, accessed September 6, 2021, https://www.nybooks.com/daily/2014/01/14/moma-loses-face/.

41   Rustow, "Façadism." Referring to the "backhanded compliment" characterizing the Folk Art building as a "bespoke suit," as MoMA officials had done, Rustow remarked that the museum always preserved its "own original bespoke suit [the Goodwin and Stone building of 1939]." (Ibid.)

42   Ibid.

43   Elizabeth Diller during "A Conversation on the Museum of Modern Art's Plan for Expansion."

44   See Nicolai Ouroussoff, "Next to MoMA, a Tower Will Reach for the Stars," *The New York Times*, November 15, 2017, accessed September 2, 2021, https://www.nytimes.com/2007/11/15/arts/design/15arch.html.

45   Kerrie Jacobs, "The Missed Opportunities of MoMA's Expansion," *Architect*, December 19, 2019, accessed September 2, 2021, https://www.architectmagazine.com/design/the-missed-opportunities-of-momas-expansion_o. See also Stephens, "Museum of Modern Art Addition": "Architectural cognoscenti note that the [new] building is named for developer Jerry Speyer, chairman emeritus of MoMA's board, and his wife, Katherine Farley, for whom Williams and Tsien developed a townhouse on the Upper East Side."

46   Herbert Muschamp, "Fireside Intimacy for Folk Art Museum," *The New York Times*, December 14, 2001, accessed September 2, 2021, https://www.nytimes.com/2001/12/14/arts/architecture-review-fireside-intimacy-for-folk-art-museum.html.

47   Elizabeth Diller during "A Conversation on the Museum of Modern Art's Plan for Expansion."

48   Kimmelman, "$450 Million Expansion."

49   Joseph Giovannini, "MoMA: Expanded and Refreshed," *Los Angeles Review of Books*, November 8, 2019, accessed September 2, 2021, https://lareviewofbooks.org/article/moma-expanded-refreshed/.

50   Ibid.

"... six stories of reticent white chambers, tucked under Pelli's overbearing gray-and-brown glass tower, melt into the cityscape and form, with their treasures, an invisible cathedral."[54] This kind of invisibility, despite the gigantic materialistic presence, was precisely what Linda Nochlin, a leading force in feminist art history, cautioned against in her review for *Art in America*, stating: "The moment I walked into the new MoMA, I thought about power: how it is exercised, and how it is concealed within an institutional setting."[55] Finally, scholar Cynthia Davidson, joining a group of distinguished male professors in a comprehensive feature for the influential New York-based *Artforum*, reminded the readers that with its 1932 *Modern Architecture: International Exhibition* by Johnson and Henry-Russell Hitchcock, MoMA had already "all but eliminated the political ideology of the Left, a tenet of modern architecture that was beginning to be abandoned."[56] Davidson concluded: "Few museums have the kind of influence in modern and contemporary art that MoMA has attained, but its new building is not likely to enhance its influence in contemporary architecture."[57]

By commissioning a building expansion not even ten years after the Taniguchi complex had been completed, MoMA this time focused on internal changes, including the rearrangement of its collection with eyes on its general cultural mission in a global context. Did the resulting subtler—and not "sweeping"—expansion by DS+R prompt architectural critics to comment on it rather than to critique it?[58]

In 1991, Miriam Gusevich asserted, "Criticism is riskier than commentary. It is willing to judge and to condemn, to stake out and substantiate a particular position.... By conferring judgment, criticism exercises power. This power works indirectly by effectively establishing the canon; and it works directly by making and undoing reputations."[59] Gusevich furthermore observed: "While criticism might not seem necessary to actually build, it is crucial to the act of establishing architecture as a cultural institution."[60] Goldberger, however, highly doubted the power of architectural critics, but rather assigned "authority" to them, because they have the general ability to make people more aware of and literate about the built environment that no one is able to escape from.[61] While critics used to control the relationship "between

fig. 9
The American Folk Art Museum (2001–2004), staircase. Photo: Giles Ashford. Courtesy of Tod Williams Billie Tsien Architects | Partners. © Giles Ashford.

fig. 10
The Museum of Modern Art, "Blade Stair," designed by Diller Scofidio + Renfro, completed in 2019. Photo: Iwan Baan. © Iwan Baan.

[51] Ada Louise Huxtable, "MoMA's Big, New, Elegantly Understated Home," *Wall Street Journal* (December 7, 2004), reprinted in: Ada Louise Huxtable, *On Architecture. Collected Reflections on a Century of Change* (New York: Walker Publishing Company, 2008), 364–71, 367. Huxtable added: "In the galleries, circulation displaces contemplation" (ibid., 366). Huxtable worked at MoMA as an assistant curator under Philip Johnson between 1946 and 1950. See Paul Goldberger, "Ada Louise Huxtable (1921–2013)," *Journal of the Society of Architectural Historians* 72, 2 (2013): 130–33, here 131.

[52] Stephens, "Yoshio Taniguchi's Design," 95, 103. "Critics can scream and shout about its not being avant-garde or spectacular, but one thing's for sure—you know you're at MoMA." (Ibid., 97)

[53] Paul Goldberger, "Outside the Box: Yoshio Taniguchi's Elegant Expansion of the Modern," *The New Yorker*, November 7, 2004, accessed September 2, 2021, https://www.newyorker.com/magazine/2004/11/15/outside-the-box.

[54] John Updike, "Invisible Cathedral: A Walk Through the New Modern," *The New Yorker*, November 7, 2004, accessed September 2, 2021, https://www.newyorker.com/magazine/2004/11/15/invisible-cathedral.

[55] Linda Nochlin, "The New Modern: Itineraries,"

the profession of architecture and the world," he stated that neither architects nor their critics can "change the world."[62] Goldberger's successor at *The New York Times*, Muschamp, referred to the nineteenth-century English critic Walter Pater by paraphrasing that "the critic's most important asset is the power to be moved in the presence of beautiful objects."[63] Muschamp understood this as "an active not a passive power".[64] In contrast, the architect and critic Michael Sorkin, who used to attack power structures with verve and wit, did not resort to a focus on aesthetics when he considered the primary task of criticism to "situate the nature of its own urgency."[65] In Sorkin's case this was a fight against "the architecture of neo-liberalism, driven by a market to which it offers not the slightest resistance."[66] As a fierce critic, Sorkin addressed architectural professionals six years prior, when DS+R was already focused on a new building design for the site where the American Folk Art Museum had just been torn down: "Our job is not to adjudicate nitpicking questions of academic status but to help save the world."[67] While Sorkin worked with arguments that were developed by the New Left in the course of the 1960s, which other authors, most prominently David Harvey, understand as partially enabling neoliberalism in the first place, it is worthwhile to keep asking what architectural critics can actually do in opposition to a perpetuation of "elite power."[68] Themselves part of elitist circles, which architects inevitably engage with, arguing for a transparency of power structures related to the built environment appears to be one of the critic's most important tasks. In the particular case of MoMA and the American Folk Art Museum, none of the critics was able to save the smaller museum, which not everyone involved even deemed worth saving. Rather than to fundamentally review its position, the intensity of criticism from various sites led MoMA to "keep the facade." Whereas their active power will always remain in question, it is nevertheless the critics, who are needed to educate the public about ways of how to look behind it.

Biography

Martin Hartung is a doctoral fellow at the Institute for the History and Theory of Architecture (gta) at ETH Zurich, conducting research for his thesis "Values of Representation: Architecture in the Art Market" (2014–2022). He was a visiting scholar at Columbia University in New York (2016) and has worked on various exhibition and publication projects.

Art in America, March 2005, 51–52, 54, here 51.

[56] Cynthia Davidson, "On the Modern and Architecture," *Artforum* 43, 6 (February 2005): 135, 194, here 135.

[57] Ibid. In 1984, Kramer came to a similar conclusion with regard to the Pelli expansion (see Kramer, "MOMA Reopened").

[58] See Diller, "A Conversation."

[59] Miriam Gusevich, "The Architecture of Criticism," in *Drawing/Building/Text. Essays in Architectural Theory*, ed. Andrea Kahn (New York: Princeton Architectural Press, 1991), 8–24, 14–15. See also Pattabi G. Raman and Richard Coyne, "The Production of Architectural Criticism," *Architectural Theory Review* 5, 1 (2000): 83–103, and Jane Rendell, Jonathan Hill, Murray Fraser, and Mark Dorrian, eds., *Critical Architecture* (London and New York: Routledge, 2007).

[60] Gusevich, "The Architecture of Criticism," 11.

[61] "Paul Goldberger, On Criticism," *Architect's Newspaper*, November 16, 2005, accessed September 2, 2021, https://www.archpaper.com/2005/11/on-criticism-2.

[62] Paul Goldberger, "Criticism, Architecture & the Age of Twitter," lecture, Southern California Institute of Architecture, Los Angeles, September 19, 2012, accessed October 7, 2021, https://www.youtube.com/watch?v=-vfN6jjshWQ.

[63] See Davidson and Berman, "A Conversation with Herbert Muschamp," 16.

[64] Ibid.

[65] Michael Sorkin, "Critical Measure: Why Architectural Criticism Matters," *Architectural Review*, May 28, 2014, accessed September 2, 2021, https://www.architectural-review.com/essays/critical-mass-why-architectural-criticism-matters.

[66] Sorkin, "Critical Measure."

[67] Ibid.

[68] David Harvey, *A Brief History of Neoliberalism* (New York: Oxford University Press, 2005), 19.

On Lina Bo Bardi's Iconography: Three Drawings

Cláudia Costa Cabral

fig. 1
Lina Bo Bardi, MASP, São Paulo (1957–1968). View of the belvedere, 1965.
India ink and oil pastel on tracing paper, 49.9 × 69.5 cm. Instituto Bardi/Casa de Vidro.

Both the images of the lighthouse and the flashlight can be related to what should be the general purpose of criticism: to shed light on existing things. Nevertheless, they address two opposing models for architectural criticism. While the lighthouse stands for an idea of criticism grounded on the commitment, either ethical or aesthetical, to show the safe and true route for an audience presumably in need of guidance, the flashlight is a hand-scale tool, more suitable to illuminate specific angles. This paper uses the flashlight. Examining three drawings of the MASP's belvedere by Lina Bo Bardi, the paper expects to uncover aspects that may have remained unseen under the bright, but homogenizing, halo of the lighthouse.

Introduction

A Brazilian journalist and art critic once said that critics often confused a flashlight with a lighthouse and stayed lost.[1] Such an amusing statement was also making a serious and honest point about the difficulties faced by those who decide to navigate the murky and turbulent waters of art and architectural criticism. Both the image of the lighthouse and the image of the flashlight refer to what should be the general purpose of criticism as an intellectual activity: to shed light on existing things. Nevertheless, we may use this pair of images, the lighthouse and the flashlight, to address two opposing models of architectural criticism.

The lighthouse can symbolize an idea of criticism predominantly grounded in the commitment, either ethical or aesthetic, to show the safe and true route for an audience presumably in need of guidance. Casting its uniform light upon a large surface, and from a detached and fixed point of view, the lighthouse evokes the nature of the great explanatory systems and agendas that, so often, preexist the critic's work in itself.

The flashlight, on the contrary, is a hand-sized tool, more suitable for searching for and illuminating specific perspectives. This essay chooses the flashlight. The objects of our examination are three drawings by Lina Bo Bardi (1914–1992) depicting the famous empty space under the Museum of Art of São Paulo (MASP, 1957–1968) on Paulista Avenue. By taking these three drawings not as illustrations of a previous discourse but as starting points, the essay will uncover aspects that may have remained unseen under the bright, but homogenizing, halo of the lighthouse.

Lina Bo Bardi was the author of an original and diversified body of work, ranging from furniture design to architecture and urban proposals and from editorial activity to scenography and museography.[2] Unlike others of manifold character, such as Le Corbusier or Clorindo Testa, she did not pursue a separate career as a painter. Even so, paintings and drawings, as bidimensional artifacts, played a central role in her architectural practice, even surpassing the conventional function of the architectural drawing. Edward Robbins' inquiry on how and why architects draw starts from the premise that architectural drawing basically has to do with the various stages of design, from conception through construction, as part of the set of cognitive and creative efforts to clarify the circumstances of a problem and develop an architectural solution.[3] These three drawings, however, were done when Lina had already conceived the new MASP building's parti. Chronologically arranged, the first is a bottom-up view of

keywords:

Lina Bo Bardi; MASP; iconography; Brazilian modern architecture

[1] Daniel Piza, "O valor da crítica," in *Questão de Gosto: ensaios e resenhas* (Rio de Janeiro: Record, 2000), 39.

[2] See Marcelo Ferraz, ed., *Lina Bo Bardi* (São Paulo: Instituto Lina Bo e P.M. Bardi, 1994).

[3] Edward Robbins, *Why Architects Draw* (Cambridge: The MIT Press, 1997), 53.

the reinforced concrete slab that covers the clear span of 246 feet, signed and dated on November 5, 1965 **(fig. 1)**. The second is not dated but was published in 1967 as an illustration for the article "O novo Trianon 1957–67" in the magazine *Mirante das Artes* **(fig. 2)**. The third shows the rear facade of the museum acting as a background for an open-air exhibition with interactive sculptures for children. It is dated May 4, 1968, a few months before the museum's opening at the new location on Paulista Avenue **(fig. 3)**.[4]

fig. 2
Lina Bo Bardi, MASP, São Paulo (1957–1968). View of the belvedere, 1967. Graphite, India ink and collage on paper, 47.2 × 69.8 cm. Instituto Bardi/Casa de Vidro.

Lina's account of the "new Trianon" in *Mirante das Artes* may be useful to start placing these three drawings within the chronology of the museum's conception and construction. She begins in 1957, mentioning the empty sloping site on Paulista Avenue, facing the Siqueira Campos Park where once had stood the old Belvedere Trianon. Designed by Ramos de Azevedo and inaugurated in 1916, with a sunny terrace and views to the Anhangabaú Valley, it held a significant place in São Paulo's political and social life.[5]

MASP was founded by the Brazilian press tycoon and patron of the arts Assis Chateaubriand in 1947, and since the beginning was directed by Pietro Maria Bardi, Lina's husband. For ten years, the museum functioned on the first two floors of the Diarios Associados office building in downtown São Paulo, along with the Museum of Modern Art (MAM) created by industrialist Francisco Matarazzo, also a patron of the arts and promoter of the São Paulo Art Biennial. In this building Lina was responsible for MASP's gallery design and the design of the innovative display screens on steel tubing. Henrique Mindlin included her work on the museum's galleries in his 1956 survey on Brazilian modern architecture, highlighting the creation of a particularly pleasant feeling of spaciousness.[6] In 1951, the Paulista site housed the temporary pavilion of the first Biennial, and in 1952 Matarazzo commissioned Affonso Eduardo Reidy to design a new MAM building there, which was never built.[7] By the end of the 1950s, Lina must have felt that the still-vacant site at Paulista, collective and architecturally meaningful, was the right place to build a new home for MASP.[8]

According to Lina's account, despite earlier attempts to get support from municipal authorities, the idea would not be accepted before 1960. The uneven building process stopped in 1962 and was resumed in 1966.[9] Thus, the overall conception of the building was already established before she made the three drawings being examined here.

The Rise of the Big Span

Two of the drawings are taken from the same point of view: the first, made in 1965, showing the huge concrete slab suspended over an empty space, and the second, showing the same space occupied by a group of sculptures. In both drawings the observer is placed under the building's gigantic free span. Lina assumes a fixed one-point perspective, staging almost symmetrical scenes with the central vanishing point of Renaissance perspective.

The ground-level plaza is a central feature of the MASP project. Lina's scheme split the building into two independent bodies. Using the site's slope, a half-buried basement comprises the complementary program (auditoriums, library, restaurant, and the civic hall), generating

[4] The museum was officially inaugurated on November 7, 1968, although it was not truly finished. The first exhibitions opened to the public on April 7, 1969. Zeuler R.M. de A. Lima, *Lina Bo Bardi* (New Haven: Yale University Press, 2013), 125.
[5] Lina Bo Bardi "O novo Trianon 1957–67," *Mirante das Artes* 5, September/October 1967, 20.
[6] Henrique Mindlin, *Modern Architecture in Brazil* (Rio de Janeiro and Amsterdam: Colibris, 1956), 182–83.
[7] Nabil Bonduki, ed., *Affonso Eduardo Reidy* (Lisbon: Editorial Blau; São Paulo: Instituto Lina Bo e P.M. Bardi, 1999), 154.
[8] It seems that competition between the two museums was not out of the question. Lina Bo Bardi wrote in *Habitat* (1952) that the Museum of Art of São Paulo collection was "worthy of figuring in any European or American museum and at present the only collection of value in South America." Lina Bo Bardi, "Balanços e perspectivas museográficas. Um Museu de Arte em São Vicente," *Habitat*, no. 8, July/September 1952, 3.
[9] According to Lina's account. See Lina Bo Bardi, "Museu de Arte di San Paolo del Brasile," *L'architettura. Cronache e Storia*, no. 210, April 1973, 777–99. Spanish version published in Mara Sánchez Llorens, Manuel Fontán del Junco, and María Toledo Gutiérrez, eds., *Lina Bo Bardi: Tupí or not Tupí. Brasil, 1946–1992* (Madrid: Fundación March, 2018), 512–13. According to Zeuler Lima the construction site reopened in 1964. Lima, *Lina Bo Bardi*, 112.

the flat, continuous terrace at the street level. The main rooms for the collection and temporary exhibitions are housed in a volume suspended above the plaza. Lina's comments stressed that the free ground floor was mandatory. The parcel had been left to the municipality by the former owners with the condition that the terrace should remain open to the public. The new belvedere should be "column-free," as she claimed; the ceiling above it should be eight meters high, and the building itself should not exceed two floors.[10]

fig. 3
Lina Bo Bardi, MASP, São Paulo (1957–1968). View of the belvedere, 1968. India ink and watercolor on paper, 56.3 × 76.5 cm. Collection MASP.

However, it is more likely that the idea of a fully unobstructed ground-level plaza had asserted itself during the process of design. Early sketches display a solution perhaps closer to Lina's earlier "seaside museum" in São Vicente (1951), never constructed but published in *Habitat* in 1951.[11] In both, a rectangular volume is raised on a supporting structure formed by a sequence of transversal concrete frames, taking advantage of the shorter span length. Although the main exhibition room would be free of columns in this early scheme, the ground level would be punctuated by at least six columns on each side *(fig. 4)*. This sort of rhythmic structure is related to Reidy's Museum of Modern Art in Rio (MAM, 1953–1967), a building also provided with an open ground-floor space beneath a huge concrete slab.[12] Further sketches show that Lina decided to rotate the porticoes and reduce them to two, heading toward a less economical solution that would demand the use of prestressed beams to overcome the span length. Although vertical supports were condensed to just four points, the plaza remained occupied by a centralized, compact nucleus of vertical circulation set against a wall, with stairs and two lifts, and by a generous, elastic helicoidal staircase spreading over one side of the open floor plan *(fig. 5)*.

Her definitive grasp on the problem appears in a quick pen sketch taken from the same viewpoint as the drawings discussed here. A bridge-like structure covers a space that has been entirely swept of obstacles *(fig. 6)*. The expansive helicoidal staircases, which recalled the striking one Reidy had designed for MAM Rio, are replaced by unassuming orthogonal stairs and a single lift confined to the far end of the span. With this move, Lina downplayed the connection between the superimposed levels and increased the significance of the span. Clearly, it is not an open-air hall, a subsidiary and preparatory space for the architectural experience of the above's museum. It stands for itself.

The Asphalt

According to Lina's account, the building work stopped in 1962 with the four large columns emerging from the terrace. The deserted construction site served as a parking lot and a carpentry workshop where fire pits were lit, darkening a structure that she believed to be in a "precarious aesthetic situation" due to the lack of care in the process of execution.[13] She probably drew the asphalt-like surface of the huge reinforced concrete slab over the clear span after work had stopped and before it was fully resumed. An atmosphere of abandonment pervades the drawing, calling to mind the no-man's-lands under bridges and viaducts, scribbled and scratched upon by anonymous hands *(fig. 1)*. So, to a certain extent it fits into

[10] Bardi, "O novo Trianon 1957–67," 20.
[11] Lina Bo Bardi, "Museu à beira do oceano," *Habitat*, no. 8, July/September 1952, 6–11.
[12] See Maria Alice Junqueira Bastos and Ruth Verde Zein, *Brasil: arquiteturas após 1950* (São Paulo: Perspectiva, 2010), 60–61; Carlos Eduardo Comas, "The Poetics of Development: Notes on Two Brazilian Schools," in *Latin American in Construction: Architecture 1955–1980*, ed. Barry Bergdoll, Carlos Eduardo Comas, Jorge Francisco Liernur, and Patricio del Real (New York: The Museum of Modern Art, 2015), 50–51.
[13] Bardi, "Museu de Arte di San Paolo del Brasile," 512.
[14] See Nestor Goulart Reis, *Dois Séculos de Projetos no Estado de São Paulo. Grandes obras e urbanização*, vol. 3, *1930–2000* (São Paulo: Editora da Universidade de São Paulo, 2010), 20–21.

 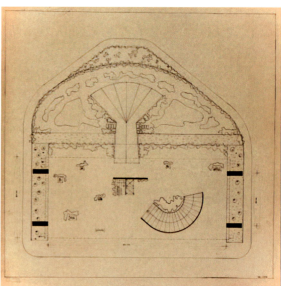

her description of the neglected construction site. Nevertheless, the drawing is not likely to be a literal representation of the state of the structure. If her account is truthful, the work had stopped on the columns and the suspended slab could not yet exist. She probably imagined the future plaza's ceiling in that specific way at the time, which gives the drawing a deeper and more complex connotation.

Notwithstanding the raw concrete finishing, MASP's structural solution was sophisticated. The use of prestressed beams, developed and executed by Brazilian engineer José Carlos de Figueiredo Ferraz, was a technological breakthrough. Concrete technology had been fully incorporated into Brazilian construction patterns between the 1920s and the 1940s and employed in major road works and buildings.[14] Oswaldo Bratke built the first large concrete viaduct in downtown São Paulo in 1932, Rino Levi concluded the Columbus Building (1934), followed by Álvaro Vital Brazil's Esther Building (1935), and the twenty-four-story tower of the Municipal Library by Jacques Pilon (1935). During the 1950s São Paulo's downtown urban landscape was quickly changed by high-rise concrete buildings, such as Niemeyer's Copan (1951), Franz Heep's Itália Building (1956), and David Libeskind's Conjunto Nacional (1955) at Paulista Avenue.

Prestressed concrete was employed for the first time in 1953 in the construction of the Boa Vista Viaduct over the Santos-Jundiaí railroad bed. The innovative bridge-like structure developed by Figueiredo Ferraz for the MASP building would be the first architectural use of a prestressed structure in São Paulo.

The building of the new museum coincided with both a sensitive change of scale in the city's urban environment and a vertiginous process of territorial reconstruction that was not limited to the verticalization of downtown areas, but was also largely incorporated into the expansion of major road infrastructure works. Although the city's vertical growth expressed by the architecture of high-rise buildings was perhaps quantitatively more impressive, Lina's MASP had no parallel as a technical tour de force, except in the engineering realm of viaducts and bridges.[15]

Lina's drawing responds to São Paulo's transformation into an asphalt jungle, or to the city's "growth fever,"[16] in a double and perhaps ambivalent way. The fixed Renaissance perspective and the placing of Alberti's "*linea del centro*" near the bottom of the page seems to downplay the pavement, or the plaza's usable space, and overstate the ceiling. Emphasizing the gigantic concrete slab, the perspective reinforces the idea of the building as a statement

fig. 4
Lina Bo Bardi, MASP, São Paulo (1957–1968). Perspective, early studies. India ink and watercolor on paper card, 34.3 × 48.6 cm. Instituto Bardi/Casa de Vidro.

fig. 5
Lina Bo Bardi, MASP, São Paulo (1957–1968). Floor plan, belvedere level, early studies, 56 × 56 cm. Instituto Bardi/Casa de Vidro.

[15] A theme she would later revisit in her entry to the competition for the Anhangabaú Valley in São Paulo (1981), which consisted of a bridge-like steel structure for carrying high-speed traffic, as an "aqueduct of cars" following the valley, raised over a park. See Cláudia Costa Cabral, "On Circulation: Lina Bo and CIAM's Fourth Function," in *Adaptive Reuse. The Modern Movement towards the Future. 14th International Conference Proceedings*, ed. Ana Tostões and Zara Ferreira (Lisbon: Docomomo International, Casa da Arquitectura, 2016) 788–93.

[16] Lina Bo Bardi, "Arranha-céus e o espírito," *Habitat*, no. 8, July/September 1952, 1.

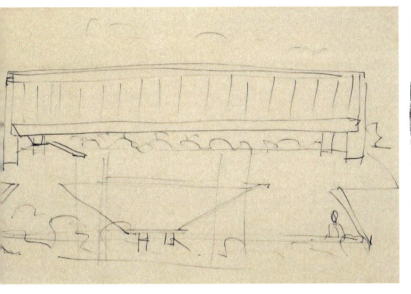 

on technical capacity, aligned to modern architecture's commitment to technical rationality and its implicit confidence in social progress through scientific advance.

Nevertheless, the huge concrete slab is not depicted as a neutral architectural surface. It also acts as a giant screen holding an independent significance. The building is presented simultaneously as the result of a technical triumph and as a dark surface marred by scars and scrawls, an informal support to a random discourse of incomplete words.

This sort of "picture inside the picture" strategy suggests the interweaving of distinct sensibilities. The "inside picture," the asphaltic trapezoidal figure spread over the upper part of the page, may be compared to Jean Dubuffet's sooty landscapes of the 1940s, inspired by street graffiti and the idea that life should be "offered raw" by the artist *(fig. 7)*.[17] Dubuffet was interested in vulgar and unstable materials like the rugous *hautes* pâtes that included mortars and asphalt, and his technical experiments led him to seriously consider weight as well as precarity. Lina's portrayal of her work as tainted by blurs and scratches recalls Dubuffet's engagement in a "game of destruction," and his acceptance of the accidental, the dirty, and the arbitrary as the truthful representation of a formless and chaotic reality.[18]

The allusion to the less bright aspects of modernity can also be found in the way she depicts the free space below the concrete slab. At the bottom of the page Lina wrote "L'ombra della sera." The expression can be literally translated from Italian as "the shadow of the evening," but it also refers to the famous small Etruscan statue called *Ombra della sera*, probably from the third century BC, representing a nude male with an extremely elongated body, which is frequently associated with Alberto Giacometti's slender sculptures *(figs. 8-9)*.[19] Despite more recent insistence on MASP's large span as a place made for intense use by people, it looks silent and uninhabited in this drawing—except for the very small human figures at the bottom of the drawing, whose shadows stretch out like the little Etruscan statue or Giacometti's skeletal, almost evanescent figures from the postwar period, cast in rough bronze and exposing human fragility in a world increasingly shaped by technological power.

Nature's Revenge

The next drawing was published in 1967 as an illustration for the previously mentioned article "O novo Trianon 1957–67," bearing the caption "study for an open-air exhibition."[20] Mixing drawing and collage, Lina presents MASP's large span populated with large sculptures—seemingly

fig. 6
Lina Bo Bardi, MASP, São Paulo (1957–1968). Sketches with a view of belvedere level, 15.5 × 24.7 cm. Instituto Bardi/Casa de Vidro.

fig. 7
Jean Dubuffet, *Wall with Parachute*, 1945. Source: Eleanor Nairne, *Jean Dubuffet: Brutal Beauty* (Munich, London, and New York: Prestel, Barbican, 2021).

[17] For example: *Wall with Parachute* (1945); *Wall with Inscriptions* (1945); *Large Black Landscape* (1948). Eleanor Nairne, *Jean Dubuffet: Brutal Beauty* (Munich, London, and New York: Prestel, Barbican, 2021), 7.

[18] See Rachel E. Perry, "Painting in Danger: Jean Dubuffet's Hautes Pâtes," *RIHA Journal*, no. 0221 (August 2019), https://doi.org/10.11588/riha.2019.0.

[19] For example: *Walking Woman* (1932–1934); *Femme Leonie* (1947); *Walking Man* (1947); *City Square* (1948). Christian Klemm, *Alberto Giacometti* (New York: The Museum of Modern Art, Kunsthaus Zürich, and Harry N. Abrams, 2001).

fig. 8
Ombra della sera (probably third century BC), 57.5 cm. Jnn95, CC BY-SA 4.0, https://creativecommons.org/licenses/by-sa/4.0, via Wikimedia Commons.

fig. 9
Alberto Giacometti, *City Square*, 1948.

primitive African idols and totemic columns—surrounded by visitors **(fig. 2)**. The drawing can be related to Lina's earlier collages for large-scale exhibitions published in *Habitat*, which also incorporated cropped photographs. Two of them belonged to the study for the seaside museum in São Vicente (1951);[21] the other was described by her as "an ideal and free project" for the exhibition marking the fourth centennial of São Paulo, to be celebrated at Ibirapuera Park in 1954 **(fig. 10)**.[22] In these collages, the architectural space was defined by homogeneous flat surfaces, with neat flat ceilings mirroring clean unpolluted floors. Against these neutral backgrounds she displayed a collection of drifting things—artworks or industrial objects (in the case of the Ibirapuera proposal)—whose position in space seemed to be independent from architecture, giving the impression of a sort of imaginary landscape made of realistic figures. Nature entered the scene from behind the glass walls. Even in the seaside museum collage for an open-air exhibition area, a tree trunk and the sea were framed into a rectangular stripe in the background **(fig. 11)**.

The MASP collage conveys a slightly different strategy in the placement of objects and a less predictable approach to the relationship between building and nature. The symmetrical underlying perspectival structure of the drawing converges at a single vanishing point located behind the stairs and two columns, overemphasizing the actual span length. The plaza's floor is covered by a geometrical grid that does not match the small-scale texture of the stone pavement eventually executed. Nevertheless, as in the architecturally determined perspectival space of Renaissance painting, the squared pavement has a connective role, building both a sense of depth and a sense of narrative.[23] It convincingly places the smaller figural elements—the people designed by Lina and the cut-and-pasted photographs of sculptures—within a unifying architectural scene framed by the larger architectural elements.

In a sense, more than the earlier collages, the "study for an open-air exhibition" anticipates the way in which the permanent collection would be arranged inside the building: in the

[20] Bardi, "O novo Trianon 1957–67," 21.
[21] These two collages can be related to those belonging to Mies van der Rohe's Museum for a Small City project (1942–1943). See Bardi, "Museu à beira do oceano," 8, 11.
[22] Lina Bo Bardi, "Ibirapuera," *Habitat*, no. 11, April/June 1953, 3.
[23] See Amanda Lillie, "Constructing the Picture," in *Building the Picture: Architecture in Italian Renaissance Painting* (London: The National Gallery, 2014), accessed July 20, 2021, https://www.nationalgallery.org.uk/research/research-resources/exhibition-catalogues/building-the-picture/constructing-the-picture/introduction.

upper floor and according to Lina's conception of a desacralizing and nonhierarchical system for displaying the works of art.[24] The conventional practice of hanging paintings on the walls was rejected in favor of using transparent glass easels designed by Lina, allowing visitors to simultaneously perceive all the paintings and the continuous architectural space—entirely free of columns—achieved by her bold structural solution. Moreover, the easels gave the paintings a sort of tridimensional presence, acting as freestanding objects in space in the same way sculptures do. Although paintings are gathered without any stylistic or chronologically structured criteria, the arrangement has a front and a back, since all the glass easels are placed facing the entrance. In the collage for the open-air exhibition, objects also hold a fixed position in relation to architecture and are frontally arranged as if they were the components of a large staged scene.

Compared with Lina's previous asphalt-like view of the span *(fig. 1)*, the concrete slab is represented as a brighter surface, starting from the center of the composition and vanishing toward the top of the page. Nevertheless, it is not depicted as a neat, smooth surface, but as one already aged, marked by small fracture lines and taken over by vegetation like an abandoned structure. Yet the powerful suspended slab, whose dimensions are even exaggerated by perspective, is contrasted by an implied atmosphere of ruin and decay where nature has eventually had its revenge.

In fact, this furtive presence of vegetation, spreading over the building, may be related to Lina's earlier ideas for the MASP facade. The glazed facades were not her first choice: Sketches dated 1963 show the suspended box as an opaque volume. In them she studied an exterior system of enclosure including precast panels, upon which random patterns of vegetation should grow and flourish. She referred to them as "epiphytic" plants, suggesting a sort of symbiotic, mutable relationship between the architecture and nature *(fig. 12)*.

The drawing featuring the imaginary open-air exhibition seems to express the expectation of an unmediated relation between art and people and between building and nature. It followed an article that featured a complete documentation of the final project, as well as a full technical description of the structural system and a photograph of the building's structure already complete. As an illustration to the so precisely described, and just about to be completed, "new Trianon," it has an intriguingly fictional component. The new Trianon is pictured as if it possessed an organic life, alongside which reinforced concrete, a material with a shorter life span than stones and bricks, would somehow return to its stone and mineral origins. Perhaps the article contains a clue: due to construction problems,

fig. 10
Lina Bo Bardi, "Ideal and free" project for installation in the building of the fourth centennial of São Paulo, Ibirapuera Park. *Habitat*, no. 11 (1953).

fig. 11
Lina Bo Bardi, Seaside Museum, São Vicente, 1951. Collage. *Habitat*, no. 8 (1951).

[24] See Renato Anelli, "O Museu de Arte de São Paulo: o museu transparente e a dessacralização da arte," *Arquitextos* 112 (September 2009), accessed July 21, 2021, http://vitruvius.com.br/read/arquitextos/10.112/22; Lima, *Lina Bo Bardi*, 131–32.

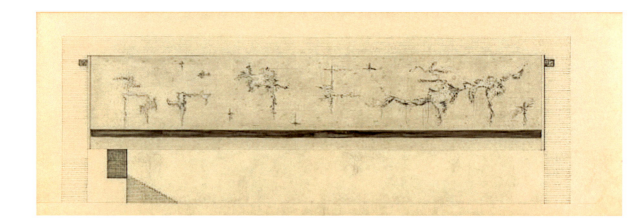

fig. 12
Lina Bo Bardi, MASP, São Paulo (1957–1968). Facade with precast panels and plants, 31.8 × 90.7 cm. Instituto Bardi/Casa de Vidro.

Lina had to accept an addition to the columns, one that she decided not to disguise. She used it to stand for a "rationalist" position stripped of any "idealist heritage" and prepared "to face, within reality, the architectural incident."[25] Later on, the incident would provoke other accepted changes in the building. In 1990, facing the necessity of waterproofing the prestressed beams, she had the structure painted red.[26]

The Playground

The third drawing also belongs to a study for an open-air exhibition, this time with large practicable sculptures meant for children. However, it required a change of viewpoint. It is not an eye-level perspective, but an aerial view of the whole architectural ensemble, taken from the Anhangabaú Valley side. It shows the exposed concrete structure rising from the ground, supporting the glazed exhibition rooms and the entire length of the terrace built over the building's half-buried base *(fig. 3)*.

Executed in India ink and watercolor, the drawing is still based on a symmetrically structured composition that follows the strict regularity of the museum's exterior volume. The rear facade, stretched horizontally against the green mass of Siqueiras Campos Park across Paulista Avenue, is the wide canvas for the myriad little stories taking place throughout the terrace on a sunny day, in a happy atmosphere reminiscent of children's books.

The gentle colors, the fine lines, the multifocal composition, with multiple scenes portrayed in a single visual field, recall a younger Lina's watercolors, such as *Summer Watermelon* (1929) or *Festa de Noantri in Trastevere* (1929), and her father Enrico Bo's narrative paintings. Unlike his friend Giorgio De Chirico's deserted metaphysic landscapes, Enrico Bo's urban scenes were intensely inhabited. In *Piazza Guglielmo Pepe*, the city is depicted as a lively place, a joyfully shared space crowded by people. *Sunday, Escape from the Circus* is a meticulously realistic painting with the atmosphere of a fairy tale, showing a symmetric circus tent and an orderly line of animals coming out of a hole in a wall.[27] Lina claimed that the painting, dedicated to her, was in fact composed by her father with animals taken from a big illustrated book with which she had learned to read.[28]

Instead of the dramatic or melancholic overtones of the views from beneath the span, the panoramic view of the museum and the plaza has an optimistic atmosphere, but also one that erases the real city. The museum and the belvedere seem to have been separated from the city by their own small green belt. This sweet vision of a hard building in a hard city, perhaps inspired by Enrico Bo's affinities with magic realism and its commitment to making improbable visions plausible, as Alfred Barr put it,[29] presents the belvedere as a sort of urban oasis, where the massive volume of the building safeguards the generous and luminous urban square, surrounded by greenery and, finally, overrun by people.

[25] Bardi, "O novo Trianon 1957–67," 21.
[26] See "MASP. Museu ganha vigas e lajes vermelhas," *Projeto*, no. 134 (August 1990): 106.
[27] Enrico Bo's paintings are published in Ferraz, *Lina Bo Bardi*, 33.
[28] Flávio Ferreira, "Manuscritos e quadro pintado pelo pai de Lina Bo Bardi revelam memórias da arquiteta," *Folha de São Paulo*, February 2, 2015, www.folha.uol.com.br/ilustrada/2015/02/1583796-manuscritos-e-quadro-pintado-pelo-pai-de-lina-bo-bardi-revelam-memorias-da-arquiteta.

Conclusion

These three drawings were not part of an investigation intended to arrive at an architectural solution (which by the time they were produced was already decided), nor were they further instructions for the construction of the building. But they speak about the project. The heterogeneous and sometimes cryptic visual discourse furthered by these drawings can be contrasted with Lina's verbal one.

Later, she proudly referred to MASP as an "ugly" building. She said she expected that SESC Pompéia, her masterpiece from 1977, would be "ugly, much uglier than the Museum of Art of São Paulo," because "the Beautiful" was easy, while "the Ugly, the truly ugly" was difficult. She would also describe SESC as "Poor Architecture," not in the sense of indigence, but owing to its use of "minor and humble means."[30]

Afterward, the "poor" would be incorporated into her narrative on MASP's architecture and associated with her five-year experience in northeastern Brazil:

> **By means of a popular experiment, I arrived at what may be called Poor Architecture. I insist, not from the ethical point of view. I feel that in São Paulo Art Museum I eliminated all the cultural snobbery so dearly beloved by the intellectuals (and today's architects), opting for direct, raw solutions. Concrete as it comes from the forms, the lack of finishing, may shock a whole group of people.**[31]

Despite her insistence in separating the "poor" from the "ethical," this later narrative on MASP would better suit the contemporary assessment of her work as a socially engaged activity rather than an artistic endeavor, and therefore as something that could be considered a libel against formalism—supposedly in opposition to those who had defended architecture as an art, like her contemporaries Oscar Niemeyer and Lucio Costa. Instead, Lina's iconography regarding MASP resists oversimplification. Rather than a lack of interest in formal or aesthetic problems, her drawings might precisely reveal the way in which these issues were being reworked into the cultural and artistic field. In 1970, the American art critic Harold Rosenberg used the expression "de-aestheticization" to explain the trajectory of art since the postwar period, which reflected a growing interest in working "into the nature itself," as a "fragment of the real within the real." Rosenberg's samples included Donald Judd's preference for authentic brown dirt instead of artificial brown paint and the acceptance, by other artists, of the effects of chemical, biological, physical, or seasonal forces over the original materials, changing or even destroying them.[32] Lina's alleged search for the "difficult ugly" and the "accepted incident" might well be understood as the awareness of these artistic concerns and anxieties, following Guillaume Apollinaire's prediction in 1913: "Beauty, that monster, is not eternal."[33]

Biography

Cláudia Costa Cabral
Born in Porto Alegre, Brazil; architect, Federal University of Rio Grande do Sul (Brazil); doctorate, Escuela Tècnica Superior d'Arquitectura de Barcelona (ETSAB/UPC, Spain); full professor of the Faculty of Architecture, Federal University of Rio Grande do Sul; researcher at the National Council of Scientific and Technological Development (CNPq) in Brazil; chair of Docomomo Brazil, 2012–2013; interested in modern and contemporary architecture in Latin America and the relationship between architectural culture, art, and technology; author of several articles and book chapters on these themes.

[29] Dorothy C. Miller and Alfred H. Barr, Jr., eds., *American Realists and Magic Realists* (New York: The Museum of Modern Art, 1943).

[30] Lina Bo Bardi, "SESC—Fábrica da Pompéia," in Ferraz, *Lina Bo Bardi*, 220, 230.

[31] Lina Bo Bardi, "Museu de Arte de São Paulo," in *Museu de Arte de São Paulo. São Paulo Art Museum. Lina Bo Bardi 1957–1968*, ed. Marcelo Ferraz and Isa Grinspun Ferraz (São Paulo and Lisbon: Instituto Lina Bo e P.M. Bardi, Blau Portfolio Series, 1997), 8.

[32] Harold Rosenberg, "De-aestheticization," *New Yorker*, January 24, 1970, 61.

[33] Guillaume Apollinaire, *Los pintores cubistas. Meditaciones estéticas*, vol. 13 (Buenos Aires: Nueva Visión, 1957).

Imported Starchitect in a Local Market

Seda Zafer

fig. 1
Renovated traditional Odunpazarı houses in Eskişehir (author's archive, 2021).

The destiny of most architectures intended to create an icon or to be perceived on an urban scale is similar: to be the focus of fair or unfair criticism. The targets of this criticism are the contradictions of an iconic architectural object bearing the fame of its starchitect and his intentions on a global level. The architectural object in question is the "Odunpazarı Modern Museum" in Eskişehir, Turkey, designed by Kengo Kuma in 2019. Does a museum imported from the geography of the starchitect and differentiated within its context by its form make that building pioneering? Does architectural criticism have an ability or a duty to be pioneering, new, experimental? These are the questions that are addressed by this essay.

Introduction

The practice of criticism today includes efforts to understand the way in which any object or phenomenon came to exist. The basic expectation of architectural criticism is to understand the processes and the systems of relations in design, and to open the design object in question to new interpretations rather than to reach a final judgment. Architectural criticism also attempts to analyze the intention and point of view of the designer of the building. The concept of criticism, understood in a neutral sense, inevitably involves evaluation of a building in relation to the previous designs or tendencies of the architect within his/her own theoretical framework. In this complex process, the final verdict may describe both positive and negative impacts at the same time. In this article, architectural criticism is approached with a method that analyzes, makes sense of relations, questions meaning, and reinterprets that meaning.

The Critical Dimension of Architecture

The structure of the traditional, which does not allow change, has been turned upside down by modern social structure, and everything that is called unchangeable has become changeable. Any image, form, or object is an image that can be consumed. This process can be seen in various architectural products, from buildings to images and writing. When architectural discourse gained new critical dimensions, especially in the 1980s, attitudes such as academicism, aestheticism, and formalism came to the fore. With such perspectives, critics such as Neil Smith and Mike Davies have offered supportive considerations for marginalized and disadvantaged groups and situations.[1,2] Also, Robert Venturi and Denise Scott Brown, who gained notoriety with their radical ideas on the history of architecture, brought up issues that had been beyond the scope of criticism until the 1960s, from lavishly decorated streets to illuminated advertising signs in their study, *Learning From Las Vegas*.[3] Radical criticism in architecture can sometimes also be put forward as a direct design. For example, Sant'Elia's futuristic new city project, the utopian projects of the Archigram group, and early projects by architects such as Frank Gehry, Peter Eisenman, and Bernard Tschumi questioned prevailed thought and popularized radical criticism.[4] At their core, critical designs or projects should have elements that are incompatible with the existing order and develop the creative tension between what is and what could be.

keywords:

architectural criticism, Kengo Kuma, starchitect, modern museum, anti-object

[1] Neil Smith, "Of Yuppies and Housing: Gentrification, Social Restructuring, and the Urban Dream," *Environment and Planning D: Society and Space* 5.2 (1987), 151–72.
[2] Mike Davis, *City of Quartz: Excavating the Future in Los Angeles (New Edition)* (New York and London: Verso Books), 2006.
[3] Robert Venturi, Denise Scott Brown, and Steven Izenour, *Learning From Las Vegas* (Abingdon: Routledge, 2013).
[4] Charles Jencks, *The Story of Post-Modernism: Five Decades of the Ironic, Iconic and Critical in Architecture* (Hoboken: John Wiley & Sons), 2012.

By its mere existence, architecture transforms its context, revealing cultural structures and allowing brand new insights and intuitions. In this way, architecture both glorifies criticism and becomes the focus of criticism—it crosses borders. Characteristics such as being pioneering, experimental, or original privilege a work of architecture by allowing the formation of a critical grounding. These features encourage the evaluation of the designed building as a finished product or object because of the popularity of the building, its socially acquired functionality, and its representational value. In architectural criticism of such buildings, the measure is often the level of consistency between the developmental concepts of the design and the end result. This may be closer to an acceptance of the design than a criticism thereof.

In this context, it can be said that one of the most frequently criticized issues of contemporary museum buildings is their focus on exhibiting themselves as objects rather than the objects they contain. Bilbao, for example, was a city that no one wanted to visit before the Guggenheim Museum was built; afterwards it became one of the most famous tourism centers in the world. This was due to the building becoming an iconic symbol for the city.[5] Gehry's innovation in contemporary architecture and its resulting impact on the globalization of design were criticized from many perspectives. The titanium material, a unique tectonic at the time, was the most prominent feature that contributed to this iconic connotation. While cities that want visibility on the world stage aim to be illuminated by the light of a star architect, contemporary museums have become their architectural marketing symbols.

fig. 2
Odunpazarı Modern Museum aerial view (NAARO, 2019).

[5] Joan Ockman, "New politics of the spectacle: 'Bilbao' and the Global Imagination", *Architecture and Tourism: Perception, Performance and Place*, ed. Medina Lasansky and Brian McLaren (Oxford and New York: Berg 2004), 227–40.

The Odunpazarı Modern Museum (OMM)

The Odunpazarı Modern Museum (OMM) was designed by the world-famous Japanese architect Kengo Kuma in Eskişehir, an Anatolian city, not as uninspiring as Bilbao was before its transformation, but on the contrary a dynamic and heavily-visited city where we can discuss the twenty-first-century counterpart of the Bilbao Effect. Although the museum, which was built in 2019, has its own iconic and touristic symbols, the touristic brand of the historic environment (Odunpazarı) where the building is located has already been formed by the restoration of traditional wooden houses in the local environment *(fig. 1)*. For this reason, the Bilbao Guggenheim Museum's iconic effect cannot be compared to the OMM in either temporal or environmental terms, but in its modern values and the intention to raise the city to the global stage. So, it is possible to say that the goals of the two museums were similar.

Contemporary museums are most noticeable by their attitude to the surroundings and their facade design. The most distinctive feature of the OMM is the big masses consisting entirely of wooden piles in an otherwise very traditional and human-scaled local area. A businessman and art collector, Erol Tabanca, wanted the OMM to be a unique and iconic building in his hometown that would be visited from all around the world. To provide such an impact, Kengo Kuma and his partner Yuki Ikeguchi were chosen, and they envisaged the museum as an inviting meeting point for the city, inspired by the local surroundings. At this point, it is inevitable that we question why Kengo Kuma and his team were the ones building an iconic museum in a city in the middle of Anatolia and why Tabanca did not work with the notable architects of his own country. Perhaps it was the belief that Kuma's world-renowned wood tectonics would integrate effectively with the local tradition of Odunpazarı.

The design process, from the first sketch to its implementation and completion, is a process in which the architect's desires need constant reconciliation with the demands and effects

of all other actors. Here, there was an expectation to produce an iconic space in Odunpazarı style, but the bond the designer establishes with his object, his unique point of view, and his ideological stance must be evaluated. The presence of the distinctive wooden tectonics that made Kuma a starchitect, based on traditional Japanese construction, constitutes the contextual discourse that he termed *anti-object*—standing against object-formalism and establishing a healthy relationship with outside becomes debatable and superficial in the OMM. To define it more clearly, it is Kuma's opposition against the clear separation of the architectural work from its surroundings which he defines as anti-object. According to him, the mentality of transforming almost everything into a commodity, including architecture, under the current global economic system precludes establishing a healthy relationship with the outside world.[6] With this idea, Kuma, who created a contemporary tectonic language from the Japanese wood-making tradition, opposes producing objects/forms. Although there are points where the OMM avoids being an object by establishing a strong connection with the city and being a good neighbor to the environment, the key terms—such as geometry, light, clustering, and wood—that are put forward by the design team makes this debatable.[7] The intention seems to be more one of selling the architecture, as it was in Bilbao **(fig. 2)**.

The name Odunpazarı, a combination of the words wood and market, originates from a time when both were central to daily life—something far removed from our modern lives today. By referring to this, it is insinuated that the goal of the design team was to establish a strong bond between the building and its location by blending context and architecture.[8] The design team states that they developed their design concept by the fact that this environment was originally a place where wood materials were bought and sold. This also gives reference to the wooden building envelope and cantilevered volumes. The traditional arrangement of the surrounding residential fabric as random clusters is considered a precedent for the fragmented mass of the OMM. However, the effect of the traditional fabric on the articulation is only reflected visually in the design. There is no analysis or inference made concerning the coming together of the houses in the traditional pattern. This deficiency can be read through the structure's fragmented integrity and scale, which, by consisting entirely of wood, gains a sculpture-like appearance **(fig. 3)**. The wooden elements and tectonic language, which are identified with Kuma's designs, are the main elements in creating the clustering effect of this entire building, while the bay window design

fig. 3
OMM entrance adjacent to the restored traditional houses (author's archive, 2021).

fig. 4
OMM wooden facade and clustered volumes (author's archive, 2019).

[6] Kengo Kuma, *Anti-Object: The Dissolution and Disintegration of Architecture*, vol. 2, ed. Brett Steele. (London: Architectural Association, 2013).
[7] "The Building," Odunpazarı Modern Museum, accessed October 24, 2021, https://omm.art/en/details/the-building.
[8] María Francisca González, curator, "Odunpazarı Modern Art Museum" ArchDaily. September 10, 2019. https://www.archdaily.com/924542/odunpazari-modern-art-museum-kengo-kuma-and-associates.

of the traditional houses is unconvincingly reflected by the withdrawals in the masses of the building in a contemporary and abstract language *(fig. 4)*.

As a design strategy, it is clear that consolidating the volume was more about an architecture that asserts itself on an urban scale than on the scale of the houses surrounding the museum. One could say that this intention created a new cultural focal point in dialogue with the region. On the other hand, the structural system of the building is reinforced concrete, and the wood is used as a curtain wall. The fact that the visible material, rather than the structural material, is wood can only be interpreted as contemporary rather than as a reference to the past *(fig. 5)*. If the building had intended to be in dialogue with the area tectonically, wood would have been an integral factor instead of just a cladding. The fact that the Odunpazarı Modern Museum is contemporary, which is emphasized by its "modern" name, creates a certain expectation: that a modern building in a traditional environment will inevitably be monumental and iconic. When Kengo Kuma is the architect of a modern museum, wood becomes both an element to be expressed and a modern iconic indicator. Thus, an exterior wooden envelope becomes a predominantly visual element that is far from a reinterpretation of the traditional construction systems and tectonic thinking. The use of wood as a cladding material continues to shape not only the exterior, but also the interior spaces. As one enters the museum, the objectified wooden context of the outside is interrupted. It is possible to feel the tectonics of the wood in the interior with effects such as the fashioning of the surfaces created into seating areas and light voids *(figs. 6, 7)*.

Charles Jencks believed that as monuments lose their power to create lasting impressions, so the desire for buildings to become more dramatic increases.[9] The growing scale of contemporary buildings reflects the characteristics of the time we live in as well as the characteristics of architects who produce forms to attract attention and become iconic. Some museums are so sculptural that it is impossible for works of art to compete with them. The compulsive need to monopolize visual interest in architecture thus creates the unwelcome necessity for artists to respond to architecture. On the other hand, the characterization of museums as empty warehouses that can contain gigantic works of art results in giant atriums, and these spaces, although they are useful for museums as activity areas, can be challenging when used as art galleries. In the OMM, the atrium that starts at the entrance and continues through the lower level and the wooden elements that comprise it, by echoing the overlapping form of the exterior, provides a qualified integrity

fig. 5
The contemporary wooden facade of the OMM in relation to the traditional renovated facades of the area (author's archive, 2021).

fig. 6
Seating area and light well on the museum's ground level (author's archive, 2020).

fig. 7
Gallery space and light well on the first level (author's archive, 2020).

with its surrounding circulation and non-colossal scale. As if the combination of wooden elements throughout the entire building has not been emphasized enough, the gallery space located in the center of the building is made an object of interest as it wanders through the upper levels extending upwards as a light well. This area is left blank, as if encouraging the user to come, pause, and look up. It seems the architect cannot let go of objectification in the interior, either **(fig. 8)**.

The desire to be seen, to be special, and to attract touristic flows guides the belief that the main goal of contemporary architecture in the globalizing world is to design iconic buildings. There are also many projects that try to capture the "wow" effect with unusual forms or visual codes that are shocking in what they represent (for example, Norman Foster's Gherkin building in London or Frank Gehry's Walt Disney Concert Hall). The presence of the wow factor reveals that a building is not truly set out to create open and public spaces, leaving the subtext of poetics and meaning ignored. It would not be wrong to say that the learning process from Las Vegas is still not completed. In a small Anatolian city like Eskişehir, although a public and cultural museum building is naively desired, a structure that displays the starchitect and his way of doing things, with the emphasis on being modern, is what eventually emerges.

The silhouette forming the image of the city and the complex historical visual effect, the identity of the environment, appear to be in conflict with the OMM. In cities, it's generally desired that the silhouette is defined by typological, classical, and historic structures such as mosques and churches. The essence of this historic environment, of which traditional houses form the silhouette, suddenly changes with the fragmented integrity of the new building. At the same time, the steps surrounding the building offer users the opportunity to gather between the main road on the lower level and the intermediate streets on the upper level **(fig. 9)**. Surrounding the museum with wide steps creates an island, highlighting the building's presence in a sculptural way, while providing the users with a vantage for taking photos and spending time. This clearly shows that, in the touristic world, architecture as a spectacle is not limited to the image of the building: the programs are transformed as well. Besides being iconic and touristic by design, the program is planned to accommodate and separate the touristic circulation.

The desire for the museum to be discernable from all corners of the city here determines not only the facade and the mass, but also the larger circulation of the city environment.

fig. 8
Gallery space and light well in lower level (author's archive, 2020).

[9] Jencks, *The Story of Post-Modernism: Five Decades of the Ironic, Iconic and Critical in Architecture*, 32.

The side streets leading to the OMM trace back and forth from point to point within the sequential texture of Eskişehir's traditional houses, resulting in a defined visual effect where the striking facade of the OMM is slightly obscured. While this creates a mysterious effect and an organic complexity, it also contributes to the fragmented focal point of the contemporary museum.

It is difficult to estimate how much the intention of the designers to recreate the traditional street inside is achieved as one circulates through the building and the exhibition areas. However, the richness of space they have created on an area of approximately 3,000 square meters is diverse. This quality is underlined by the fact that the individual volumes in elevation each have different schemes in the plan, by the voids created by pulling the masses back and forth at different levels, and the fact that the floors form voids at varying heights The effort to create exhibition spaces and installation areas of different sizes inside makes the building's fragmented, box-like appearance functional.

Hal Foster's article, "After the White Cube," emphasized that what contemporary art requires is a diversity of exhibition spaces and spaces that can double as alternate programs.[10] In the context of making museums effective, Theodor Adorno indicated that museum halls devoid of any kinds of decorative details represent interior spaces created to accentuate the artist's work, but the design of more active spaces can become a means of revival rather than reification [11]. All this legitimizes the museum as a lively and busy place, for the benefit of both its administrators and its audience. The OMM, as a museum coming after the white cube era, is concerned about combining an old residential area with a new city as well as a cultural center. We can see that the museum attempts to do this by framing various city vistas using the openings, open terraces on the upper levels, and the steps extending around the building, forming a wide plaza that invites public use **(figs. 10, 11)**. At the same time, we could say that the abstract trend towards the white interiors of "modern" museums is broken by the wood, but the wood does not step beyond it.

fig. 9
Sketches of the museum surrounding silhouette and section (author, 2021).

fig. 10
Seating area and light well on the museum's ground level (author's archive, 2020).

fig. 11
Gallery space and light wellon the first level (author's archive, 2020).

[10] Hal Foster, "After the White Cube," *London Review of Books*, 37 no. 60 (2015), 25–27.
[11] Catherine Lui, "Art escapes criticism, or Adorno's museum," *Cultural Critique*, no. 60 (spring 2005), 217–244.

Beyond the design idea and its dynamics, the effects on the users who physically experience the space cannot be ignored. Based on Roland Barthes' discourse that "the text often contradicts the author's tendencies, and a new text is constructed in each reading," Jonathan Hill emphasized that a similar perspective can be developed for the relationship between the designer and the user from an architectural point of view.[12] The user is just as effective as the architect in evaluating the designed space because, just like the person reading the text, they constantly use the building in ways that the architect never envisaged; that is, they reconstruct it. The iconic image created by the OMM in the local environment has already become an object of love and interest for local inhabitants. It seems that constantly changing exhibitions in contemporary art are attractive to the public, especially when these take part in a new and distinctive cultural discourse.

[12] Jonathan Hill, *Occupying Architecture: Between the Architect and the User.* (Abingdon: Routledge, 1998), 77–90.

Conclusion

While contemporary architecture is expected to be radical and present itself as an anti-object by producing its own criticism, it can become a symbol, message, or representation when it comes to museums. It is clear that every new modern museum can reproduce the Bilbao effect on its own, as for years the articles and criticisms concerning contemporary museums have not escaped the echoes of the Bilbao debate. The OMM, as a recent example of a contemporary museum, was the case study for this essay, because it is a prominent building brought to a local market through a starchitect.

It is seen that Kuma's point of view, which wants to focus on material character by avoiding heroic gestures, becomes in itself a representational value in the focus of the modern museum's image. The building's modern emphasis and the projection of its own name also shows that it seeks to become a center of attraction to add value to the city and to attract tourists. Choosing a starchitect for such a building further contributes to the idea of creating popular value, and may open the door to naive criticisms such as those asserting this is an adequate contemporary reinterpretation of the context's traditional wood tectonics. But still, when contemporary architecture is thought of as a background for life, it would not be wrong to expect the modern museum to contain features that can go beyond the object itself. Rather than the building's own architecture, the routes and public interactions created at the ground level go beyond this.

While architectural criticism evaluates the functionality and representational value of a realized design on a social basis, it should reveal conflicting ideas between the stated values of the designer and the values borne out by the building. It is thought that this critical essay produces investigations and inquiries into the potential of a modern museum that could override the object's own design intentions.

Biography

Seda Zafer was born in 1994 in Eskişehir, Turkey. She graduated from the Eskişehir Osmangazi University Department of Architecture in 2017. After a three-month internship in Barcelona at the Institute for Advanced Architecture of Catalonia (IAAC) in the same year, she started her master's education at the Istanbul Technical University Architectural Design Program. At the same time she worked at Mithralstanbul and took part in museum and exhibition projects. She graduated in 2019, with her master's thesis researching the changing collective spatial production and issues of collective memory associated with social media tools. She currently works as lecturer and studio instructor in Altınbaş University's Architecture Department and is a PhD candidate at Yıldız Technical University in the Faculty of Architecture, Architectural Design.

3 Criticism and Its Effects

The Role of Architectural Criticism in the Design of Twenty-first-century History Surveys

Ruth Verde Zein

fig. 1
Aerial view of São Paulo, Brazil. Photo: Ruth Verde Zein, 2020.

Criticism is fundamental in nurturing and sustaining efforts to both challenge and deconstruct prejudices and biases that exist in the canonical books on modern architectural history. It is essential to build new comprehensive surveys fit to represent the mindset, concerns, and challenges of the twenty-first century. On that subject, this essay will consider the ideas of two Argentinian architects and professors: Marina Waisman on architectural criticism, theory, and history, and Juan Pablo Bonta on the making of canonical interpretations as important contributions in the creation and diffusion of architectural culture.

My life in architecture began in a small-scale design practice and as an architectural journalist and critic; I became a professor and researcher later. As architectural praxis, criticism, theory, and history have always been intertwined in my professional activities, I do not find it easy to distinguish any clean-cut boundaries between them. Thus, in this essay they will also be intricately combined.

I shall propose a bold hypothesis in three points, the first two being:
1. All books containing panoramic historical surveys on the architecture of the last 200 years rely upon limited, exclusive, skewed, and biased narratives—and we already know about that.[1] **2.** A comprehensive, inclusive account of modern architecture fit to represent the mindset, concerns, and challenges of the twenty-first century is yet to be written—and we should care about that.[2]

Nobody wants to write great narratives anymore. It is not an easy task, and in the best case it will take a decade or more to complete; right from the start it is doomed to be imperfect and problematic. So, even though we are all aware of the faults of the existing surveys, it is complicated to try to change the situation, as few people would be interested in working on the creation of alternatives. For the moment, and until further notice, professors, students, and architects, all over the world, will continue to use the same old (and some recent, but still) biased books due to the lack of something better to lean on. This situation is probably more critical where it concerns architectural education, but is still problematic in a broader context, since inadequately educated architects will likely carry that skewed, biased worldview with them for another half a century of productive work. And let us not fool ourselves: the crystallized interpretations and their biases that appear in those canonical texts are not only present in history classes, they also permeate design classes perhaps in an even more pervasive way—they tend to be treated most uncritically as very present but unspoken touchstones.

From where I stand—as a Latin-American, female architect from Brazil—this situation is even more compounded, since we—the so-called "others": the non-white, non-male, non-European, non-etc., Global South—and our works represent most of the forgotten pieces that are conspicuously absent from those incomplete and distorted narratives. And when our realities do happen to be acknowledged, they are often displayed as bad examples for their supposed faults and mistakes.

[1] The debates on the subject of "post-colonial" revisions of canonical surveys has gained prominence since the late twentieth century, especially with the writings of Sibel Bozdogan ("Architectural History in Professional Education: Reflections on Postcolonial Challenges to the Modern Survey," *Journal of Architectural Education* 52, no. 4 (1999), 207–215) and many other authors (Meltem Ö. Gürel and Kathryn H. Anthony, "The Canon and the Void: Gender, Race, and Architectural History Texts," *Journal of Architectural Education* 59, no. 3 (2006), 66–76; Charles Jencks, "Canons in Crossfire," *Harvard Design Magazine*, no. 14 (2001), 43–49; David Leatherbarrow, "What Goes Unnoticed," *Harvard Design Magazine*, no. 14 (2001), 16–23; Hélène Lipstadt, "Learning from Saint Louis," *Harvard Design Magazine*, no. 14 (2001), 4–15). It has been recently revived by the decolonial debates (Fernando Luiz Lara, "Urbis Americana: Thoughts on Our Shared (and Exclusionary) Traditions," in *Urban Latin America: Images, Words, Flows and the Built Environment*, eds. Bianca Freire-Medeiros and Julia O'Donnel (London: Routledge, 2018), 10–15). In Latin America, debates on the necessity of constructing inclusive appropriated historical narratives have been in the arena at least since the SAL (Seminários de Arquitectura Latinoamericana, especially the ones held from 1985 to 1995), consolidated in the seminal contribution of Marina Waisman (*El interior de la historia. Historiografía para uso de latinoamericanos* (Bogotá: Escala, 1990); *La arquitectura descentrada* (Bogotá: Escala, 1995)).

[2] On the subject, see Ruth Verde Zein, *Critical Readings* (Austin; São Paulo: Platform Nhamerica & Romano Guerra, 2019); and Ruth Verde Zein, *The Meaningful Emptiness of the Canon*, V!RUS, São Carlos, no. 20, 2020. [online] Available at: http://www.nomads.usp.br/virus/virus20/?sec=4&item=1&lang=en [accessed: October 20, 2021]. Some authors have been successful in

This is a most unsustainable situation. Sooner or later, something must change and, hopefully, for the better.

For any change to happen many steps need be considered before we commit ourselves to such a demanding task aimed at nothing less than transforming the world of architectural education and practice. As in any long-term task, it is important to reflect and to consider the risks, thereby avoiding setting out on a long journey with the best of intentions only to end at the same old point that we wanted to transcend.

On the one hand it is essential to begin by clearly and even harshly exposing the biases and exclusions of the Western canon, deconstructing its myths, flawed narratives, one-sided points of view, distorted facts, and its concealed—though to the keen observer quite evident—single-minded, white, male, straight, imperialist, and conservative stance.

On the other hand, let us be careful not to hastily discard all the accumulated knowledge on the history of modern architecture that has been gathered over the last century; knowledge that has been widely disseminated despite being produced relatively recently. For there is no point in repeating the naive avant-garde illusion of discarding the past and trying to invent the world anew every other Monday morning. We must move forward, but, for the moment—and for a little while—this past historiographic tradition and its books are so ubiquitous that they cannot be fully avoided, much less eliminated in a coup de grace. We must learn how to keep living with those books, and we will probably continue to use them for some time yet; however, we do not have to continue accepting them in a blindfolded, naive way as an entirely unquestionable standard.

fig. 2
Aerial view of São Paulo, Brazil.
Photo: Ruth Verde Zein, 2020.

That leads to my third point:

3. Criticism has played and will continue to play a fundamental role in the task ahead. Criticism is fundamental in nurturing and sustaining the efforts to properly challenge existing canonical books that will remain in use for a while yet. At the same time, we—or more precisely, perhaps not me, but the next generations of architects and architectural historians—shall make an effort and a commitment to build new comprehensive surveys that will be needed in the education of future generations of architects.

That is, if we finally realize that such a kind of literature—the all-encompassing panoramic survey—is the best alternative for architectural education and practice. But let us also be open to the possibility that perhaps other alternatives may come to be asserted as more suitable for that endeavor.

But why am I writing about the making of architectural history if the subject here should be architectural criticism? Is there a clear-cut distinction between them? If there is, how do we distinguish one domain from the other? In order to build my argument, I shall be guided by tradition—my tradition.

In her seminal 1990 book, *El interior de la historia. Historiografía arquitectónica para uso de latinoamericanos* (The inside of history. Architectural historiography for the use of Latin Americans), Argentinian architect, historian, and critic Marina Waisman (1920–1997)[3] affirms that "history, theory and criticism are three modes of reflecting on architecture, intimately intertwined, often confused, differing in their methods and objectives, and fulfilling different functions for architectural thought and practice."[4] She states that since "architecture is a concrete

going beyond these limitations and experimenting with other possibilities; for example, Kathleen James-Chakraborty (*Architecture Since 1400* (Minneapolis: University of Minnesota Press, 2014)).

[3] Marina Waisman was born in Buenos Aires. She graduated as an architect from the National University of Córdoba in 1944. She was a professor at the same university from 1948, when the first Chair of Contemporary Architecture was created, until 1971. Between 1956 and 1959, she taught at the National University of Tucumán with Enrico Tedeschi and Francisco Bullrich, creating the IIDEHA—Instituto Interuniversitario de Historia de Arquitectura (Interuniversity Institute of History of Architecture). In 1974, she joined the Faculty of Architecture of the Catholic University of Cordoba where she formed the Instituto de Historia y Preservación del Patrimonio (Institute of History and Heritage Preservation; now called the Marina Waisman Institute). She founded and developed SAL—Seminarios de Arquitectura Latinoamericana (Latin-American Architecture Seminar)—in 1985 in Buenos Aires. In 1987, she was awarded the America Prize for her work and critical contributions to Latin-American architecture. In 1991, she was appointed professor emeritus of the National University of Córdoba. The following year, she

and practical activity, any type of reflection on it will retain a more or less direct relationship with praxis,"[5] which means she believes—and I concur—that in the field of architecture, no theoretical, historical, or critical approach to the subject should occur in a disembodied way. As she says further on in the book, "praxis provides the objects of reflection; reflection in turn provides the concepts that will guide praxis."[6] She also states that, according to Benedetto Croce and other authors, history's contemporaneous character is well established. As such, criticism—as the primary reflexive approach in observing praxis—is in a leading position to help in the building of new comprehensive historical surveys, especially (since it is my field of interest in research) in the field of modern architecture. And, of course, criticism has already been the seminal tool with which all previous panoramic accounts have been constructed.

I will never get tired of praising the work and deeds of Marina Waisman, whom I consider a mentor. I first got to know her by reading her articles and books while a student, then continued by the privilege of a warm friendship, despite the distances in time and space. However, if you are not a Latin-American, you probably have never heard of her work, a lack of awareness that, for me, is one of the proofs of the selective blindness of the "international" historical surveys on twentieth-century architectural theory, history, and criticism. Anyone would certainly benefit from becoming familiar with her work, but until now, every attempt others and I have made to promote her contribution in international forums on architectural history has failed. At last, it seems the situation is changing. A recent book organized by Fernando Lara[7] includes a most enlightened text about the work of Marina Waisman, written by Louise Noelle.[8] But still, there is much more to be known about her work.

In any case—to stay on the subject of the duty and power of criticism—it is worth mentioning some details of the debates organized by Marina Waisman from the 1960s onward on the possible relationships between history, theory, and criticism, if for no other reason than to demonstrate that this text has no intention of "inaugurating" a field, of being "original," or of bringing some "breakthrough" novelty to the arena. The aim here is not to be "innovative"—this persistent myth of modernity—but to present evidence of a well-established and objective approach to the issue subject. Leading a debate does not necessarily mean having to be in the front looking ahead and turning your back on everything that is left behind. It may also be legitimate to look back and to acknowledge everyone's contributions, of everyone around, as a better way to guarantee that the paths we are going to build are grounded well enough to help us succeed. The search for adequate alternatives to properly construct a truly comprehensive historical survey will set us on a journey without a foreseeable ending: it is probably something like a permanent quest. Of course, the authors of those twentieth-century and early twenty-first-century canonical books—that, while we may find them outdated, are still meaningful—were aware of that. So, while it is necessary to assume a radical as much as a critical stance in examining these past contributions, we should not discard everything that was done and said by the last century's history books with the aim of inaugurating some brave perfect new world. Realistically speaking, it may suffice if some good comes from the current will to change.

In the mid-1950s Marina Waisman and a group of architects, historians, and professors from the University of Tucumán in Argentina founded the IIDEHA—Instituto Interuniversitario de Historia de la Arquitectura (Interuniversity Institute of History of Architecture)—and organized some very meaningful debates in the 1960s. This group included the Argentina-based Italian architect Enrico Tedeschi and Francisco Bullrich, who would later author the first panoramic survey on Latin-American architecture written by a Latin-American. There is not space here for a more complete account of the deeds and works of the group, so only a reference is made to a seminar held in Cordoba, Argentina, in 1968 that had among its guests the British critic Reyner Banham, who presented research in progress that was to be published as a book the following year.[9]

According to the accounts of the event from Waisman[10] and others,[11] Banham stated during the seminar that the critic's role was to observe reality, and find interesting architectural

returned to the National University of Córdoba, creating there the Center for Research Training in History, Theory, and Criticism of Architecture, now called the Marina Waisman Center. She was a member of the Instituto Universitario Nacional del Arte. Waisman died in 1997 in Río Cuarto, Córdoba. Source: https://en.wikipedia.org/wiki/Marina_Waisman [accessed: October 11, 2021]. That entry was created based on the research organized by the collective "Un día una arquitecta" (A day, a (female) architect), which has published the biographies of a thousand female architects (Cf. https://undiaunaarquitecta.wordpress.com/2015/05/27/marina-waisman/ [accessed: October 25, 2021]).

4   Marina Waisman, *El interior de la historia. Historiografía para uso de latinoamericanos* (Bogotá: Escala, 1990), 29.

5   Ibid., 35.

6   Ibid.

7   Fernando Lara is a Brazilian-American author, activist, architect, husband, father, and professor of architecture. He holds the R. G. Roessner Centennial Professorship in Architecture at the University of Texas at Austin, where he currently serves as director of the PhD in Architecture program.

8   Louise Noelle, "Marina Waisman and 'The Decentering of the Discipline,'" in *Decolonizing the Spatial History of the Americas*, ed. Fernando Luiz Lara (Austin: University of Texas Press, 2021), 68–75.

9   Reyner Banham, *The Architecture of the Well-Tempered Environment* (London: Architectural Press, 1969). I cannot help but notice that Banham acknowledged many people in the beginning of his book, but failed to mention his stay in Argentina, and how that sojourn had an effect on his work, something that was clearly reported by several people who had been present at the time; for example, Cesar Naselli, "Seminario de Reyner Banham y la arquitectura ambientalista adecuada a su contexto," in *Historia de la arquitectura argentina. Reflexiones de medio siglo, 1957–2007* – IIDEHA (Cordoba: Centro Marina Waisman, 2008), 49–51.

10   Waisman, *El interior de la historia*, 30–31.

11   Naselli, "Seminario de Reyner Banham", 49.

facts and attract general attention to them. Referring to that talk in her subsequent book,[12] Waisman further explained that in this first moment of acknowledgment of something new or unknown, it is necessary to momentarily suspend judgment until our understanding expands, rendering it possible to define new parameters to help illuminate that new phenomena's significant structure. Waisman then took this idea to its logical conclusions. She stated that this "suspension" was absolutely necessary in the first analytical moment. In other words, before comparing a new fact with others that are already well known (or, better, before applying a decontextualized ready-made set of rules to judge anything new to us), firstly we have to honestly acknowledge that whatever appears new to us may be a well-known fact to others. Secondly, we have to proceed carefully and not hastily force the comparison of those new phenomena with other supposedly similar examples that are better known to us. Measuring the new information with some sort of ruler designed to evaluate other kinds of situations may be a completely or partially inappropriate way to assess the quality and importance of different phenomena.

While this appears to be quite obvious, it would be easy to show hundreds of examples of how Latin-American modern cities have been judged in canonical history books, when their authors care to refer to them at all, as "not proper cities," or words to that effect, because their construction and development have not followed the same unjustly universalized rules of European cities. Brasilia would be the most notorious case: it continues to be addressed and judged through smoky lenses blurred by prejudices born from misleading and mistaken information about it and from external scales of measurement.

So, the first step is to suspend judgment and examine the facts themselves. But then (quoting Waisman again), "the prolongation of this suspension of judgment beyond the establishment of proper guidelines to judge is negative since it leads to the indiscriminate acceptance of all examined phenomena. The fear of mistaking the judgment about a new proposal tends to limit the critic to a mere description, without risking any evaluation. But the critics' function is precisely to make judgments if they are to render real services to the professional community."[13]

Besides, critics are not compelled to find the truth. Instead, they should accept errors as part of the potential outcome in the evaluation of new phenomena. For it is very likely that even a well-founded and carefully crafted critique may not have come from a full understanding of a situation; or worse, an evaluation may simply be wrong about a phenomenon.[14] Personally, I doubt there is a "truth content" imbued in any building or ensemble, one that is to be assessed once and for all, as all human works are contingent and limited, just like our minds and bodies. Criticism must try to be informed and precise, but it is not our task to be correct all the time. That would be a preposterous and arrogant proposition.

Therefore, since there will never be a single truth to lean on as a perfect interpretation, it is necessary to gather different and diverse critical evaluations by a variety of authors before assessing the importance of a given phenomenon. These would serve as a basis for legitimate inclusion in any historical universal panoramic narrative (or any other kind of historical narrative). For a built phenomenon to be included, at least two conditions must be fulfilled:

a) A phenomenon should be thoroughly studied by collecting an ample amount of information about it[15] so that the critic/historian will be able to arrive at a more complex and detailed assessment of its significance.

b) A phenomenon must display enough substance to justify that it is meaningful to a wider community beyond the immediate people and place it affects.

While this seems quite obvious, it is not what usually happens. To begin with, if the phenomenon in question is located in a "central" part of the world, it is often already deemed to have universal value no matter what, thus avoiding application of the second condition. Most of the phenomena included in canonical books have acquired this status based on incomplete, inadequate, even biased and misinformed data and interpretations, thus not meeting the first condition. Of course, this can be seen as an interesting achievement of

12 Waisman, *El interior de la historia*, 30.
13 Ibid., 31.
14 Besides, any critical evaluation of a given phenomenon will carry the marks of its time and place, embodied in the critic's personality and beliefs. So even if it results in a correct assessment, future readers will certainly find its faults and/or shortcomings. Better to be humble and accept that even our best efforts will be transient.
15 Collecting information is not to appropriate and use the work of other researchers and authors without giving the proper credits. The authority of future panoramic surveys will not be asserted by occulting sources, but quite the contrary.

the canonization process: it has provided us all, critics and researchers, with plenty to do for decades in unravelling mistakes.

However, this is as good as it is bad. Should we remain preoccupied with approving or disproving these old narratives? Should they turn all of us into hamsters inside the library wheel of old books? Why are we so attached to them? Are we so afraid of "losing" something in the process of widening and enlarging our knowledge of the last two centuries of modern architecture that we should be doomed to never transcend the old canons? Should we keep on assuming that modern architecture has a geographically limited origin, even after data on modern buildings that has been collected by researchers and scholars from all continents clearly shows us that it was a phenomenon that happened simultaneously, everywhere? Despite the geographical differences, we have been willingly or unintendedly full participants of the modernization process that has steamrolled the planet (to use an expression coined by the philosopher Agnes Heller[16]). Still, we are afraid of abandoning some incorrect assumptions. the parti pris, namely, that some parts of the world—the ones that colonized and exploited—are the best, or the original ones, by divine right, while other parts of the world—those that were colonized and exploited—are doubly penalized. Is it right that the latter will never, ever have the right either to denounce such imposed inequalities or to look at themselves (ourselves) with pride and care about the value and high quality of their (our) contributions to the field of modern architecture?

But perhaps the problem is being solved nowadays—and wonder of wonders—by the same group of people that created it in the first place, with the new enlarged editions of canonical books already in preparation, containing new chapters that include us, "the others." Problem solved?

Well, from where I stand—here, in the so-called Global South background of the planet—or better, from where I was placed by the status quo, along with Marina Waisman—and so many other colleagues of previous and more recent generations—what I see is quite a different scenario. Yes, there is already a great deal of information about "world architecture" that has been painstakingly collected and organized by countless people situated all over the world, doing primary research almost without funds, but fueled by idealistic motivation. And yes, this important sum of information is in the process of being cannibalized and reduced into conformity by the same old authors and their canonical books. From where I stand, what I see is that all our collective hard work is in the process of being impudently appropriated, once again. And in a few years, we may even be accused of plagiarism, since nobody will believe that a woman from the "Global South" was the primary source of that information or interpretation, and not the prestigious professor who writes about her country's architecture even though he was absolutely ignorant about it previously. So, no, the problem is not solved, far from it. These "expanded" revisions of the same old accounts may even be seen as benign, and perhaps they are, up to a certain point. But they are not at all a meaningful step on the path to change, the change that I am claiming as being necessary.

It is from the perspective of that pseudo-change that a recurrent question is raised, a question that tends to be asked when someone is talking about the establishment efforts

fig. 3
Aerial view of São Paulo, Brazil.
Photo: Ruth Verde Zein, 2020.

[16] "The consciousness of reflected generality has already gained momentum. Modernity is general; it steamrolls over the entire Earth. Now, once again, the whole world with all of its people shares the same stage; and if it shared nothing else, it still would share historical consciousness." Agnes Heller, *A Theory of History* (New York: Routledge, 2016), 4.

to keep alive what is actually dying. The question is "what should I exclude in order to include?," and after enunciating it, the questioner looks at us—the excluded—with piteous eyes for the ordeal we, the "others," are cunningly, deviously making the questioner suffer to accommodate our built phenomena.

This question is a false one. It is false because it implies—subtly, but powerfully—that there is one, and only one way to tell history. Ask historians: they will tell you that there is not. This question implies the established and canonical way of narrating the history of modern architecture, one that was assembled in the last century, is forever sound for unquestionable reasons—reasons that are never to be completely elucidated or else the contradictions of this position would become evident. This question implies that, supported by their unproven belief in the one and only "right" way to tell history, they are thus absolved of any fault in its making. (As a matter of fact, architectural historians rarely acknowledge there may be faults.) And finally, the question implies that in order not to lose anything of such unquestionable (auto-attributed) importance structure, it will be enough just to give us all, the "others," some minor superficial subchapter at the end of a book—but only in the edition published in our language or region.

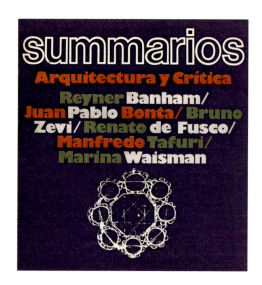

fig. 3
Magazine cover of *Summarios Arquitectura y Crítica* #5, March 1977.

In fact, there is no need to be afraid of "losing" examples if you want to devote yourself to the contemporary and necessary task of revising canonical panoramic surveys. This should not come as a surprise, since all "truths" and "paradigms" are impermanent; indeed, they must be constantly challenged and revised if they are to retain their raison d'être. The good news is that the process of inclusion/exclusion tends to be cyclical. And someday, all things will have not only their fifteen minutes of fame, but also their fifteen years of neglect, followed by a comeback, and so on . . .

In any case, the intention here is not to tear down statues, but to assume an optimistic position, believing in the reality, necessity, and inevitability of change. Criticism is and always will be a fundamental tool to foster that effort. Harsh criticism of the status quo is the first step to be taken. Considering the limited length of this essay, it is sufficient to mention that I am also engaged in constructive assignments paving the path of change. Beginning by cleaning my own house, I have been examining the crystallized narratives on Brazilian modern architecture, a very interesting experimental case.[17] This is helping me to establish proper bases to continue the quest into examining Latin-American and then so-called worldwide historical narratives.

And that is why—because my studies are also challenged by these changes—I realized how the process of canonization is perhaps quite inevitable. "Eliminating any sort of 'canon' may be an impossible task, doomed to failure, since the establishment and propagation of a canon may be an inevitable and/or recurrent tool among practice-based research and professional fields—as for example, in architecture (Foqué, 2010). [So], for now, the immediate goal is, at least, to promote a more general awareness of the prevailing canon limitations."[18] In this sense, it is not so bad to promote its continuation and engorgement—which, of course, from a purely pragmatic point of view, is better than nothing. But the real goal is to change and renovate the canons.

If canonizing processes are inevitable, it does not mean that they have to occur in a blind way. In this regard it is important to examine the work of another Argentinian architect and critic, Juan Pablo Bonta, who was already teaching abroad when Marina Waisman invited him to contribute to *Summarios #5*,[19] a publication dedicated to architecture and criticism. Edited by Waisman, it also included original texts by Reyner Banham, Bruno Zevi, Renato de Fusco, and "one of the most prominent critics of the new generation," namely Manfredo Tafuri, as well as Marina Waisman's own article on the subject. She prefaced the

[17] This is the subject of my recent book: Ruth Verde Zein, *Historiographical Revisions: Modern Architecture in Brazil* (Rio de Janeiro: Riobooks, 2021).
[18] Zein, 2020.
[19] *Summarios #5*, March 1977. I am indebted to architect Horacio Torrent, who kindly digitalized this issue for me from his personal collection (since access to the university's library was impeded during the Covid-19 pandemic).

publication by stating: "There is no doubt that our knowledge and opinions on the architecture of the past and present are guided by the writings of critics and historians, who in turn interpret historical reality based on the basic codes provided by the society of their time, to which they add the characteristics of their own personality. In order for this orientation not to become a simple imposition, it is necessary for the reader to assume a critical position upon the contents of their messages, and for that it will be very useful to become aware of the codes handled by the issuer."[20]

In his essay, Bonta argued that, despite the widespread idea that we should first and foremost look at the buildings and not what has been said about them, writings are also a striking part of cultural reality, especially when the task at hand is to assess the importance and significance of a building. As he wrote, "the paradigm according to which the direct experience of the work of art or architecture surpasses the immediate experience offered by criticism is arbitrary and limiting. It ignores an important part of the conditions in which architectural and artistic culture develops." He then proposed a most interesting model on how the canons—or more precisely, the canonical interpretations—are born, developed, crystallized, and surpassed, until a new interpretative wave replaces the former established canons and new ones are devised. For this to happen, as Bonta stated, criticism will always have a most fundamental role. "The proposed model [designed by Bonta to understand the canonization process] departs from the traditional paradigm insofar as it recognizes critique as a fundamental participant in the process, not only in the propagation but also in the generation of architectural culture. The model assigns to verbal articulation or the written word a gravitas that traditional approaches, especially those of architects themselves, deny."[21]

In conclusion, let me reiterate my third point. Criticism is fundamental in nurturing and sustaining the efforts to properly challenge or criticize existing canonical books that will still be in use for some time yet. Criticism has played and will continue to play a fundamental role in the task ahead: to commit to the effort of building new comprehensive surveys that will be needed in the education of future generations of architects. And I hope that a new generation of researchers will be inspired to contribute to that challenge.

[20] Ibid., 2.
[21] Juan Pablo Bonta, "Arquitectura hablada," *Summarios #5*, March 1977, 6–8.

Biography

Ruth Verde Zein is an architect, FAU-USP, Brazil, 1977. PhD in Theory, History and Critique, PROPAR-UFRGS, Brazil, 2005; winner of the Capes Prize 2006; professor of Modern and Contemporary Architecture and Design in Graduated and Post-Graduated Studios at Mackenzie Presbyterian University, São Paulo, since 1997; member of DOCOMOMO, SAH, EAHN, CICA; former senior editor of *Projeto* (1983–1996); former member of the editorial board of *Architectural Histories Journal* (2015–2018); member of the editorial board of *En Blanco* journal and *Arquitexto/ Vitruvius*. She is a frequent contributor to Brazilian and Iberoamerican magazines and participant in international seminars, debates, conferences, and courses as a visiting professor. She is the author of articles and books, including *Critical Readings* (Austin/São Paulo: Nhamérica/Romano Guerra, 2019), which was awarded the Bruno Zevi CICA Prize 2020, and *Historiographical Revisions: Modern Brazilian Architecture* (Rio de Janeiro: Riobooks, 2022).

Architectural Criticism in the Space for the Unexpected

Jasna Galjer

fig. 1
Zagreb's new urban identity: University Boulevard, south-facing view, 1960s.
Source: Croatian State Archive CO 2199/49-TABLO F.14222 AG FOTO.

Taking architectural criticism's mediating role between architecture and its audiences as its basis, this essay will discuss how criticism has adapted to different media. The focus is on the analysis of the multifunctional institutional building the Workers' University, known today as the Public Open University Zagreb (1955–1961), promoted locally and globally as a paradigmatic example of socially engaged architecture within socialist modernism.
Looking at specific models of architectural criticism, ranging from authoritative academic scholarship, international networking (CIAM, Team 10), and journalism to participatory approaches, the aim is to examine the effectiveness of contemporary criticism's practices and to raise the question of its relevance today.

1. Architectural criticism's role in constructing historiographic narratives: the case study of socialist modernism

The Yugoslav model of "socialism with a human face," which appeared to be extremely successful in the 1950s and 1960s, found its architectural analogy in the concept of the socialist functional city. To achieve this project, modernization in Yugoslavia became inseparable from democratization and general societal progress. In the field of visual culture, abstraction soon became a symbol of creative freedom; however, the fields of architecture and urbanism were instead defined by the significantly more complex meanings of socialist modernism, as well as by their (self-)representational relationship with the centers of political power. The opening up of a discourse on architecture and urbanism to include the public speaks volumes about how criticism played a mediating role in the democratization of decision-making on key political issues. The affirmation of an interdisciplinary approach to designing urban planning strategies contributed significantly to this change.[1] Open forms, organic growth, polycentrism: these were all topics emerging in the field of architecture and art during the 1960s.

This text considers the role of critique from the (self-)representational discourse of the 1950s politics of socialist enlightenment and 1960s self-management in Yugoslavia, through to the reformist transformations in "acculturation" processes, up to the period when the Yugoslav socialist system disintegrated in the transitional 1990s,[2] and on to the critical and historiographical narratives after the first decade of the twenty-first century. Despite the breakdown of the country's socialist political, cultural, and social system in the 1990s, what links these periods is a thesis on how socially engaged architecture's modernity was conditional on political ideology and the revealing of an "absent presence"[3] of that modernity in the "in-between space" amid the cultural dominance of the East and the West.[4]

Recent historiography has increasingly taken an interest in architecture from the socialist Yugoslav period.[5] It has generated numerous interpretive models, among which the phrase "socialism and modernity"[6] is one of the most common. After the year 2000, this conceptual pair started being used to codify a cultural and social identity. As a consequence, a critical distance and analytical apparatus is often lacking, which results in mythologized narratives about a heroic age in which emerged modern society "from nothing."[7] One illustrative example of how curation can be instrumentalized for critical practices is the exhibition *Towards a Concrete Utopia: Architecture in Yugoslavia 1948–1980*, held by MoMA in 2018. This exhibition used an ostentatious format to resemanticize theoretical and critical

keywords:

architectural criticism, societal modernization, socialism, structuralism, Team 10, socially engaged architecture

[1] A typical example is the radicalization in the 1980s of urban sociology and the emergence of critiques of the "socialist concept of the city" as a humanized place that should satisfy all the needs of contemporary working people.
[2] After the breakup of Yugoslavia, 1990–1992, former federal republics Slovenia, Croatia, Macedonia, Bosnia and Herzegovina, Serbia and Montenegro became independent states.
[3] Victor Buchli and Gavin Lucas, eds., *The Absent Present: Archaeologies of the Contemporary Past* (London: Routledge, 2001), 3–18.
[4] The journals *Architectural Review, L'Architecture d'Aujourd'Hui, Casabella, Baumeister,* and others regularly publish contributions on the scope of Yugoslav architecture. One key example is the pavilion at Expo 58 (the 1958 Brussels World's Fair), which was judged to be one of the most successful architectural creations of the period.
[5] The period from 1945 to 1992 is often described as the time frame of the "Other," that is, of the socialist Yugoslavia.
[6] The tendency became a trend after the publishing of Peter Beilharz's influential book, *Socialism and Modernity* (Minneapolis: University of Minnesota Press, 2009).
[7] A telling example is the book and exhibition of the same name by Ljiljana Kolešnik, ed., *Socijalizam i modernost: Umjetnost, kultura, politika 1950–1974* [Socialism and modernity: art, culture, politics 1950–1974] (Zagreb: IPU, MSU, 2012). It aims to represent the topic from an interdisciplinary perspective along the lines of Beilharz's methodology, but without stating the aforementioned template.

fig. 2
"Aménagement de L'avenue des Brigades prolétaires, Zagreb, Yougoslavie." Source: *L'Architecture d'aujourd'hui*, 87 (1959/1960), 101.

concepts in order to establish a "new" historiographic narrative of socialist modernism which relied on patterns of continuity with the (neo)avant-garde and the transfer of ideas and ideologies to twentieth-century architecture. However, it did not clarify the provocative question of how the Yugoslav version differed from other paradigmatic examples of socialist modernism or the issue of it being part of the postwar New Humanist movement.[8] This lack was particularly visible in the exhibition catalog, a photograph-heavy volume consisting mainly of a sequence of monumentalized "iconic" fragments that have survived the bygone state; there are no distinguishing marks of a whole.[9] These fragments include the Moša Pijade Workers' University in Zagreb, defined in postmodernist terms as a "double-coded" construction. What is problematic here is that both functional and iconic "codes" are defined by a political determinism that insists on architecture having a role in political propaganda.[10]

This is also the problem underpinning the exhibition's conceptual basis. In transposing the methodologies of multicultural and postcolonial theoretical models, such as one taking "the Balkans" as an "Other,"[11] the exhibition attempted to popularize and institutionalize these categories, positioning them as a historiographic interpretive model. Thus, the text states that the Workers' University building anticipates the phenomenology of the Mat-Buildings,[12] while the relations between architecture and urban culture—which Tom Avermaete has defined in terms of the concept of acculturation[13]—remain outside the focus, as does the social framework (in which political ideology is just one factor among many). More detailed insights into international networking in the 1950s reveal analogies with the organizational principles of "Groundscrapers"—a prime example is the conceptualization of urban density in the project for the Free University in Berlin by Candilis, Josic, and Woods (1963–1973).[14]

Eve Blau and Ivan Rupnik's 2007 study, *Project Zagreb*, offers a different interpretative model to the previously mentioned exhibition.[15] It researches alternative discourses of architectural and urban culture in a much wider context, attempting to conceptualize the

[8] No shift has occurred since the predominant reinterpretation of historiography found in relation to the reinterpreting of historiography found in Ákos Moravánszky and Judith Hopfengärtner, eds., *Re-Humanizing Architecture: New Forms of Community, 1950–1970* (Basel: Birkhäuser Verlag, 2017); Ákos Moravánszky and Karl R. Kegler, eds., *Re-Scaling the Environment: New Landscapes of Design, 1960–1980* (Basel: Birkhäuser Verlag, 2017); Ákos Moravánszky and Torsten Lange, eds., *Re-Framing Identities: Architecture's Turn to History, 1970–1990* (Basel: Birkhäuser Verlag, 2017).

[9] Martino Stierli and Vladimir Kulić, eds., *Toward a Concrete Utopia: Architecture in Yugoslavia 1948–1980* (New York: MoMA, 2018).

[10] Occasions that feature political propaganda in everyday life, such as the tenth anniversary of the liberation in 1955 or the first assembly of the nonaligned in 1961, have been groundlessly attributed structural meanings in the emergence of architectural typologies: Tamara Bjažić Klarin, "Moša Pijade Workers' University," in Stierli and Kulić, *Toward a Concrete Utopia*, 125.

[11] The thesis comes from Maria Todorova, "The Balkans. From Discovery to Invention," *Slavic Review* 53 (1994), 453–82.

[12] By the early 1960s, observations of the Workers' University were featured in the local daily press, describing it as a "groundscraper" (literally: horizontal skyscraper): Krešo Špeletić, "Horizontalni neboder" [Groundscraper], *Večernji list*, January 1, 1962, 13.

[13] Tom Avermaete, "Acculturation of the Modern: Mass Tourism, Consumer Culture and the Work of Candilis-Josic-Woods," in *Architecture Culture and the Challenges of Globalisation* (conference proceedings, ACSA International Conference, Havana, June 21–24, 2002), 380–90.

[14] Dina Krunic, "The Groundscraper: Candilis-Josic-Woods and the Free University Building in Berlin," *ARRIS* 23 (2012), 30–49.

[15] Eve Blau and Ivan Rupnik, eds., *Project Zagreb: Transition as Condition, Strategy, Practice* (Barcelona: Actar, 2007).

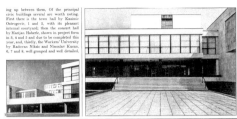
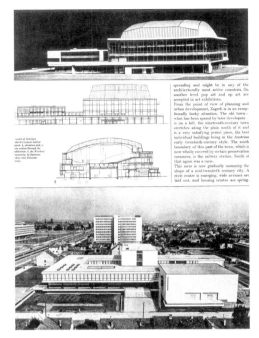

city's dynamic of practice while avoiding "manufacturing" the history of the city. The authors believe that in a transitional environment, the stability required for normative planning is not present, and therefore architects and urbanists have developed methods that are now cutting edge across the globe—an indication that this transitional environment is ubiquitous.[16] In this context, Blau and Rupnik find the main signs of the transitional condition in the "feeling for the city as a project," from the socialist "functional city," with its realized metropolitan forms, to the establishing of "urban rules" in the chaos of the 1990s transition after the collapse of Yugoslavia. Such a reading implies a revaluing of the cultural legacy of Zagreb and a conceptualizing of future urban practices.

The transdisciplinary method of "reading the city" as an open, unfinished work forms the point of departure for Dennison Rusinow's theses on the "Yugoslav experiment based on socialist self-management."[17] The appearance of the innovative architectural concept of a multifunctional complex for adult education was therefore—completely justifiably—interpreted in terms of the urban concept of the functional city. Blau and Rupnik highlighted that the Workers' University was one of the key projects of the Zagreb mayor, Većeslav Holjevac, aimed at reconfiguring the relations between the city and industry. Architecture was thus ascribed a position of exceptional influence in the power relations of the city. This was particularly the case as the focal point for decision-making on questions of key political importance, such as worker education, shifted from the centralized federal authorities to the level of the city administration.[18] As a result of a central location on University Boulevard (a wide street along which many key Zagreb University faculties are located) being chosen for its site, the building also became a symbol of the relationship that the socialist society of the time had with academic institutions and the relation of academic knowledge to social transformation. To explain the stratification of these relations and the multiplication of meanings of urban culture, Blau and Rupnik used hybrid means of presentation, including collages, mapping, diagrams, layering, analytical models, animations, projects, and stop-motion photographs. Architectural photography, in the form of photo albums and photojournalism from the 1950s up to recent photographic records of the devastated and dilapidated building,

fig. 3
"Zagreb." Source: *Architectural Review*, 838 (1966), 456–57.

[16] Eve Blau, "City as Open Work," in Blau and Rupnik, *Project Zagreb*, 8–25.
[17] Dennison Rusinow, *The Yugoslav Experiment 1948–1974* (Berkeley and Los Angeles: University of California Press, 1977).
[18] Blau and Rupnik, *Project Zagreb*, 200.

has documented changes to the "main" and "secondary" meaning of architecture exemplified by the Workers' University. Coincidentally, the visual language and conceptual basis of architectural journals in socialist Yugoslavia of the 1950s and, especially, the 1960s displays great similarity to contemporary examples in Portugal, Spain, or Brazil, as well as examples in Romania, Bulgaria, and Greece. These analogies are based on the representational codes of the interaction between architecture and photography, while they also hint at transfers of architectural ideas and ideologies across different media in media space. One example are the thematic photojournalist pieces on Zagreb's contemporary architecture in the journals *L'Architecture d'Aujourd'hui*[19] and *Architectural Review*.[20] Like the "universally comprehensible" language of contemporary visual culture, structured communicative codes were established that could not be unambiguously defined in terms of the East's or the West's political framework.

fig. 4
Frames from the film *Zagrebačke paralele* (1962): a film adaptation of the concept "The Future Is Now." Source: Zagreb film Archive.

[19] Anonymous, "Aménagement de L'avenue des Brigades prolétaires, Zagreb, Yougoslavie," *L'Architecture d'Aujourd'hui* 87 (1959/1960), 100–101.
[20] Anonymous, "Zagreb," *Architectural Review* 838 (1966), 455–58.
[21] Branko Majer directed the film, and it was produced by Zagreb Film.

2. Mediated representations and the construction of architecture's contested meaning

The dynamic of Zagreb's transition during the 1950s and the early 1960s was documented in the film *Zagrebačke paralele* (1962), which offered various perspectives of the metropolization of the city.[21] It used a newsreel format to record the clash between the old and the new: the disappearing urban periphery and the construction of the modern city. The film's focus is on a critical depiction of the ideology of progress that destroys small, old houses. Beside the accelerated pace of construction, the film's message included the stepping away from tradition, which was equated with the negative features of capitalist society. Large-scale architecture, residential settlements, factories, schools and hotels, exhibition facilities, and socially engaged architecture for public purposes were all depicted as recognizable and as visual motifs of socialist architecture. From close-up shots of facades and views from the air to dramatically composed low-angle shots designed to accentuate monumental presence, architectural photographs unambiguously transmitted a message of prosperity and interpreted architecture as a symbol of collective progress.

Much more radicalized interpretations appeared in the film *The Trial* by Orson Welles (1962), where these spaces are depicted as a dystopian world from which there is no escape.

fig. 5
David Maljković,
Recalling Frames, 2010
b/w print from collage on negative
108 × 127.8 cm (framed).
Courtesy of Sprueth Magers Berlin
London Los Angeles.

This was diametrically opposed to the dominant conception of the modernist architecture of the Workers' University; in the film's case, the university was a scene of anguish and hopeless alienation. Flexibility regarding the building's spatial dispositions—its main functional units and its relation to the city—took on Kafkaesque features in the style of film noir: in a nightmarish atmosphere, the boundaries between space and time in the (then still abandoned) Paris Gare d'Orsay melded with the elementarism of the Workers' University in Zagreb. Regarding interpretations of Welles's film as an explicit critique of the social and political system, the director's reasoning for his choice of Zagreb—and modernist environments that evoke the disappearance of the "old social order" under attack from the modernization of the New World—is provocative.[22] We find recollections of this critical interpretation of the city's (and its architecture's) vision of the time "in line with human needs" in the series of photographs titled *Recalling Frames* (2010) by the contemporary artist David Maljković. In the tradition of objets trouvés, frames from *The Trial* are used to form a "ready-made" collage of appropriated images of the current state of the building. By multiplying the points of view and manipulating the photographic images, the patterns in relations between time and space are deconstructed. In comparison with the methodology of the *Project Zagreb* study, Maljković also researched the historical and cultural legacy of the socialist modernist project. The reconfiguring of the layers of film and photography—their fictions and documentations—highlights the transformation in the urban environment from the early 1960s to the contemporary period and the complete absence of whole, stable categories of spatial meaning, in this case at the Workers' University.

[22] Frank Brady, *Citizen Welles: A Biography of Orson Welles* (New York: Charles Scribner's Sons, 1989), 529.

3. Appropriating structuralism amid social change: "The story of another idea"

Despite close links with the ideology of the socialist political and social system, the Workers' University is also an example of openness toward transfers of architectural culture, which intensified from the 1950s onward. In 1953, a group of like-minded participants in the ninth International Congress of Modern Architecture (CIAM) who went by the name Team 10 challenged the prevailing modernist doctrine of the congress, particularly in its social and

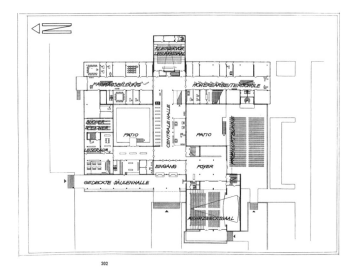

fig. 6
Radovan Nikšić explains his work at the CIAM meeting in Otterlo in 1959 (above); floor plan of the ground floor of the Workers' University in Zagreb. Source: Oscar Newman, CIAM '59 in *Otterlo: Documents of Modern Architecture*, 202.

fig. 7
Radovan Nikšić and Ninoslav Kučan (coauthor), floor plan of the ground floor, conceptual sketch (project as part of a project tender for the construction of the Workers' University in Zagreb), 1955. Source: HAZU Croatian Museum of Architecture, Zagreb. Radovan Nikšić's personal archival collection.

[23] Team 10 was a group of architects, whose core participants were Jaap Bakema, Georges Candilis, Giancarlo De Carlo, Aldo van Eyck, Alison and Peter Smithson, and Shadrach Woods. The group disbanded the CIAM organization in order to revitalize the "other" modern tradition of urbanism. Team 10 did not include separate branches of architects from Eastern Europe. The participants of Team 10 meetings (1953–1981) included architects from Eastern Europe (Oskar Hansen and Jerzy Soltan from Poland, Charles Polóny from Hungary, and Radovan Nikšić from Zagreb, then in Yugoslavia, as well as followers from Yugoslavia and Czechoslovakia), who shared with their colleagues from Western Europe the aims to advance architecture and urban design in postwar society.
[24] Łukasz Stanek, ed., *Team 10 East: Revisionist Architecture in Real Existing Modernism* (Warsaw: Museum of Modern Art, 2014).
[25] Renata Margaretić Urlić and Karin Šerman, "Workers' University Zagreb: Team 10 Ideas in the Service of Socialist Enlightenment," in Stanek, *Team 10 East*, 157–63.
[26] Tamara Bjažić Klarin, "CIAM Networking—International Congress of Modern Architecture and Croatian Architects in the 50s," *Život umjetnosti* 99 (2016): 40–57; Jasna Galjer, "Radical or Not at All? Architectural Criticism as a Vehicle of CIAM and Team 10 Networking in Socialist Yugoslavia," in *REVISITING POST-CIAM GENERATION. Debates, Proposals and Intellectual Framework*, ed. Nuno, Correia, Maria Helena Maia, and Rute Figueiredo (Porto: CEAA/ESAP-CESAP, 2019), 149–66, accessed July 13, 2021, https://comum.rcaap.pt/handle/10400.26/28351?mode=full.
[27] In the Hague, Nikšić held a lecture on Yugoslavia's contemporary architecture and later, in Zagreb, organized a lecture by Reinder Blijstra, the literary critic and editor of the architectural magazine *Forum*, on Dutch architecture with a special focus on the urban regeneration of Rotterdam and contemporary completed works by Bakema and Van den Broek.

urbanistic dimensions, and are often cited as a crucial point of divergence in modernist dogma.[23] The book *Team 10 East: Revisionist Architecture in Real Existing Modernism*[24] is a valuable example of dispassionate analysis that sheds light on the exchange of ideas between the East and the West, wherein the Workers' University assumes a prominent position. The article "Workers' University Zagreb: Team 10 Ideas in the Service of Socialist Enlightenment" stands out among the contributions to the book as a particularly egregious example of a tendency toward the critical revision of linear historiographic narratives. It does so principally with a thesis on the conditionality of the ideology of socialist enlightenment, which, its authors surmise, resulted in an innovative approach to the conceptualization of space. However, what is lacking is a contextual analysis of space as a facilitator for social interaction; that is, the thing that makes the "eastern" wing of Team 10's conceptualization of space closer to contemporary principles.[25] In early 1956, immediately after the successful tender for the Workers' University project was published, the building's architect Radovan Nikšić departed for the Netherlands on a six-month study where he worked as an associate in the office of Johannes H. Van den Broek and Jacob Bakema, researching architectural projects intended for education and everyday living.[26] This period had a formative influence on both his later actions and his networking engagements between the Dutch and Yugoslav architectural scenes.[27]

Undoubtedly, the most significant contribution to networking at that time was Nikšić's participation in the final official meeting of the International Congress of Modern Architecture (CIAM) in Otterlo in 1959, where he gave a presentation on the then incomplete Workers' University in Zagreb. There were forty-three participants in the congress, from twenty European, North and South American, and Asian states, who presented projects to the

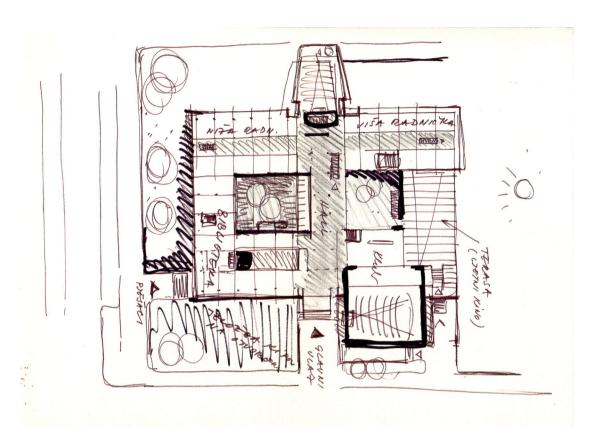

whole group before a discussion. In the introductory text to the monograph *CIAM '59 in Otterlo*, Jacob Bakema stated that these participants were invited as individuals and not as representatives of political, national, ideological, social, regional, or religious positions.[28] Thanks to this extensively documented publication we can reconstruct the meeting's program, which was conceived as a workshop for the exchange of opinions.[29] The congress gathered participants of a generation then in their forties, who had matured professionally after 1945, and who had actively participated in the previous CIAM meetings. This confirms the thesis that Team 10 emerged as a critique of the modern movement that ignited a debate on the scale of technocracy and the sustainability of the functionalist categories of the 1933 Athens Charter; they advocated a "perspective on the transformation of places" along more human lines and a regard for social life when shaping spaces.

In his presentation on the Workers' University, Nikšić, after an introduction in which he informed the participants about the specificities of self-managing socialism, explained the project's goal of forming a more flexible space that workers would accept as their second home and which would stimulate a "feeling for measure, form and good style."[30] Afterward, he explained a modular system based on a complex of interpersonally linked spatial configurations where the spatial unit was also the foundation of educational activities for groups of fifteen to twenty participants. Given that most users would be workers, one key intention was to design a space that would stimulate the creation of new cultural activities in people's free time. The surface area of the space was 20,000 square meters, and it was designed to accommodate 5,000 visitors a day as a multifunctional complex analogous to a small town. It was to have a grid of interlinked streets and squares, open interior courtyards, corridors, classrooms, and rest areas, creating a "continuous" space.

[28] Jacob B. Bakema, "Introduction," in *CIAM '59 in Otterlo: Documents of Modern Architecture*, ed. Oscar Newman (Stuttgart: Karl Krämer Verlag, 1961), 9. A practically identical statement can be found in the foreword/preface of the same publication, signed by Oscar Newman (p. 8).
[29] Interestingly, the index in Eric Mumford's book *The CIAM Discourse on Urbanism, 1928–1960* (Cambridge and London: The MIT Press, 2000) does not list data on the authors and publications of CIAM '59 in Otterlo.
[30] Newman, *CIAM '59 in Otterlo*, 203.
[31] Jasna Galjer and Sanja Lončar, "Socially Engaged Architecture of the 1950s and Its Transformations. The Example of Zagreb's Workers' University," *Etnološka tribina: godišnjak Hrvatskog etnološkog društva* 49 (2019), 194–222.
[32] When presenting the project in Otterlo, Nikšić stated that the chief intention was to invite young artists and architects to participate in shaping a total-design environment that would have a stimulating effect on the understanding of art. The presentation was published as "Zgrada Radničkog sveučilišta—model odgojno obrazovne ustanove" (The Workers' University Building—a model of an educational institution), in Newman, *CIAM '59 in Otterlo*, 203–204.

Special attention was paid to "islands for resting" that were carefully distributed and linked by stairs.[31] The use of top-quality fittings in the space was designed to generate an awareness about the role of design in shaping the quality of everyday life. The ultimate goal was the acceptance of a synthesis of architecture, painting, and sculpture.[32]

The stated arguments thinking through the concepts of identity and the collective—that is, the focus on harmonizing individual needs and community belonging—confirm preoccupations that became critical examinations of how space is shaped as a flexible framework for possible interactions and communications. At that time, this was the focus of Team 10's actions, and this focus consequently eluded the conventions of modern architecture's historiography.[33] Twenty-five years after CIAM, in the text "Sarabande for CIAM," Nikšić commented on his participation in the meeting in Otterlo. He admitted that, for him, "CIAM was the first architectural literature from even my student days." He recalled that most of the participants had wanted to keep CIAM going but in a reorganized form. In the end everyone went their separate ways without any discussion of what happened in Otterlo.[34] To conclude, let us consider the final part of Bakema's introduction to the book *CIAM '59 in Otterlo*. In it, the conceptual basis of most of the projects presented is described as an orientation toward a new architectural language that could respond to current individual and social needs. The Workers' University project was deservedly placed in this category.

In the mediatic popularization of architectural culture in the second half of the 1950s, the journal *Forum* played a crucial role.[35] The first issue of the new journal was published with the title "The Story of Another Idea," and it was distributed to participants at the meeting in Otterlo, who steadfastly displayed their dissatisfaction with the existing opportunities available to architects current trajectory of architecture. On the same occasion, Aldo van Eyck presented a theory based on concepts of a "space in-between" and a "space of encounter." As confirmed by recent interpretations of Van Eyck's works, generated by analyses of his texts published in *Forum*,[36] these concepts emerged under the influence of Martin Buber's philosophical discourse. The shaping of architectural design is defined by the "anthropology" of space as a place of dialogue and interaction, which new experiences, encounters, and events always make afresh.[37] As part of his presentation, Van Eyck also presented his own recent projects based on a modular principle and the dynamic composition of spatial units, analogous to the principles also applied in the project for the Workers' University. These included an orphanage in Amsterdam now regarded as an paradigmatic example of structuralism. A concept of space that encourages the development of social relations in the project for the Workers' University is most clearly manifest in the network of "indoor streets" that feature islands equipped with comfortable furniture, inviting visitors to sit down and socialize or rest. In this way, the building takes on a function analogous to that of public spaces in urban environments, and the spaces are interlinked and interpermeated.

Besides the "formal" features, analogies can be found in the optimal balance between closed and open concepts of interlinked spatial units of the Workers' University. Configurations of smaller and larger functional units are linked with diagonal and axial arterials of movement that "network" them in a complete orthogonal structure. As with Van Eyck's project for an orphanage in Amsterdam, the Workers' University also understands the principles of contemporary urban planning as manifest in the actions of the Team 10 group. This is especially the case in relation to a shift away from the rigidly rationalist CIAM doctrine[38] that opposed the idea of social relations and communication as driving forces in design. Van Eyck's contribution to the CIAM program is key to defining his concept of "in-between space"[39] as a place of encounter and unification. The starting point is the thesis that categories which appear to be opposed (such as open and closed, subject and object, small and large) are not mutually exclusive but rather complementary, and the conviction that a totality is always complex. The concept of an "in-between space" determines how the balance between categories is established. This is like a person's nature and—just like a person—this balance needs to breathe.

[33] Max Risselada and Dirk van den Heuvel, *Team 10, 1953–1981: In Search of a Utopia of the Present* (Rotterdam: NAi Publishers, 2005).

[34] Radovan Nikšić, "Sarabanda za CIAM" [Sarabande for CIAM], *Arhitektura* 189–95 (1984/1985), 38–41.

[35] Starting in 1959, *Forum* was edited by a group of young Dutch architects: Aldo van Eyck, Jacob B. Bakema, Dick C. Apon, Gerrit Boon, Joop Hardy, Herman Hertzberger, and Jurriaan Schrofer.

[36] Francis Strauven, "Aldo van Eyck—Shaping the New Reality from the In-between to the Aesthetics of Number," in *CCA Study Centre* (Montreal, 2007), accessed July 12, 2021, https://www.cca.qc.ca/cca.media/files/1491/1392/Mellon12-FS.pdf.

[37] Georges Teyssot, "Aldo van Eyck's Threshold: The Story of an Idea," *Log* 11 (2008), 33–48.

[38] This rationalism relates to a rigid division of built space in line with basic functions: working, living, circulation, and everyday life.

[39] Strauven, "Aldo van Eyck," 10.

During a climate of educational reform in the first half of the 1970s, the political significance of architecture and the need to articulate new strategies grew. Stipe Šuvar, one of the founders of urban sociology in Croatia, analyzed sociological aspects of spatial development using Zagreb as an example. It is telling that Šuvar, in representing the focal point of political power,[40] points to a crisis in the "city as a social community," highlighting the inadequately developed network of basic social institutions.[41] Given that Zagreb's urban planning was based on micro-neighborhoods, each with a complete infrastructure designed to function as a "miniature city," Šuvar concluded that Zagreb's transformation into a metropolis was unsatisfactory. In the conclusion, alongside an illustration depicting a view of the Workers' University complex and the aforementioned University Boulevard, the author suggests that structured and decentralized urban planning would help create more specialized, multifunctional spaces designed to resolve social problems more easily. The problem's complexity was described in the greatest detail in a Consultation on Cultural Community Centers conducted in 1976 in Kumrovec, organized by the Association of Yugoslav Architects. The discussion's key thematic features can be reconstructed from a special issue of the journal Arhitektura,[42] in which 115 architects and representatives from related fields participated, as did representatives from the social and political sphere from across the entire territory of Yugoslavia. The commencement of a debate intended to include a broader expert public at the federal level coincided with a redefining of the social function that dominated in multifunctional buildings of various workers' universities in the previous period.

Like most of the multifunctional centers for culture that faced the loss of their previous functions in the early 1990s, the former Workers' University, which was highlighted as an emblematic example of socially engaged architecture from the 1950s to the 1980s, became a symptom of the deconstruction of these roles, and no appropriate alternative emerged in its place. One of the main arguments in favor of this specific building at that time was the potential flexibility of its space, but no such initiatives were implemented. However, the

fig. 8
Interior of the Workers' University in Zagreb (1961), entrance hall with "islands for resting," 1961. Source: Library of the Public Open University Zagreb. Photo: Željko Krčadinac.

fig. 9
Interior of the Workers' University in Zagreb, library. Design of equipment: Bernardo Bernardi. Reproduction: Miličević-Nikolić, "Radničko sveučilište Moša Pijade u Zagrebu," Source: HAZU Croatian Museum of Architecture, Zagreb. Radovan Nikšić's personal archival collection. Photo: Željko Krčadinac.

[40] Stipe Šuvar (1936–2004) was a prominent Croatian and Yugoslav politician who was the Secretary for Education and Culture of the Republic of Croatia from 1974 to 1982 (a position at the republic level analogous to the minister of the department for culture).

[41] Stipe Šuvar, "Sociološki aspekti prostornog razvoja Zagreba: ljudski problem u velegradu" [Sociological aspects relating to the spatial development of Zagreb: the human problem in a large city], Arhitektura 106 (1970), 60–66.

[42] Arhitektura 158–59 (1976). The special issue was edited by Andrija Mutnjaković and Darko Venturini.

urbanist seminars Frames of the Metropolis (Okviri metropole), of which the first was held in 1995 in the former Workers' University building (then the Open University), demonstrate that the 1990s did not have an exclusively negative legacy in relation to this architecture and its memory.[43]

The seminars discussed experimental methods and theories through contemporary urban topics, problems, and questions, chiefly those which were "flashpoints." In the workshops, lectures, and accompanying programs, they scrutinized possible urban strategies for resolving problematic spaces.[44] The 1995 seminar was organized as a workshop in which around ten groups of architects gave their suggestions on how to renovate these spaces; that is, how they could once again establish a link between the individual components of the city's structure. Besides its importance for architectural practice, it also opened a series of questions of interest to a wider public, as well as providing an opportunity to "learn from history."

The guest lecturers included Kenneth Frampton, Herman Hertzberger, and Raoul Bunschoten. Hertzberger, who was then the dean of the Berlage Institute, held a lecture called "Spaces for the Unexpected" in which he clarified his own foundations in architecture: architecture as an expression of identity and the strong individuality of expression. It is here that the common ground and related sensibilities with Nikšić's mode of thinking are most visible. Hertzberger also advocated an architecture that did not offer ready-made solutions but instead spatial frameworks with room to be accoutered in line with users' needs: the building has to be made like a city, it must possess a city's clarity, and it dare not confuse [users] with its programmatic attitudes.[45] This architect's motto was not to create space, but to live space. In the building of what was then the Open University, Hertzberger saw programmatic ideas of structuralism: the primary task was to create "spaces for the unexpected," which, instead of predetermined relationships, facilitated a polyvalence. Furthermore, this idea furthered the contention that architecture ought to have a good basis (not only in the physical sense, but also in the spiritual sense) in order to be able to be reinterpreted in various ways and in line with the needs of the time. This is a long-term and holistic process, within which readings can shift relationships more in line with current needs or ways of thinking. This is, according to Hertzberger, structuralism's foundational idea.

One characteristic feature of the transitional 1990s is the transmission of new architectural ideas, whose torchbearers were Croatian architects linked to the Dutch scene gathered around the Berlage Institute's research programs. Small Changes (Male Promjene, 1999), the third in a series of experimental urbanist seminars in collaboration with the Berlage Institute, confirmed the hypothesis that transitional planning must be radically different from the socialist historical model. In total, fifty-eight projects demonstrated a range of innovative suggestions for democratizing public spaces in Zagreb, which, by respecting tradition, considered new strategies for the development of urban culture.[46] Even though necessary institutional reforms for achieving these changes have since been in short supply, numerous activist initiatives[47] have pursued various tactics—from Jane's Walk[48] to the popularization of the "archaeology of the recent past"—and conducted thematic round tables and conservation studies discussing the former Workers' University. These demonstrate the critical potential of the acute dissatisfaction that the city's people have with its quality and structure. Given the lack of institutional reforms, these strategies based on "small changes" still come closer to achieving a space of identity. Paradoxically, their effects are in fact far closer to the utopian ideals of "immediate democracy" than are spectacularized narratives that relate to the political side of architectural ideas and the production of space.

The case studies examined in this chapter demonstrate the double-sidedness of architectural criticism: its persuasive power in mediating the meaning of architecture vis-à-vis its lack of impact outside the architectural field, an impact we would expect to be a precondition for the founding of a relevant "critical project." The affirmation of criticism in multidisciplinary contextual perspectives, or the formation of compelling experimental mod-

[43] During that period, the institution operated with the name the Open University, and later the Public Open University Zagreb.

[44] For the seminar program, see Vladimir Mattioni, ed., Okviri metropole [Frames of the metropolis] (Zagreb: Grad Zagreb/ Gradski zavod za planiranje razvoja i zaštitu čovjekova okoliša, 1996).

[45] Stated in the following conversation with Herman Hertzberger: "Arhitekt na krovu," (Architect on the roof), in Vijenac (Zagreb) , 18 May 1995, no. 36 III.; p. 25.

[46] Vedran Mimica, "Democratization of Public Space," in The Berlage Affair, ed. Vedran Mimica (New York and Barcelona: Actar; Chicago: IITAC Press, 2017), 301–302. Not only architects, urban planners, and designers but also actors and visual artists supervised the research and work on the projects.

[47] After the 2000s, these included Pravo na grad, Zelena akcija, Mapiranje Trešnjevke, and Centar oblikovanja svakodnevice.

[48] Participatory practices organized by a network of city organizers around the world, to honor and activate the ideas of Jane Jacobs (1916–2006) a writer, urbanist and activist.

fig. 10
Transfers of 1990s architectural design ideas: the Workers' University as a "space for the unexpected." Source: *Okviri metropole,* Zagreb, 1996, 84–85.

els for reinterpreting urban and architectural relations, can be much more readily adjusted to reality than can attempts to aestheticize both politics and architecture by constructing narratives that rely on a exhibitionist media space. As it is the case in the field of art, there is a critical call to reconnect architecture with its political and social context, wherein architectural criticism should challenge preconceptions and question values but at the same time acknowledge the social realities that are manifested in the built environment as it exists. When determining the quality of this particular building, the question is: why is it still there, in this town, surrounded by other "iconic ruins"?

Translated by Andrew Hodges

Biography

Jasna Galjer is an art historian and professor in the Department of the History of Art and Architecture at the University of Zagreb. Prior to joining the University she worked at the Museum of Arts and Crafts in Zagreb as a curator of the collection of architecture and design. Her research interests focus on twentieth- and early twenty-first-century history, theory, and criticism of architecture and design. She is interested especially in transfers and mediations of ideas, ideologies and discourses, in the context of cultural history from the early 1950s to the end of the 1970s. She is the author of various essays and monographs on architectural criticism, cultural history of periodicals, architectural photography, history of exhibitions and design.

Aphaeresis and Urban Policies

Konstantinos Petrakos

fig. 1
Book cover *Critical Spatial Practice 4: Subtraction*,
Kelly Easterling (Berlin: Sternberg Press, 2014).

The prevailing superficial and overweening treatment of architecture should be sidelined, and a focus on contextual dynamics should be prioritized. In a design culture focused on the excellent, destruction appears a secondary concern. While our built environment is the product of many forces, the act of removal provides a space for critical thought on economic, political, and social contexts. The act of aphaeresis in architecture is proposed not as a mere theoretical concept, but as both a design tool in architectural practice and an apparatus of critical thinking: a means to understand and critically dismantle the visible aspects of architecture while synthesizing the invisible.

Introduction

The broader scope of this essay is to interrogate the epistemological question of architectural praxis intrinsically. As many scholars have already pointed out, architecture is inextricably intertwined with the act of building. The prevailing view is that architectural praxis is wholly realized in the process of designing and erecting a structure; from Laugier's primitive hut to contemporary discourse, architecture is constantly portrayed as a process of addition. There are very few instances in which architecture is discussed otherwise, and this is precisely the area of study that I am focusing on. That is, I am investigating the possibility of an architecture that is produced not by addition but by the reverse process, the act of aphaeresis.

The term aphaeresis is already well known and used primarily in medical science. Etymologically the word consists of the prefix aph- (ἀφ, "off") and the verb hairéō (αἱρέω, "to take") and it means to take something away from the totality of which it is part. The reason for employing the above term is because I wanted to avoid synonymous words that would cause misunderstandings. Notably, as will be discussed, the words that I wanted to avoid are: subtraction and abstraction. Both have already been used excessively in architectural theory and thus bear powerful connotations.

Our built environment is the product of many forces. As aptly described in the competition "Taking Buildings Down,"[1] its production can dialectically be reduced to the tensions between creation and destruction, addition and subtraction, and erection and demolition. Having the above *problematique* as our basis, the main objective of this essay is to investigate the potential of architecture to act as an interpretive tool in the erasure of buildings, structures, and infrastructures. Specifically, it explores the possibility of subtraction and the production of voids as a creative act. The act of adding in architecture has always been associated with adding value. Subtraction, however, can often add value that cannot be quantified, assessed, or even predicted: the act of removal provides a space for critical thought on its economic, political, and social context. Through this application of "unbuilding" as a culture-shaping force, we will investigate the pragmatic and conceptual effects of creation and destruction upon a cultural landscape.

keywords:

aphaeresis, unbuilding, landscape, abstraction, subtraction

[1] "Taking Buildings Down" (competition, Storefront for Art and Architecture, New York, January 2016).

Methodology

A case study methodology was employed to examine this problematic. A strong theoretical framework was deemed crucial for a more profound understanding of the case studies and the concept of aphaeresis; thus, research began with a study of the theoretical frameworks of similar acts as an attempt to challenge the established conceptions of "built" and "unbuilt."[2] This critique guided the development of the following case studies, revealing the cultural values implicit in the established relationship between tourism, landscape, and architecture, and presenting a design strategy that could assess, challenge, and redefine the above relation. The theoretical concepts on which the theoretical framework is built are subtraction, minor architecture, and abstraction.

Subtraction is not a novel concept, but rather a common phenomenon in real estate, transportation management, and city planning. In his 1993 project "Erasing Detroit," the architect Dan Hoffman was the first to note that "unbuilding has surpassed building as the city's major architectural activity."[3] Ten years later, we have the exhibition *Shrinking Cities*,[4] which analyzed overgrown cities under urban crisis, including Detroit. Subtraction was linked with Keller Easterling's theory **(fig. 1)**, where she argues that unbuilding has been transformed into currency and calls on architects to contribute to policymaking. Through this lens, we can understand architecture not merely as an act of addition but also as an interplay of values where demolition is often an agent for growth rather than a symbol of

[2] Keller Easterling, *Critical Spatial Practice 4: Subtraction* (Berlin: Sternberg Press, 2014), 73.
[3] Dan Hoffman, "Erasing Detroit," in *Stalking Detroit*, ed. Georgia Daskalakis, Charles Waldheim, and Jason Young (Barcelona: Editorial Actar, 2001), 101.
[4] "Shrinking Cities" (exhibition, KW Institute for Contemporary Art, Berlin, September 2004).

fig. 2
Acropolis of Athens in the Ottoman map of 1827. Source: K. Stathi, 2015.

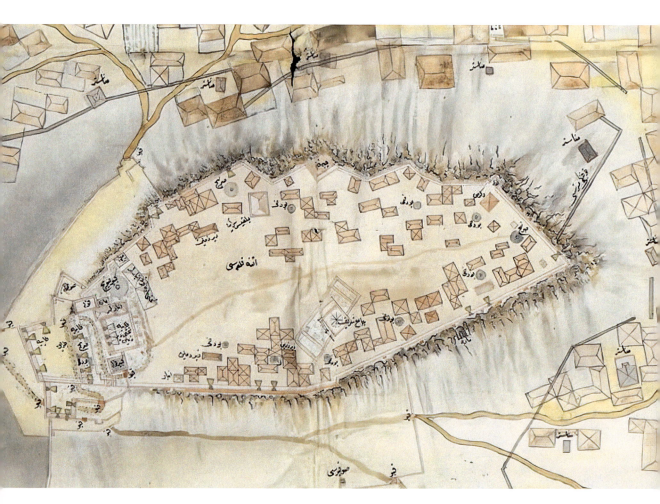

violence. A deeper inquiry reveals a significant corpus of literature on the topic. Some note-worthy studies are Jill Stoner's *Toward a Minor Architecture* and Julia Schulz-Dornburg's "Modern Ruins, a Topography of Profit." However, like Easterling, most of these scholars focus primarily on financial factors, such as the transformation of buildings into currency, and less on the potential of such an act in the architectural praxis of space formation.

Keller Easterling believes that an economy of subtraction could be both destructive and creative as it would not erase information but instead release a flood of information, correlations, and interactions. It could use both material and immaterial means to shape the conditions, composition, or organization of space. According to her, if every act of building is both addition and subtraction, every act of unbuilding is also addition and subtraction. This economy of subtraction almost exists already. Unfortunately, it lacks the political momentum to escape from the destructive cycles of the free market, among other political impasses.[5]

In her book *Toward a Minor Architecture*, Jill Stoner states that architecture can no longer limit itself to the act of making buildings. Stoner presents a radical and optimistic re-visioning of the contemporary built environment and landscape of late capitalism. She provocatively promotes a new discourse, one that moves away from design and toward perception of architecture as a political act. She asks us to consider alternative models of operation, investing in the future of cities by way of their past: reusing existing buildings instead of building new ones.[6] Minor architecture is less obsessed with affecting skylines and more interested in transforming the existing urban context by way of program, history, systems, technology, and material. Minor architecture represents a radical shift from the egocentric and iconic to the invisible and contextual.

Abstraction in architecture is a very ambiguous term compared to abstraction in art and literature. In *The Production of Space*, Henri Lefebvre defines two types of abstract space: the political as a product of violence and war and the institutional established by a state.[7] More recently, in a lecture titled "Design Without Qualities: Architecture and the Rise of Abstraction" at the Architectural Association,[8] Pier Vittorio Aureli stated that abstraction could be a useful creative concept in a design world increasingly dominated by redundant forms and superficial architecture. The point of abstraction in an academic context and in architectural practice is to challenge the traditional reflex that the solution to any problem is a building.

As already mentioned, to signify the different trajectory my research takes regarding the act of removal-demolition in architecture, I will use the term aphaeresis. Specifically, in my study I aim to investigate the act of aphaeresis in architecture, not as a mere theoretical concept but as a design tool in architectural practice, giving aphaeresis the same weight one would give addition in the transformation of space. While destruction appears a sec-ondary concern in a design culture focused on the superlative—the tallest, the newest, the priciest—my criticism aspires to problematize the complex relationship between the social, political, cultural, and historical contexts by developing a novel design strategy, one predicated upon the potential of aphaeresis.

In this regard, I will examine the transformation and production of space through the act of removal in three archetypical projects across the past three centuries. The first case study is the cleansing/purification of the Acropolis of Athens (1837), which expresses the rising nationalism of the mid-nineteenth century. The second is Le Corbusier's Plan Voisin for Paris (1922), a symbol of the modern movement's dismissive attitude toward the past. The last project is a very recent landscape intervention and was crucial in understanding the nuances and particularities of such a complex topic: the Tudela-Culip Restoration in Cap de Creus, Spain, by EMF landscape architects and Ton Ardèvol (2011) is a project with profound political and social impact that has instigated heated debate on preservation, ecology, and design. All three cases are products of political forces instituted by a state or a designer. I am proposing aphaeresis as an apparatus of critical thinking, a means to understand and critically dismantle the character of the above cases.

[5] Easterling, *Critical Spatial Practice 4*, 73.
[6] Jill Stoner, *Toward a Minor Architecture* (New York: Random House Publishing Group, 2012).
[7] Henri Lefebvre, *The Production of Space*, trans. Donald Nicholson Smith (Paris: Anthropos, 1991).
[8] Pier Vittorio Aureli, *"Design Without Qualities: Architecture and the Rise of Abstraction"* (lecture, Architectural Association, London, October 2015).

Acropolis of Athens

Between 1831 and 1835, during the establishment of the Modern Greek State, national identity was constructed through aphaeresis. After moving the capital of Greece from Nafplio to Athens, Bavarian King Otto and his team of architects, Stamatios Kleanthis and Eduard Schaubert, called for the employment of antiquities to form the new national identity. This operational demand led to a series of destructions, particularly on the Acropolis hill. The Acropolis represented the two contradicting elements of the early Modern Greek State: On the one hand, the small Ottoman town on the rock reflected the collective conception of "Romiossini" (citizen of the Roman empire).[9] On the other hand, the ruins of the Acropolis connoted a glorious past of "Hellenism." Here, aphaeresis was used as a spatial and ideological tool to create the phantom of an invisible culture: the contrived culture of ancient Athens. In reality, the Acropolis was a small settlement for the Ottoman garrison of Athens rather than the monument we see now *(fig. 2)*.[10] Besides the Parthenon, several tiny houses have been recorded on the hill; it served as military infrastructure for the city, closed for hundreds of years to visitors. Contemporary travelers, in their depictions, deliberately ignored the Ottoman buildings of the settlement and placed more emphasis on the classical antiquities of the hill.

The redesign of the Acropolis was not based on a master plan but instead on a series of independent actions and subjective decisions by all those involved in the process. Each design decision was made according to what was worth doing on the hill—that is, according to the respective mastermind. Therefore, this multifarious process can be fragmented and classified into several planned interventions that contain decisions, actions, and gestures of strategically designed removals and abstractions on the Acropolis hill.

Paradoxically different proposals for the final configuration of the modern Acropolis were formulated, like that of Karl Friedrich Schinkel. He proposed the palatial complex be built on the Acropolis summit. On the other hand, Leo von Klenze tried to compose a European landscape of eternal ruins, one with dramatic effect but no usability. What prevailed, in the end, was a naked and strictly demarcated archaeological monument, establishing the national identity and the possibility of an aphaeretic architecture.

Plan Voisin

Exhibited at the Salon d'Automne in 1922, Le Corbusier's project La Ville Contemporaine established the ideology of the modern movement. In the history of urbanism, the Plan Voisin has often served as a symbol of the modern movement's dismissive attitude toward the past. Many architects and theorists such as Colin Rowe, Stanislaus von Moos, and Richard Sennett argue that the Plan Voisin treated the historical context of Paris as a tabula rasa.

One aspect that suggests otherwise is the presence of historical monuments in the first draft of Le Corbusier's Plan Voisin *(fig. 3)*.[11] This gesture indicates an interrelation of subtraction and preservation. Within the modernist ambition to erase the past, a strategy toward the historical urban context can be read, one which is related to aphaeresis. A subtractive protocol is applied as a filter to the historical context of Paris. The interplay of preservation options is a protocol of aphaeresis in this case: objects of conservation are "constructed" through the process of selection—they might be singled out as culturally significant, rare, or representative of their age—yet once they are preserved in preference to others, they reveal a distance between what they are and what they were through the very act of representing their cultural value.

Critical conservation work is a means of unraveling hierarchies in architecture. In Le Corbusier's Plan Voisin, the close relationship between destruction and preservation is clear: objects of conservation are constructed through a process of selection. The goal of critical conservation is to integrate growth and preservation into one interrelated process of urban improvement, rather than simply working with preservation and "architecture" as independent disciplines.

[9] Michael Herzfeld, *Ours Once More: Folklore, Ideology, and the Making of Modern Greece* (Austin: University of Texas Press, 1982).

[10] Katheri Stathi, "Athens in the Ottoman Map of 1827," in *Athens Social Atlas*, ed. Thomas Maloutas and Stavros Nikiforos Spyrellis (2015), http://www.athenssocialatlas.gr/en/article/ottoman-map-1827/.

[11] Thordis Arrhenius, "Restoration in the Machine Age: Themes of Conservation in Le Corbusier's Plan Voisin," *AA Files*, no. 38 (spring 1999): 10–22.

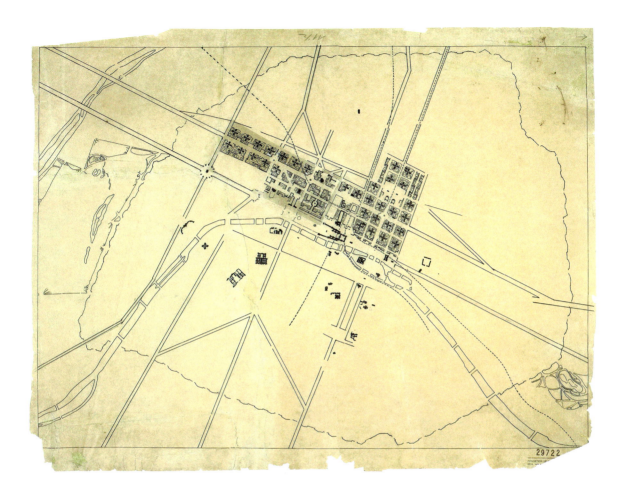

fig. 3
Le Corbusier, Plan Voisin, Paris, 1925. © F.L.C. / Adagp, Paris 2022. Photo: F.L.C. / Adagp Images.

The transformation of existing buildings lies in the space between architecture, preservation, and urban planning. Architecture tends to focus on new constructions, conservation on original conditions and maintenance conditions, and urban planning on a scale much more extensive than either. So, it is essential to bring these disciplines into a dialogue. How might architects recontextualize the historical? How could one think about architectural form as operating, relationally, in response to structures already there? Does this approach require a different set of design tools? What kind of design issues come up while working with existing architecture? Preservation is always politically loaded and, as such, is very different from the design practice of stand-alone buildings; it requires a relational process, constantly analyzing and responding to something that is already there.

Cap de Creus

A similar subtractive protocol was used to reappropriate the tourist infrastructure of Club Med in the Cap de Creus. The peninsula of Cap de Creus lies twenty-five kilometers south of the French border, at the far northeastern corner of Catalonia. In 1961 a small "vacation village" was built by the French company Club Med SAS, which developed some of the first "all-inclusive" summer resorts on the Mediterranean coast. The Club Med in Cap de Creus was planned to accommodate 1,200 people, mostly French, in a friendly setting emphasizing leisure activities and sensual pleasures. By 1980, similar resorts had been developed across the Mediterranean coast. However, in 1998 the whole area around the Club Med village

was declared a natural park.¹² The very point where the resort was built was classified as a territory with the highest levels of protection due to its outstanding geological and botanical value. This declaration was the beginning of the end for the Club Med. In the summer of 2003, the small vacation village received its very last visitors.

Club Med's tourist infrastructure lay abandoned for the next couple of years and gradually turned into a picturesque destination for curious visitors of all kinds: architecture lovers, hikers, and ecologists. Finally, in 2005, the Spanish government bought the property for approximately €4 million from the State Administration and the Department of the Environment, intending to restore and return the developed land to the integral natural reserved ecosystem of Cap de Creus. A few years later, and after many ferocious debates, one of the most significant restoration projects in the Mediterranean Basin began. Led by landscape architects Estudi Martí Franch (EMF) and architect Ton Ardèvol, the ecological interventions were considered innovative and documented as prototypical methods for ecological practice. These interventions throughout the landscape, with a network of paths aiming to highlight the contrast between the memory of the vacation village and the current revived picturesque image, created a framework of abstract programs and uses.

EMF and Ardèvol's novel design strategy at Cap des Creus reappropriates a sensitive landscape *(fig. 4)*. The landscape is made a cultural experience through aphaeresis, the ideal topography designed based on subtraction—a counterstrategy to prevailing modes of development. The most important part of this project is not the minimalistic design of the additions but the designed process of aphaeresis as an architectural tool.

Here subtraction functioned as a design tool in a set of exchanges, advances, aggressions, and attritions. Various architects and communities endlessly debated the relationship

fig. 4
EMF Landscape Architects + J/T Ardèvol S.L.: Tudela-Culip Restoration Project on Cap de Creus, Spain, 2010– 2013; above: the site after restoration, below: the site before restoration. Photos: © Martí Franch.

¹² Paris Tsartas, "Tourism Development in Greek Insular and Coastal Areas: Sociocultural Changes and Crucial Policy Issues," *Journal of Sustainable Tourism* 11, no. 2/3 (2003), 116–32.

between architecture, territory, and tourism before the decision was made to "subtract" all constructions, along with all the cultural values associated with them. As Julia Schulz-Dornburg poignantly notes, the project at Cap de Creus is a story of "unbuilding" where, after the subtraction of the Club Med infrastructure, the landscape was reclaimed by nature.[13] The exciting thing about this radical project is the dematerialization of time and space. The critical decision to tear apart the famous resort became a bold political statement; a robust design gesture of erasure transformed a seemingly ordinary landscape into a significant political terrain. Club Med's subtractive project vividly illustrates that the landscape itself is the primary reason for touristic development and, paradoxically, the first thing to be sacrificed for this development. Thus, subtraction in this case emerges not as a mere act of removal and destruction but as a critical tool for political and architectural reappropriation.

Conclusion

"It's much easier to imagine the end of all life on earth than a much more modest radical change in capitalism" *(Slavoj Žižek)*

It is always important to keep in mind that architectural and urban forms are the result of political and economic forces. As Žižek's provocative quote suggests, those forces are impossible to tame. Therefore, it would be naive to think or imagine that new architectural methods and design strategies can transform underlying socioeconomic structures. However, growing arguments and endeavors for a more sustainable relationship between these forces and the built landscape are rendering subtraction a key design strategy and a way out of the current deadlock. Like any other capitalist venture, the tourism industry has the extraction of revenue and the maximization of profit as a primary aim. The proposed design strategy of aphaeresis challenges the existing pattern by introducing an alternative method for a socially and environmentally responsible cultural economy.

To sum up, as Manuel Shvartzberg Carrió aptly notes, from Vitruvius to modern discourses, a distinction has been made between architecture as building and as culture.[14] Building upon this distinction, I pursue the cultural aspect of architecture by stressing the act of aphaeresis as a way to transform the established relation between culture and landscape. Although the design strategy of aphaeresis was tailored to the peculiarities of the Acropolis, Cap de Creus, and the Plan Voisin, this seminal idea could be further developed into a more integrated and broadly applicable model.

Finally, one of the seminal conclusions of this formative work is that the "landscape" remains a highly political discourse in the etymological sense of the term (*politikos*, "relating to citizens"). Pier Vittorio Aureli, in his article "The Theology of Tabula Rasa," re-actualized Walter Benjamin's "political theology" when he concluded that "we are no longer expected to do something; rather, we should make room."[15] The design strategy of aphaeresis could leverage the critical resources of a place to "make room" and instigate a new balance between culture, landscape, and architecture.

[13] Julia Schulz-Dornburg, *Ruinas modernas, una topografía de lucro* (Barcelona: Àmbit Serveis Editorials, 2012).

[14] Manuel Shvartzberg-Carrió, "Architecture: The Geontopolitics of Knowledge and Time," Archinect, January 4, 2018, https://archinect.com/activity.

[15] Pier Vittorio Aureli, "The Theology of Tabula Rasa: Walter Benjamin and Architecture in the Age of Precarity," *Log*, no. 27 (2013), 111–27.

Biography

Konstantinos Petrakos is an adjunct faculty of architecture at the University of Patras, Greece, where he teaches studios and courses. He is research coordinator of the ongoing design research www.coastaldomains.upatras.gr. He is currently a PhD candidate in architectural theory at the University of Patras and he was awarded a master of architecture from Cornell University in 2017. His academic research focuses on ethical and aesthetic questions that arise from aphaeresis in urbanism. He investigates the influence or relevancy of subtraction on contemporary architectural practice from a philosophical and social point of view.

Nineteen Verdicts on the Viking Ship Hall

Morten Birk Jørgensen

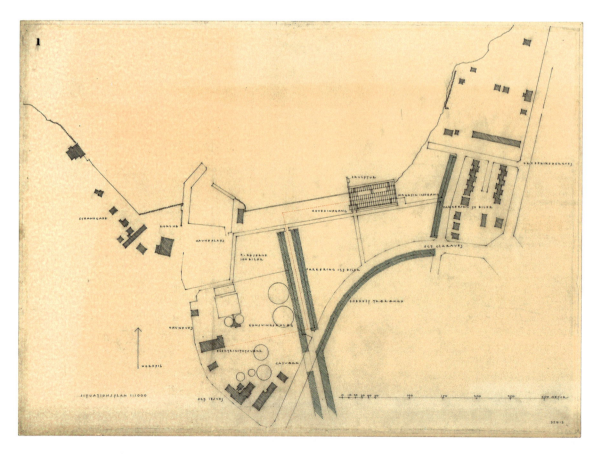

fig. 1
The site plan shows the Viking Ship Hall situated where the free coastline meets a straight stone edge.
Credit: The Danish Art Library. Drawing: Erik Christian Sørensen.

This essay examines the unsettled history of the Viking Ship Hall, opened in 1969 and designed by architect Erik Christian Sørensen. A publicly accessible exposed concrete structure for the exhibition of five Viking ships from an adjacent archaeological site, the building was immediately celebrated for its architectural values and listed less than thirty years after its inauguration. However, technical deficiencies in the building became apparent, and since a storm surge threatened to harm the ships, the future of the building has been uncertain. Through an exposition of acclamations and condemnations, the essay discusses the effect of architectural criticism and judgment.

Architectural criticism is oftentimes considered an evaluative enterprise. The object of criticism must exist before criticism itself, and when that object is a built piece of architecture, the critical assessment rarely directly influences its presence, we suppose. This essay concerns a case where it has. Architectural judgment, whether in favor or in disdain of the building, has determined its fate multiple times. The building in question is a hall built for the assembling and exhibition of five Viking ships found in the late 1950s on the seabed in Roskilde Fjord. In this essay, a range of events, assessments, judgments, and statements are gathered as nineteen verdicts on the life and death of the building. Passed by persons, institutions, materials, or meteorological incidents, each contributes to the unsettled case. Discussing the outcome of the verdicts showcases which effects architectural criticism had, could have had, or maybe should have had in this case or in similar cases in the future.

Verdict 1 **The Architect's Intention**

Soon after the excavation of the ships, the National Museum of Denmark arranged an invited competition for the design of a museum hall, won by Erik Christian Sørensen, dean and professor at the Royal Danish Academy. The first public commentary on the Viking Ship Hall was published in the Danish journal *Arkitekten* following the competition in 1963 and included an extract of the project description and a statement from the jury. "Verdict I" is the project description, where the siting of the building was rationalized by three main arguments: the shape of the coastline where a stone pier meets the free coastline; the view over the fjord from the town rising to the south; and the connection with a park. Consideration of the building can be made from a "purely aesthetic, direct juxtaposition of the ship hulls and the human size," Sørensen declared.[1] The closeness to the water and the silhouette of the ships cast onto the surface of the sea is crucial. The structure is a system of coordinates in which the curved hulls can be read. Displacement of the floor level permits the viewer to have an overview, seeing the ships at a distance; it optimizes the use of space. No barriers or railings separate the viewer from the ships and innovative skylights regulate daylight on the scale of both the day and the year. The surfaces are a particular collocation of concrete cast in situ with visible imprints from the formwork, precast columns, white-painted bricks, plastered surfaces, and a ceiling of pine planks. Apart from the ceiling, wood does not appear elsewhere in the building to pay regard to the ships. A request in the program for an open-air restaurant is

keywords:

architecture criticism, judgment, cultural heritage, Viking Ship Hall, Erik Christian Sørensen

[1] Erik Christian Sørensen, "Et vikinge-skibsmuseum I Roskilde," *Arkitekten* 13 (1963): 245, my translation.

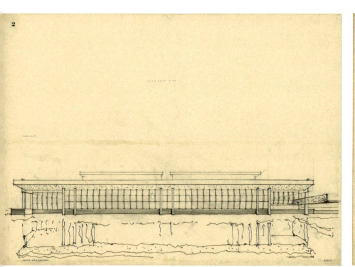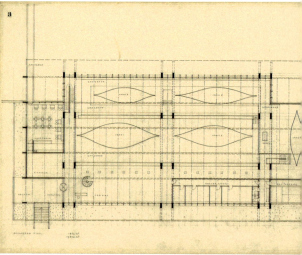

considered, by Erik Christian Sørensen, to be in conflict with the position and the character of the building. "By an exposed museum hall, an open-air restaurant 'family garden'-atmosphere will be intolerable," he asserts.[2]

Verdict 2 **Assessing the Vision**

The jury statement printed along with the project description was the first external verdict on the proposed Viking Ship Hall. It emphasized the well-chosen location that allowed for views over the fjord from the town of Roskilde and supported the planned tree-lined avenue between the cathedral and the fjord. The architecture was described as "interesting"; the position of the ships was considered felicitous both architecturally and curatorially, as it provided visitors an overview while also enabling viewing from various vertical and horizontal perspectives. The view of the ships in silhouette with the fjord as background was of great importance, and the proposal worked "seriously"[3] with light problems, incorporating both daylight and artificial lighting. The statement welcomed the design's accommodation for early visitation, during which the public could follow the work of placing the ships into their final position. It was stressed that the project would be of a moderate volume. It was a valuable solution to the brief, and the jury unanimously selected it as the winner.

Verdict 3 **Approving the Result**

In 1969, the year of inauguration for the Viking Ship Hall, Erik Christian Sørensen was bestowed with the then acclaimed Wood Award. Chairman of the jury was Poul Erik Skriver, a prominent Danish architecture critic and editor. His ceremonial speech was published in *Arkitekten* and focused mainly on the Viking Ship Hall.[4] Skriver began with a reflection that the Wood Award was awarded to an architect whose chief work was a concrete building; a choice he justified by virtue of the wood formwork, whose grain structure clearly appeared as ornamentation. Following a reiteration of the qualities outlined in the project description, he emphasized that the building was prepared for extension, something considered exemplary in a time where everything was changing so rapidly. The ostensibly unshakable surroundings seemed a comforting safeguard for the ships, which by coincidence have survived the human desire to discard and renew. "In this building, the old ships will always remain the primary zone of attention," Skriver stated. "Relatively, it is only for this brief observation that our focus has been distracted and drawn to the building and its architect, who will probably be the first to acknowledge that also this is a quality of the building, that it will eventually occupy a more neutral and less conspicuous role in this museum environment."

fig. 2
The elevation of the building facade reflected in the water.
Credit: The Danish Art Library. Drawing: Erik Christian Sørensen.

fig. 3
The plan shows the organization in a system of coordinates that emphasize the curves of the ship hulls.
Credit: The Danish Art Library. Drawing: Erik Christian Sørensen.

[2] Sørensen, "Et vikingeskibsmuseum I Roskilde," 246, my translation.
[3] "Et vikingeskibsmuseum i Roskilde," *Arkitekten* 13 (1963), 245, my translation.
[4] Poul Erik Skriver, "Træprisen 1969," *Arkitekten* 20 (1969), 476–77.

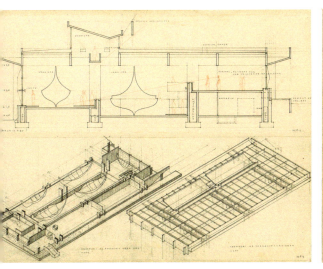 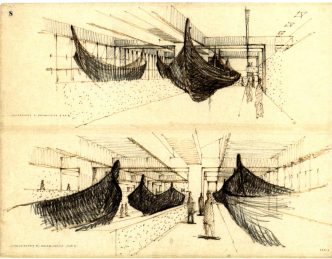

Verdict 4 **Prescient Engineers with Critical Curiosity**

Parallel to the attention the Viking Ship Hall received in architectural media, the weekly engineering journal *The Engineer* followed the case. During construction in 1967 they described the challenges of placing a building on the brink of the fjord and how pillars were cast twelve meters below ground with the risk of flooding the formwork.[5] Prior to the inauguration in 1969, they published an interview with the museum director, curator, and civil engineer Ole Crumlin-Pedersen that asked critical questions regarding climate control in the hall. They had a "very fine"[6] climate system that could bring the humidity down to 65 percent in half an hour, even after a thunderstorm, Crumlin-Pedersen asserted. Another question cast doubt upon the economic conditions of the self-governing museum, which had funded construction with a loan. Crumlin-Pedersen replied that the museum hoped to generate a profit from the visitors to invest in future maritime excavations, several of which were on hold. Another interview in *The Engineer* also revealed public skepticism toward the new museum: "Many passers-by have sulked that the museum is built in raw concrete. Unpleasant things have been said about this building . . . ."[7]

Verdict 5 **New Situation and Request for Extension**

After the initial attention surrounding the construction abated, a good twenty years went by without public verdicts. Around 1992, the museum initiated preparations for an extension of the Viking Ship Hall. Now that the excavations, assembly, and studies of the archaeological find were well in progress, they wished for facilities for the construction of replicas of the Viking ships, better research facilities, and a more engaging museum. With these plans, new attention arose around the museum and Viking Ship Hall, and the journal *Arkitektur DK* published an article on the building including an extension proposal by Erik Christian Sørensen. It was written by the same Poul Erik Skriver who had chaired the Wood Award twenty-three years earlier, and who now claimed the Viking Ship Hall to be "among Denmark's finest museum buildings."[8] Despite the praise from Skriver, a postscript clarified that the extension proposal by Sørensen had now been canceled in favor of a museum island further west. To support a public discussion, the Roskilde municipality published a folder outlining possible futures for the museum island. In response to this, the members of the local council from the Socialist People's Party filed a minority declaration criticizing how "the intentions in the discussion paper are marked by a tourist-centered thinking."[9] Despite extensive objections to the plan,[10] the museum island was put out to tender and constructed in only two years as a fundamentally different building cluster some hundred meters west of the Viking Ship Hall.

fig. 4
Displacement of the floor levels as shown in the section allows the visitor to view the ships from multiple perspectives.
Credit: The Danish Art Library.
Drawing: Erik Christian Sørensen.

fig. 5
The hulls are placed on a bedrock of sea stones which establish a clear limit for the visitors that eliminates the need for fences or strings as seen in these perspective drawings.
Credit: The Danish Art Library. Drawing: Erik Christian Sørensen.

[5] Museumsrejsegilde," *Tidsskrift for Ingeniør- og Bygningsvæsen*, September 22, 1967, https://www.e-pages.dk/ingarkiv/6306/?page=17&query=vikingeskibshallen.

[6] "I juni åbnes Vikingeskibshallen, hvor Danmark største puslespil lægges," *Ingeniør- og Bygningsvæsen*, May 16, 1969, 3–4, https://www.e-pages.dk/ingarkiv/10049/?page=4&query=vikingeskibshallen.

[7] "Et 'bådeskur' til 5,5 millioner," *Ingeniør- og Bygningsvæsen*, May 16, 1969, 12, my translation, https://www.e-pages.dk/ingarkiv/6410/?page=12&query=vikingehallen.

[8] Poul Erik Skriver, "Vikingeskibshallen," *Arkitektur DK* 8 (1992), 438–44.

[9] *Helhedsplan for havneområdet—Debatoplæg*, Roskilde Kommune, 1992, Appendix: Mindretalsudtalelse fra Socialistisk Folkeparti.

[10] Among these were an objection from the state council in artistic matters who asked architects not to participate due to the tender being based on honorarium alone. "Arkitekter siger fra overfor ny priskonkurrence," *Politiken*, February 25, 1995, Section 2, p. 12, www.Infomedia.dk.

Verdict 6 A Youngster Listed as National Heritage

A likely reason for the hasty extension process is that in 1995, only twenty-six years after its inauguration, the Viking Ship Hall had been recommended for listed status. (Buildings listed as cultural heritage in Denmark are managed by a governmental office under the Cultural Ministry, hereafter called the heritage authorities.) Two years later, as the museum island opened, the listing of the Viking Ship Hall was completed. The listing description reiterated some points from the project description, but it also provided additional historical and stylistic considerations, describing a "structural clarity and raw finish under influence of Japanese architecture and the architectural mindset that goes under the term 'brutalism.'"[11]

Verdict 7 Wrecked Ambitions for Further Extensions

In 1997, with the new museum island open and the listing complete, the Viking Ship Hall entered another period of being ignored by the national media. The local press in Roskilde, however, kept an eye on the museum, and in December 2005 the newspaper *Dagbladet Roskilde* reported that the museum had new plans for a "restoration and extension"[12] of the listed hall. The project was again designed in collaboration with Erik Christian Sørensen and consisted of a building entirely enclosing the original hall, including some restoration and improved accessibility. In the proposal description, Sørensen called the original hall a "coffin ship,"[13] referring to the technical condition of the structure. The following year, the newspaper reported that the application was rejected by the heritage authorities, who found that the proposal compromised the listing's values.[14]

Verdict 8 A Sinking Ship

In 2010, the Viking Ship Hall once again hit the national media. A report to assess the building's overall condition had been opened after discovery of extensive decay in the concrete structure.[15] The conclusion was that most of the assessed building parts were still functional, but comprehensive restoration was urgently needed. The principal reason was corroding reinforcement that had been placed too close to the concrete surface. Earlier attempts to stop the corrosion with surface treatments had covered the imprint of the wooden formwork on the facades, compromising the architectural expression of the building and thereby the heritage value.[16]

fig. 6
The Viking Ship Hall on the brink of the fjord shortly after construction.
Credit: The Danish Art Library.
Photo: Keld Helmer-Petersen.

fig. 7
The temple-like facade facing land is met by a large, empty lawn.
Credit: The Danish Art Library.
Photo: Keld Helmer-Petersen.

[11] "Vikingeskibshallen," Fredede og Bevaringsværdige Bygninger, Ministry of Culture, accessed July 26, 2021, https://www.kulturarv.dk/fbb/sagvis.pub?sag=7396666.

[12] "Vikingeskibsmuseet vil udvide vikingeskibshallen," *Dagbladet Roskilde*, December 24, 2005, Section 2, p. 2, www.infomedia.dk.

[13] This is referred to in the first application for delisting, see Joy Mogensen and Tinna Damgård-Sørensen, "Ansøgning om affredning af Vikingeskibshallen i Roskilde," Vikingeskibsmuseet, 2016, https://www.vikingeskibsmuseet.dk/frontend/Dokumenter/Ansoegning_om_affredning_af_Vikingeskibshallen_27.09.2016.pdf.

[14] "Styrelse siger nej til udbygningsplan," *Dagbladet Roskilde*, February 3, 2007, Section 2, p. 3, www.infomedia.dk.

[15] "Fredet museum for vikingeskibe ruster og krakelerer," *Ingeniøren*, October 19, 2010.

[16] Erik Møller Arkitekter, "Notat vedr. status på forprojekt for restaurering af Vikingeskibsmuseet," November 11, 2010, https://www.vikingeskibsmuseet.dk/frontend/Grafik/TI-findings.GIF.

fig. 8
The short facade facing west.
Credit: The Danish Art Library.
Photo: Keld Helmer-Petersen.

fig. 9
The skeleton for the ships resting on the sea stones prior to the assembling of the wood pieces.
Credit: The Danish Art Library.
Photo: Keld Helmer-Petersen.

Verdict 9 **Recapitulation**

Erik Christian Sørensen died in 2011, and the obituary underscored the significance of the Viking Ship Hall in his oeuvre. The architecture critic Torben Weirup, in *Berlingske Tidende*, described Sørensen as "one of the twentieth century's most important Danish architects"[17] and the Viking Ship Hall as a "chief work in Modern Danish architecture."[18] In *Politiken*, Professor Christoffer Harlang also positioned Sørensen as one of the principle figures in Danish architecture, though also someone who was considered by many to embody an "elitist aesthetic."[19]

Verdict 10 **Preserving Concrete Heritage**

In 2013, Professor Christoffer Harlang gave an interview in *Arkitekten* that focused on the heritage and listing of postwar concrete buildings. Harlang was the chairman of a governmental heritage council (hereafter referred to as the heritage council) that advised the cultural minister on heritage matters. He described the concrete buildings from the period as being in a fragile situation where technical problems often motivated large renovation projects. Focusing on the development of the Viking Ship Hall, Harlang referred to the recently finished report on its technical condition and stated that the biggest problem was the surface treatment done some fifteen years prior that covered the concrete with a plastic paint. Beforehand, the building had been sandblasted, so even a cleaning procedure would not be able to recover the architecturally important formwork imprint. The main problem of concrete peeling off had been caused by an incorrect type of aggregate in the original structure. The only solution would be to remove the entire concrete surface and cast a new one with formwork like the original.[20]

Verdict 11 **A Meteorological Sentence**

On December 6 in the same year, a winter storm hit northwestern Europe and caused an extraordinary storm surge in Roskilde Fjord, where the water rose above the windows of the Viking Ship Hall. Water entered the exhibition space and only a brave fight with sandbags by a group of museum employees and local volunteers prevented damage to the ships. The story of the Viking Ship Hall under water and the alarming photos taken that night reached all major national newspapers in the days following.

[17] Torben Weirup, "Banebrydende arkitekt," *Berlingske Tidende*, August 23, 2011, Section 1, p. 23, www.infomedia.dk.
[18] Ibid.
[19] Christoffer Harlang, "En vital og generøs aristokrat," *Politiken*, August 22, 2011, 9, www.infomedia.dk.
[20] Henrik Schafranek, "Værdig Beton," *Arkitekten* 2 (2013): 55, www.infomedia.dk.

fig. 10
When entering the Viking Ship Hall, the large hulls appear in silhouette against the fjord where they once sailed.
Credit: The Danish Art Library.
Photo: Keld Helmer-Petersen.

Verdict 12 **A Political Sentence**

The Viking Ship Hall's next storm arose in the media in January 2016 when Alex Ahrendsen, cultural spokesman for the far-right Danish People's Party, proposed to tear down the building and erect a new one on the site. The existing building was decaying, and there were problems with heating and daylight, Ahrendsen argued, continuing as follows: "[T]he present building [is], to put it nicely, a monstrosity from the late 1960s which doesn't visually communicate that this is a unique Viking attraction. So, rather than renovating something which is not very appealing to renovate—because it is, building-wise and aesthetically, constructed wrong—it is better to remove the building and erect a new one."[21] Instead of refurbishing the existing building, Ahrendsen proposed erecting an "iconic building in Viking style"[22] and further pushed this proposal, saying: "We find ourselves in an international Viking competition where Norway is especially far ahead. They aim very high. So it would be aggravating if we sit back and leave Denmark with a disintegrating concrete museum which scares away the tourists."[23] Several architects, architectural writers, and cultural critics and journalists reacted to the proposal. The editor of *Arkitekten* wrote an editorial that accused Ahrendsen of interfering in matters outside of his domain as a politician.[24] Christoffer Harlang compared the proposal with the iconoclastic actions of the Taliban and Islamic State, to which Ahrendsen replied as follows: "Architects have over time changed from being craftsmen in service of the people to acting like artists with some kind of divine sight from above. This is the entire tradition from the Bauhaus and Le Corbusier, through Cultural Radicalism and to the modernist Stalinist buildings in the east. My political vision is that architecture once again becomes the servant of the people."[25]

Verdict 13 **Requested Release from Listing**

In September 2016, the museum submitted an application to the heritage authorities for the delisting of the Viking Ship Hall. They no longer saw it as a realistic opportunity for a project that would satisfy all actors and which could raise the necessary funding. They concluded that the priority was now to save the Viking ships rather than the Viking Ship Hall. Along with the application they provided thorough documentation of the case, including restoration proposals and more than a dozen technical reports. They included statements from various

[21] Nicolaj Heltoft, "DF vil rive Vikingeskibsmuseet ned og rejse et nyt i 'vikingestil' samme sted," *Politiken*, January 27, 2016, 3, www.infomedia.dk.
[22] Ibid.
[23] Ibid.
[24] Martin Keiding, "Kvalitetssikring," *Arkitekten* 2 (2016): 5, www.infomedia.dk.
[25] Nikolaj Heltoft, "Arkitekturstorm mod DF-forslag om nedrivning af fredet museumshal," *Politiken*, January 28, 2016, 5, www.infomedia.dk.

professional consultants describing technical problems applying to all vital building components and functional problems concerning climate, accessibility, infrastructural inadequacies, and lack of potential for contemporary outreach. One of the last reports from the Technological Institute estimated the lifetime of the vital building elements to be eight to ten years.[26]

Verdict 14 **Keeping Control**

On December 19, 2017, the heritage authorities rejected the application with a fifteen-page statement explaining the case, the process, and their stance as authority. The rejection was backed by the heritage council, who stated that the heritage values of the Viking Ship Hall were still present. They were open, however, to potential modifications to the building due to the fact that they considered the heritage values to be of a "general character." [27] A range of the recent technical reports found that the technical state of the building was not as bad as previously thought.

Verdict 15 **Trying the Case with the Minister**

The decision from the heritage authorities could be appealed directly to the minister of culture within four weeks, and on January 15, 2018, the museum submitted a complaint concerning the retention of the listing. The museum disagreed with the heritage authorities' reading of the technical reports and refuted the idea that the existing building could remain a safe place for the ships in the long term. They further did not agree with the economic considerations in the retention letter that suggested a restoration was possible in the current economy.[28]

Verdict 16 **Justifying Concrete Architecture**

While the decision from the cultural minister was pending, a book on Danish concrete architecture was published with prominent examples selected, one of them being the Viking Ship Hall. The author, Jørgen Hegner Christiansen, wrote that it is "probably the most expressive brutalist facility in Denmark." [29] The preface by Professor Carsten Thau touched on the hesitant view of the material among laypeople, asserting that "concrete is the modern material par excellence." [30]

Verdict 17 **Political Decree**

Still in 2018, on August 30 the Cultural Ministry replied to the complaint in what they called a final decision. Across seventy-five pages, the ministry justified the decision to abolish the listing on the grounds that the listing values, due to the rising water levels and many other reasons, could not be sustained in the Viking Ship Hall.[31]

Verdict 18 **Architectural Condemnation**

The delisting of the Viking Ship Hall triggered fierce reactions both nationally and internationally. The International Union of Architects wrote to the Danish cultural minister, stating that "the Viking Ship Hall is a unique representation of the Danish architectural canon and is internationally recognized as an eminent contribution to modern architecture." [32] The International Council on Monuments and Sites (ICOMOS) published a heritage alert stating that "Vikingeskibshallen (The Viking Ship Hall) is a masterwork of modern Danish architecture. It is a unique structure that creatively integrates museum, setting and archaeology in a way that transcends historic definitions." [33] The Danish Association of Architects established an entire webpage on the case, compiling a range of articles. In a column from October 2018, Danish architect Søren Johansen stated that "Everything considered, it is hard not to suspect that the delisting and the plan to demolish the hall originates from political pressure and a general displeasure towards the building." [34] Professor Mogens Morgen, former head of the heritage authority, described how the delisting, conducted by the cultural minister against her professional heritage authorities and heritage council, undermined the listing system.[35] The director and the head of the Danish Association of Architects wrote an open letter to the minister of culture stating that the delisting was "cultural-historical vandalism" and that they considered the delisting to be politically motivated.[36]

[26] Joy Mogensen and Tinna Damgård-Sørensen, "Ansøgning om affredning af Vikingeskibshallen i Roskilde," Vikingeskibsmuseet, 2016, https://www.vikingeskibsmuseet.dk/frontend/Dokumenter/Ansoegning_om_affredning_af_Vikingeskibshallen_27.09.2016.pdf.

[27] "Fastholdelse af fredningen af Vikingeskibshallen," *Slots- og Kulturstyrelsen*, December 19, 2017, 2, my translation, https://www.vikingeskibsmuseet.dk/frontend/Dokumenter/WEB_Afgoerelse_Vikingeskibshallen_Roskilde_-_afslag_affredning_2017.pdf.

[28] Joy Mogensen and Tinna Damgaard-Sørensen, "Klage over afgørelse i sag om affredning af Vikingeskibshallen i Roskilde," January 15, 2018, https://www.vikingeskibsmuseet.dk/frontend/Dokumenter/Klage_over_afgoerelse_-_affredning_Vikingeskibshallen_2018-01-15.pdf.

[29] Jørgen Hegner Christiansen, *Dansk Betonarkitektur* (Copenhagen: Forlaget Vandkunsten, 2018).

[30] Carsten Thau, "Beton—den flydende sten," in *Dansk Betonarkitektur*, ed. Jørgen Hegner Christiansen (Copenhagen: Forlaget Vandkunsten, 2018), 9.

[31] Katrine Tarp, "Kulturministeriets afgørelse vedr. klage over Slots- og Kulturstyrelsens afslag på at ophæve fredningen af Vikingskibshallen," Kulturministeriet, August 30, 2018, https://www.vikingeskibsmuseet.dk/frontend/Dokumenter/Endelig_afgoerelse_om_Vikingeskibshallen_575414_16_0.pdf.

[32] Thomas Vonier, December 10, 2018, https://www.google.com/url?sa=t&rct=j&q=&esrc=s&source=web&cd=&ved=2ahUKEwirlu26p_bxAhUaHewKHadhAjgQFjAPegQIMxAD&url=https%3A%2F%2Fwww.icomos.org%2Fimages%2F181210_LetterViking-Ship-Hall.pdf&usg=AOvVaw3slWSolPfMac6UonvBQZ85.

[33] ICOMOS, "Heritage Alert: The Viking Ship Hall—Roskilde, Denmark," December 19, 2018, https://www.icomos.org/en/get-involved/inform-us/heritage-alert/current-alerts/53198-heritage-alert-the-viking-ship-hall-roskilde-denmark.

[34] Søren Johansen, "Et tempel i rå beton," *Arkitekten* 8 (2018).

[35] Cecilie Frydenlund Nielsen, "Affredning er en underminering af fredningsredskabet," The Danish Association for Architects, accessed July 26, 2021, https://arkitektforeningen.dk/nyheder/affredning-er-en-underminering-af-fredningsredskabet/.

[36] Lars Autrup and Natalie Mossin, "Kulturhistorisk Vandalisme," arkitektforeningen.dk, accessed July 26, 2021, https://arkitektforeningen.dk/nyheder/kulturhistorisk-vandalisme-2/.

fig. 11
The flooding of the building during a storm in 2013.
Credit: The Viking Ship Museum in Roskilde. Photo: Werner Karrasch.

Verdict 19 **New Prospects**
Following the delisting, the Viking Ship Museum published a prospect for a new museum in March 2019. In the foreword it is stated that: "The new museum shall pass on the unique values and permit a complete renewal of the histories and dissemination activities of the museum. The launch pad shall be maritime and the view global. The history shall be relevant for all visitors of the museum, including the many foreign guests."[37]

Reviewing the Verdicts
These nineteen verdicts are a chronological exposition of the main events in the life of the Viking Ship Hall. Some are passed by architecture critics, others by heritage professionals, and yet others by politicians. They are pronounced by an aggregate used in the concrete in 1967/68, heralded by engineers as messengers some forty years later, and by climate changes that result in larger and more frequent storm surges. The increased influence of the experience economy has overridden former museum priorities, or is it the understanding of strong historical dissemination that is altered? Whether one verdict is more valid than another is not the focus of this essay. What consequences they have had, however, is.

Limiting the verdicts to those addressed to the architectural community presents a remarkably boring trajectory. From the jury statement, to the Wood Award, to the most recent writings in *Arkitekten* and the book on Danish concrete, they all praise the characteristics described by Erik Christian Sørensen in his competition proposal. The only clear evolution is the extent to which the value of the building is ascribed, and it peaks with the delisting. None of them bother to add new readings or counter-analyses that could reveal new insights. Did Sørensen really manage to describe all major qualities so precisely that there is not anything to add? Or do the architects lack the capacities to experience the building anew? If the Viking Ship Hall is so valuable, as is argued, then criticism ought to be able to generate such new insights from a continued rereading of its architecture.

    Looking back at the coverage in *The Engineer* during the 1960s is more surprising, as they seem to have foreseen several issues that have plagued the building up until today. In their coverage and interviews they focus on the technical conditions, announce a laypeople

[37] "Prospekt for et nyt Vikingeskibsmuseum," Vikingeskibsmuseet, March, 2019, https://www.vikingeskibsmuseet.dk/frontend/Dokumenter/Vikingeskibsmuseum_prospekt_060319_low.pdf.

fig. 12
The facade was reinforced to avoid the glass panes cracking and the ships were covered for protection during the storm surge.
Credit: The Viking Ship Museum in Roskilde. Photo: Werner Karrasch.

opposition to the concrete structure, and find interest in the economic value of the Viking Ship Hall to the museum. I will follow these three tracks. First, the technical difficulties of placing a building for highly valuable and fragile objects on the brink of a fjord: while the coverage rested on a technical interest in the solution of casting the foundation, it also triggered critical questions about the control of the indoor climate. Both decay in the concrete and the problem of securing the ships result from the technically challenging position. Since the problems with the concrete received public attention in 2010, the technical issues have been the main center of attention. Second, *The Engineer* reports of the problem of laypeople opposing the concrete structure: the opposition may not be considerably surprising, as concrete has always been a source of contention, but if the Viking Ship Hall is a prime example of the use of concrete in architecture, then it ought to be a good case to address this disagreement and bridge the divide between architects and laypeople. Christoffer Harlang touched upon the elitist view of Erik Christian Sørensen in his obituary, and this "elite versus the people" dynamic seems vital in this case. In what appears to be a pivotal verdict, Alex Ahrendsen stood forward as a representative of the people, distancing himself from the architectural elite that believe they have a "divine sight." These political oppositions are suggested by the director and president of the Danish Association of Architects as the actual motivation for the final delisting by the cultural minister against her own advisors. Third, *The Engineer* probe of the economic conditions surrounding the hall: despite the many entangled motivations behind the requests for continuous extensions and rebuilds from the museum, it is hard not to see the economic motivation for increased tourism as one of them. This "tourist-thinking," as opposed by the Socialist People's Party in 1992, continues in an ungraceful alliance with the stylistic and ideological criticism by Ahrendsen and even stands out clearly in the prospects for the museum following the delisting. All these tracks, absent in the architectural coverage, appeared in *The Engineer* already at the time of the inauguration.

The exposition of these nineteen verdicts on the Viking Ship Hall prompts much speculation on which of the many motivations are really the strongest, and to whom. Were the heritage authorities and advisory board always too conservative in their views and unworldly in their decisions, or has the museum always tried to sneak hidden agendas into its extension requests?

fig. 13
The Viking Ship Hall with the medieval Roskilde Cathedral in the background.
Credit: The Viking Ship Museum in Roskilde. Photo: Werner Karrasch.

Did Erik Christian Sørensen refuse all common sense by insisting on building these slender concrete girders on the brink of a fjord, or should he rather be seen as a part of a liberating architectural movement? Has climate change simply altered the conditions of architecture, leaving us with no other choice than to relinquish pivotal works of modernism, or should we alternatively just accept the cost of their preservation? Is it a wave of populist nationalist romanticism that presently utilizes a position of strength for iconoclastic purposes? Is it a museum that wants to jump on the bandwagon of the experience economy and prioritize their profit over the preservation of cultural heritage? The answers to such questions will probably never find mutual agreement.

Zooming in again on the actions of the architectural community, there is one major achievement to note. With relatively few public announcements, the Viking Ship Hall gained a reputation strong enough to get it listed when less than thirty years old. It is fair to say that architects play a considerable role in the heritage authority in Denmark, and that the listing of the Viking Ship Hall rests on the architectural qualities rather than the cultural-historical significance. On the technocratic level, the architectural community has managed to establish an impressive reputation for the building. In this case, it is, however, also an achievement with a time limit. Other roles of critique were neglected. Architectural critique did not manage to mobilize a public appreciation of the building to an extent that politicians might fight for its preservation. Instead, the political sentence was passed by a single opponent and realized by an uncommitted cultural minister. While the professional criticism that established the work in the architectural community has been important, a focus on an inclusive discussion might have been favorable in the long run.

The focus of all architectural commentary and coverage on the Viking Ship Hall for the first forty years was on the spatial and aesthetic qualities of the building. These qualities can reasonably be said to reside at the core of the architectural discipline. However, aspects other than these have been demonstrated as crucial for this specific building. Its technical capacities have become a central topic of discussion. A strong architectural criticism could have been engaged with the negotiations between architect and engineer on the slenderness of the girders. A public disdain for concrete was apparent in the 1960s and has become decisive for the building. A strong architectural criticism could have engaged in discussions on this topic, too. As museums have become more engaging and playful, a strong architectural criticism could have defended the Viking Ship Hall for its capacity to convey historical artifacts in another manner. As such, the case suggests a discipline of architectural criticism that is preoccupied with architecture per se, but also one which ought to engage more with the affairs of adjacent disciplines and societal matters at large. It could likely stimulate public concern for a case like the Viking Ship Hall, and it might also skew the focus of the architectural discipline toward new domains.

As mentioned in the first paragraphs of this essay, architectural criticism on the Viking Ship Hall has had direct influence on its presence and on its uncertain future. With this essay, I suggest that a more explicit criticism, one that honestly engaged with the paradoxes inherent in the building, could have laid the foundation for a proper discussion on the actions needed to safeguard its qualities. I furthermore suggest that architectural criticism needs to engage in a more straightforward manner with the positions and concerns of the public if architecture is to escape the populist accusation of elitism. The architecture of the Viking Ship Hall has much to offer future generations in their conception of the past. In its present state of uncertainty it is doubtful if it will, and, as critics, we ought to acknowledge our complicity and reform our engagement with architecture.

Biography

Morten Birk Jørgensen is an architect, researcher, and critic. He is associate professor at the Institute of Architecture and Culture at the Royal Academy in Copenhagen and is affiliated with the research groups Cultural Heritage, Transformation and Restoration, and Meaning & Measure in Architecture. His primary research field is the practice of judgments in architecture with particular attention to criticism, valuation, certification, and awards. Jørgensen has cofounded the platform Damn critics! for experiments with architecture and criticism. He has initiated the relaunch of the Copenhagen-based architecture award Årets Arne from the Danish Association of Architects with a focus on criteria, evaluation process, transparency, and the contribution to public discourse. He is the editor of the newly established *Magasin for Bygningskunst og Kultur*, published by the Institute of Architecture and Culture at the Royal Danish Academy.

Architectural Criticism on Post–World War II Collective Housing: Complicit in a Historical Prejudice?

Carolina Chaves

fig. 1
Robin Hood Gardens (1968–1972) by Alison and Peter Smithson showing the "streets in the air." Photo taken on a Twentieth Century Society visit to Robin Hood Gardens in 2008. © Steve Cadman.

Architectural criticism of the 1960s and 1970s contributed to the unpopularity of post–World War II collective housing, while criticism of the 1980s and 1990s rendered it obsolete. To this day, unpopularity and obsolescence are buzzwords used to justify demolitions and disfigurement, neglecting both the cultural significance and the social dimensions of these ensembles. The Robin Hood Gardens (RHG) estate will be used as an example to analyze how architectural criticism may have contributed to this culture of erasure by examining the public struggle to preserve the building in local journals and architectural magazines, confronting historical and contemporary discourses with the building itself.

Architectural Criticism on Post–World War II Collective Housing

"A false or malicious criticism may do much injury to the minds of others; a stupid invention, either in prose or verse, is quite harmless."[1]

Matthew Arnold's judgment, though referring to literary criticism, can easily be applied to architecture. It is common for our opinion of a place or site to come from what we have read or heard about it rather than from the actual experience on site. Even film[2] has a significant influence on how we frame our assessment.

The architectural criticism of the 1960s and 1970s contributed to the general unpopularity of post–World War II collective housing, while the criticism of the 1980s and 1990s made it obsolete. Unpopularity and obsolescence are still the buzzwords used today to justify demolitions and disfigurement, neglecting both the cultural significance and social dimensions of these ensembles. Justified by "urban regeneration projects" and supported by historical prejudice, a global wave of demolition is bearing down on the masterpieces of postwar modernist heritage.

The Heygate Estate (London, 1971–1974 / 2011–2014), Rochor Centre (Singapore, 1977 / 2018), and Monmousseau Building (Lyon, 1965–1973 / 2005–2021) are just some of the cases where postwar collective housing around the world has been demolished in the past decade. It is noteworthy that all these cases were justified with arguments emphasizing the low incomes of the tenants, the lack of maintenance, the failure to create a sense of community, and the reputations for crime, drugs, prostitution, and vandalism. However, there was no mention of the fact that these housing estates were located on land of high value. In this sense, Maya Dukmasova[3] lucidly argues that:

What was once a public asset has been drained of its value, disassembled, and redistributed into private hands. For this to happen, a wide consensus had to emerge that public housing couldn't be fixed. We had to believe that problems in public housing were inevitable because there is something naturally wrong with poor people living together.

keywords:

Robin Hood Gardens, historical bias, architectural criticism, historic preservation

[1] Matthew Arnold, "The Function of Criticism in the Present Time," in *Essays in Criticism* (London and Cambridge: Macmillan and Co., 1865), 3.

[2] It is worth mentioning that numerous fictional movies between the 1960s and the 1980s have used social housing as a setting, and the representation of postwar residential architecture, especially the high-rise typology, is associated with antisocial behavior, anarchy, and chaos: *Cathy Come* Home, directed by Ken Loach (1966), 75 min; *A Clockwork Orange*, directed by Stanley Kubrick (Warner Bros, 1971), 133 min; *High Hopes*, directed by Mike Leigh (Skouras Films, 1988), 112 min. Even recently, residential towers are still featuring as marginal spaces in commercial films: *Attack the Block*, directed by Joe Cornish (Optimum Releasing, 2011), 88 min; *High-Rise*, directed by Ben Wheatley (Studio Canal, 2015), 119 min.

[3] Maya Dukmasova, "Tricknology 101. The Destruction of Public Housing in Atlanta and Chicago Exposes Capitalism's Violent Order," *Jacobin*, nos. 15–16, March 2014, accessed July 2, 2021, https://www.jacobinmag.com/2014/10/tricknology-101.

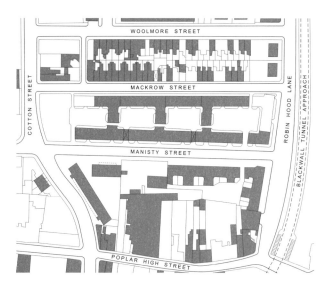
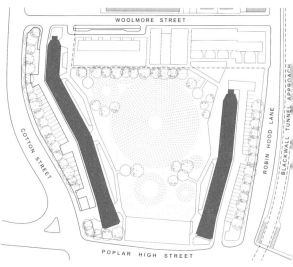

This narrative was underpinned by the argument that the modernist project had failed in its social ambitions. In fact, this argument is a "mystification"[4] (Bristol, 1991) or a "manufactured reality"[5] in service of financial interests and neoliberal policy. Stephen Graham[6] explains, "myths about the inevitable failure of vertical public housing have been generalized to be endlessly repeated as accepted 'facts' in many Western societies." Moreover, it becomes a major problem when these "accepted facts" are used to advocate the destruction of buildings by obscuring their cultural value.

In 2008, Robin Hood Gardens (RHG) became a controversial preservation case, triggering an international plea for its heritage recognition—one which was ultimately unsuccessful. By 2018, demolition of the western block had been completed. Alan Powers[7] described a historically biased critique of RHG that judged it "against a set of standards represented by a different imaginary ideal building," the opposite of a disinterested criticism that takes the object as it really is.

Criticism as a cultural product is deeply enmeshed with its own time, and therefore the present generation, reflecting on its contemporaneity, has a duty to review past critiques and consider them in their social, cultural, and political context. Powers's statement offers an opportunity to update the critique of post–World War II collective housing and reframe the debate—weaving new interpretations and recontextualizing the role of these architectural and urban achievements in contemporary culture, accounting fairly for what the buildings actually represent.

Reflecting upon the RHG case, this paper will analyze how architectural criticism (its methods and strategies) operated by examining the public struggle to preserve the building in local journals and architectural magazines, confronting historical and contemporary discourses around the building itself.

Robin Hood Gardens: Born in a Condemned Context

In an open letter to the English Heritage Advisory Committee in 2008, John Allan,[8] as a member of the committee, argued that Robin Hood Gardens (1966–1972) did not fit all the criteria for listing as a heritage site because it was an out-of-date project that had already been born obsolete. According to his interpretation, the RHG project is a late realization of a thesis elaborated by Peter and Alison Smithson twenty years earlier in their proposed

fig. 2
Sequence of site plans, Poplar, London Borough of Tower Hamlets: 1. site plan of Poplar's urban fabric in the 1950s, © Carolina Chaves; 2. redrawn RHG site layout and proposed landscaping by Alison and Peter Smithson for GLC, © Carolina Chaves; 3. RHG aerial view from 2000 (map data: Google), © 2021 Infoterra Ltd and Bluesky; 4. RHG aerial view from 2021 (map data: Google), © 2021 Landsat/Copernicus.

[4] Katherine Bristol, "The Pruitt-Igoe Myth," Journal of Architecture Education 44, no. 3 (May 1991), 163–71.
[5] Dukmasova, "Tricknology 101. The Destruction of Public Housing in Atlanta and Chicago Exposes Capitalism's Violent Order."
[6] Stephen Graham, "Luxified Skies: How Vertical Urban Housing Became an Elite Preserve," City. Analysis of Urban Change, Theory, Action, no. 5 (2015), 618–45. DOI: 10.1080/13604813.2015.1071113.
[7] Alan Powers, "Fixes, Fluxes and Futures," in Robin Hood Gardens: Re-visions (London: The Twentieth Century Society, 2010), 15–23.
[8] John Allan, "Robin Hood Gardens, Poplar, London," in English Heritage Conservation Bulletin, no. 59 (December 2008), 31.

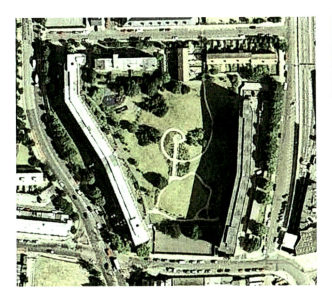

Golden Lane Project (1952), with an outcome inferior to other similar projects (e.g., Park Hill Sheffield and the Barbican Estate). The conclusion was that "the case for *historic* interest is also lost precisely because the project came so late in this phase of modernist architecture in Britain, without however representing a glorious culmination."[9]

After thirty-six years, these arguments echo the very first reviews of RHG, one written by Peter Eisenman,[10] published in *Architectural Design* (September 1972) under the title "Robin Hood Gardens, London E14," and the other by Anthony Pangaro,[11] published in *Architecture Plus* (May 1973) under the title "Beyond Golden Lane, Robin Hood Gardens." It seems no coincidence that both critics are North American architects condemning a modernist housing project completed in the same year as the demolition of Pruitt-Igoe (1972–1976). The point, then, is to understand the building relative to its cultural background, which represents a turning point in the way housing policies and the social agenda of architecture have been interpreted from the 1970s onward.

In this sense, the low level of magazine coverage as evidence of lack of importance, mentioned in the *English Heritage Bulletin*[12] as an argument against listing, speaks more about the cultural context of housing policy and the role of architects and architecture at the time than about the building itself. The special issues entitled "Manplan" published by *The Architectural Review* at the turn of the 1970s (from September 1969 to September 1970, eight issues in total) provide perspective on a period devoted to rethinking categories of society and the role of architects, reflecting a growing interest in the social environment and behavioral approaches. Far from being an isolated case, one can also recall the Italian magazine *Casabella*, which distributed and sponsored "Fotoromanzo": three issues that "describe the housing problem and rethink the role of the architect."[13]

In "Manplan," Hubert de Cronin Hastings, embedded in the revisionist spirit of the 1960s, did not say "that architects are responsible for the mess we're in" but argued, "we've got to accept a large measure of responsibility for the environmental crisis."[14] The 1970s critique, however, would find in the social crisis of the modernist housing program the culmination of an architectural culture that had permission to erase past mistakes: "*If it doesn't work out ... Erase it*,"[15] as published in *The Architectural Forum* (May 1972) and illustrated with a photograph of the falling Pruitt-Igoe.

It is more than relevant to remember that RHG was born in the same year that the modern movement and high-rise public housing, seen as the causes of Pruitt-Igoe's failure,

[9] Ibid.
[10] Peter Eisenman, "Robin Hood Gardens, London E14," in *Architectural Design*, no. 42 (1972), 557–73. The text was later reprinted in *Oppositions*, no. 1 (September 1973) as "From Golden Lane to Robin Hood Gardens; or if You Follow the Yellow Brick Road, it May Not Lead to Golders Green."
[11] Anthony Pangaro, "Beyond Golden Lane, Robin Hood Gardens," in *Architecture Plus*, no. 6 (1973), 560–70.
[12] Allan, "Robin Hood Gardens, Poplar, London," 31.
[13] Carlos Machado e Moura, "Narrative Takes Command: Revisiting Manplan and Fotoromanzo, Photo Sequences in Architectural Magazines around 1970," *Sophia Journal* 2, no. 1 (2017). DOI 10.24840/2183-8976_2017-0002_0001_05.
[14] Hubert de Cronin Hastings, "Manplan: Frustation," in "Manplan 1," special issue, *The Architectural Review* (September 1969).
[15] "St. Louis Blues," *The Architectural Forum* 136 (May 1972), 18.

fig. 3
Robin Hood Gardens (1968–1972) by Alison and Peter Smithson showing the "streets in the air." Scenes from the "Street life in Robin Hood Gardens" event in 2006.
© Erect Architecture.

were condemned and sentenced to death. Katherine Bristol[16] discussed in the early 1990s how this myth was forged with the support of architects and architectural critics, strongly reinforced by Oscar Newman's *Defensible Space,* which William Marlin[17] called "not just the most important housing book in recent years [but] the most important *human* book as well," and which constituted a static indictment of high-rise public housing. For Bristol,[18] however, *Defensible Space* "is a subtle form of blaming the victim. . . . It naturalizes the presence of crime among the low-income populations rather than seeing it as a product of institutionalized economic and racial oppression."

In the mid-1970s, Pruitt-Igoe was unceasingly used to illustrate the failure of the modern movement. First, Colin Rowe and Fred Koetter in *Collage City* (1976) represented the failure of the city of modern architecture and how "the former city of deliverance is every day found increasingly inadequate,"[19] by illustrating it through a sequence of photographs beginning with Le Corbusier's designs for La Ville Contemporaine (1922) and Le Plan Voisin (1925), followed by high-rise public housing in Lower Manhattan (New York), and La Défense and Bobigny (Paris), and ending with the demolition of Pruitt-Igoe in St. Louis (USA). Although these cases are not mentioned in the text, this is indeed a very eloquent frame: from the ideal and conceptual modern city, to the real city center, and then to the demolition where the high-rise building was elected as the great symbol.

This interpretation reached an extreme position with Charles Jencks's[20] *The Language of Post-Modern Architecture* (1977). In the first part of his book, Jencks announces the death of modern architecture:

> **Modern Architecture died in St. Louis, Missouri on July 15, 1972, at 3.32 p.m. (or thereabouts), when the famous Pruitt-Igoe scheme, or rather several of its slab blocks, were given the final coup de grâce by dynamite.**

Furthermore, Jencks argues that the ruins of Pruitt-Igoe should be preserved as a reminder of a great failure in order to avoid its repetition, equating the ruins with the Berlin Wall and the collapse of Ronan Point (a high-rise block in England, 1968). Considering this background, the lack of interest in and even condemnation of high-rise housing projects is more than understandable; it is expected.

[16] Bristol, "The Pruitt-Igoe Myth," 163–71.
[17] William Marlin, "Forum. A Monthly Review of Events and Ideas," *The Architectural Forum* 137, no. 4 (November 1972), 25.
[18] Bristol, "The Pruitt-Igoe Myth," 167–68.
[19] Colin Rowe and Fred Koetter, *Collage City* (Cambridge: MIT Press, 1976), 6.
[20] Charles Jencks, *The Language of Post-Modern Architecture* (New York: Rizzoli, 1977), 9–10.

fig.4
Urban views from "streets in the air" at Robin Hood Gardens,
© Leandro Cruz, 2012.

Built in the same year that modern architecture was declared dead, RHG was interpreted as a residual outcome of the brutalist experience, and in terms of the Smithsons' work it was, after all, the realization of their social theory on housing. Contradicting the Smithsons' intention to create a sense of community and enhance identity in London's East End, Jencks argues that all the positive aims were "denied by the built form."

> It suppresses this [the identity of each house] in favour of visual syncopation, a partially randomised set of vertical fins, and horizontal continuity — the notion of a communal street deck. These "streets in the air" have, surprisingly, all the faults which the Smithsons had recognised in other similar schemes. They are under-used; the collective entries are paltry and a few have been vandalised. Indeed, they are dark, smelly, dank passage-ways. Little sense of place, few collective facilities and fewer 'identifying elements', which the architects had reasonably said were needed in modern buildings.[21]

A series of biased criticisms sealed the fate of RHG and have had a major impact on its recent history. In contemporary architectural culture, it was considered that the building had nothing more to offer and should remain in silence. Neglected by the public administration, the decay of the building fabric was just a matter of time.

> In comparing the critical climate of both its completion and demolition, the physical lifespan of Robin Hood Gardens was neatly bookended by damning reviews — at both points in time, backed by different authorities, the architecture itself had nothing of significance to say.[22]

Recognition of Cultural Values: An Attempt at Salvation

In 2007, the silence was broken after the Blackwall Reach Regeneration Project of the Tower Hamlets Borough Council announced the demolition of the RHG estate. Faced with the possibility that the building might be listed, the council applied for a Certificate of Immunity from Listing (COI)[23] with a report from Peter Stewart Consultancy arguing that "the Robin Hood Gardens buildings do not bear comparison either with other post-war

[21] Ibid., 23.
[22] Ang Li, "Raised by Association: Robin Hood Gardens and Its Interpretations," *Thresholds*, no. 43 (2015), 117, accessed July 21, 2021, http://www.jstor.org/stable/43892699.

housing projects that have been listed, or with other projects by the Smithsons that have been listed. They do not reach the high standard required for them to be listed. A certificate of immunity should therefore be issued."[24]

Stewart's analysis echoes old criticisms from Anthony Pangaro and Charles Jencks, which are reinforced by the idea of "bad design"[25] in the context of housing estate production. Another report written in 2012 by Graham Stewart[26] follows the same trail of references and employs similar arguments.

The first resolution came in July 2008, when Minister of Culture Margaret Hodge announced that "Robin Hood Gardens was not innovative or appropriate in terms of the concept of 'streets-in-the-air.'" In the aftermath of this decision, a campaign was launched by *Building Design* magazine and the Twentieth Century Society (C20), with the support of many eminent architects, to overturn the decision. However, in May 2009, Culture Secretary Andy Burnham upheld the previous decision and granted the COI, making RHG ineligible for listing for the following five years (2009–2014).

The arguments made by English Heritage (government advisors) and others to legitimize this erasure process relied on a historical prejudice built in the 1970s that was based on justifications such as the inadequacy of the project in fulfilling inhabitants' expectations; misconceptions of the design process, such as the architects' intention to stimulate community life through the "streets in the air"; the lack of innovation; and the repetitive and monotonous facades. Henrietta Billings, from C20, stated that:

> **The architecture has been misunderstood and underappreciated, and also unfairly maligned due to maintenance issues and underinvestment over a long period of time. This has added to the perception that it's the fault of the architecture rather than other issues around things like maintenance and general upkeep.[27]**

Therefore, this process adopts old-fashioned arguments without bothering to contextualize the flaws inherently related to the construction of a building "in an especially isolated location, surrounded not only by trunk roads, but when first constructed, by the wider desolation of the closed London docks"[28] and without further consideration of the pace of material and social transformations. "The sense of isolation at least has changed, and the estate which once towered over a surrounding wasteland is now increasingly overshadowed by new neighbors, bringing with them an expanding residential community"[29] to which the greenery created by the Smithsons brings a strong contribution.

To give the community a voice, in 2008 *Building Design* published the article "It's a Great Place to Live, Absolutely,"[30] which presented residents' views on their living conditions in RHG:

> **Look out my kitchen window, what do you see? Trees, grass, very pleasant surroundings. It's a great place to live, absolutely. This is the most peaceful part of the borough with plenty of facilities.**
> **When this was first built it was very modern and people were fighting to get in here. It was very cleverly built. . . . The way it has upside down maisonettes, you never hear noise from anyone else. And the nice thing is that every room has plenty of light – one wall is all windows and you're not looking into someone else's house. I don't think these people who are proposing thousands of new homes for this site have a clue. (Shirley Magnitsky, tenant since 1995)**

The RHG project comprises 214 flats (including thirty-eight flats on the ground floor for the elderly) in two independent blocks of seven (West, Cotton St.) and ten (East, Blackwall Tunnel) stories, resulting in a density of 142 inhabitants/acre, slightly above the density required by the Greater London Council (GLC). The two blocks were built running north–south, with

[23] A Certificate of Immunity from Listing is a document that guarantees that a building will not be statutorily listed for the subsequent five years.

[24] Peter Stewart Consultancy, *Robin Hood Gardens: Report on Potential Listing*, 2007.

[25] The same idea behind the "Pruitt-Igoe Myth" (see Bristol, note 12), one, since then, constantly used to justify the failure of post-World War II social housing programs, depicting them as troubled.

[26] Graham Stewart, *Robin Hood Gardens Blackwall Reach: The Search for a Sense of Place* (London: WILD ReSEARCH, 2012).

[27] Tamlin Magee, "Politician Calls for Immediate Demolition of Robin Hood Gardens After Listing Bid Fails," *Dezeen*, August 2015, https://www.dezeen.com/2015/08/05/politician-calls-immediate-demolition-robin-hood-gardens-listing-bid-fails-historic-england-brutalism/.

[28] Dickon Robinson, "Fit for Purpose," in *Robin Hood Gardens Re-vision* (London: The Twentieth Century Society, 2010), 127.

[29] Ibid., 127.

[30] Rory Olcayto, "It's a Great Place to Live, Absolutely," *Building Design*, February 2008, 8–9.

slight rhythmic deflections following the urban fabric and embracing an internal public green space ("stress-free zone"), resulting in an integrated relationship between the buildings and the landscape designed to improve quality of life and allow social integration *(fig. 2)*. The perimeter walls and the buildings themselves shielded the inhabitants from traffic noise, offering suitable spaces for "connective possibilities" in line with the designers' concerns and struggle toward a more democratic urbanism.

From urban scale to constructive details, RHG was planned to fulfill human needs and rights for better and more dignified living conditions, but balancing all the budget constraints the GLC imposed on social housing schemes required narrowing the street decks (which were not only the means of access to the maisonettes but also common spaces of conviviality). The flats had three or four bedrooms—with generous interiors in accordance with the Parker Morris Committee standards—provided with direct lighting, cross-ventilation, and visual contact with the outside from both the east and the west facades.

The residential "streets in the air" are the primary realization of Alison and Peter Smithson's urban design principles, which in RHG reflect an evolution of the Golden Lane project, associated with their lived experience in the East End. More than a passage, they "are intended to be ample spaces, wide enough for two mothers with prams to stop to talk and still leave room to pass."[31] They were designed as elements of both social and spatial connectivity, linking people and houses, but with the potential strength to knit together a district and, ultimately, a city.

In the Smithsons' words, "the street is not only a means of access but also an arena for social expression," and the street decks were their way to redesign this "arena" in an era of changing values, one where streets were "invalidated by the motor car."[32] Even if people kept fighting against the motor car in that "social arena," the "streets in the air" became a potential element of a new sense of community, as shown by the "Street life in Robin Hood Gardens" event, which took place during Open House London in 2006 *(figs. 3, 4)*.

This idea of conviviality has been lost with the demolition of the western block. The downsizing and fragmentation of the public green area and the floor plans of the new blocks reveal a different composition of values, asserting the individual over the collective *(figs. 5, 6)*. A small hall and private balconies where there is no space for social expression have replaced all the "communitarian" potential of the street decks. The residential street that

fig. 5
Collage drawings of RHG western block deployment (map data: Google, © 2000) with the floor plan of "streets-in-the-air" (from Google Earth), and the drawing of Blackwall Reach Regeneration Project phase 2. Images produced by the author.

[31] Alison Smithson and Peter Smithson, *Urban Structuring: Studies of Peter and Alison Smithson* (London: Studio Vista, 1967).
[32] Ibid., 10.

allowed all inhabitants the opportunity for a casual gathering, for children's games, or just to take a moment to appreciate the urban landscape, was split into small, private balconies for a few. Even if one argues that those streets were detached from the ground, losing connection with urban life, their conception was intrinsically linked to public areas adding a new urban element based on values such as social equity, allowing people to move through urban space into permeable buildings that are not only livable at height but also walkable at height.

A second COI was granted in 2015 (2015–2020) and demolition of the western block took place in 2017–2018. Underpinning this ruthless determination to knock down the RHG estate, there is an economic interest so strong that no cultural or social argument could dissuade it: "The land it stands on has become increasingly valuable as London's centre of gravity has shifted eastwards. Housing providers are being forced to take an increasingly commercial approach to their assets. The fate of the residents often takes second place."[33]

If the local authorities and specialists were unable to recognize the cultural value of this architectural masterpiece and there is no longer a home for it in the city, at least the Victoria and Albert Museum acknowledged its merit and decided to buy a fragment of the building (a maisonette from the demolished block) and give it a new address in which it could remain. An aftereffect far from what Peter and Alison Smithson envisioned as "a more enjoyable way of living in an old industrial part of a city," "a new mode of urban organisation" that they wanted to build "for successive occupying generations."[34]

Yet, against all odds, the eastern block still stands, and the second COI has now expired. Is this the chance for a turning point?

Robin Hood Gardens: A Plea for Revision

Despite all its misfortune, in the history of Robin Hood Gardens not all was silence. A new generation of scholars who devote their research to the post–World War II period have brought new interpretations to the project, as Dirk van den Heuvel[35] did with several pieces reviewing Peter and Alison Smithson's contribution and, particularly, the historic, cultural, and artistic value of the RHG estate.

> **The astounding achievement of RHG is that it succeeds in absorbing classic elements of modern architecture, such as Miesian repetition, and Le Corbusier's call for a "Virgilian" cityspace, while at the same time transposing these things into something altogether new, specific to its time and location, something which can be recognised as wholly British, yet appeals to an international audience.[36]**
>
> **The site planning might be considered the result of an expanded "As Found" approach, a careful observing of existing patterns, connecting routes, the few remaining neighbourhood shops, and responding to the special features of the site.[37]**

Even voices from the real-estate sector realize the importance of avoiding demolition. As part of the C20's request for a review of the decision not to list RHG, Dickon Robinson's analysis casts light on RHG's potential to remain a viable space for living: "RHG has provided generously sized and well-planned homes for over thirty years in an unattractive area of East London. While it has suffered from all the trials and tribulations of any social housing estate, there is little or no real evidence to suggest that it has been more or less popular with residents."[38] Urban Splash founder Tom Bloxham,[39] responsible for the Park Hill Sheffield refurbishment, also agrees that it would be completely possible to save RHG from demolition if there was the political will to do so.

The reason for preserving RHG goes beyond its authorship or its status as a brutalist masterpiece; its design resilience remains a manifesto toward a more democratic urbanism.

33 Colin Wiles, "A Tale of Two Brutalist Housing Estates: One Thriving, One Facing Demolition," *Guardian,* January 2016, https://www.theguardian.com/profile/colin-wiles.

34 "The Smithsons on Housing," in *Broadcast* (London: BBC2, July 10, 1970).

35 Just to mention some of his works related to this article's theme: Max Risselada and Dirk van den Heuvel, *Team 10—In Search of a Utopia of the Present* (Rotterdam: NAI Uitgevers/ Publishers Stichting, 2005); Max Risselada, Alison Smithson, Peter Smithson and Dirk van den Heuvel, *Alison and Peter Smithson—From the House of the Future to a House of Today* (Rotterdam: 010 Publishers, 2004). Both these publications were produced in collaboration with Max Risselada; see Max Risselada, "Alison and Peter Smithson: A Brutalist Story Involving the House, the City and the Everyday (Plus a Couple of Other Things)" (PhD diss., TU Delft, 2013), DOI 10.4233/uuid:7e9d6f1f-9b3e-4b85-a4ce-72f7eca919ba. Mark Swenarton, Tom Avermaete, and Dirk van den Heuvel, *Architecture and the Welfare State* (London: Routledge, 2015).

36 Dirk van den Heuvel, "A Virgilian Cityspace," in *Robin Hood Gardens Re-vision* (London: The Twentieth Century Society, 2010), 47–49.

37 Dirk van den Heuvel, "A Brutalist Story," 228.

38 Dickon Robinson, "Fit for Purpose," 123–29. Robinson is a housing expert and director of development and technical services at the Peabody Trust, which operates as a housing association.

39 Elisabeth Hopkirk, "Robin Hood Gardens Easier to Redevelop than Park Hill, Says Urban Splash Founder," *Building Design,* July 2015.

fig. 6
Aerial view from the eastern block of RHG and Blackwall Reach Regeneration Project (map data: Google). © 2021 Landsat/Copernicus.

The "streets in the air" represent this struggle and the belief in human conviviality rather than individualism. In the end, this is the message that is worth getting across.

Anne Power[40] argues that demolition is not an option, and the reasons why are not only "carbon-related justifications" but also social and cultural. Certainly, not every housing estate will be (nor should be) recognized as a heritage asset. But the only way to identify and assess this important group of modernist architectural and social achievements is by building new interpretations of them and their current cultural significance, updating the critiques from the 1970s and the 1980s—especially historical prejudices associated with high-density estates and social behavior within them.

[40] Anne Power, "Council Estates: Why Demolition Is Anything but the Solution," LSE Housing and Communities Blog, March 2016, accessed July 19, 2021, https://blogs.lse.ac.uk/politicsandpolicy/sink-estates-demolition/.

Biography

Carolina Chaves is an architect and assistant professor at the University of Sergipe (Brazil) and deputy coordinator of the Laboratory of Project Teaching and Memory (LaPEM) research group, leading the scientific inquiry "History of architecture and the city: critical investigations and new narratives." In 2012, she graduated with a masters degree from IAUUSP-São Carlos (SP). Since 2019, she has been a PhD student at Instituto Superior Técnico (University of Lisbon). Her research area is the critical history and theory of twentieth-century architecture, focusing on the critical revision of current and canonical narratives on Brazilian architecture. In 2018 she was awarded an honorable mention for the research project "Contemporary Brazilian Architecture: a critical review of the architectural magazines Projeto and AU (1970–1990)." She also has a special interest in modernist heritage and its conservation. Between 2016 and 2018, she led research projects on the dissemination of modern architecture in Northeast Brazil and on modern heritage documentation using BIM technology (HBIM).

4 Explicit Criticism

Architectural Criticism in the Emergent Urbanscapes of the Global South

Philippa Tumubweinee

fig. 1
Andrew Makin, RSA Constitutional Court in context, 2004. Often referred to as the Light on the Hill, the Constitutional Court presents a warmth and dignity of place that reflects the beginning of an open, equal, and just South African landscape and society. Photo: Constitutional Court, Johannesburg, https://www.designworkshop.co.za/project/constitutional-court-of-south-africa.

The purpose of this essay is to make the case for an inclusionary approach to practice in the construction of architecture within an emergent urbanscape.[1] Given the scale of processes for the development of many of Africa's cities or, more precisely, the scales across which decision-making happens in the new master plans for these urban environments, this approach builds on how architectural designs, as creative manifestations, fit into the complexities of the challenges and absences found in African cities.[2]

With the help of three architectural projects, this essay aims to provide orientating information on the political, social, cultural, and environmental dynamics in South Africa. Conversations with the projects' architects allow us to explore how, in a South African context, the design process can move beyond concerns around the quality of architecture to become a part of the rationalities of developmental processes in the creation of place.[3] Each conversation reveals design processes that respond to place-based knowledge systems and possibilities that are built into the transitional, at times rogue, and at times ad hoc, characteristics of the continent's emergent urban landscape.[4] Embedded from the beginning was the process of the conception of architecture, as well as its realization in the particularities of place-based concerns. This approach biases a design process such that it moves through connections and intersections and across scales to position the architecture in the tensions between shifting temporalities. The conversations with the architects show that this approach allows for each project to critically speak to broader decision- and place-making processes in society; they present how a differentiated practice can successfully engage with the temporalities of a colonial and postcolonial history, with governance and oversight issues, and with the act of place-making in informal and marginalized communities. In this way, architecture as a process becomes a way of thinking through place-specific knowledge so that it can serve societal needs and concerns.

All three conversations reveal how the respective architecture aims to appropriately address and respond to contextual knowledge and concerns that in turn can be harnessed to create active and dynamic intersections between the individual client–architect relationship and the broader community and society. In all three projects, the design and construction processes transformed a collective conception of an architecture—one that is grounded in and of the place in which it is located—into physical reality.

Three Projects

At a national level, the Constitutional Court in Braamfontein, Johannesburg was designed by OMM Design Workshop (architects: Janina Masojada and Andrew Makin) and Urban Solutions (architect/urban designer: Paul Wygers). As South Africa's supreme court, the Constitutional Court is the custodian of its democracy and a symbol of the transition from apartheid to democracy. The Constitutional Court is located on the site of what was once a notorious prison under the apartheid regime.[5]

[1] Cf. https://www.futureofcities.ox.ac.uk/video/vanessa-watson/ (accessed October 1, 2021).
[2] Edgar Pieterse, "Cityness and African Urban Development," Urban Forum 21 (2010), 205–219.
[3] Vanessa Watson, "Conflicting Rationalities: Implications for Planning Theory and Ethics," Planning Theory & Practice 4, no. 4 (2003), 395–407.
[4] Edgar Pieterse, "Grasping the Unknowable: Coming to Grips with African Urbanisms," Social Dynamics 37, no. 1 (2011), 5–23.
[5] Bronwyn Law-Viljoen, ed., Light on a Hill: Building the Constitutional Court of South Africa (Johannesburg: David Krut Publishing, 2006).

fig. 2
Andrew Makin, Constitutional Court entrance foyer, 2004. The slanted columns with mosaic-clad capitals in the entrance foyer of the Constitutional Court, which is flooded with dappled natural light, are a metaphor for a forest of trees. It speaks to the manner in which, in rural South Africa, discussion and debate often take place under the shade of a tree. Photo: Constitutional Court, Johannesburg, https://www.designworkshop.co.za/project/constitutional-court-of-south-africa.

At a regional level, Vukuzakhe, designed by Koop Design (architect: Richard Stretton) in 2013, is an architectural response to the poor levels of public services in South Africa. With the advent of democracy, there was an immediate need to provide services for previously marginalized and disenfranchised communities. Over the past two decades—aggravated by a lack of institutional capacity—complex and problematic procurement processes, corruption, and maladministration have led to poor performance by local governments in delivering services and infrastructure to these communities.[6] This resulted in widespread protests[7] in which public infrastructure such as schools, fire stations, clinics, and community centers have borne the brunt of communities' ire.

At a community level, the Emergent Common Spaces project in Macassar was designed and built in 2019 by Studiolight—founded and run by the architect and academic Clint Abrahams. Abrahams carried out this project in collaboration with the School of Architecture, Planning and Geomatics (APG) at the University of Cape Town (UCT); the Cape Peninsula University of Technology (CPUT); Germany's Rheinisch-Westfälische Technische Hochschule (RWTH), Aachen University; and the Peter Behrens School of Arts (PBSA) at the University of Applied Sciences Düsseldorf. The project, run as a summer/winter school, was funded by the Deutscher Akademischer Austauschdienst (DAAD). The architecture developed from a project that was realized with youth from the community of Macassar, culminating in the photographic exhibition *Macassar: Who We Are.*

[6] Azwifaneli Managa, "Unfulfilled Promises and Their Consequences: A Reflection on Local Government Performance and the Critical Issue of Poor Service Delivery in South Africa, Briefing no. 76," 2021, https://media.africaportal.org/documents/No.-76.-Unfulfilled-promises-and-their-consequences.-.pdf.
[7] Penwell Dlamini, "Gauteng under Shack Attack," TimesLIVE, 2014, https://www.timeslive.co.za/news/south-africa/2014-04-02-gauteng-under-shack-attack/.

Three Conversations
1 Janina Masojada and the Constitutional Court

The Constitutional Court project emerged from a key moment in the history of South Africa: the birth of the democratic republic. The design for the Constitutional Court is the result of an international architectural competition held in 1997. The winning submission by OMM Design Workshop and Urban Solutions highlighted how an architectural intervention can, from a grassroots-development perspective, produce an outcome grounded in a consultative process that supports the development of relationships with disenfranchised communities—those who have little or no experience of speaking up, no record, no voice, and no concept of how to make themselves heard. This approach favored the development of an architecture that underscored the tenet of the South African Bill of Rights in its foregrounding of broad public consultation over a prescribed architectural style or notion.

fig. 3
Andrew Makin, Court Chamber, 2004. The circular form of the court chamber breaks the austerity and hierarchy of court proceedings and the low-lying ribbon of glass above the judges' bench speaks to the transparency of its processes. Photo: Constitutional Court, Johannesburg, https://www.design-workshop.co.za/project/constitutional-court-of-south-africa.

> The adjudicators of the competition asked if they would meet with us. They had two concerns. The first thing was, they still didn't know what the building looks like, which is very unusual in a competition. And then they wanted to see if we would participate in a process during the conceptual development of the project, which included some of the adjudicators and the judges, to ensure that we continued with the same positioning of our architectural response throughout the design development.[8]

Because of the architects' focus on the consultative process as a design generator, the architecture itself became a small component of the brief, with an emphasis being placed on iterative conversations between the architects' understanding of the brief and the processes and frameworks that defined its context—a democratic South Africa. The relationship between the brief and its context informed an evolving architectural outcome, one which grew incrementally beyond both the architect and the client to include the communities in the immediate urban context and the complex history of the site, showing how, from a complicated and divided past, the idea of an inclusive democratic constitution could emerge and create connections across constructed boundaries that divide and separate society.

> Basically, there is no front elevation to the building; it is their big statement. And it's interesting now looking at when they do show the Constitutional Court in the newspaper prints or when there's a hearing or something, they often show an interior image of a court chamber with the judges sitting at the bench it's not . . . a big intimidating front facade, which is exactly what the intention of it was. It is a fragmented building that is supposed to be something that is completely knitted into the fabric of the site—as an evolving and incremental collection of aggregated pieces that, together, are the Constitutional Court.[9]

An important conceptual approach in the actual construction of the building was to include as many hands as possible as a tangible realization of an inclusive and democratic architecture that relates to and identifies with as many people as possible. For example, the west elevation

[8] Janina Masojada, in discussion with Philippa Tumubweinee, 2021.
[9] Janina Masojada, in discussion with Philippa Tumubweinee, 2021.

sunscreen was developed through a series of sub-competitions targeted at excavating stories and narratives from the communities near the site, to incorporate living histories and memories. As such, the western elevation that frames the "African Steps" of Section Four and Section Five of the prison is an illustration and recording of the narratives of prisoners who had spent time on the site and residents who had lived alongside the site where these atrocities took place, literally across the street from them.

> And that process of recording and hearing and storytelling, I think became a very integral part to the Court's acceptance into that location by the immediate surrounding communities. So, . . . at a very different scale to the urban and the architecture, the building presents itself intimately and personally.[10]

The integration of diverse voices, communities, stories, and memories into architecture has resulted in national reverence toward, and relevance of, the building. The building gives rise to a sense of pride of place; people who visit the site respect it not only because of the architecture but also because of its embodiment of inclusive narratives and histories with which they can relate and identify.

The Constitutional Court can be navigated without a guided tour and without paying to access this symbol of the birth of an inclusive and democratic society. It is in this accessibility that the evolving and incremental nature of the architecture can be experienced, as a place that records the feeling of upliftment and achievement that deserved to be celebrated just as much as the seriousness of what the South African Constitution had accomplished needed to be expressed. The architecture speaks of the people's silent emotions and hopes in a physical form, and its critique thereof must accommodate the democratic design process, bringing with it a gravitas that seeks neither to elevate the building nor to intimidate. Rather, the gravitas of the building lies in its inherent accessibility as a place and symbol—historically, socially, culturally, and spatially. Through this accessibility, the building signals the clarity of intent behind the design and development of an architecture of relevance to South Africa. The architecture of the Constitutional Court is a manifestation of conversations that were going on at the time.

2 Richard Stretton and Vukuzakhe: Emerging Contractor Development Programme

Protest in South Africa is innate, and Jane Duncan argues that it is a right.[11] In the democratic republic post-1994, protests have become the most common form by which previously marginalized communities express their dissatisfaction with national and local government's inability to deliver basic services and infrastructure. Njabulo S. Ndebele argues that the rate of escalation of protests over the last decade in connection with poor service and infrastructure delivery may soon take on an organized character, starting as discrete formations and then coalescing into a full-blown movement.[12] Solutions are desperately needed to rapidly deliver services and infrastructure in marginalized and disenfranchised communities. These needs exist in urban contexts characterized by sprawl, given that municipalities continue to provide social housing and public infrastructure that are both detached and located further and further away from the economic centers of cities and towns in South Africa.[13] As such, the need to deliver basic services and infrastructure to these communities is immediate and urgent so that they can become viable and functional. In the case of the city of Durban, where the Vukuzakhe Emerging Contractor Development Programme was conceptualized, there is a need for over 2,000 community buildings such as clinics, schools, community halls, and fire and police stations.

The delivery of infrastructure to communities is hampered by various problems, including the inefficiencies of onerous bureaucratic procurement rules and complex as well as irregular fiscal oversight and management. The challenges are thus: how should an architect conceive the design of these public buildings to beneficially implement them; and what processes should

[10] Janina Masojada, in discussion with Philippa Tumubweinee, 2021.
[11] Jane Duncan, *Protest Nation: The Right to Protest in South Africa* (University of KwaZulu-Natal Press, 2016).
[12] Njabulo S. Ndebele, "Liberation Betrayed by Bloodshed," *Social Dynamics* 39, no. 1 (2013): 111–114.
[13] Vanessa Watson, "Conflicting Rationalities," 395–407.

an architect put in place to ensure that the architecture is not only useful but also adequate to address deeply problematic governance and urban realities? These questions demand solutions that not only intersect with the particularities of place but also are grounded in the determinants that define that place.

As an architectural response, Vukuzakhe adopted a system that simply and easily supported people with existing construction skills while considering the economy of how buildings are realized. With Vukuzakhe, the architect consolidated research and observations on the city authorities' lack of critical thought regarding urban development needs in South African cities. The architect developed systems for the delivery of an alternative building typology by offering a framework in which the construction process can be harnessed to address not only the problems posed by procurement bureaucracy but also the immediate and dire need for job creation and thus economic empowerment.

The proposed delivery systems combine sensitive, inclusive site planning, intensive local labor for site preparation, and simple pre-fabrication. Local economies are stimulated by developing an easily adaptable and replicated component-based building system suitable for small to medium-sized businesses. This system focuses on viable procurement and construction processes in which the singular functioning of the architecture as a "thing" incorporates components that fit together seamlessly when they arrive on site, while also allowing for the independent production of parts prior to assembly on site.

figs. 8–10
The Vukuzakhe Systems Model is a proposed delivery system that combines sensitive, inclusive site planning and intensive local labor for site preparation with simultaneous simple prefabricated building component production.
It aims to resolve materials choices and systems required for holistic co-ordination of municipal buildings within an alternative building typology. Concept sketch and photographs: Richard Stretton. Vukuzakhe Systems Model, 2019.

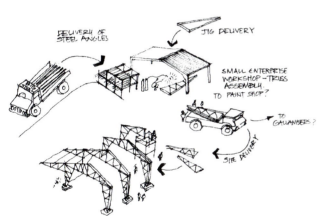
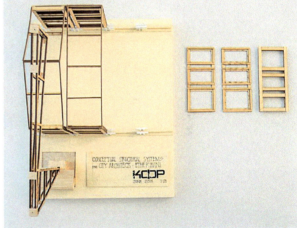
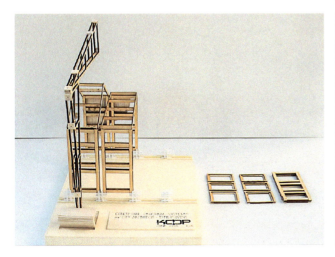

> **The conceptualization of Vukuzakhe is premised on maximizing the economic benefit to the community for whom the building is provided. Simply employing people through the building process and leaving them jobless after the building is completed is pointless. It is sought at every opportunity to generate economic opportunity through the manner by which the site is developed. The pursuit of form as a driver of architecture is becoming unpopular. The austerity of global economics is fast marginalizing the indulgence of architects in pure form. Architecture is assessed in terms of the opportunity it creates for the maximization of resource and return. Closed loop production guides where opportunity exists.[14]**

Vukuzakhe shows how architecture as a practice can present an opportunity for pursuing a wide range of relevant solutions to what is, in essence, an economic and governance problem. In this instance, breaking up the construction process into components directly embeds it in the community in which the architecture is located. In this program, the role of the architect extends beyond the object to engage the realm of processes and frameworks that define its context. The system developed in Vukuzakhe not only provides for much needed public infrastructure but also activates an environment in which communities are resourced and supported through economic empowerment and the development of skills. Here, the architecture makes a meaningful contribution on a very personal level as it allows for people in the community to take charge not only of the conceptualization of the architecture but also of the procurement and construction processes through which the architecture is delivered.

The systems and solutions developed in Vukuzakhe are architectural in the widest sense. Vukuzakhe, in its support of small businesses and sustained quality jobs, presents an architecture that is concerned with the economic freedom of the people for whom public service delivery buildings are intended.

3 Clint Abrahams and Macassar

In 2018, Clint Abrahams conceived and staged the photographic exhibition *Macassar: Who We Are* through his non-profit organization Studiolight in collaboration with young adults in the community. The photographs, taken by youth, framed their understanding of everyday experiences in Macassar. The exhibition shifted perceptions expressed in dominant narratives about place and place-making that marginalize the embedded knowledge about materials and materiality in communities such as Macassar. It set the stage for what Abrahams refers to as a "rescripting" of socio-spatial narratives and for how this process critically engages with the postcolonial challenges of previously displaced communities in South Africa. The project won the 2019 UCT Creative Works Award.

In response to both the images on display and the exposure enjoyed thanks to being shown in different venues in Macassar, the exhibition initiated a series of intergenerational conversations and encouraged broader community participation. It was these conversations around shared understandings of Macassar as a material and immaterial concept that unearthed the need for a common space for the sustained formation of community identity and resilience through the act of storytelling.

In collaboration with students and academics across five institutions, and with various colleagues at UCT, Abrahams explored how intergenerational practices of self-made constructions had informed and developed the material and architectural tectonic found in Macassar. Abrahams argues that, through engagement with the emergent architectural tectonics of self-made constructions, architects can "make visible marginalized knowledge" that supports the conceptualization and realization of architecture to better serve and represent the particularity of places and their communities.

[14] Richard Stretton, in discussion with Philippa Tumubweinee, 2021.

figs. 8, 9, 12
Clint Abrahams, street view of the *Macassar: Who We Are* temporary exhibition that has moved across three spaces in Macassar. The exhibition was designed and built by the non-profit Studiolight along with local youth in cooperation with students from the University of Cape Town (UCT) to showcase photographs taken and stories told by young people in Macassar.
Clint Abrahams, *Macassar: Who We Are* exhibition at the Macassar Public Library, Western Cape (South Africa), 2018. Photo: Macassar, Cape Town. https://liveprojectsnetwork.org/project/who-we-are/

The Emergent Common Spaces project is a result of an ethnographic reading and study of self-made constructions in Macassar, based on the intersections between storytelling and local intergenerational communal knowledge. As such, the architecture is founded on and biases what Abrahams refers to as restorative architectural practice. This form of practice shows how the design process is informed by place-based knowledge systems and concerns when the architect—as the expert citizen—relinquishes control of the architecture's conception to the citizen expert—the community. Meaning thus found in the everyday can produce something new and singular that is of its place.[15] It is in this shifted relationship from the expert citizen to the citizen expert that Abrahams explores the new role of architecture as a restorative practice.

In Conclusion

The purpose of this essay was to make the case for why a much more differentiated approach to practice is required within an emergent urbanscape in the process of constructing architecture. The discussion of three projects with three architects biases the tension between understanding architecture as an abstraction from its context and place-based design processes. The bias was used to frame the complexities of the architect's role in a contemporary Global South urbanscape. This brings into focus the "novelty and originality of this [urbanscape . . .] to pay sufficient attention to that which is unknown about it, or to find order in the apparent mess of its past and the chaos of the present."[16] For architecture to retain any relevance there needs to be a real acknowledgement of the creative practice that is composed and invented by a society in a specific place. If the values that ground the conceptualization and realization of the architecture are place-specific, then the ethics of its critique can move beyond contextualizing firsthand knowledge and individual client–architect relationships to speak to the realities of the ongoing societal concerns.

    In each of the three projects, and in conversation with the architects, the process of conceptualization of the architecture, both inclusionary and participatory, is used as a tool to address and work through societal concerns. The architect relinquishes control of the process of conceptualization in favor of broader decision- and place-making processes as well as frameworks. As a result, the architect can locate the realization of the project across different modalities, temporalities, and histories. In the case of the Constitutional Court, the process of design conceptualization positions the resultant architecture as a symbol of healing and of the future direction of a nation that, at the time, was constructing a narrative to legitimate itself as a democratic political legal entity. The architects of the Constitutional Court took a back seat and enabled active participatory engagement to capture a significant moment in time—the birth of a democratic republic. In the Vukuzakhe Emerging Contractor Development

figs. 10, 11
The Storytelling Shack, a community common space, is the product of a collaborative project between UCT's School of Architecture, Planning and Geomatics; the Cape Peninsula University of Technology (CPUT); Germany's Rheinisch-Westfälische Technische Hochschule (RWTH) Aachen University and the Peter Behrens School of Arts (PBSA) at the University of Applied Sciences Düsseldorf; led by Studiolight. Clint Abrahams. Storytelling Shack. 2019. Photo: Macassar, Cape Town, https://ait-xia-dialog.de/ait-dialog-themen/buildingcommunity/

[15] J. Achille Mbembe and Sarah Nuttall, "Writing the World from an African Metropolis," *Public Culture* 16, no. 3 (2004): 347–72.
[16] Ibid., 348.

Programme, there is an appreciation that, in the South African context, it is necessary to think through the process and logistics of procurement in which the delivery of architecture functions. In this case, the need to adapt to the stymied and problematic realities in which architects find themselves realigns and redefines their creative work. Architectural practice cannot be limited to the individualized client–architect relationship; it must take on the tensions borne from that which is *seen* to be formal and that which is *said* to be informal. In the South African urban context, the differentiation between the formal and the informal city presents an opportunity for architects to extend architectural practice as a bridge across this binary opposition; the Emergent Common Spaces project in Macassar is such an example. In a design process that is informed and governed by local knowledge systems, the resultant architecture is a product of locally available materials and technologies. Thus, the bias of place-based knowledge roots the architecture deeply in the socio-spatial environment for which it is intended.

In the Global South, architecture is tasked with acknowledging the ongoing negotiations between what is and what could be[17] to identify points of entry and exit within the design process for the possibilities embedded in the nature of the emergent urban landscape. This can be achieved through an inclusionary and participatory process that fosters intersections between the individualized objectives of the architecture and the knowledge systems and concerns of the designated place. For architects to remain relevant, there needs to be a pivotal shift towards the conceptualization of architectural design processes that are borne from place-specific knowledge systems and concerns. This active engagement with and in our communities will result in an architecture that can be experienced as meaningful and inclusionary of all of us that live in it.

[17] Jean-Luc Nancy, *The Sense of the World* (Minneapolis: University of Minnesota Press, 1997), 9.

Biography

Philippa Nyakato Tumubweinee was born in Kampala, Uganda. She was awarded her masters degree in architecture at the University of Pretoria, graduated with a DPhil in higher education studies from the University of the Free State, Bloemfontein. She is a co founder and director of IZUBA INafrica Architects, a senior lecturer, and the immediate past Head of School at the School of Architecture, Planning & Geomatics at the University of Cape Town. Her teaching focuses on the experience of architectural education in the first-year architecture studio.

"The Lightest Parliament in the World":[1] Hans Schwippert's Bundeshaus (1949)

Lynnette Widder

fig. 1
Hans Schwippert's Bundeshaus under construction, seen from the far side of the Rhine River. TU Munich Architecture Museum, Schwi-92-3.

Designed and built in less than a year, while the German Federal Republic was constituted, Hans Schwippert's Bundeshaus was a laboratory for the formulation of a modern architecture that embodied the period's ethical aspirations. Its spatial expression references theological and philosophical traditions uniquely meaningful during Germany's post-Nazi "Year Zero." The building is no less remarkable for the fact that it has, throughout its history, been received as "transparent" at a moment when the materials of modern architecture – glass, steel, concrete – were available only in very limited quantities and forms. These two aspects, the theoretical and the material, are inextricable.

The transfer of sovereignty in 1948/49 from the Allied occupying forces to the new government of West Germany carried a mandate to replace the old capitol of Berlin and all it had represented with an entirely different kind of architectural expression. After much political wrangling, the Parliamentary Council, precedent to the Bundestag, voted on May 10, 1949 to locate its new provisional capitol in Bonn instead of in its competitor city, Frankfurt. That decision foreclosed any remaining possibility of architectural association with the past: Frankfurt's Paulskirche, renovated as part of the unsuccessful capital city bid and designed to house the Bundestag by Rudolf Schwarz and a team of other architects, had been the site of Germany's first constitutional congress in 1848. Instead, the new West German parliament would meet in an addition to a Weimar-period building originally designed as a teachers' college. Bonn's Pedagogic Academy had no relevance to Germany's political history at all.

Hans Schwippert, the architect charged with renovating the Pedagogic Academy for its new role, received the commission directly, without tender or competition. As director of construction for the Rhineland in 1945 and 1946, he had favorably impressed Hermann Wandsleben, the man then serving as minister-director and head of the state chancellery, who had led Bonn's successful campaign.[2] The ease with which the commission was granted would be more than compensated for by the incredible difficulty of its execution. During Bonn's bid, Schwippert had begun the preliminary design in November 1948.[3] Over the first weeks of 1949, he produced numerous sketches of the complex. His office moved quickly to finalize the design. The groundbreaking for the plenary was in April, and the hall was inaugurated to great fanfare[4] on September 7 of the same year.[5] Everything occurred at breakneck speed.

The pressure to design, detail, source, schedule, and oversee construction of the building within this ten-month period is difficult to imagine. Further difficulty arose from the dire shortage of construction labor and material in Bonn. Less than a year before construction began on Schwippert's parliament, one observer described a city barely managing to rebuild from its rubble:

While an army of "rubble-seekers" were out – people who searched through the ruins for useful objects for their own building projects – there were already transport groups in the old city who brought hand-cleaned bricks to trucks and brick fragments to a set-up that made new blocks from milled brick and a cement mixture.[6]

---

[1] Will Grohmann, "Das hellste Parliament der Welt," *Die Neue Zeitung*, March 4, 1951, 53.

[2] Werner Durth and Paul Sigel, *Baukultur: Spiegel gesellschaftlichen Wandels* (Berlin: Jovis Verlag, 2009), 420.

[3] Agatha Buslei-Wuppermann and Andreas Zeising, *Das Bundeshaus von Hans Schwippert in Bonn: architektonische Moderne und demokratischer Geist* (Düsseldorf: Grupello, 2009), 44.

[4] Benedikt Wintgens, "'Neues Parliament, neue Bilder?' Die Fotografin Erma Wagner-Hemke und Ihr Blick auf den Bundestag," in *Die ideale Parliament: Erich Salomon als Fotograf in Berlin und Den Haag, 1938–1940*, eds. Andreas Biefang and Marji Leenders (Berlin: Droste Verlag 2014), 309–12.

[5] Buslei-Wuppermann and Zeising, *Das Bundeshaus*, 52.

[6] *Bonn zwischen Kriegsende und Währungsreform: Erinnerungsberichte von Zeitzeugen* (Bonn: Bouvier, 1991), 183–84.

According to other firsthand reports, it had been impossible to find enough cement to reinforce the banks of the Rhine. Revetment construction therefore necessitated the grueling work of breaking basalt, which was then transported in wheelbarrows. Conditions were similar throughout the country.[7] There were few obvious resources upon which the construction of the new parliament could draw, either locally or nationally.

No less dire than material privation was the sense of distress that pervaded consideration of architecture's ethical dimensions. With cities decimated, the occupying forces, citing reasons of expediency, had quickly reinstated politically compromised urban planners and architects to government positions. The transition from a leading position in Albert Speer's Arbeitsstab für den Wiederaufbau kriegszerstörter Städte to an important role in postwar reconstruction proceeded with little interruption.[8] Guilt was a matter of degree, a fact of which all were conscious.[9] Friedrich Tamms, a member of Speer's "internal staff,"[10] summarized the situation as follows: "The comfortable simplification: modern—democratic, traditional—national socialist has no credibility. Conceptual discussion crosses political boundaries. It is apolitical."[11] Modernism had lost its ethical aura. It needed new rules.

This dilemma dictated a reconceived theoretical foundation. *Baukunst und Werkform*,[12] the journal of the reinstated German Werkbund, of which Schwippert would become president, was among the first publications to respond. A 1947 statement in its first issue by its editorial board, on which Schwippert, Rudolf Schwarz, Otto Bartning, Egon Eiermann, and others served, made it clear that continuity was impossible, but a total break with the past unsupportable:

> **The collapse destroyed the visible world of our lives and work. With a sense of liberation, we thought then that we could return to action. Today, two years later, we recognize the degree to which the visible collapse is only an expression of spiritual erosion and we could lose ourselves in desperation. We are left to return to the foundation of things, it is from this point that our responsibility is to be understood . . .[13]**

In 1951, three and a half years after this editorial statement and less than two years after the inauguration of the Bundeshaus, Schwippert and his colleagues set out to take stock of theory's status at the second Darmstädter Gespräche, a series of annual conferences sponsored by the city of Darmstadt. The topic, "*Mensch und Raum*" (human being and space), represented precisely that "return to the foundation of things." It was an occasion to imagine architecture's purpose within a broad story of humanity; to explain space's origins in theology and human perception; and to rewrite the founding myths that resonated in interwar manifestos and pronouncements, many of which had been coauthored by the organizers as young avant-gardists during the 1920s.

Schwippert's Bundeshaus is remarkable in its status as a laboratory for the ideas that Schwippert framed at the 1951 Gespräche. It is no less remarkable for the sleight of hand and architectural prowess that allowed him to realize a building that has, throughout its history, been received as "transparent" at a moment when the materials of modern architecture—glass, steel, concrete—were available only in very limited quantities and forms. It nonetheless begs the question of Schwippert's apparent conviction, despite Tamms's pointed diagnosis, that transparency would somehow, magically, affirm democratic governance. These aspects, theoretical and material, are inextricable.

Religious belief, expressed early in Christian Democratic politics, was woven through the social fabric of West Germany in the late 1940s and 1950s. In 1946, 96 percent of all Germans identified as practicing Protestants or Catholics.[14] No other element of society was so widely shared or respected, despite the acknowledged moral failings of both Catholic and Protestant churches under the Nazi regime. The Allied occupying forces recognized that religious institutions were the only intact structures with which to partner

7 Dirk Dorsemagen, *Büro und Geschäftshäuser der 50er Jahre konservatorische Probleme am Beispiel West-Berlin* (Band I., diss., Berlin Technical University, 2004), 6.

8 Werner Durth, *Deutsche Architekten Biographische Verflechtungen 1900-1970* (Braunschweig and Wiesbaden: Vieweg, 1986). Cf. Gutschow in Hamburg, Wolters in Coesfeld, and Tamms in Lübeck, and the scandal surrounding the appointment of Julius Schulte-Frohlinde in Düsseldorf.

9 Durth, *Deutsche Architekten*, 326.

10 Durth, *Deutsche Architekten*, 212.

11 Durth, *Deutsche Architekten*, 326.

12 Johannes Busmann, *Die revidierte Moderne: der Architekt Alfons Leitl 1909-1975* (Wuppertal: Müller und Busmann, 1995), 59.

13 Durth, *Deutsche Architekten*, 59.

14 Heike Springhart, "'Dass es eine Hoffnung gibt für Deutschland ...' Religion und Kirchen im Nachkriegsdeutschland als gesellschaftliche Institutionen der Reeducation," in *Die lange Stunde Null: gelenkter sozialer Wandel in Westdeutschland nach 1945*, eds. Hans Braun, Uta Gerhardt, and Everhard Holtmann (Baden-Baden: Nomos, 2007), 95.

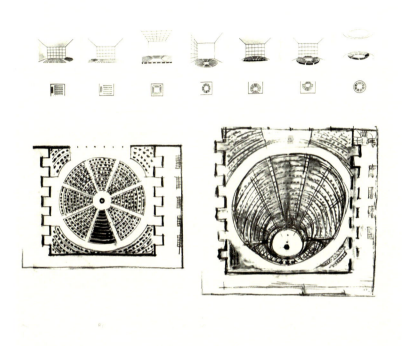

fig. 2
Hans Schwippert, studies for the plenary, 1948. TU Munich Architecture Museum. Schwi-92-31.

in rebuilding. Even in the Soviet-occupied sector, at least initially and in contravention to anti-religious Communist tenets, the two major denominations were allowed to persist.[15] But in the American and British zones, support for both Protestant and Catholic clergy was inscribed in official policy. The occupying forces could distribute aid through churches and clergy, track a populace in motion, and begin stabilization efforts, which included moral reeducation. "Democracy ... lives from Christianity and alone protects law and liberty. It is the responsibility, therefore, of the church to foster democracy," stated Pastor Martin Niemoller at the Treysa Conference of August 1945, convened with support from the occupying forces in a small Hessian town to address the future of the German Protestant church. Churches needed intact spaces for their work, and that need offered a much-desired opportunity for architects who aspired to capture a new vision for German society. "The existential had precedence, no one wanted to live in cellars ..." as Ulrich Conrads, the assistant editor of *Baukunst und Werkform*, said of the early days after the war, and "therefore spatial building was only possible in church building."[16] Especially in the design of the plenary and in the sequence of spaces through which delegates proceeded, Schwippert's Bundeshaus bears out this confluence of organized religion, architectural design, and statecraft.

Even before he had conceived the new complex as a whole, Schwippert had begun to study the plenary in a series of sketches completed in November 1948. He worked through a progression of lighting conditions and seating geometries: uninflected parallel rows of seats to face a speaker, a configuration replicating the former gymnasium then in use as a temporary plenary hall; a similar frontal organization, although slightly curved and inflected at the podium; seating in a square, with delegates facing one another, centered below zenithal light; and a series of circular seating schemes with four different light conditions. The first two in the series reinforced the traditional hierarchy of delegate and leadership.

[15] American pastor and OSS operative Stewart Herman wrote in a September 1945 report: "The Russian attitude toward the church work seems to be quite free and reasonable, except perhaps in the matter of Christian organization for the youth, which goes beyond catechetical instruction." It is noteworthy that religious instruction was allowed but civil instruction restricted. See Gerhard Besier, "Ökumenische Mission in Nachkriegsdeutschland: Die Berichte von Stewart W. Herman über die Verhältnisse in der evangelischen Kirche 1945/46. 2. Teil," in *Kirchliche Zeitgeschichte* 1, no. 2 (October 1988): 336.

[16] Ulrich Conrads, in discussion with the author, February 3, 2004, Berlin.

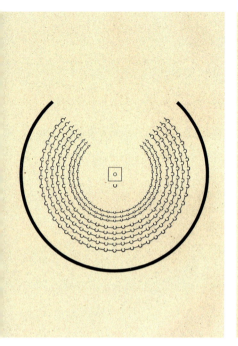 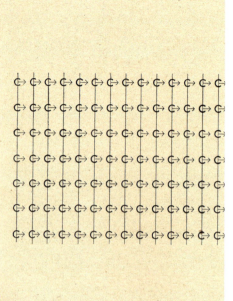 

fig. 3
Church types from Rudolf Schwarz's *Vom Bau der Kirche.*

The versions that followed seem in search of parity between audience and speaker, while the location of light source—backlit, side lit, top lit as represented by the gridded and glazed surfaces shown in the sketches—amplifies or equilibrates the relationships between those in the room and the place from which light emanates: the heavens, perhaps God. At stake in these glazed surfaces was not, or not only, the view inward that allowed the electorate to see their delegates, nor the view outward, to remind the delegates that they were beholden to their people. Transmission of light, and the transcendental bonds it signified, was just as important. The enormous glazed surfaces with which Schwippert experimented in these sketches would find their way into the realized design; the gridded zenithal surface in the third sketch ultimately took a more pragmatic turn, in the custom light ceiling he designed with the manufacturer Osram.

 Schwippert's exploration clearly references the theories published by his mentor, collaborator, and friend Rudolf Schwarz in *Vom Bau der Kirche* in 1947, republished in Chicago with the assistance of Ludwig Mies van der Rohe in 1958 under the more apt title *The Church Incarnate*. Schwarz, like Mies a Rhineland Catholic and acolyte of theologian Romano Guardini, had interrupted his architectural education in Berlin to study theology. Unlike Schwippert or Mies, he left behind voluminous architectural theoretical writing best described as a turgid, intertextual philosophy of architecture. But speaking through the architecture of his churches, Schwarz was eloquent and precise: his churches embody with real clarity ideas he developed in his writing. The diagrams in *Vom Bau der Kirche* that apparently inspired Schwippert exemplify this synergy between theory and design.[17] Each chapter of the book explored a spatial typology in terms of its putative correspondence to a different stage in a human life, then considered its distinct liturgical genesis. The chapter titles bespoke this connection. The "open ring," for example, centered and circular, bore the imprint of a congregation created by the joining of hands, whereas a frontal organization, "the path," registered in its array of forward-looking visions the act of pilgrimage. His final chapter, "the cathedral of all eras," combined all preceding types to conjoin the acts of centering and passage, culminating in the radiating moment he called the *Heiliges All*, or

[17] Thomas Hasler offers a thorough discussion of these typologies relative to Schwarz's interpretation of Gestalt theory in *Architektur als Ausdruck—Rudolf Schwarz* (Zurich and Berlin: gta / Gebr. Mann Verlag, 2000), 64ff.

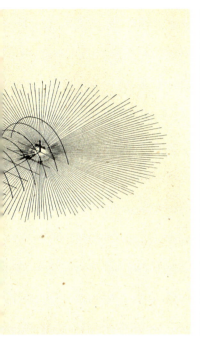

fig. 4
Bundeshaus plenary hall with square Osram-manufactured fluorescent-tube-light ceiling. TU Munich Architecture Museum. Schwi-92-49.

"all-encompassing holy space." His choice of the word *All* implied the space of the universe rather than the experiential space denoted by the more quotidian German word *Raum*. Schwarz's renovation of the circular Paulskirche in Frankfurt was an étude for Schwippert's plenary and for the transposition of liturgical space to the space of parliamentary democracy.

Certainly Schwippert's abstract studies of the plenary are more than organizational schemes. They are closely associated with transcendental, spiritual space, conceived in analogy to the churches he and Schwarz designed together.[18] This analogy went beyond even fundamental geometry and its meaning. As had been the case in their churches, light is integral to all of Schwippert's variations. Light was more than a corollary of transparency. It embodied both the light of the world and the light of God. Schwippert's design sketches ponder the way geometry constructs the relationship among the building's occupants, and the importance of those relationships to a transcendent space that light intimates.

In early 1949, just after receiving the commission and over the course of a single week, Schwippert produced numerous sketches for the complex as a whole. His drawings beautifully render volumes and landscape but are also careful to depict glazing precisely, as dark gridded surfaces. Glass was essential to Schwippert's ambition to make this the "lightest parliament in the world." It was constitutive of his vision for the plenary in which the new West German parliament would take shape. Still, while much has been written about the obvious symbolism—transparent glass to represent transparent democracy—few have taken into account the near impossibility of building in glass at the time. Fewer still have acknowledged that, actually, very little of the project was glass. But this making-do-in-spite-of is at the heart of Schwippert's achievement.

The drawing in figure 5 marks Schwippert's first use of a surface grid to articulate facades even where there is no glass. It also describes an entry sequence quite similar to what was realized, in which the two-story gymnasium, where delegates had been meeting provisionally, became the lobby or *Wandelhalle* for the new plenary. Sketched across all the new facades, the grid unifies the rangy complex. But it also implies that the building is wrapped in a skeleton structure, much as a curtain wall or glass building would have been.

[18] Schwippert and Schwarz's collaboration extended beyond the date usually given of 1934: in December 1949, they submitted an unsuccessful competition entry for the rebuilding of the Maria-Himmelfahrt Kirche in Wesel. Letters between Schwarz and Schwippert, 7.12.49–22.2.50, unnumbered binder, Schwippert Archive, Germanisches Museum.

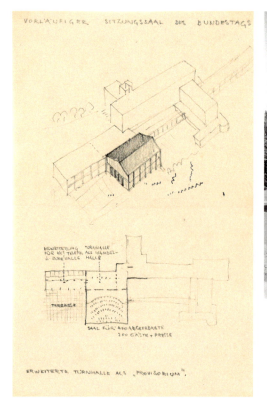

The grid implies glazing and transparency where there is none. The facade of the complex's administrative wings shows how Schwippert's optical illusion worked. Conventional windows were set within a surface of darker stone, crossed by a superordinate lighter grid. The low relief has conjoined in a single field the inset windows with the spandrels below them; as the photo makes plain, one might easily mistake this for the inset glass of a glazed office building facade. The sleight of hand that Schwippert employed in his facade grid emerges in all his details, if one looks carefully.

Consider the glazed side walls of the plenary. On the exterior, the windows lay flat within a steel grid. On the interior they are angled, with one edge coplanar with the innermost point of the steel flange and the other coplanar with the exterior glazing. In actuality, the steel grid in which the windows sit is part of the building's bearing structure, not its enclosure: each primary vertical mullion supports the roof and each intermediary horizontal mullion, equally deep, resists the horizontal force of the wind coming off the Rhine. The window frame, window structure, and bearing structure are conflated so that these large glazed areas appear instead as a single, delicate glass surface. A row of conventional shopfront glazing with awning windows fronts the restaurant that flanks the plenary. But otherwise Schwippert's building is made transparent not by glass but by the suggestive powers of its surface relief and by the experience of its spatial configuration.

Schwippert's orchestration of interior spatial sequence calibrates daylighting, dimension, controlled view, color and texture, asymmetry, and orienting movement to establish drama and hierarchy without recourse to the typical architectural language of civic buildings. Transparency— the view through, the view out, the view in, the view across—is tightly controlled, almost stingy throughout the entry sequence. Once in the building and able to move into the plenary and the restaurant, then onto the open terrace with its dramatic vistas towards the Rhine, however, the visitor experiences space as expansive. The building's primary entrance from the street

fig. 5
Sketch of Bundeshaus complex with original gymnasium as lobby. TU Munich Architecture Museum. Schwi-92-56.

fig. 6
Administrative offices, Bundeshaus. TU Munich Architecture Museum. Schwi-92-4.

led up four flights of stairs. Steps and entry door seem radically underdimensioned, smaller in width than the interior doors that gave onto the plenary hall. The rare published photographs shot along the entry facade show the building's white stuccoed surface, continuous with the original building, punctured by only a few unspectacular high windows. From the front, Schwippert's addition is entirely indistinguishable from the original building.

Upon entry, before the building was dismantled just prior to German reunification, visitors stood in one corner of an elongated room that ended at a solid wall. To their left, stretching perpendicular to the entry and more or less the same in its dimensions, was a space that connected to the corridor of the older building. Outfitted with small seating groups, and with access to the coat check and bathrooms, this was the so-called *Ruhehalle* or lounge. These two initial spaces were defined by heavy walls, which also supported the buildings above. Neither entrance nor the adjacent transitional space provided the visitor any view to the outdoors. The sparse daylight came from the entry doors at the visitors' backs.

Only as the visitor proceeded towards the entrance space's rear wall did two sets of glass doors, one to the right and one to the left, provide a sense of what was to come. On the left, the doors opened onto the restaurant, its ceiling supported on narrow steel columns and its Rhine-facing glass facade eliding the indoors with the enormous outdoor terrace. Expansive, flooded with natural light, dominated by the view of the Rhine, the restaurant was a dramatic contrast to the entry sequence. On the right was the *Wandelhalle*, two stories high, with three large windows that faced the street and a concrete staircase that floated without visible support from a U-shaped balcony to land at the dark, rectangular-gridded stone floor. The main entrance to the plenary sat asymmetrically in this foyer, on the wall opposite the windows. Only upon entering the plenary were visitors repositioned on axis; every other element of the sequence, from entry point onwards, was organized on the oblique. Even the symmetrical plenary, in the experience of its users, would rarely be entirely balanced: its two enormous glass walls, facing east and west, would have produced variable lighting conditions over the course of a day. The shadows and lighting effects Schwippert had been careful to render in his perspective sketches underlined these changing effects.

Schwippert's sense of gratification and accomplishment upon the completion of the Bundeshaus was sadly short-lived. Less than a year after completion, highly publicized repairs had to be made, leading to accusations that his project had been poorly built. But as an early, symbolic attempt to "return to the foundation of things," as Schwippert and his *Baukunst und Werkform* cohort had written in 1947, the Bundeshaus provided much from which he could extrapolate. The central question of transparency as independent of the materials and methods once used to validate modern architecture was precisely his interest at the 1951 Darmstädter Gespräche.

Schwippert spoke on the second day of the conference after a series of prepared lectures by Jose Ortega y Gasset, Martin Heidegger, and Rudolf Schwarz. Without explicitly referencing the preceding speeches, Schwippert began by describing the mythic reciprocity between an era's spiritual urges and the spaces it inhabits. To describe that reciprocity, he used his own neologism *Wohnwollen*—the will to dwell or inhabit—clearly referencing Aloïs Riegl's *Kunstwollen*, an era's will to appropriate expression in art. *Wohnwollen* was transcendent and affirming. It was an expression of ideals and ethics. But it was not articulate without space to occupy.

Inverting the typical modernist argument, Schwippert went on to suggest that genuine *Wohnwollen* might be independent of an era's physical reality. This was an important possibility in impoverished postwar Germany:

What does the directive of building look like for us today? How does this dwelling appear to us, if we are to make it into building? It seems to me that there is something quite peculiar here. In a time characterized by unrest, fear and threat . . . we sense around the world a directive of

fig. 7
Interior and exterior views of the plenary. TU Munich Architecture Museum. Schwi-92-29 and 30.

[19] Ulrich Conrads and Peter Neitzke, ed., *Mensch und Raum: das Darmstädter Gespräche* (Braunschweig: Vieweg, 1991), 104–105.
[20] Conrads and Neitzke, *Mensch und Raum*, 104–105.
[21] Conrads and Neitzke, *Mensch und Raum*, 106.

building which is anything but a bastion of refuge.... If dwelling precedes building, then we have to ask: is the affinity between the brightness and lightness of our spatial desire on the one hand, and the technical means of contemporary building on the other—is this affinity between these two things the only possibility given to us to build concretely in accordance to the internal directive?... If we had neither steel nor glass ... would then spatial building in the sense of the kind of dwelling we desire and require be forever eliminated? In other words, is that spatial being which most precisely bespeaks our dwelling on the earth today tied to the materials of today, or is this *Wohnwollen* so strong that it can form all simple materials, even all other methods, even all older forms of building—that it can penetrate them?[19]

To decouple material progress from spatial expression was a radical act. Material progress as a mandate to architecture had long been modernist canon. Perhaps pragmatism spoke here, born of the experience of the Bundeshaus. The new parliament comprised an architecture to house a new, light, aspirational West Germany *in spite of* material scarcity. But Schwippert offered another, more sinister, inverse scenario, too. Was it not "thinkable that someone could misuse the means of today... to make spaces that bear no relation to us?"[20] The experience of modernist architecture in the Third Reich had proved that architectural style was no guarantee of democratic politics.

Schwippert's questions cut both ways. If *Wohnwollen* were dependent upon both material and architectural style, then the lack or misuse of material might be tantamount to "an end to spatial building."[21] Spatial building, a term with which Schwippert invoked both Schwarz's and Heidegger's considerations from the previous day of the conference, was the fundamental human activity through which community was formed. If it were merely material dependent or, perhaps worse, corruptible by virtue of materials misused, then there was little hope of any architectural ethics.

In his role as moderator, Schwippert left his audience to ponder three distinct scenarios: that an affinity between spatial desire and technical means could be "the only possibility given to us to build concretely in accordance with the internal directive"; that spatial desire could be "so

strong that it can form all simple materials, even all older forms of construction"; or that someone could "misuse the means of today ... to make spaces that bear no relation to us."[22] He offered no answer to the questions he had posed. But in his role as architect of the Bundeshaus he had made clear: architecture was the practice of sensing, embodying, and providing for the needs of *Wohnwollen* under any circumstances.

    Amidst such considerations, beyond Tamms's "comfortable simplification,"[23] why insist upon an architecture associated with light and transparency, with glass and steel? *"Das bunte Glas/zerstört den Hass"* had been engraved above the door of Bruno Taut's 1914 glass pavilion, a militantly utopian credo at the threshold of an unimaginably violent future, as though glass could make politics. Writing forty years later about the first pavilion staged by West Germany at a World's Fair, Schwippert countered. He described the life-world around him, one in which light and lightness had effected change through subtle, individual efforts: "The glass walls of new construction, the new brightness of the office; the workshop, the factory, the delicate lines of the new furnishings; the friendliness of living amidst greenery, the transformation of clothing and decorative arts—these together are the great efforts of human resistance to threat, to darkness, to looming chaos."[24] Glass, simply a means to provide both light and transparency, no longer embodied in Schwippert's words the messianic promise it had before the two world wars. Lightness, couched as a demand that came from the bottom up, from the people in their bright offices and transformed clothes and delicate furnishings, was democratic in the most basic sense. The architecture of the Bundeshaus was, in this context, a manifestation of a groundswell, neither a symbol of aspiration to good governance nor a literal mechanism to check bad.

[22] Conrads and Neitzke, *Mensch und Raum*, 106.
[23] Tamms quoted in Durth, *Deutsche Architekten*, 236.
[24] Hans Schwippert, "Notizen zur deutschen Beteiligung an der Weltausstellung zu Brüssel 1958," typescript dated October 14, 1955. DKA Nachlass Schwippert, Germanisches Nationalmuseum Nuremberg.

Biography

Lynnette Widder is associate professor at Columbia University. She has written for *Daidalos, Bauwolt, Manifest, Kritische Berichte*, and *Journal of Industrial Ecology*, and authored *Year Zero to Economic Miracle: Hans Schwippert and Sept Ruf in Postwar West German Building Culture* (gta, 2022). Her work with aardvarchitecture has been published internationally. She holds Institute for Ideas and Imagination and MacDowell fellowships (2020–2022) and has received grants from the Graham Foundation, DAAD, UNDP Guinea, and the Mellon Foundation.

Whose Architecture? Whose Criticism?: Applying Stakeholder Theory to the Process of Criticism

Alexandra Staub

fig. 1
The Bank of America Tower in the New York skyline.
Photo: COOKFOX/Ryan Browne.

The duty of architectural criticism is to be honest without bias. In an era of increased branding, where the internet allows for a broad and rapid influence of perceptions, architectural criticism should strive for transparency in how buildings are assessed while at the same time maintaining rigor of method in such assessments. This paper will present a tripartite method to critique buildings based on stakeholder theory[1] and architectural ethics. The first layer of analysis explores the process by which a building is commissioned, designed, and constructed. The second layer examines the building's aesthetic coding, while the third layer considers the building as an expression of power over users versus their empowerment. Each of these layers takes into account a series of stakeholders and their interests to better understand buildings and urban ensembles, especially when their production is embedded in complex power relations. As a case study, the Bank of America Tower at One Bryant Park in New York City (Cook + Fox Architects, 2010) will be critiqued.

In 2010, the Bank of America Tower at One Bryant Park in midtown Manhattan opened to much acclaim as the first Leadership in Energy and Environmental Design (LEED) Platinum-certified commercial skyscraper in history. The developer's aims were lofty: to create "the highest quality modern workplace emphasizing daylight, fresh air, and an intrinsic connection to the outdoors," with a slew of advanced technologies to "save energy, use less water, generate less construction waste, and provide healthier and more comfortable indoor environments."[2] Just as lofty were the expected investment returns, as the tower became one of the latest gems in an area that had seen spectacular new construction and extensive refurbishment of older buildings, sending commercial rents "through the roof."[3]

In the context of the neoliberalism that has shaped the US economy since the 1980s, a focus on making immense financial profits through a philanthropic approach that "gives back" to the community is not unusual. Yet who ultimately judges the success of these efforts? The Bank of America Tower is an example of architect and developer branding that, repeated throughout the internet, has shaped an evaluative narrative that broadly and rapidly molded the building's image. Faced with this "critique" that fuels the perception of a building's success, how can we begin to form a more nuanced evaluation of the building in question?

Starting from the premise that architectural criticism should strive for transparency in establishing the criteria by which buildings are assessed, I propose a method of criticism based on an analysis of stakeholder agency and interests as a key to understanding and critiquing a building's ethical merit. This method interlinks three analytical layers: a consideration of stakeholder interests in the design process, an analysis of the building's aesthetic qualities and their reflection of stakeholder interests, and a study of how the building's setting and spatial qualities either empower stakeholders or grant power over them.

As used here, the term "stakeholder" was first proposed by business management professor R. Edward Freeman in the 1980s as an adaptation of the word "shareholder." Freeman defined stakeholders as "groups and individuals that have a valid interest in the activities and outcomes of a firm and whom the firm relies on to achieve its objectives."[4] In contrast to the prevalent management theory of the era, which addressed only shareholder profits, stakeholder theory sought to generate value for a firm by taking into

keywords:

architectural ethics, stakeholder theory, Bank of America Tower

[1] The definition of stakeholders as "groups and individuals that have a valid interest in the activities and outcomes of a firm and on whom the firm relies to achieve its objectives" is adapted from a management strategy outlined in R. Edward Freeman, Jeffrey S. Harrison, and Stelios Zyglidopoulos, *Stakeholder Theory: Concepts and Strategies* (Cambridge: Cambridge University Press, 2018), 1. Initially seen as a value-creation tactic, the approach is now used in business ethics as well.

[2] Durst Organization, accessed July 28, 2021, https://www.durst.org/properties/one-bryant-park.

[3] Jeremy Quittner, "42nd St.'s Midsection Expands: New Towers, Pricey Renovations Upgrade Area East of Sixth Avenue," *Crain's New York Business* 21, no. 3 (2005): 34.

[4] Freeman, Harrison, and Zyglidopoulos, *Stakeholder Theory*, 1.

fig. 2
The Bank of America Tower from Bryant Park.
Photo: COOKFOX/Ryan Browne.

account stakeholder interests. Over time, stakeholder theory became part of the moral foundation in business practice, and it expanded into other fields such as law, healthcare, public policy, and environmental policy.[5]

Stakeholder theory may readily be adapted to architectural production. Primary stakeholders in architecture can be defined as the client, the developer, the architects, and the building's users. Secondary stakeholders, meaning those who engage with the building through the primary stakeholders, are typically banks, various regulators, construction firms, suppliers, the community at large, and, when considering a building's sustainability, the environment, as well as future generations.

Stakeholder interests vary and can sometimes be at odds with one another. In the Bank of America Tower, the primary stakeholders can be seen as: the Durst Organization as the project developer; the Bank of America as the primary tenant; other building tenants, which included a law firm, two restaurants, and Al Gore's Generation Investment Management firm; Cook + Fox as the project architects; the building's users, including office workers, staff, and visitors; and, finally, future generations, who benefit from ecologically sustainable buildings that counter climate problems and who were defined by both the developer and the architects as major stakeholders whose interests they wished to address.

Secondary stakeholders can be defined as: the US Green Building Council (a national certification board), which sought validation of its LEED certification system; the architectural profession, which was interested in seeing an example of a high-tech ecological building realized as a precedent for further development in the field; and the public at large, who live in the urban spaces that developers and architects create.

[5] Ibid., 163ff.

The First Layer of Analysis: Stakeholders and the Decision-making Process

The decision to build the Bank of America Tower came about, like many such decisions, through a series of opportunities. The Durst Organization had spent decades buying up properties in a somewhat run-down pocket of Manhattan, and in 2003 took the final steps of assembling a site for a major new project. As two owners of existing buildings on the site declined to sell, the State of New York informed the Durst Organization that if it were able to find an anchor tenant for the project, it could enact eminent domain to have the remaining buildings condemned and torn down, even though they were not in a "blighted" neighborhood. Once the Bank of America signed on as the anchor tenant, the remaining holdouts sold quickly, and the Durst Organization was able to move forward with the project.[6]

The contentious use of eminent domain illustrates how, as a developer, the Durst Organization was willing to use its position to achieve financial gain from a major new building in a gentrifying area. Yet the organization also regarded the new building as a public relations boost that would highlight the company's perceived leadership and innovation among New York realtors. Heralding the tower as a "new standard in sustainable commercial construction" and "the first skyscraper in North America to achieve LEED Platinum certification," the developer touted the fifty-five-story, 2.2-million-square-foot building as visionary, a workplace of the highest quality.[7] The developer did not just list benefits for the tenants and their employees, the firm highlighted portions of the building that would be available to the public as well, including a ground-floor "Urban Garden Room," a pedestrian passageway, and a restored, 50,000-square-foot theater on the site.[8] The Urban Garden Room was touted as an indoor extension of nearby Bryant Park, owned by the New York City Department of Parks and Recreation but managed by a private corporation. As such, the Bank of America Tower continued a neoliberal tradition that gave private entities special rights over public lands.

In 2003, the Durst Organization approached Richard Cook of Cook + Fox Architects who had designed the Ross Institute in East Hampton, where "connecting the user with

[6] Terry Pristin, "Developers Can't Imagine a World without Eminent Domain," *The New York Times*, January 18, 2006, https://www.nytimes.com/2006/01/18/realestate/developers-cant-imagine-a-world-without-eminent-domain.html.

[7] Cf. Durst, https://www.durst.org/properties/one-bryant-park; cookfox.com, accessed July 28, 2021, https://cookfox.com/projects/one-bryant-park/.

[8] Durst, https://www.durst.org/properties/one-bryant-park.

fig. 3
The Bank of America Tower lobby
Photo: COOKFOX/David Sundberg/Esto.

nature" had been a central design focus.[9] The architects saw a need for more sustainable development in urban centers, stating that "[i]nefficient, outdated urbanity places an unsustainable demand on our sources of energy; therefore, it is imperative that we consider not only how much energy we use, but also where it is coming from and how it is made."[10] The architects saw the Bank of America Tower as an opportunity to "establish a new benchmark for high-performance buildings" that would use state-of-the-art technology while incorporating the city's transit infrastructure through access to a major underground transit hub.[11] Technology implemented included an on-site electricity-generation plant and other features to avoid daytime demand on the city's power grid, use of the site's gray water (from rain and snow), waterless urinals and low-flow toilets and faucets, exterior glazing to minimize solar heat gain, and an automated lighting system to dim lighting during daytime hours. Recycled materials were used in the building's construction, while a "hospital grade" air-filtration system was designed to provide clean air for the building's inhabitants.[12] These features in and of themselves were not technologically new; what was novel was the architect's desire to incorporate so many of them in a single, large-scale office building. While the architect saw the Bank of America project as an opportunity to innovatively merge technology and urban transit planning into a symbiotic push for "global human health and well-being,"[13] and a holistic "back to nature" experience, the many claims regarding the building's sustainability were designed to also market the firm as a sustainability innovator.

The building was frequently touted as "the first skyscraper in North America to achieve LEED Platinum certification."[14] As such, the US Green Building Council became an important stakeholder in the design and building process. Certification of such a high-profile skyscraper—which is fee-based and completely voluntary—was an opportunity for the US Green Building Council to further LEED's reputation as the criterion of successful sustainable architecture.

Both the developer's and the architect's claims of sustainability came under question in 2015 as it became evident that, with more than double the energy use per square foot of other office towers, the Bank of America Tower, rather than being an energy miser, was one of the largest energy consumers in New York City when compared to both "all bank / financial institution" buildings and "peer buildings"; that is, buildings of a similar age, building type, and size.[15] Outrage came swiftly. *The Guardian* criticized the LEED system as a "brand [that] has been embraced by designers looking to establish themselves as innovative, real estate brokers looking to boost rents and companies looking to proclaim their sustainability bona fides."[16] The new city data also called into question the definition of "sustainability" suggested by the building's LEED Platinum rating, which had implied that the building was a model for the future. What had gone wrong?

It soon became clear that energy use as a LEED and marketing strategy had not realistically considered the building in use. For example, since LEED ratings are based on comparisons to "conventional" buildings rather than on a quantifiable standard, an architect or engineer could propose improvements to a very inefficient design in order to achieve a high LEED rating.[17] The architect's and developer's claims of energy savings were equally misleading, as they described such savings without defining comparison objects or standards.[18] Once comparable buildings in Manhattan were brought into play through the Mayor's Office of Sustainability's Energy and Water Performance Map, the architect's and developer's optimistic calculations of vast energy savings evaporated.

When an article in *The New Republic* titled "Bank of America's Toxic Tower" criticized the LEED system for having created an unrealistically positive impression of the building's ecological footprint, the senior vice president of LEED at the US Green Building Council wrote a scathing rebuttal in which he attempted to absolve his agency of all responsibility for LEED's failure to address the discrepancy between the building's LEED rating and its actual energy consumption.[19] Clearly, the Green Building Council feared that LEED's reputation, as well as its marketing potential, was at stake.

[9] Richard Cook, "Sustainable Skyscrapers and the Well-Being of the City," in *Practicing Sustainability*, ed. Guru Madhavan, Barbara Oakley, David Green, David Koon, and Penny Low (New York: Springer, 2012), 25–30.
[10] Ibid.
[11] Ibid.
[12] Durst, https://www.durst.org/properties/one-bryant-park.
[13] Cook, *op. cit.*
[14] Durst, https://www.durst.org/properties/one-bryant-park.
[15] NYC Energy & Water Performance Map, accessed July 28, 2021, https://benchmarking.cityofnewyork.us/#/.
[16] Bruce Watson, "The Skyscraper at the Heart of the Debate over America's Green Building Standard," *The Guardian*, November 6, 2015, https://www.theguardian.com/sustainable-business/2015/nov/06/bank-of-america-one-bryant-park-leed-certification-sustainable-design.
[17] Ibid.
[18] Cook, *op. cit.*; Durst, https://www.durst.org/properties/one-bryant-park.
[19] Sam Roudman, "Bank of America's Toxic Tower," *The New Republic*, July 28, 2013, https://newrepublic.com/article/113942/bank-america-tower-and-leed-ratings-racket.

Part of the problem was separating assessment of the building's performance from the performance of what happened within; that is, differentiating between the building as a container for a generic program and the energy use of the building's occupants. As architectural commentator Craig Schwitter put it, "putting the LEED stamp on a building doesn't necessarily mean it's all that climate-friendly . . . . The problem is that not wasting energy isn't the same thing as using less of it."[20] For example, the building's combined heat and power (CHP) system used a natural gas-fired cogeneration plant that was only economical if operated continuously. Since nighttime electrical needs were vastly reduced, the excess electricity was used to generate ice that was then used to cool the building during the day.[21] While this system allowed daytime peak electrical demand to be reduced by 30 percent, hardly anyone noted that the system required more energy than usual outside of peak hours. Another energy challenge was presented by the facade's transparency, as energy loss was balanced against a desire for better views that would command higher rents.[22] Finally, the many computers used on the bank's six trading floors required an enormous amount of energy that no one had accounted for.[23]

In ignoring such factors, architectural critics and the architectural industry lauded the architects and developers for producing a building shell, while the architects had set themselves the lofty goal of designing the building as a holistic system that would serve the users' and even future generations' health and happiness. Compounding this discrepancy, three crucial stakeholders in the building's production—the developer, the architect, and the LEED certification board—had seen the Bank of America Tower as an opportunity to market themselves as front-runners in sustainability. Architectural writers failed to realize the discrepancy between the architect's holistic vision and the building's piecemeal approach to wellness and energy savings or that claims of energy savings never defined a baseline measure. The literature applauding the Bank of America Tower as ushering in a new era of climate-friendly high-rises had conflated architectural marketing with building critique, all the while taking a misleadingly narrow view of the issue indeed.

fig. 4
The Bank of America Tower "Urban Garden Room."
Photo: COOKFOX/Ryan Browne.

[20] Tim McDonnell, "There's Been a Boom in Energy-Efficient Skyscraper Construction—But There's a Catch," Grist, September 16, 2015, https://grist.org/climate-energy/theres-been-a-boom-in-energy-efficient-skyscraper-construction/.

[21] Joann Gonchar, "Case Study: Bank of America Tower," GreenSource: The Magazine of Sustainable Design 5, no. 6 (2010): 78–83.

[22] Ibid.

[23] Bryan Walsh, "The Surprisingly Large Energy Footprint of the Digital Economy [UPDATE]," Time Magazine, August 14, 2013, https://science.time.com/2013/08/14/power-drain-the-digital-cloud-is-using-more-energy-than-you-think/.

[24] Simon Guy and Graham Farmer, "Contested Constructions: The Competing Logics of Green Buildings and Ethics," in Ethics and the Built Environment, ed. Warwick Fox (London and New York: Routledge, 2000), 73–87.

The Second Layer of Analysis: Aesthetics as Ethics

In 2000, Simon Guy and Graham Farmer described six often competing concepts of "green" buildings and their ethical premises in their essay "Contested Constructions." Noting that "the debate around green buildings can be visualized as a landscape of often fragmented, contradictory and competing values and interests," they analyzed buildings according to factors such as building image, design strategy, scale, space, and technology, correlating such tangible aspects with ethical concerns each of their "logics" sought to address. The Bank of America Tower falls squarely into two of their listed logics: "Smart" and "Aesthetic." The Smart idiom sees buildings as assets, while the Aesthetic idiom strives for buildings that are iconic. The corresponding design strategies and ethical concerns are to reduce energy, to achieve "futurity," and to express nature through an iconic building form.[24]

The Bank of America Tower's architects used aesthetics in the form of futuristic design with inserted fragments of "nature" to signal both market-driven corporate power

and ecological values, with an emphasis arguably placed on the former. This focus mirrors how LEED's system of evaluating green buildings has evolved into a vehicle for promoting premium real estate. As Rick Fedrizzi, one of LEED's founders, states: "In the 1980s and 1990s, people were getting turned on by building materials that looked great ... [T]op buildings were largely defined by aesthetics. There was no connection to air quality, water and energy usage, or the waste produced onsite .... A big part of promoting LEED was making people understand what a high-performance building is."[25] As Fedrizzi makes clear, LEED's green building approach was driven by public perception from the outset, born of a negotiation between the consumer's aesthetic desires and the builder's attempts at resource-saving technical functionality, a union that has carried through into the Bank of America Tower.

In large part, buildings like the Bank of America Tower do not have a stereotypically "green" aesthetic. The tower uses largely high-tech methods to reduce energy consumption and waste, and many systems are hidden. The developer and the architect were interested in producing an iconic building that would stand out in the New York skyline—there is much mention of the building as the "second-tallest building in New York," a nod to the idea that superlative height makes for striking buildings—yet they also realized that the building's tenants and users, important stakeholders in the building's perceived success, demanded an agreeable environment for their day-to-day activities. The architects theorized about users' interests based on their own experience, leading to a focus on views, fresh air, and abundant natural light as important design (and perceived sustainability) criteria. With Manhattan's environment so shaped by humans to begin with, the architects' ad hoc approach became visible as Richard Cook mused how users' connection to nature is necessary because it "feels good" and because appreciation of nature is important in "the long-term efforts of practicing sustainability."[26]

The building's aesthetic logic was further advanced through an emphasis on its faceted facade. Project architect Serge Appel discussed how the irregularly jagged building shape was inspired by a quartz crystal "and the way in which light diffuses through its facets," the angles designed to create a perspectival play so the building appears less imposing to pedestrians looking upward.[27] The architects further accommodated the pedestrian and the general public through the 3,500-square-foot "Urban Garden Room": a ground-floor space that would be open to the public as a type of weather-protected lounge. Although

fig. 5
The Bank of America Tower, corner conference room with view of Bryant Park. Image: Author.

fig. 6
The Bank of America Tower, interior corridor of an office suite. Image: Author.

fig. 7
The Bank of America Tower, view of a trading floor. Image: ABCO Peerless.

[25] Quoted in Watson, "America's Green Building Standard."
[26] Cook, *op. cit.*
[27] Murrye Bernard, "Designing a NYC Icon: One Bryant Park/Bank of America Tower," *Buildipedia.com*, January 4, 2012, http://buildipedia.com/aec-pros/featured-architecture/designing-a-nyc-icon-one-bryant-park-/-bank-of-america-tower.

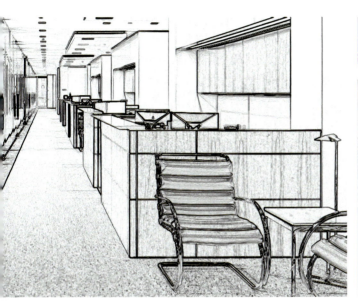 

this lobby space is not directly adjacent to Bryant Park, and its materials—hewn stone, metal, and glass—are characteristic of the built rather than the natural environment, the architects nevertheless emphasized how they saw the popular Bryant Park as a central concept for their design.[28]

A 9.6-acre public park that is listed on the National Register of Historic Places and is designated as a New York City Landmark, Bryant Park became a symbolic element for the tower. Located southeast of the tower and expanding from the neoclassical New York Public Library building, the park includes a formal arrangement of sculptures, memorials, food stands, a carousel, and restrooms, as well as a large lawn and shade trees. A nineteenth-century vision of tamed nature, the park presents an incarnation of highly cultivated recreational spaces within the urban grid.

In their metaphorical use of natural elements such as quartz crystal and vegetation, the architects merged a conventional expression of corporate power-architecture—emphasizing hard-edged tech-modernism—with a softer focus on the ideals of greenery, fresh air, and ecology through references to the park and through the building's ventilation system, finishes, and furnishings. The latter included a bamboo ceiling in the lobby area, entryway door handles made of wood, the Urban Garden Room's bistro-style seating (similar to that of the adjoining Bryant Park), and the room's large, blob-like shrubs sculpted of espaliered English ivy. These fittings stood in for the nature that Manhattan's hard urbanity was loath to provide.

The interior design of the upper floors was more conventional, with a clean-lined aesthetic typical of modernist-inspired corporate clients. Furnishings included metal-framed and leather-padded office seating, elegant glass and wood partition walls, glossy color accents, and sand-colored flooring.[29] As in most office towers, natural lighting is limited by opportunities for window placement. While executive offices and conference rooms on the building's perimeter do have access to views and natural daylight, the six trading floors are artificially lit, open-plan office spaces with bleak white columns stoically placed between vast rows of office desks, each topped with five monitors and other computer equipment.[30]

Overall, the building's aesthetic language vacillates between the status expectations of a high-end corporate client and the assumed user desires of working in "nature." The former is expressed through the elegant furniture and finishes that, being aesthetically

[28] Ibid.
[29] Arenson Office Furniture Sales, accessed July 28, 2021, https://www.aof.com/projects/one-bryant-park.
[30] Ibid.

modern, express the client's forward-looking values. This is mirrored in the futuristic glass sheath of the building envelope itself, which expresses the tenants' cutting-edge status in a competitive urban marketplace. Connection to nature is purportedly realized through features that incorporate daylight, filtered air, and wooden accents. Some offices have views of Bryant Park, and there is a green space within the building. That such nature-inspired features are limited makes clear the difficulty of including "nature" within buildings that are set in the complex and dense urban system typified by midtown Manhattan. In terms of its sustainability, the tower's powerful mechanical features remain aesthetically invisible to the observer, while its fixtures and finishes, highly touted as connecting the user to nature, remain largely metaphorical in their association.

The Third Layer of Analysis: Power over Stakeholders Versus Their Empowerment

Kim Dovey, in his book *Framing Places: Mediating Power in Built Form,* has outlined five ways in which buildings exert power over the user. These methods can be overt, such as when barriers restrict the user's access, or latent, such as when public monuments signify state power. Users can be manipulated, for example when spaces are organized so that users unconsciously perform actions in a certain way, or they can be "seduced," for example through advertising. Finally, trappings of authority, such as signs, can direct the user of a building.[31]

The Bank of America Tower, largely hailed by critics as a new precedent for sustainable building, was first presented by the stakeholders who designed and developed it. This included the Durst Organization and Cook + Fox Architects, whose seductive writing about the tower sounded informative and analytic as they theorized about the urban condition, discussed the building's features, and offered a quantitative, albeit incomplete, analysis for their sustainability claims.

In setting the tone for this early narrative, sustainability features dominated the discussion and soon translated into monetary rewards, not only for the developer, who saw himself able to charge tenants higher rents than he could in a conventional building, but also for the building's tenants. In a 2009 interview, Douglas Durst noted, "[i]ncreased productivity is the big attraction for companies seeking green workplaces .... For a company with highly paid knowledge workers, even a small increase in productivity yields immediate bottom-line benefits .... Increased productivity is much more important to green building tenants than the much smaller savings from reduced energy and water use."[32] Commenting on the role of the US Green Building Council's LEED rating as a marketing mechanism, Durst added: "Today's marketing forces virtually require that an upgraded building offer the green-benefits guarantee of a LEED rating."[33] Would the developer be willing to build "green" for the sake of the environment and future generations alone? The question remains unanswered.

It is not easy to evaluate a building as complex as the Bank of America Tower. While separate aspects of the building, such as its energy-saving features or design features that aim to generate specific user experiences, can be evaluated individually, once the architect advances claims of a more holistic, synergistic nature, the building must be seen as more than the sum of its parts. In the Bank of America Tower, the user experience could only be speculative. Was the "Urban Garden Room" with its sculptural ivy blobs a unique continuation of Bryant Park, or simply another high-rise lobby space? What about the functional requirements of the Bank of America, with its six floors of trading areas dominated by small workspaces stacked with monitors? Not only did these areas require large amounts of energy to run the equipment, they hardly offered their users access to nature. One could even ask if designing a single biophilic building within the dense urbanity of midtown Manhattan can achieve the type of holistic experience of "nature" the architects aimed for, or if we would be better off rethinking our urban experiences and the workplaces

[31] Kim Dovey, *Framing Places: Mediating Power in Built Form,* 2nd ed. (London and New York: Routledge, 2008), 12–15.

[32] Charles Lockwood, "Q&A with Douglas Durst," *Urban Land* 68, no. 9 (September 2009): 132–133.

[33] Ibid.

in them at a much larger scale—that of the city itself.

The Bank of America Tower has many handsome architectural features that architectural critics readily picked up on. The lobby is elegantly proportioned, the materiality is modern and understated with an agreeable blend of colors and textures, and spaces along the building's perimeter are well lit. Many of the sustainability features, such as the power-generation plant or the water-saving features, are excellent concepts. Yet in critiquing a building of this nature, is it enough to speak of spatial, material, and lighting qualities or to list technological features? Should critics take into account more holistic social and environmental factors and their influence on various stakeholders? Especially when both the developer and the architect make claims that they have redefined a building typology to incorporate nature into the urban workplace in groundbreaking ways, the critic would be well-served to closely examine such assertions.

Built structures present us with a complex interplay of social, technological, aesthetic, and symbolic factors, and often represent different things to different stakeholders. In the interest of transparency, architectural critique should help us unravel a building's intertwined narratives in order to build up a more holistic picture of its architectural merits. One way of achieving this is to consider the interests of all stakeholders involved, not just a vocal few. Examining the building's process, aesthetics, and spatial language through the lens of the stakeholders involved brings us closer to a fair and independent critique.

Research assistance for this article was provided by Audrey Buck and Aleah Davis, graduate students in the Penn State University Department of Architecture.

Biography

Alexandra Staub is a professor of architecture at Penn State University (USA) and an affiliate faculty of Penn State's Rock Ethics Institute. Her research focuses on how our built environment shapes, and is shaped by, our understanding of culture. This interest leads her to examine not just what we build, but also how we get there: design processes and their social implications, the economic, ecological, and social sustainability of architecture and urban systems, interpretations of private and public spaces, architectural ethics understood as questions of power and empowerment, and how social class or gender shapes our expectations for the use of space.

Staub's current work examines ethics and stakeholder theory as a framework for spatial production. She has published extensively on the intersection of architecture and power, ethics, and gender. Her 2018 edited volume *The Routledge Companion to Modernity, Space and Gender*, examines how modernity has defined various cultural contexts, how this concept is expressed spatially through architecture and urban form, and how this has affected women in their everyday lives. *Conflicted Identities: Housing and the Politics of Cultural Representation* examines, using West Germany of the 1950s and 60s as a case study, how nation states use officially sanctioned architecture to create a national identity that often diverges greatly from an identity represented by the vast realm of domestic space defined largely by those who occupy it.

Staub completed her BA in psychology at Barnard College in New York before gaining a professional architecture degree (Dipl.-Ing. Arch) at the University of the Arts in Berlin. She completed her PhD at the Brandenburg Technical University (BTU) in Cottbus, Germany. Before joining the faculty at Penn State, she worked as an architect and an architectural journalist, translator and editor in Berlin, as well as a junior faculty member at the BTU Cottbus.

The Lost Battle for Memory: The European Solidarity Centre in Gdańsk and Architectural Criticism in Poland

Błażej Ciarkowski

fig. 1
The European Solidarity Centre seen from the edge of the city. © Błażej Ciarkowski.

The inauguration of the European Solidarity Centre (ECS) in Gdańsk became a great opportunity to discuss the heritage of the "Solidarity" Trade Union. Media praised the building as a new architectural icon and a central European agora for discussing issues of social justice. However, the unintended symbolism of the edifice depicts something different. The monumental, rusting corten-clad hull of an imaginary ship located at a failing shipyard that is slowly turning into an elite housing estate illustrates the fall of social solidarity as an ideal. Instead of becoming a platform for the exchange of thoughts and ideas, the ECS is a monument to a one-sided narrative.

Harbor cranes by the docks of the Gdańsk Shipyard, the inconspicuous steel gate leading to the plant, and the shipyard itself—the home to the Independent Self-Governing Trade Union "Solidarity" (NSZZ "Solidarność")—have together become one of the most widely recognized symbols of post-socialist transformation in Poland. In its vicinity, the construction of the new European Solidarity Centre (ECS) commenced on the thirtieth anniversary of the agreement between the striking trade unionists and the representatives of the communist authorities.

With great difficulty, the cranes were defended against being sold for scrap (and it is uncertain how much longer they may avoid such a fate). Gate No.2 is now recognized as a national monument. The shipyard area has been divided into smaller units that are less and less part of a genius loci. In this context, questions arise: what is the role of the ECS in the narrative of this extraordinary space and the recent history of Poland? What messages, both intentional and unintentional, are transmitted by the architecture of the ECS? Finally, what does this edifice in Gdańsk tell us about the role of architectural criticism in contemporary Poland and the condition of our domestic architecture?

The Truth and the Myth

The ECS was supposed to become a manifestation of the great success of post-socialist transformation in Poland, a monument to the creation myth of the Third Polish Republic. It was supposed to tell the story of a bloodless revolution, and its heroes, who led Poland and Poles from real socialism to the promised land of capitalism, from communist oppression to democracy. "The new edifice of ECS will be an agora for people and ideas which support the building and development of a civil society, a meeting place for those who care about the future of the world,"[1] declared the architects representing FORT design studio, who won the international contest for the edifice in 2007.

Bronisław Komorowski, the president of Poland, officially inaugurated the ECS on August 30, 2014. He spoke about the supra-local dimension of the social protest movement, which was Solidarity at its core. He recalled the people who nowadays are perceived as the icons of Poland's road to democracy. One of them, Lech Wałęsa, described the purported role of the ECS during the inauguration, with the assembled crowd cheering every sentence: "Once again, we will gather together the people who will remind us how to win in a different way. Those people will search for the solutions to contemporary problems in contemporary times."[2] However,

keywords:

Solidarity, European Solidarity Centre, Polish architecture, architectural criticism in Poland

[1] Anna Cymer, "Europejskie Centrum Solidarności," accessed June 30, 2021, www.culture.pl.

"those people" whom the former president of Poland mentioned were not present at the celebration. From a distance, from behind the fence, the shipbuilders' cloudy gazes followed the limousines which passed the edifice of the ECS. "Those people"—trade unionists and workers, the foundation of Solidarity—had not been invited to the inauguration. Grzegorz Klaman, the Gdańsk-based artist most associated with the shipyard, described the situation as follows: "They watched us as they would watch monkeys in the cage."[3] Thus, the grand opening of the ECS has become a manifestation of a certain version of the recent history of Poland and a parade of self-proclaimed depositaries of memory.

The relics of this memory were placed in a reliquary made of steel and concrete: the edifice of the European Solidarity Centre. The building, erected from 2010 to 2014, is nearly 200,000 cubic meters in volume and cost around 230,000,000 PLN (over 50,000,000 euros). The compact shape with slanted walls represents an industrial aesthetic. The walls are covered with corten steel plates with visible seams, oxidizing more readily than most steel to change their color over time. The rusty surfaces of the walls are pierced with horizontal stripes of windows. Vertical rifts between different sections of the building were glazed over and covered with lamellas. In the interior, the architects exposed the reinforced concrete beams and steel struts, which provide structural stiffness and, at the same time, complete the industrial character of the edifice. According to its designers, the building as a whole was intended to support the story about the heritage of Solidarity and the place where it was born—the Gdańsk Shipyard. It was to testify about hope, heroism, and the desire for freedom.

fig. 2
The Solidarity Square preceding Gate No. 2 of the Gdańsk Shipyard with three monumental crosses dedicated to the victims of the 1970 protests in the center.
© Błażej Ciarkowski.

As often happens, the intended narrative became its own parody. The architecture, which was supposed to reinforce a reassuring myth, revealed the (inconvenient) truth. It became the unintended metaphor of the post-socialist transformation, its negative results, and exclusion.

Between the Gate, the Crosses, and Tatlin's Tower

The ECS narrative is constructed on two different levels: the architectural envelope and the exposition inside. Both equally (and against the designers' intentions!) illustrate the history of how the Warsaw and Gdańsk–based elites have stolen the legend of the people's social movement.

The first and most eye-catching aspect is the location of the ECS in relation to the shipyard. The building was erected near Gate No. 2 of the Gdańsk Shipyard; it was there, in 1968, that the people of Gdańsk left flowers to express their solidarity with striking shipbuilders. It was where Lech Wałęsa climbed the fence in August 1980 to announce the end of the strike and the reaching of an agreement with communist authorities. In front of Gate No. 2, on the city's side, is Solidarity Square. A low epitaph wall limits a space paved with granite, but its focal point is three forty-two-meter-tall crosses—a monument designed by Bogdan Pietruszka, Elżbieta Szczodrowska-Peplińska, Robert Pepliński, and Wiesław Szyślak, and dedicated to the Fallen Shipyard Workers, victims of the 1970 protests.

Next to Gate No. 2, an inconspicuous reception pavilion leads to the shipyard. Once one passes through, an astonishing landscape appears. A field of grass and weeds foregrounds historical buildings and shipyard machinery, their silhouettes looming on the horizon. Near the reception, surrounded by high grass and thistles, are two neglected structures—the gates created by Grzegorz Klaman. The first one is made of rusty steel, the same as the hulls of the ships, and it resembles the bow of a sinking vessel. Inside the structure, screens display quotations and slogans, which, according to the artist, turn into a cacophony of meaningless

[2] Wiadomości, "W Gdańsku otwarto Europejskie Centrum Solidarności," accessed July 2, 2021, www.dzieje.pl.
[3] Grzegorz Klaman, interview by Błażej Ciarkowski, Sobieszewo, June 25, 2021.

phrases. The other has an "international" character and represents the deconstructed Third International Tower of Vladimir Tatlin—the symbol of a communist utopia whose decay (deconstruction) started in Gdańsk.[4]

We can easily indicate different strategies of commemoration and other methods of building relations with the past. Gate No. 2 has become a historical monument and a *lieux de memoire*, even though it was originally a purely utilitarian infrastructural element. The monument imposes one dominant, official narrative. Klaman's installations, on the other hand, elude any obvious, simple interpretations while attempting to place the heritage of Solidarity in a broader context.

In such an extraordinary space, permeated with different meanings and symbols, the monumental edifice of the ECS has been raised.

The Edifice and its Message

The architect Wojciech Targowski declared that one of his aims was to create a building that would become a platform for social dialogue. Critics spoke in a similar manner echoing the narrative established by the authors of the building.[5] According to them, the *architecture parlante* of the ECS "serves to promote Solidarity's ideas of social movement": slanted, reinforced concrete walls clad with corten steel rest against one another, just like the letters in the Solidarity logo, designed by artist Jerzy Janiszewski. Rusty steel plates refer to the hulls of ships built in the shipyard. A spacious internal atrium filled with greenery is a platform of intellectual dialogue. The square paved with gray granite and the fountains in front of the building reflect the popular dream of a better world. "Regarding the popular character of Solidarity, the message had to be clear and easy to understand,"[6] wrote Targowski.

Being fully aware of the author's intentions, one should consider whether the message is truly "clear." Who is its recipient? Is it possible to interpret it in a different way from what the architects intended? Is the architect unknowingly becoming a teacher who aims to subconsciously educate the users of the building, and at the same time to take away their right to reflect on its meaning in their own way? Isn't it a sin of pride to exclude from the official narrative those who were pushed to the margins of society by the post-socialist transformation, including the shipbuilders who were not invited to the opening ceremony? Isn't this "sin" one of the original sins of Solidarity, which transformed from a bottom-up movement of the masses into the elite "institution"?

Reliquary, or Who Has Stolen the Legend of Solidarity

At the beginning of the third decade of the twenty-first century, the history of transformation (and Solidarity) is increasingly the subject of critical analysis. The activist Jan Śpiewak often makes references to this issue. His opinions reach mass consciousness and result in a slow, gradual deconstruction of the creation myths of post-communist Poland. Maybe it is time to revise the official narrative created by the elite, who steered the direction of the Solidarity movement's evolution in the 1980s and, thirty years later, became the only (official) depositaries of its memory, which materialized in steel and concrete at the ECS.

The myth's deconstruction can happen in many different ways—from a rebellion against it to total negation. One of the tools of the revision can be irony.[7] It takes down the monuments raised on foundations made of pathos and punctures the balloon of solemn, hollow slogans. A critical-ironic analysis of architecture allows one to keep cognitive distance from the analyzed asset, placing the critic in the position of a flaneur who traverses the space but does not interact. The lack of personal relationship with the subject of analysis and critique sharpens the judgment and clears the vision. The critic reaches for the sting of criticism, hits the target, and cuts deeply. What can the flaneur see while approaching the ECS? The rusting hull of the ORP (Okręt Rzeczypospolitej Polskiej, Ship of the Republic of Poland) *Solidarity* caught on a sandbar of capitalism? Or maybe a never-completed ship that the failing shipyard has never launched? Are the sloping walls a homage to the people who, as Grzegorz Stiasny claimed, made "the earth

4 Maciej Śmietański, "*Bramy* Grzegorza Klamana czyli gdańska tragedia antyczna," *Sztuka i Dokumentacja/ Art and Documentation*, no. 23 (2020): 233–39.

5 See Henryk Woźniakowski, "Europejskie Centrum Solidarności otwarte!," *Znak*, no. 11 (2014).

6 Wojciech Targowski, "W odniesieniu do placu i pomnika," *Architektura-murator*, no. 2 (2015).

7 See Naim Garnica, "Critical Irony or the Lovers of Ruins: The Aesthete, the Dandy and the Flaneur," *Tópicos, Revista de Filosofía*, no. 52 (2017): 151–72.

rise on new foundations"[8] or rather the sign that collective activism, which years ago resulted in the first independent trade union in communist Poland, has now faltered and disappeared?

The architecture of the ECS was designed to consolidate the significance of the exposition hidden in its heart. Is that really the case? The modern narrative exhibition presents the history of social protest in the Polish People's Republic, the birth of Solidarity, its history, and the collapse of the communist system. It is presented in an accessible manner but, at the same time, not without unfair oversimplification. What other word can be used to describe juxtaposing reconstructions of the cells in which communist authorities imprisoned their enemies with a room from a prefabricated house? Did people responsible for the exposition design really want to create an equivalence between the regime's oppression and the social program that provided millions of Polish people with decent living conditions? There are many more similar issues, but the most severe reproach is the reduction of the mass protest movement to few well-known individuals—the icons.

The architecture of the ECS does not support the exhibition, which exists somehow in isolation from the iconic building. It is not akin to Daniel Libeskind's Jewish Museum in Berlin—where the space, not the exhibits, creates the narrative—but is rather a monstrous corten-clad reliquary in which the saints of Solidarity's memorabilia have been placed—Anna Walentynowicz's overhead crane, Jacek Kuroń's desk, Wałęsa's election poster...

As a whole, it is a story of a Warsaw and Gdańsk-based elite, a white-collar (even though in reality they wore shabby sweaters) narrative about the birth of Free Poland. It is a story that can be locked in a display case, which will be admired and dignified, but which shall not become a living inspiration for subsequent generations. In fact, no elite, no authority—political or intellectual—wants solidarity. Because solidarity means rebellion.

Farther and Farther from the Shipyard

Petrified memory taken out of its social context is secure; it does not endanger the established order or the established interpretation of the past. The ECS exists somehow out of time and out of space. It is a neutral construct, a preparation that can be used as an illustrative material during history lessons but will never become a spark that incites revolution.

A granite piazza and an impressive fountain are the edifice's foreground. If one considers them "a dream of a better world," the future appears to be inhuman. They seem to exemplify the problem that echoes throughout contemporary Poland and concerns the low quality of dehumanized public space. The only signs of life can be noticed near the main entrance, which faces the Freedom Road—the way into the shipyard. A few tourists

fig. 3
Two different representations of Solidarity: the deconstructed Tatlin's Tower by Grzegorz Klaman and the monumental edifice of the ECS. © Błażej Ciarkowski.

fig. 4
Aesthetics of a shopping mall or the returning to nature of the shipyard? Atrium of the European Solidarity Centre. © Błażej Ciarkowski.

[8] Grzegorz Stiasny, "Pałac Solidarności," *Architektura-murator*, no. 2 (2015).

sit at tables in the shade of sun-heated corten steel walls, sipping cappuccinos. Inside the building, lone visitors wander through the five-story-high atrium. Someone sits on one of the minimalistic benches placed among the neatly arranged greenery.

Bushes and several-meter-high trees were supposed to symbolize the returning to nature of the post-industrial area. However, instead of wild vegetation that reclaims the territory taken away by humans decades ago (an example of which can be found at a former steel mill in Bochum, Germany), one can observe a careful arrangement. Grzegorz Klaman ironically comments, "This is an aesthetic of the shopping mall." [9] It is hard to disagree with the artist—black olive trees and parlour palms have nothing in common with Gdańsk and the shipyard. The internal space of the ECS ... it is easy to imagine it housing nearly any other program—an office, a commercial or leisure function.

The lack of local flora inside the edifice appears to be even more flagrant. The richness of the shipyard's biosphere is presented only within one of the social-artistic activities led by Klaman.[10] Like the workers mentioned earlier in this article, industrial plants seem to be an undesired context for the ECS. The edifice, originally planned on the border between the city and the shipyard, is getting further away from the latter. It is separated from brick halls and hangars, docks and cranes by a two-lane road which, in the near future, is to become a main thoroughfare of the planned new district—Młode Miasto (Young City). Around the ECS, new office and apartment buildings are being (or will be) raised. Soon Gate No. 2 and the ECS will no longer be a part of the Gdańsk Shipyard; they will be isolated relics without context.

This gradual "drifting apart" appears to be another unintended symbol of post-socialist transformation. Solidarity was taken away from the shipyard. Instead, it hit the political salons, to be absorbed by the liberal world.

Solidarity and Solidarity. The Political Role of Architecture (Criticism)

Solidarity is considered a popular mass movement whose membership peaked at ten million in 1981, and it influenced the shape of Polish architecture (and architectural criticism) in the era of the decline of communism. It coincided with the global revision of the modernist doctrine, the rise of postmodernism's popularity, and a crusade against the modern movement in architecture. It's no mistake that the design of the cover of *Architektura*, the most popular Polish architectural journal, imitated the style of the Solidarity logo in June 1980. At the same time, during the UIA Congress in Warsaw, only the architect-dissident Czesław Bielecki and his associates from DiM—Dom i Miasto (House and City)—architecture studio presented an openly political critical message.[11]

fig. 5
A new road and building plots separate the European Solidarity Centre from the area of the shipyard. © Błażej Ciarkowski.

fig. 6
Rusting hull on a sandbar? The European Solidarity Centre seen from the shipyard's edge. © Błażej Ciarkowski.

[9] Grzegorz Klaman, interview.
[10] Aneta Szyłak and Karolina Sikorska, *Błędnik codzienności. Książka praktyk Alternativa/Garden of Everyday Errors. Alternativa Book of Practices* (Gdańsk: Fundacja Wyspa Progress, 2015).
[11] Czesław Bielecki, "Karta DiM," in *Teksty modernizmu. Antologia polskiej teorii i krytyki architektury 1918–1981, Tom 1: Źródła*, eds. Dorota Jędruch, Marta Karpińska, and Dorota Leśniak-Rychlak (Cracow: Instytut Architektury, 2018), 353.

Instead of Solidarity, Polish architects chose solidarity (with themselves). Political declarations and actions, in consequence, would inevitably lead to conflict within the architectural community. And such a conflict was avoided like the plague, which can be proven by the marginal commitment of professional architectural bodies to any social protests against the communist authorities.[12] But what do individual choices and attitudes in the 1980s tell us about the situation of architecture in Poland now? Admittedly, an analysis of the activities of an entire discipline is not an easy task; yet once again, irony appears to be a helpful research tool for the distanced observer.

The apolitical attitude (alleged or actual) of Polish architects became one of the cardinal sins of the entire discipline. It resulted in a withdrawal of the vast majority of architects from any political discourse and froze architectural criticism for years.

Considering the opinions of contemporary Polish architects, we can conclude that they regard their profession as morally pure. "So why do we need politics?" they seem to say. "Let's focus on architecture!" As if architecture has never and nowhere been dependent on politics . . . For the past hundred years, architects have built a cocoon, a shield bearing the values established by Vitruvius: beauty, functionality, durability. It has been perceived as an armor that protects the big and the small against the consequences of their choices. Unsuccessful projects remained architectural orphans; buildings were raised without the participation of the creator. The investors and politicians held responsibility. Architects remained innocent.

Meanwhile, we should repeat in the wake of Michael Sorkin that architecture is never nonpolitical.[13] We need to agree with Bruno Zevi and Ernesto Tafuri and admit that it is a part of the economic, political, and social game. It is a battlefield for memory—just like the ECS. As long as we continue to deny those facts, architectural criticism in Poland will remain stagnant. As long as this falsely conceived professional solidarity limits the debate on contemporary architecture, we will be stuck in a stuffy atmosphere saturated with the reticence of inconvenient facts, endlessly repeating the same clichés.

Why Does Architectural Criticism in Poland Remain Silent?

If the political nature of architecture is beyond any doubt, then architectural criticism is political as well. Its purpose should be to provoke creative ferment, question widely accepted dogmas, snap designers out of their blissful state of complacency. Criticism understood in this way should be uncompromising. Unfortunately, apparent objectivity and ideological neutrality, which contemporary Polish architects refer to, hampers the development of criticism and limits its force of impact.

Like history, criticism is never fully objective, and the researcher (or critic) is never fully transparent. Personal beliefs and experience have an impact on the judgment of all phenomena—including architecture. One of the luminaries of postwar architectural criticism, Bruno Zevi, was never shy about his left-wing anti-fascist views. Moreover, they became one of the foundations of his critical approach toward contemporary architecture.[14] So, can we follow in his footsteps and, *toutes proportions gardées*, build the analysis of the edifice of the ECS on the contestation of the founding myths of the Third Polish Republic?

Unfortunately, in the reality of the Polish architectural community, the notion of criticism is too often identified with negative assessment. The problem has escalated recently with the rising influence of social media. Criticism is not criticism any longer—it is considered as haters' comments. Any assessment which is not unequivocally positive is often viewed as an attack. Moreover, community dependencies and mutual relations and affections sometimes determine how a specific building is described and evaluated. Concerning the arbitrarily established canon, there is often only one binding version of a narrative. Questioning its legitimacy may even lead to ostracism.

Architects, under falsely conceived professional solidarity, avoid criticism. They are reluctant to question the meaning of their colleagues' works. Although the younger generation

[12] Andrzej Basista, *Betonowe dziedzictwo. Architektura w Polsce czasów komunizmu* (Cracow-Warsaw: PWN, 2001).

[13] Alexandra Wagner, "Against the Wall. Interview with Michael Sorkin," *Covjek i Prostor*, no. 7–8 (2006): 39–47.

[14] Thomas Muirhead, "Bruno Zevi. Architectural Philosopher Who Railed against the Evils of Classicism," accessed June 30, 2021, www.theguardian.com.

tries to break the decades-old deadlock and breathe new life into dead architectural criticism, the unwritten law says that (architectural) success has many factors while (design) failure is an orphan. The criticism often refers to selected phenomena, not particular buildings. It is conducted in the realm of abstract notions, not in the real world, where those notions take very material shape.

We can find hope for the future by looking at the approach taken recently by Polish historiography. The positivist methods of analyzing the past give way to postmodern pluralism. If we are willing to accept different narratives on Solidarity, why can we not introduce differing narratives on the ECS's architecture? In 2017, the architect Jacek Droszcz, author of the Museum of the Second World War, described Gdańsk as "The City of Historical Memory";[15] and nobody wondered what hid beneath this sophisticated yet ambiguous title. So far, the ECS has not received a reliable critical architectural analysis. It has merely been described as a new icon of Gdańsk, the beginning of the former shipyard's transformation.

Thoughtlessly repeated platitudes do not have a positive impact on architecture itself. On the contrary, they impoverish it, depriving it of its multidimensional characteristics which arise from myriad interpretations. The ECS deserves an extensive critical analysis for many reasons. Let it become the beginning of a transformation aimed at bringing architecture where it belongs—from the heights of the Vitruvian Olympus to the lows of reality, to the political-social-economic puzzle of everyday life.

[15] Marta Kulawik, "Muzeum II Wojny Światowej w Gdańsku," *Architektura & Biznes*, no. 5 (2017).

Biography

Błażej Ciarkowski received his MSc and PhD in architecture from the Lodz University of Technology and his MA in the history of art from the University of Lodz. Since 2010, he has been an associate professor in the Institute of Art History, University of Lodz. From 2017 to 2021, he was an assistant professor at the Institute of Architecture and Urban Planning, Lodz University of Technology. He is the author of numerous articles and books on modern architecture and the preservation of the modern movement's heritage. His current research focuses on post war modernist architecture, mutual relations between architecture and politics in totalitarian and authoritarian systems, preservation of modernist architecture, and architectural criticism.

The New Istanbul Museum of Painting and Sculpture as a Case for Multi-perspectival Criticism in Contemporary Turkish Architecture

Özlem Erdoğdu Erkarslan, Burak Altınışık, Batu Kepekcioğlu

fig. 1
Digitized version of the original drawings of the entrepôt buildings designed by Sedad Hakkı Eldem circa early 1950s. © SALT Archives.

Prologue

This essay is a critical reading of the Istanbul Museum of Painting and Sculpture, designed by Emre Arolat Architects in Salıpazarı, which is the transformation of an existing warehouse building called Entrepôt Number 5, designed in the 1950s by Sedad Hakkı Eldem *(fig. 1)*. The new museum was completed recently and received its first unofficial guests in 2019 during the 16th Istanbul Biennial. It was officially inaugurated in the fall of 2021.

Authorship and authority are considered crucial in architecture. Despite the shift of architectural design from sole authorship to a complex process of interdisciplinary teamwork in recent years, these two issues remain intact. Architectural criticism is also associated with such power mechanisms.

In this essay, two layers are formulated with the aim of deconstructing the author and authorship arguments. The first experiments with a different type of architectural criticism: a collaborative essay of three critics, progressively exchanging ideas about a singular building. This process provided us with a flow of criticisms and counter comments that mutually informed one another. It is also crucial to mention that cross-references to Arolat were used so that he may be interpreted as the fourth author. The criticisms are based on the contradiction between the claims of the architect and the facts, calling into question the sincerity, authenticity, and integrity of the building.

The second layer is the archaeology of authorship in architecture. Arolat sees himself as an author and defines his role as "guarding the legacy of Eldem" just as he frequently compares himself with the masters of modernity or the well-established architects of his epoch. Although Eldem's and Arolat's practices represent two different types of architectural culture in Turkey, both are seen as competent, successful, and appreciated relative to their own time and circumstances. Eldem (1908–1988) is widely respected in Turkish architectural culture: a legendary name in modern architecture and a very influential professor of the Academy of Fine Arts. Therefore, renewing one of his buildings would be an important and intimidating commission for any architect.

Biases Versus Facts

The Emre Arolat Architects (EAA) website defines their strategy of transformation as one preserving the concrete structure while removing the walls and slabs to create a convenient void in which to position the "shipping containers." The museum interior is described as an open space visually connected to the city of Istanbul, which will be viewed from the ramps and bridges when passing from one "container-gallery" to the next.[1]

Contrary to these claims of the architect, the following facts become the basis of the critical debate presented here:

1. EAA justifies the preservation of the former building by highlighting the structural "carcass" that is acclaimed as an archetypal and distinctive element of traditional Turkish architecture by Eldem. (See note 13 for a full discussion of the term "carcass".) However, the street facade of the former building was reconstructed and modified[2] *(fig. 2)*.

2. EAA claims the project is sensitive to collective memory by preserving some traces of the site, using shipping containers as a ready-made material, for example. The official presentations of EAA misleadingly displayed the containers as if they had already been there waiting to be upcycled. However, there had never before been containers on the site[3] *(fig. 3)*.

3. The exhibition boxes, labeled as "containers" in the museum, are not infrastructural plug-ins but rather spectacular installations of building hardware. The boxes are not stacked within the structural grid; instead, they are conventionally fabricated in situ and affixed to the framework *(fig. 4)*.

4. Although EAA describes the "containers" housing the museum collection as "white cubes" and refers to them as neutral spaces, the superimposition of the existing structural system and the containers leaves beams and columns exposed at unexpected moments in the gallery spaces[4] *(fig. 5)*.

keywords:

architectural criticism, authorship, Sedad Hakkı Eldem, Emre Arolat, context, tradition

[1] Emre Arolat Architecture, "Istanbul Museum of Painting and Sculpture," accessed July 29, 2021, https://emrearolat.com/project/istanbul-museum-of-painting-and-sculpture/.

[2] In one of his interviews, Emre Arolat talks about the reconstruction of the street facade with additional ambiguous phrases: "The narrow and elongated office building that is adjacent to the entrepôt building on the Meclis-i Mebusan street will be reconstructed with a similar sentiment of memory regarding especially the characteristic facade." Heval Zeliha Yüksel, "Istanbul Resîm ve Heykel Müzesi Üzerîne Emre Arolat ile Söyleşi" *İstanbul Art News*, no.44 (2017): 8.

[3] "While the Prost Plan of the 1930s accelerated the transfer of Istanbul city center from the Historical Peninsula to the Beyoğlu side, it did not omit the harbor and moved the quay from the Haliç inlet to the Bosphorus shoreline of Beyoğlu at Karaköy-Salıpazarı. The port administration remained in the former center in Karaköy while the warehouse functions were deployed along the shoreline. During the process another move was made on the Asian side and the quay behind Haydarpaşa train station was transformed into a container terminal. Hence, the warehouses were on the Beyoğlu side while the containers used as freight boxes to transport the merchandise were in Haydarpaşa, distributing the port area at the intersection of Marmara, Bosphorus and the Golden Horn." For detailed information see İhsan Bilgin, "Port as Memory and Reality," in *Port City Talks. İstanbul–Antwerp* (Leuven: Exhibitions International, 2016), 38–48.

[4] The following statement belongs to Emre Arolat: "Our aim is to open up the building as much as possible while on the other hand providing sterile museum galleries to grasp the so-called 'white cube' effect." Emre Arolat, "Görsel Sanatlar Derneği Platformu (GSD_P) Müzemi İstiyorum Paneli-3/Müze Tasarımı ve Mimarisi" *Görsel Sanatlar Derneği Platformu*, Istanbul, June 21, 2014, YouTube video, accessed July 29, 2021, https://www.youtube.com/watch?v=ssoTl4VbWnU. The term "white cube" was introduced with critical connotations by Brian O'Doherty in 1986: "The ideal gallery subtracts from the artwork all cues that interfere with the fact that it is 'art.' The work is isolated from everything that would detract from its own evaluation of itself. This gives the space a presence possessed by other spaces where conventions are preserved through the repetition of a closed system of values." Brian O'Doherty, *Inside the White Cube: The Ideology of the Gallery Space* (Santa Monica: Lapis Press, 1986), 13–34.

 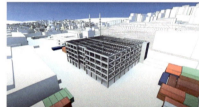

fig. 2
Street facade before and after transformation. © Engin Gerçek. 2020.

fig. 3
Screenshots from the video uploaded on EAA's official YouTube channel, https://www.youtube.com/watch?v=jqfmsreDXoA

fig. 4
Relations of existing and new beams. © Batu Kepekcioğlu, 2019.

fig. 5
An inner view of the "containers," described as being ideal "white cubes." © Engin Gerçek, 2020.

Critique by Murat Burak Altınışık

Emre Arolat considers himself to be concerned with context and situation rather than iconicity.[5] As expressed in his presentations, context covers the historical and physical patterns of the site while situation refers to the institutional, bureaucratic, sociocultural, and positional conjuncture of the project requirements. The museum design at the outset revolves around the "carcass," as referred to by Arolat, as the justification of both preserving the structure and stripping it.

Umberto Eco delineates most of architectural practice as a system of rhetorical structure, since it is a profession characterized by addressing people—convincing them to accept certain designs or to live in a particular way.[6] As mentioned in the "Biases Versus Facts" section of this essay, the site has never been a container terminal. Hence, widely circulated "container" images and references become a purely rhetorical device. It is a fictional image, a gesture of an absent signifier. In other words, the museum rhetorically resides in mythic connotations of the industrial and the port while it easily rationalizes the discursive assumptions of place and context in the architectural mise-en-scène *(fig. 6)*.

It is certain that neither the prior conditions of the port nor connotational inspiration for using "containers" correspond to the historical facts. However, EAA contrived ambivalence to put the design discourse on an opportunistic track. Another aspect of the treatment of the containers as neutral hosting boxes for the artwork is that the space allocated to each piece does not allow the viewer sufficient autonomy to immerse themselves in the work, rendering the whole gallery a compositional and consumptive configuration.

In this regard, Eco's notion of "styling" may be a notable frame for this architectural endeavor.[7] Styling provides existing and prevailing functions with symbolic disguises via a new design. Hence, it is no more than a skillful strategy to reproduce already-disseminated knowledge. Therefore, it can be claimed that the references are not tools for anchoring the conceptual to the corporeal but are instead intellectual codes to appeal to the reception of both professional and nonprofessional spectators. Hence not only material appearances but also the immaterial signifiers become acts of mimicry—be it the container, context, history, or tribute to Eldem—for the justification of all the architect's desires.

Such styling of the new museum can be considered a gentrification in which rhetorical strategies facilitated a functional, skillful, and symbolic removal of Eldem's work by complex operations of demolition, construction, reconstruction, and infill. The term "functional" should be taken as Jean Baudrillard defines it.

> "Functional" in no way qualifies what is adapted to a goal, merely what is adapted to an order or system: functionality is the ability to become integrated into an overall scheme. An object's functionality is the very

[5] Emre Arolat, "Müzemi İstiyorum Toplantısı," *Görsel Sanatlar Derneği Platformu*, Istanbul, November 11, 2014, YouTube video, accessed July 29, 2021, https://www.youtube.com/watch?v=hde5vb1J0Pg&t=2499s.

[6] The Turkish translation of Eco's *La Struttura Assente* is used as a reference for this text: Umberto Eco, *Mimarlık Göstergebilimi* (Istanbul: Daimon, 2019). For a partial English translation, readers may refer to: Umberto Eco, "Function and Sign: The Semiotics of Architecture," in *Rethinking Architecture*, ed. Neil Leach (London: Routledge, 1997), 173–95.

[7] Eco, *Mimarlık Göstergebilimi*, 43.

thing that enables it to transcend its main "function" in the direction of a secondary one, to play a part, to become a combining element, an adjustable item, within a universal system of signs.[8]

Response by Özlem: When looking at the end-product and focusing on the potentials and limitations of the original grid, it is worth appreciating that the new addition bestowed a modest expository space by raising the height of the interior and providing an opportunity for the visitor to view the original grid upon entering the building. The grandiose gallery granted by the freestanding facade brought a dramatic entry to the building that could have been more successful if it had been continued throughout the entire building. Museums are places where the building should prepare the visitors to leave the everyday world behind, and this entrance surely fulfills this task **(fig. 7)**.

What brings about questions and objections is the fact that not even one slice of the facade intervention has preserved its tectonic quality, not in its dimension, materiality, or assemblage. The grids on the west, east, and south facades are overshadowed by the dominance of the red containers. The north facade, which also creates an entry space, is a replica and keeps the original structural logic by exposing the structural and nonstructural members. On the other hand, the replica, by definition, cannot be traded with the authentic, dissatisfying any who hoped for the preservation of the former Entrepôt Number 5.

When adopting a critical approach, it becomes necessary to consider the building in its current context. Since the museum's site has now been surrounded by other development and has thus lost its presence in the port's silhouette, the north facade remains the only interface with the city—something that was clearly not envisaged by EAA during design. The red containers, although they had been thought of as the most eminent character of the entire complex, cannot be perceived either visually or spatially **(fig. 8)**.

Response by Batu: It is difficult to claim that Arolat achieved the antithesis of iconic architecture in the museum even if it was his intention to do so. The eye-catching displays of the so-called "container" cantilevers sparkle with red LEDs, accentuating the new intervention. In this way, the heavily decorated facade inevitably becomes indistinguishable from any other work of iconic architecture and is in turn marketed with the help of images narrowly framing the red cantilevers, to avoid giving any indication of their surroundings **(fig. 9)**.

Another belligerent and oxymoronic condition deliberately created by the architect is found in the exhibition spaces. Arolat attempts to establish the coexistence of sterile and non-sterile spaces, but his material and detailing choices contradict this intention. Notwithstanding the implied industrial atmosphere, the circulation spaces, which are intended to appear unsterile, are experienced as sterile zones due to the material choices such as varnished basalt stone paving

fig. 6
Exhibition box construction on site, © Burak Altınışık. 2017.

fig. 7
The new entrance gallery behind the reconstructed facade. © Engin Gerçek, 2020.

fig. 8
View of the site showing the museum with the immediate surroundings after recent development.

[8] Jean Baudrillard, *The System of Objects* (London and New York: Verso, 1996), 63.

or white pebble skirtings which generally establish the decorum of Arolat's retail space designs, while the exhibition interiors that were meant to be "white cubes" to display the artworks are unintentionally obscured with intruding columns and beams of the existing structure.

Critique by Mustafa Batu Kepekcioğlu

As mentioned previously, EAA's entire discourse on the use of containers is a fictitious narrative that claims the containers had already been on the site since the 1950s, waiting to be upcycled by the architects, which would make the adaptive reuse project an easy undertaking without the need for any extraneous constructional elements *(fig. 10)*.

Even if the fact that the containers have never been a part of the history of the site and the "capriciousness" of the container gesture—which unsettles the credibility of each assumption and argument in the project's discourse—are put aside, the "prefabricated" fantasy is still not capable of generating the promised spatial experience.[9]

Firstly, the elongated and enlarged exhibition units, or so-called containers, become gallery capsules located almost adjacent to one another being deprived of any dimensional logic, while exactly what is groundbreaking logistically about the container is the dimensional standardization that can lead to modulation.[10] Consequently, the circulation areas fall far short of being bridges linking "container" exhibition units and instead become just corridors.

Secondly, the intended three-dimensional spatial experience is not fulfilled, even though the irregular planometric superimposition at different levels forms a series of vertical voids, because the same layout is mostly repeated throughout the building volume, creating only a cacophony *(fig. 11)*. Therefore, it is inevitable to question why the former structure had been exposed to such demolition when the hollowed-out grid has simply been refilled with new floors.

Thirdly, a final problem suggests itself in the temporary exhibition hall located at the uppermost level for contemporary works outside the collection. This temporary exhibition hall is designed according to generic exhibition requirements without being attuned to the spatial sequence or the museum narrative predicated upon the axes of container and carcass. This is because the dimensions of the space, when tailored to fit the carcass span, cannot meet the requirements of contemporary artworks. Instead, we are given neither an in-between space that is adaptable to facilitate flexibility nor a characteristic space that is in dialogue with the carcass. *(fig. 12)*.

Response by Özlem: Containers became one of the most fashionable motifs of the last decade. Though their time is passing, this lightweight element continues to pervade the built environment. As mentioned in Batu's critique, a container as a standardized component has the capacity to create an industrial image and reflect an eco-friendly, conscious consumerism

fig. 9
The building is mostly represented in the media with similar photos, taken with narrow-angle lenses focusing on the building—especially when featuring the facade with the iconic container-like cantilevers—instead of panoramic photos that also frame the surroundings. © Cemal Emden, 2018.

fig. 10
The perforated corrugated metal sheets that are used to imitate the envelope of a container. © Engin Gerçek, 2020.

[9] Such an attitude is not unfamiliar to those who have an interest in the art of painting. It began with the eighteenth-century Venetian painters who produced fictitious urban landscapes, depicting realistically unreal structures belonging to different realities named *capriccio*. Similarly, Arolat bases his design in such fictitious urban landscape fantasies. Peter Parshall, "Giovanni Domenico Tiepolo: The Pastiche as Capriccio," *Print Quarterly* 28, no. 3 (2011): 327–30.

[10] Marc Levinson, "Setting the Standard", in *The Box: How the Shipping Container Made the World Smaller and the World Economy Bigger* (Princeton and Oxford: Princeton University Press, 2016), 170–201.

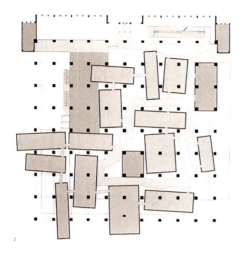
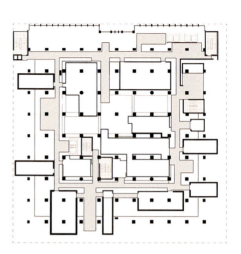

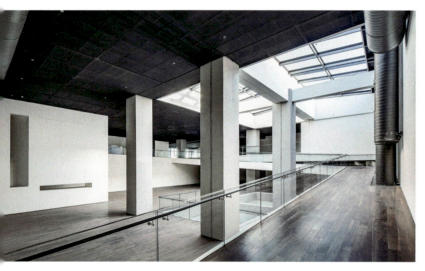

fig. 11
Two versions of plan drawings of level 2: the first version on the left published in 2016 and the second version on the right published in 2020.

fig. 12
The temporary exhibition hall, a ramped space situated at the fourth level of the museum topped by a large skylight. © Engin Gerçek, 2020.

by means of upcycling and recycling. Although some of the examples of container architecture display no limits in creativity, they have one basic duty: creating a functional space by stacking standardized capsules of which the surfaces can be expanded or glazed by means of subtraction and addition of new elements. Even if they were genuine containers as claimed by EAA, this would not change the fact that the plugged-in capsules in this museum would in no way be able to ensure fast and/or economic construction. Such a design decision automatically takes the use of containers out of the practical realm and instead associates them with the representative realm. In short, the containers, which are the most striking intervention tools of the design, are far away from providing a factual, reliable, and consistent set of references, nor can they be understood as practical design elements. When their existence can only be judged within the representative realm, it can be said that the cantilevered volumes speak out loudly and create a secondary rhythm superimposed on the pattern of the reinforced structural grid of the original building. I would describe this as a very expensive and onerous means of facade decoration. The signature of EAA on the facade that was inherited from Eldem is a clear manifestation of the temporality of architecture—which may be described as the only fairness of this building.

Response by Burak: Once the design is confined to stripping the carcass, the decision of how to refill the acquired void becomes the challenge. Upon first impression, employment of containers to overcome this challenge may appear a convincing motif. Yet not only the denotational but also the connotational aspects of containers lead to certain incompatibilities. As infrastructural vessels of logistics, containers are temporary nests used for transporting commodities. However, most of the museum collection that is hosted in the containers belongs to a world of a profoundly different mindset imbued with notions of permanence, canon, lineage, and other fixed values. In this sense, the proposed architectural design does not seem to problematize such conceptual conflicts between the content and the context it presupposes; the context is referenced only as far as the physical manifestations of the location, where the container becomes the sole icon of an alleged industrial past. The transient products of logistics are simply instrumentalized to provide permanent environments for the artworks. Therefore, the contained and the container have no reciprocal signification.

Critique by Özlem Erdoğdu Erkarslan

Many people shared that their dissatisfaction with the museum stemmed from not seeing more of the original building in the end product.[11] The idea that the valorization of buildings belongs only to the period of early modernity is an ongoing discussion and perpetuates many debates that are rooted outside the realm of the discipline of architecture. The ruling party in Turkey has been pursuing a cultural policy to erase all the institutions of the republican era before its sovereign, including the architectural heritage, for a very long time. The polarized political views in our society instrumentalize the issue of preservation of the buildings belonging to the period from 1923 to 1960, not only because each carries unique qualities, but also because they symbolize the struggle between two sets of value systems: the modernist vision of the Republican era that is now under attack by neoconservative tendencies.[12]

The distrust of the ingenuity of EAA's additions to the original building is not only an issue of fluctuating political milieu but also an unnegotiable issue to major architects and their buildings. The original warehouse building is not one of the significant buildings of Eldem and had not even been given any space in existing literature prior to the museum project. Although this cannot be the only criteria signifying the importance of the building, it simply tells us that the public was not very interested in the building and that it was not on the radar of architectural historians prior to the refurbishment plan.

Additionally, the clean, neutral, reinforced concrete structure of the Eldem design reflects the practical and semi-industrial purpose of the building, and it is not deeply associated with his "carcass" motif, with which he experimented on the residences built before 1950.[13] The word carcass was used almost like a mantra by EAA to legitimize his approach. Anachronistic and random selection of terms and themes from historical references—like using terms such as preservation and adaptive reuse as well as carcass and grid interchangeably—creates a mismatch of concepts and underlines a deep inconsistency in the design process. When architects use key terms differently from the public, creating totally different conceptions, miscommunication is inevitable.

Response by Burak: The crucial point of convergence seems to be the biographical backgrounds of the two architects pertaining to the institution as graduates of the Academy of Fine Arts. Whether a significant building or not, the entrepôts and the offices were formerly designed by Eldem and the project was granted to Arolat by the university administration as one of their graduates. Such lineage is convincingly legitimizing at different communal levels. It also utilizes a certain political correctness. Within the symbolic clashes at the present political fronts, it provides a safe position with reference to republican values and building heritage, undertaking a significant project in the vicinity of the vicious neoliberal transformation of the port quarter without officially taking part in it.

The name of Sedad Hakkı Eldem facilitates a twofold process of sophistication and legitimization. Although the former building was a relatively impotent project in Eldem's

[11] This expression has been used by Burcu Bilgiç: "Resim Heykel Müzesi İlk İzlenim ve Ardından Gelen Tuhaf Bir Hafiflik," *Arkitera,* October 3, 2019, accessed July 29, 2021, https://www.arkitera.com/gorus/resim-heykel-muzesi-ilk-izlenim-ve-ardindan-gelen-tuhaf-bir-hafiflik. A similar commentary was made by Korhan Gümüş: "Modernliğin Kurucu Paradoksu ve Yeniden Yapılanan Müzeler," *XXI,* June 27, 2019, accessed July 29, 2021, https://xxi.com.tr/i/modernligin-kurucu-paradoksu-ve-yeniden-yapilanan-muzeler.

[12] The collection was previously exhibited in Dolmabahçe Palace which was the final stage of the Late Ottoman Administration. The historiographic-symbolic value attained another critical threshold after 2010 as the ruling elites of the AKP (Justice and Development Party) proclaimed a conservative cultural discourse referring to a pre-republican era, particularly the Abdülhamid II Era. Thus, Eldem's warehouse and Dolmabahçe Palace represent these two opposite political views, whereas the collection of the museum mostly covers post-Ottoman era.

[13] The term "carcass" is an important part of Eldem's "invented tradition," which he associated with the wooden skeleton system of vernacular houses in Turkey in his early career. According to him, the wooden carcass resembled a perfect modular system which he tried to carry into modern construction systems, especially on the elements of the facade. Although such modular systems at different contexts were already well-established in the theory and practice of modern architecture at that period, Eldem provided a reference to historical vernacular houses to legitimate his practice. Additionally, he did not become persistent about the modular system he followed in his later years. However, he consistently continued to use the term carcass for standard structural skeleton systems he designed. While the former specifically aims to provide nationalist, local nuances of modern architecture, the latter has nothing to do with tradition. Although instrumentalization of vernacular carcass by Eldem is one of the most widely discussed issues, Arolat sliced the discourse of architecture (just like he physically did to Entrepôt Number 5) and instrumentalized it (again) for his own interpretation.

repository, the name alone provides a practical alibi to oppose the ongoing demolition and construction culture around the site and to insist on preserving the structure as the initial step toward continuity in collective urban memory.[14] Eldem's name also makes space to claim a legacy within a narrative that Arolat could configure himself by deciding what is and what is not significant enough to preserve in the existing structure—allowing him to showcase his sensibility while "improving" the layout, which he claims was clumsy in the first place, removing the walls and floors of the entrepôt or demolishing the office building on the street facade to conform the structure to the new museum's layout.

Response by Batu: Although Özlem's critical opinion was deliberately framed relative to Arolat's original intentions, I would like to make my comment in reference to his own words, which he communicated through different public events and mediums. It is clearly understood that the preservation of the existing building was not imposed on the architect by third parties. In one of his speeches, he noted that during the initial stages of the project the members of the Cultural and Natural Conservation Board questioned the decision to keep the existing building, which had not been officially listed.[15] Moreover, the board did not further insist on the preservation of the other mid-century buildings along the coastline with similar historic characteristics. At this point, the importance of preserving Eldem's former Entrepôt Number 5 becomes clear since it would be the only landmark left to carry the urban memory of the Salıpazarı District as well as of Eldem himself.

According to Arolat, there are two reasons for preserving this building. The first is that the building is the last piece of the former coastal silhouette in this part of Istanbul and the second is that it would give him the chance to pay tribute to Eldem.[16] From a more cynical perspective, this can be interpreted as a way of branding EAA as a firm with an emphasis on context and situation, as an alternative to the rise of iconic architecture most clearly exemplified by Bilbao's Guggenheim Museum in the 1990s. Another motivation behind Arolat's preservation of the former building is that it enables him to declare himself the sole heir of Eldem and to protect his legacy by navigating a dialogue with the structure and discourse of the former building. Whatever motivation he had, by comparing himself with major architects at the national and international level, Arolat places his name among them and creates a shield of immunity for himself.[17]

In one of his interviews, he describes his design method as a research-based approach and distinguishes himself from those who either do not necessarily incorporate research into design or get stuck in data-driven design.[18] In this way he characterizes his design as an intuitive, circumstantial approach, and favors an "instinctive method" that he repeatedly uses in his practice. This building is a typical example of his arbitrary preferences, which he picked from his basket (of data) and blended with an iconic image, like the so-called container.

Concluding Remarks

Criticism in the Turkish architectural scene is mostly limited to endorsing the conceptual intentions of the architect and providing a quasi-theoretical perspective on the built form. Defined as neutral criticism, the position of the critic is limited to the interpretation of the design intentions of the architect. Any interrogation, analysis, and comparison beyond interpretation is considered as one-sided and easily becomes an issue of complaint. Such anticipation hinders new propositions and competitive argumentation, resulting in a scene dominated by stereotypes.

Devoid of theoretical argumentations, instrumentalized concepts become vulnerable. In the case of the new museum discourse, the "context" seemed to dissolve even before the building became corporeal within the ever-changing urban setting. Functional became fictional through the idea of the container, while the contextual ended up being iconic.

Presumably, we might be familiar by now with Eric Hobsbawm's concept of "invented traditions," which argues that many traditions that appear or claim to be well-established are often quite recently constructed and invented.[19] The argument refers to a phenomenon that

[14] "I can claim that many of the architects in the Turkish architectural scene would demolish the entrepôt building to design and build something new. A very important example of where we stand." Emre Arolat, "Geçirgen ve Geçişken" [Permeable and Transitive], *Akbank Sanat Mimarlık Seminerleri*, İstanbul: Akbank Sanat, April 20, 2016, YouTube video, accessed July 29, 2021, https://www.youtube.com/watch?v=5n-jTw79oWaw.

[15] The following quotation from Emre Arolat reveals that the decision to keep the previous building is entirely that of the architectural firm: "[…] but when we designed the project and presented it to the Cultural and Natural Conservation Board, they asked us why we wanted to keep this building. I always value Republican era buildings and 1950s architectural design styles." Hatice Utkan Özden, "Keeping the Urban Memory—Istanbul Museum of Painting and Sculpture," *ArtDog Istanbul*, February 20, 2021, accessed July 29, 2021, https://www.artdogistanbul.com/english/keeping-the-urban-memory-istanbul-museum-of-painting-and-sculpture.htm.

[16] Emre Arolat declares his tribute to Sedad Hakkı Eldem in the following video: Emre Arolat, "Müzemi İstiyorum," November 4, 2014, YouTube video,- accessed July 29, 2021, https://www.youtube.com/watch?v=hde5vb1J0Pg.

[17] For instance, in an interview Emre Arolat compares himself with Zaha Hadid: "In one of the meetings we had with Cengiz Çetindoğan, he shared his satisfaction from my service by declaring his intentions to work with EAA for the museum project. However, on the other hand, he stated that the idea of working with a world star like Zaha Hadid puzzled him. I have replied to him that I am fully capable of designing a contextual building, but if the issue was worldwide recognition, I would not be able to compete with Zaha Hadid." Emre Arolat, "Nice Yerlinin Nice Yersiz Yapısı," *İstanbul Art News*, no.41 (2017): 14.

[18] "At Emre Arolat Architects (EAA), we tend to take each project as a research project. For each project, we first create a design basket, in which we collect data and add awareness to the project. After that, we start to design and draw. Most architects think as they draw designs, but I prefer to think before acting for most of the projects. An architect should follow a thought process filled with design and an architectural path. But very few architects follow this path. Not many architects follow their path of creativity. Because it is a risk to produce your architectural world, stepping aside from the bombardment of data and becoming original. If an architect wants to be like that, then he or she has to see each project as a research project, but not everyone is destined to become an architect. It is hard, and facing these difficulties is a necessity." Özden, "Keeping the Urban Memory."

[19] Eric Hobsbawm, and Terence Ranger, eds. *The Invention of Tradition* (Cambridge University Press, 2012).

is particularly prevalent in the creation of national identities to promote unity and legitimize certain institutions or cultural practices.

By taking this as a commonality between Eldem and Arolat, our multi-perspectival criticism has enabled us to read both architects reciprocally. Within this frame, Sedad Hakkı Eldem stands out as the protagonist of such "tradition invention" in the Turkish architectural scene. His analysis on "Traditional Turkish Houses" championed the wooden skeletal system as the core of the tradition to be translated into the modern architecture and reinforced concrete of Turkey.

What we have tried to argue in this essay is that invented context is not a concept that warrants an omnipotent and omnipresent or generic validity but a sustained attempt at reinvention for the particular and the singular. Such contextual reinvention seems crucial to affirm the ever-changing rhythms and flux of urban conditions, especially in the case of Istanbul, to avoid falling short within assumed categories of contextualism. Arolat deliberately misuses the term carcass and instrumentalizes its tectonics, following the footsteps of Eldem to generate/create his own context and legitimize his line of thought.

All the architectural terms—context, memory, preservation, reconstruction, carcass, container, bridge, etc.—uttered in a sophisticated manner in written or spoken forms function as discursive flavors to give the impression of intellectual zest to compensate for the weakness, even absence, of any theoretical and conceptual integrity. Nevertheless, styling demands no more. This text revealed a set of concepts that were exploited by Arolat for his "invention of context." Eldem's approach of merging the modern and the traditional is described as "invention of tradition." This alignment is one of the original findings of this essay. Although their methods of research are similarly reductionist and arbitrary, their sieves filtered different trends of professionalism and authorship.

Biographies

Özlem Erdoğdu Erkarslan was born in 1968. Following her undergraduate education in architecture in 1989, she completed her PhD thesis entitled "The Issue of Cultural Identity in the Islamic Intelligentsia and Aga Khan Awards for Architecture" in 1999 in Dokuz Eylul University, İzmir. Her research interests include architectural education, architectural criticism, and gender and identity. She is a professor in the department of architecture in Istanbul Aydın University.

Burak Altınışık was born in 1972 in Istanbul. He consecutively received his graduate degree in 1995 at 9th September University in İzmir, master's degree in 1998 at Middle East Technical University in Ankara, and PhD on architectural history and theory in 2013 at Yıldız University in Istanbul. He pursues a history and theory-oriented approach in his thinking, writing, and teaching practices. He is currently working as associate professor at Pamukkale University in Denizli.

Batu Kepekcioğlu was born in 1980. He received his graduate degree, masters degree and PhD on architectural design theory at Istanbul Technical University. He is an award-winning architect interested in expanding his scope of architectural practice spanning theory, criticism, and design. He has developed a wide range of projects of varying scales from info boxes to master plans, some of which were built. He is currently working as a lecturer at Doğuş University in Istanbul.

5 Critical Reflections

Critical Misfortune, Canonical Narratives, and the Failure of the Practical Sense: The UN-ECLAC Building in Santiago de Chile by Emilio Duhart (1960–1966)

Horacio Torrent

fig. 1
View of the facade of the CEPAL-ECLAC building in Santiago.
Photo: Fondo Emilio Duhart. © Archivo de Originales FADEU PUC.

Architectural criticism is able to generate knowledge about buildings. This paper proposes to show how architectural criticism has the power to fix analytical and conceptual structures determining canonical interpretations that are reproduced by recurrence beyond the field of architectural research. This is done by studying the United Nations building in Santiago, interpreting the impact of the idea of influence on its cultural reception and subsequent interventions to the building, thus showing the limits and possibilities of the duty and power of architectural criticism.

Introduction

One of the fundamental purposes of architectural criticism is to collaborate in the construction of a better-built environment. For this reason, it cannot avoid the good practice of knowledge production. Architectural research itself is structured to allow for architectural criticism to be linked with its processes and theoretical approaches. Criticism has the power to fix long-established analytical and conceptual structures—that is to say, those that historically go beyond their initial formation. It establishes the limits of understanding a building, shaping conditions predisposed to function as what Bourdieu called structured and structuring dispositions, generating and organizing principles of critical practice and its representation.[1] One of the powers of criticism is the establishment of durable and transmissible interpretations in the body of architectural knowledge and its dissemination in the social field. These lasting dispositions shape what Bonta called the process of constitution of the canon.[2]

Architectural criticism often coincides with the establishment of influence and recurrence. Influence is defined as a relationship in which the central value lies in the impact that one building has on another, as if it were to establish a genealogy based on physiognomy. It is an anticipatory action that places the knowledge outside the building itself; it locates it in another building or author. It does not establish recognition of the building by its differences but supposes the recognition of similarities with what would be the building's antecedent. Recurrence constitutes the frequency with which critics and historians reproduce the arguments of canonical interpretations. The dispositions of criticism, operating over a long time, create a cycle that constantly feeds and reaffirms them. The importance of criticism lies in how it impacts the comprehension of buildings—how they are understood and how they are intervened upon when necessary.

Architectural research, as a process of generating valid knowledge, can help unravel the field and break the circle of repetitions, mainly in the modality of historical knowledge and the analysis of typological series.[3] The recognition of buildings in their situation and a phenomenological approach allow us to establish differences in their spatial aspects, and a hermeneutic or explanatory hypothesis is essential to relate buildings to a larger dimension

keywords:

architectural criticism, architectural research, cultural reception, influence, United Nations buildings, UN-ECLAC building

[1] Pierre Bourdieu, *El sentido practico* (Buenos Aires: Siglo XXI editores, 2007), 85–86.
[2] Juan Pablo Bonta, *Architecture and its Interpretation: A Study of Expressive Systems in Architecture* (New York: Rizzoli, 1979).
[3] Marina Waisman, *La estructura histórica del entorno* (Buenos Aires: Nueva Visión, 1972).

of architectural knowledge. The intention is to demonstrate this process using the case of the United Nations building in Santiago de Chile—known also by its later designation as the Economic Commission for Latin America and the Caribbean (ECLAC)–*(fig. 1)*, the criticism of which initiated an interpretative process based on its influences and not the study of the building itself, and consolidated in the recurrence of these interpretations in national and international media, which defined its cultural reception and even some of the interventions for its restoration.[4] This process acquired an autonomy beyond the possibilities that architectural research proposes for interpretation, thus showing the limits and possibilities of the duty and power of architectural criticism.

Modern Architecture and Monuments: The United Nations Buildings

A key concern of the postwar period was whether modern architecture had the ability to represent monumental conditions, a concern that recognized the need for architecture to express social and community life.[5] Functionalism had to be overcome by a new monumentality to recover the lyrical value of architecture.

The criticisms of the UN Complex in New York (1947–1952) are very well known; for example, the memorable one Lewis Mumford made about the importance given to representing the bureaucratic structure over the presence of the Assembly,[6] and the criticisms of the interiors of the Assembly Building.[7] The project for the UNESCO headquarters in Paris (1953–1958) also had a controversial trajectory, with changing designers and schemes[8] and numerous criticisms of the final building. Architectural critics asserted that the buildings for the United Nations were unable to represent the spirit of the nascent international organization to the world. The new monumentality, reflecting social, political, and cultural significance, did not seem to be evident in them.

At the end of 1957, Dag Hammarskjöld, UN Secretary-General, accepted Chile's offer to build a United Nations headquarters in Santiago. In 1960 a competition was held, to which forty proposals were submitted. The jury, consisting, among others, of Henrique Mindlin and Sergio Larraín, chose four proposals that were sent to New York for the final selection by Hammarskjöld with the advice of Wallace Harrison and Philip Johnson. The first prize went to Emilio Duhart and his collaborators, Roberto Goycoolea, Christian de Groote, and Oscar Santelices *(fig. 2)*. It was not until 1966 that one of the organization's peripheral headquarters would have a building worthy of its significance.[9]

House and Monument: The UN Building in Santiago

The project statement submitted to the competition was clear and straightforward:

> **the United Nations building is conceived as a House and as a Monument. The House of the nations in community. The Monument, visible expression of their spiritual and social longing. House and Monument emerge as a plastic and functional unit, understandable to all. Monument for the nations. Monument for its gathering point: Chile, in consonance with the space of Santiago, its mountains, its land, its climate, and its flora, with the temperament of its people. A palace expressed geometrically in front of the cosmic dimension of the Andes.[10]**

The submission conceived a set of buildings, in which a central piece assumed the role of monumental representation *(figs. 3–4)*. The building's plan is based on a ninety-six by ninety-six-meter quadrangle in a clear reference to the dimensions of the traditional urban square of Ibero-American cities to confront the vast space of the local geography. Destined to house the offices, the quadrangle or ring encloses a large inner space containing three buildings: the *caracol* (snail), a conical helicoid containing the assembly rooms *(fig. 7)*; a diamond-shaped volume housing a conference room; and the services *núcleo* (core) *(fig. 8)*, all of them linked to the quadrangle by a series of pedestrian bridges. Both bridges and buildings subdivide the

[4] This work has been done as part of the FONDECYT project Nª 1140964 "La arquitectura de la gran ciudad, Chile 1930–1970." The author thanks FONDECYT for the financial support.
[5] Sigfried Giedion, Josep Lluis Sert, and Fernand Leger, "Nine Points on Monumentality," in *Sert, arquitecto en Nueva York*, ed. Xavier Costa (Barcelona: Actar, 1997), 14–17.
[6] Lewis Munford, "Workshop Invisible," (*The New Yorker*, January 17, 1953), 83.
[7] "UN General Assembly," *Architectural Forum* 97, no. 4 (October 1952), 141–149.
[8] "UNESCO House," *Architectural Forum* 97, no. 4 (October 1952), 150–157.
[9] See Alberto Montealegre, *Emilio Duhart Arquitecto* (Santiago: Ediciones ARQ, 1994), and Barry Bergdoll, "Duhart and the Transcontinental Architecture of the United Nations," in *CEPAL 1962–1966: United Nations Building, Emilio Duhart Arquitecto*, eds. Jeannette Plaut and Marcelo Sarovic (Santiago: Constructo, 2012), 14–31.
[10] Emilio Duhart, "Fragmento de la memoria, Edificio de las Naciones Unidas en Vitacura," *AUCA* 3 (April/May 1966), 29.
[11] The plans and documentation of the CEPAL Building project can be found in the Emilio Duhart collection at the Original Archives, Faculty of Architecture, Design and Urban Studies, Pontificia Universidad Católica de Chile.

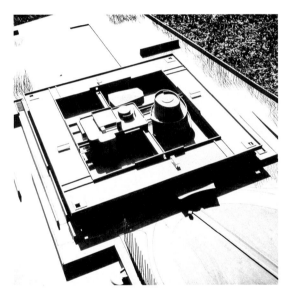

fig. 2
Aerial view of the project for the CEPAL-ECLAC building competition, showing the geography of the valley of Santiago and the Andes. Photo: Fondo Emilio Duhart.
© Archivo de Originales FADEU PUC.

fig. 3
Perspective of the project for the CEPAL-ECLAC building competition. Photo: Fondo Emilio Duhart.
© Archivo de Originales FADEU PUC.

fig. 4
Model of the project for the CEPAL-ECLAC building competition showcasing the ring, the volumes inside it, and the connection bridges. Photo: Fondo Emilio Duhart.
© Archivo de Originales FADEU PUC.

inner void into four courtyards or patios. Below the ring, an open plan establishes a new spatial dimension connecting the inner courtyards with the exterior park, the river, and the landscape.[11] The ring is an autonomous single unit, a continuous pavilion suspended over the ground level, hanging from a succession of post-tensioned concrete elements supported on two continuous lateral main beams; the latter rest on four columns aligned on each side of the quadrangle, cantilevered at the corners. Essentially a solid volume, the *núcleo* contains the services, mechanical equipment, and facilities. It also constitutes the "core" of the ensemble, reuniting the four bridges that connect the inner buildings to the quadrangle *(fig. 9)*. The diamond, never executed, was a polyhedron that would have hung high over one of the courtyards on a folded structure cantilevered from four structural points. The *caracol* is a conical helicoid contained in a truncated cone, shaped by a double skin of concrete that shifts to accommodate an external staircase, culminating in a belvedere. Constructional audacity, technical challenges,[12] structural boldness, and material prowess comprised in the design were in close connection with the building's visual expression and its monumental significance.

The structural challenges and their resultant constructive complexity were a key dimension in the configuration of the space and palace-like character of the building. This can be seen in the effort to maintain the open plan *(figs. 5-6)* under the ring, the presence of

[12] Jeannette Plaut and Marcelo Sarovic, "Between Imagining and Building: The Construction of the ECLAC United Nations Building, 1961–66," in Plaut and Sarovic, *CEPAL 1962–1966*.

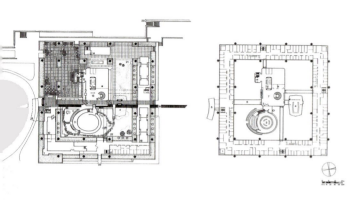
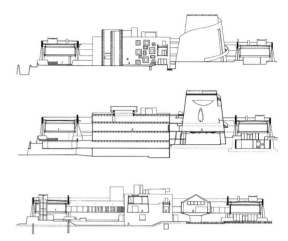

fig. 5
Floor plans of the project for the CEPAL-ECLAC building. Alberto Montealegre. *Emilio Duhart Arquitecto* (Santiago: Ediciones ARQ, 1994).

fig. 6
Sections of the project for the CEPAL-ECLAC building. Alberto Montealegre. *Emilio Duhart Arquitecto* (Santiago: Ediciones ARQ, 1994).

fig. 7
Photograph of the interior of the Assembly Room. Photo: Fondo Emilio Duhart. © Archivo de Originales FADEU PUC.

the columns and the floating corners, and the sculptural definition of the snail. These strong structural gestures contributed to the memorability of the image, further accentuated by the topographic treatment of the slopes and courtyard gardens. The inclusion of details such as the workers' hands and the bas-reliefs showcasing the history of humanity on the double skin of the *caracol* proposed a reading of cultural approximation.

Canonical Narratives

The project description was published in the local magazine *AUCA* and impacted the first interpretations **(fig. 10)**. The magazine reported that Duhart had sent images to Le Corbusier with a note that read "this project is dedicated to you. Your example has been our guide which within the greatest freedom has ensured our search."[13] *AUCA* also presented an interview providing, in the form of questions, a critical evaluation of the project's composition, structure, and ambiance. The interviewer pointed directly to the problem by asking about the most suitable composition to express the primary content of the international community. He questioned the architect's choice of an apparently hermetic volume enclosing a rich interior over an open and welcoming form. He also objected to its impossibility of growth and expansion, and argued that the complexity of the structural systems did not stem from the technical demands but were a technical exaggeration to boast the architectural design.

[13] Emilio Duhart, "Edificio de las Naciones Unidas en Vitacura," *AUCA* 3 (April/May 1966), 30.

The Argentine magazine SUMMA highlighted the symbolic value of the building not only for its institutional status but also for its formal characteristics and the plastic resources used. While noting an indebtedness to Le Corbusier, the emphasis was placed on the reflections of the local geography and traditions of Chilean architecture, achieving "something more than mere translation."[14] Through a spatial reading, an analysis of the structure, and the use of reinforced concrete, it was noted that the formal features were manifested by the architecture as an expression of technology **(fig. 11)**. Published in the same volume was Antonio Díaz's critique, evidently based on his visit to the building.[15] He argued that the project was resolved symbolically through an image and a form, and sought to define a program within this approach. He recognized that the site justified the definition based on a form and understood that the hierarchy of the architecture was visible through its structural conception.

The building was published in *Progressive Architecture* with a text based on the author's description, ending with a direct critique: "the entire complex ... seems, from these views, a rather noble and impressive concept; one marred here and there, however, by undigested Chandigarhisms such as the 'breeze intakes' in the southwest patio."[16] Then, in *Architectural Design*, the way the building "reflects the architectural tradition of Chile and the central valley plain was highlighted. The sculptural mass of the center is reminiscent of the mountain ranges that make up other prominent features of the country's geography."[17] A small note under the architect's name stated that he was "a great admirer of Le Corbusier, in whose atelier he worked during 1952; and dedicated his design for the UN building to him."[18] Duhart's international recognition was extended when the building was published in *L'Architecture d'Aujourd'hui*.[19]

The project's inclusion in the gallery of Latin American architectural masterpieces came with the publication of Francisco Bullrich's book *Arquitectura Latinoamericana 1930-1970* in the late 1960s.[20] He proposed a measured, rather admiring critique, highlighting the columns' rhythmic character and the ring's bold appearance, contrasting with the ascending form of the snail. He also highlighted the exposed concrete and considered the relationship with Le Corbusier to be one that is "more than in the finished forms, in basic attitudes."[21]

Over time, the canonical interpretation identified the building formally and physiognomically with the Assembly Palace of Le Corbusier. In 1987, Eliash warned that it was improper to understand the work under the "sole optic of Corbusian influence," although he directly affirmed the analogous relationship "in its general *parti*, materials, and language to the Assembly Palace," adding as confirmation of this the dedication of the project to Le Corbusier.[22] In 1988, with an interesting analysis, Browne still referred to the Corbusian volumetric pursuit,

fig. 8
Photograph of the outside and inside of the core volume.
Photo: Fondo Emilio Duhart.
© Archivo de Originales FADEU PUC.

fig. 9
Photograph of one of the interior courtyards and one of the suspended connection buildings.
Photo: Fondo Emilio Duhart.
© Archivo de Originales FADEU PUC.

[14] "Edificio de las Naciones Unidas, Chile, Emilio Duhart H. arq." *SUMMA* no. 8 (1967), 36.
[15] Antonio Díaz, "Comentario Crítico, Edificio de las Naciones Unidas, Chile," *SUMMA* no. 8 (1967), 37–38.
[16] "Santiago Caracol," *Progressive Architecture* 47, no. 10–11 (December 1966), 159.
[17] Emilio Duhart, "United Nations Building, Santiago Chile," *Architectural Design* 37, no. 1 (January 1967), 37.
[18] Ibid., 33.
[19] Emilio Duhart, "Edifice des Nations Unies pour l'Amérique Latine," *L'Architecture d'Aujourd'hui* 38, no. 135 (December 1967–January 1968), 54–57.
[20] Francisco Bullrich, *Arquitectura Latinoamericana 1930–1970* (Buenos Aires: Sudamericana, 1969).
[21] Francisco Bullrich, *Nuevos Caminos de la Arquitectura Latinoamericana* (Barcelona: Blume, 1969), 87.
[22] Humberto Eliash, "Cuando las arquitecturas eran blancas. Notas sobre la influencia de Le Corbusier en Chile," *ARS* no. 8–9 (September 1987), 18.
[23] Enrique Browne, *Otra arquitectura en América Latina* (Ciudad de México: Gustavo Gili, 1988), 74.

stating the project's dedication as evidence once again.[23] On the contrary, Fabry provides a notable analysis, relating the affinity of monumental conditions to pre-Columbian architecture.[24] Few have dared to change the dominant narrative, something that only happened when the ideological vision proposed an alternative interpretation. Such has been the case of Segre and López Rangel, who have considered it a representation of "the autonomy of the symbolic system of architecture concerning its social functions."[25] Pérez de Arce's approach constitutes a significant exception, emphasizing that the proximity to Le Corbusier is based only on the project's mono-material strategy, and that Duhart's building proposed a radically different appraisal of the construction process. Pérez de Arce highlighted the structure's proximity to the primary attributes of the form and the combination of two seismic strategies: "The suspension for the open-plan office ring, and load-bearing-wall construction for the specialized core buildings."[26]

Long-lasting Dispositions

The consecration of the canon occupied a preponderant place in countless publications. The paradigm of influence can be read in numerous publications where the comparison to the Assembly Palace is reiterated.[27] Pérez Oyarzún also adds La Tourette and the Baccardí project for Cuba by Mies van der Rohe as explanatory references in the most interesting study on the building.[28] The paroxysm comes in the face of attempts to prove the relationships through figurative or typological aspects. Browne displays the photographs of the Assembly Palace and the UN-ECLAC, affirming the "typological influence of the last works of the French-Swiss master,"[29] within the framework of the analysis of influences and copies.

In more recent publications, the narrative has remained unchanged. Lara and Carranza have highlighted that

> a reinforced concrete curving canopy shelters the entrance and makes a direct reference to Le Corbusier's Legislative Assembly in Chandigarh (1961), an illusion highlighted by the orthogonal arrangement of offices around a free-form auditorium. Duhart, it should be noted, had worked with Le Corbusier on the project for Chandigarh, India, in 1952.[30]

Lima has stated that the building "remains an outstanding example of both the lasting influence of Le Corbusier's ideas among his generation and of changing international political and

fig. 10
Photograph of the handprints of the workers in the pavement leading to the entrance of the building.
Photo: Fondo Emilio Duhart.
© Archivo de Originales FADEU PUC.

fig. 11
Cover of *AUCA 3* showcasing the double skin of the *caracol* containing the stairs that lead up to the viewing terrace. *AUCA 3* (April/May 1966).

[24] Elizabeth Fabry, "Consonances et affinités, Émile Duhart H. au Chili," *Techniques et Architecture* no. 334 (March 1981), 93–98.
[25] Roberto Segre and Rafael López Rangel, *Architettura e territorio nell'America Latina* (Milan: Electa, 1982), 109.
[26] Rodrigo Pérez de Arce, "Material Circumstances: The Project and its Construction," in *Chilean Modern Architecture Since 1950*, eds. Fernando Pérez Oyarzún, Rodrigo Pérez de Arce, and Horatio Torrent (Texas: A&M University Press, 2010), 63.
[27] See Osvaldo Cáceres, *La arquitectura del Chile independiente* (Concepción: Universidad del Bío Bío, 2007); Fernando Aliata, "Entre el desierto y la ciudad, naturaleza y arquitectura en América Latina," *Block* no. 2 (1998); Suzanne Frank, "Edificio CEPAL: las tribulaciones de un mito de la Arquitectura Moderna en Sudamérica," *ARQ* no. 24 (September 1993); Pablo Fuentes, "Emilio Duhart. La revancha de los latinos. Sede de las Naciones Unidas (CEPAL), Santiago, Chile, 1960–1966," in *La arquitectura moderna en Latinoamérica: Antología de autores, obras y textos*, ed. Ana Maluenda (Madrid: Reverté, 2016), 203–220; Verónica Esparza Saavedra, *Emilio Duhart Harosteguy, un arquitecto integral: 1935–1992* (PhD diss., Universidad Politécnica de Catalunya, 2016); Evelyn Meynard, *Emilio Duhart: Re-Imagining*

economic interests in Latin America."[31] The argument is reproduced in the catalogue of the 2015 exhibition about Latin American architecture at MoMA, where it is stated that

> **Duhart had worked with Le Corbusier on the new Punjab capital at Chandigarh, a project recalled here in the distinctive conical forms of the CEPAL Assembly hall, which rises above the roofline of the open rectangular frame of offices, creates a sky lighting for an inward-looking meeting room and offers a public observatory of the roof.[32]**

The recurrence of a canonical narrative is verified without a significant enrichment. Reiteration shows the permanence of the canonical arguments of criticism as dispositions that structure the possible thinking about a building.

The Failure of Practical Sense

The building's program grew during the project definition and construction phase when it was destined for the ECLAC. During the three decades following its inauguration, the functions were expanded, occupying the diaphanous floor under the ring. Towards the mid-2000s, a preservation process was initiated, which included clearing the successive additions. Faced with the effects of the 2010 earthquake, a *charette* was carried out to define the means of further intervention.[33] Following restoration, the reopening to the public took place in 2014 when ECLAC joined the celebrations of Heritage Day, an open day for visiting historical buildings. The institution instructed its staff to act as guides, preparing them with an official narrative that included repeated allusions to Le Corbusier. Guided tours, a noble resource to promote the values of the building's architecture, turned out to be merely recitations of the canon in a dissemination process. What would become of the Latin American economy if the institution applied the same criteria of truthfulness to the information used in their reports as they have applied for years to present the building to the community?

The supposed identification of the original author with the master made it possible to assume the use of Le Corbusier's color palette. Light blue, pink, and yellow from the 1920s palette have been used on the interior walls of the core. It may seem like a minor operation, but the light intensities are totally different, losing part of the spatial qualities due to the lighting effects. Likewise, the library's renovation was carried out in light blue tones of the same palette, replacing the tone of the surfaces originally made of precious woods from Suriname and Belize. This approach presupposes the existence of a symbolic capital added to the building because of the relationship between its author and the world-renowned architect; it supposes a prestige assigned by relationship, which ignores the building itself and its transcendence. Practical sense is—for Bourdieu—what makes it possible to explain that agents act in some cases as they should; that is, by performing what is assumed to be logical in action.[34] Once assumed, it seems to have become a habitual condition whose manner of acquisition is no longer clear, even appearing natural, without identifying its origin, becoming an apparently objective condition. The interpretative paradigm has dominated the practical sense of those who work in the institution, both for cultural diffusion and for architectural intervention.

Architectural Research

As we have seen, there is no shortage of critiques that repeat the discourse on the sources of influence. The project's dedication published in *AUCA* has been frequently used to affirm the similarity between the ECLAC building and the Corbusian structure. It is evident that Duhart's project has an affinity to the Assembly Palace. The dedication clearly warned that he freely followed the master's ideas, a reference that has been habitually eliminated. In some interviews Duhart established a distance from the master,[35] stating that he was "closer to a state of mind than to formal solutions."[36] When receiving the National Architecture Award, he stated that "it was good that I had enough autonomy to receive the influence of that great creator without being irradiated, as happened to some of his younger collaborators."[37]

Modernism in Finnis Terrae (MA diss., Parsons School of Design, The New School, 2021); Cristián Berríos, *Emilio Duhart: Ciudad Universitaria de Concepción. Elaboración de un espacio urbano moderno* (Santiago: LOM, 2017), 93.

[28] Fernando Pérez Oyarzún, "Emilio Duhart y el edificio Naciones Unidas en Santiago," in Plaut and Sarovic, *CEPAL 1962–1966*, 34–49.

[29] Enrique Browne, *Arquitectura: Crítica y nueva época* (Santiago: STOQ, 2011), 66.

[30] Luis Carranza and Fernando Luiz Lara, "1966 United Nations as Client and Advocate: Emilio Duhart's CEPAL Building in Santiago," in *Modern Architecture in Latin America: Art, Technology and Utopia*, eds. Luis Carranza and Fernando Luiz Lara (Austin: University of Texas Press, 2014), 242–245.

[31] Zeuler Lima, "Architectural Developments in Latin America: 1960–2010," in *A Critical History of Contemporary Architecture, 1960–2010*, eds. Elie Haddad and David Rifkind (Surrey: Ashgate, 2014), 167.

[32] Barry Bergdoll, Carlos Eduardo Comas, Jorge Francisco Liernur, and Patricio del Real, eds., *Latin America in Construction: Architecture 1955–1980*. Exhibition catalog (New York: The Museum of Modern Art, 2015), 162.

[33] Horacio Torrent, "Reuse and Transformation of a Modern Movement Masterpiece: UN-CAPL-ECLAC Building, Santiago de Chile," *Docomomo Journal* no. 52 (January 2015), 60–71.

[34] Bourdieu, *El sentido practico*, 100–104.

[35] Emilio Duhart, "Entrevista," interview by Pilar Urrejola and Fernando Pérez. Archivo de Originales SGLM-FADEU PUC, December 7, 1993, January 12, 1994.

[36] Fabry, "Consonances et affinités," 93.

The period during which Duhart worked for Le Corbusier has always been used as an argument for establishing formal connections. At the age of thirty-five, in 1952, Duhart briefly worked at Atelier 35 rue de Sèvres, by which point he had already developed a remarkable career in Chile. He did not seem a very impressionable young man. Recent research indicates he worked there between late April and early July of that year, probably after Le Corbusier returned from his third trip to Chandigarh until an accident prevented him from continuing with his assignments. His participation consisted basically of a sketch for the Secretariat Building made during May and 141 hours of work, according to the *Fiches Horaires*, dedicated to the design of the Villa Shodhan during June.[38]

It seems important to remember that during the month and a half or so that Duhart was at the atelier, the project for the Assembly Palace was still in its infancy, with no volumes protruding from the roof.[39] The most definitive version, in November 1956, shows a central hypostyle hall, with slender columns supporting the roof in the half-light, enclosed by the office blocks, and the portico with a curved slab supported by lamellar pillars and greater formal complexity in the roof.[40] Those two months working at the atelier with no direct relationship to the Assembly Palace fixed the interpretation of the building. It is clear that the critics' thinking was based on the idea of influence and a physiognomic reading that affirmed the resemblance. A typological analysis would be enough to see the differences. Indeed, the square composition and the prominence of a protruding shape seem apparent. However, the most significant disparity resides in the structure of courtyards versus the enclosed space of the hypostyle hall. This radical difference undoubtedly results from an aspect that has often gone unnoticed: the free plan of the *piano nobile* made possible by the suspension of the upper floor from the ring supported only by four columns per side. Architectural research might dismiss similarities that can otherwise be quickly established and look at the differences. "No one who knows architecture would say it is a copy," stated Duhart, further clarifying that Le Corbusier detested copycats.[41] An emphasis on spatial reading would ratify the differences.

The Power of Criticism

The power of criticism has placed a remarkable building in a troublesome position. However, the revelations offered by buildings assuming uncomfortable canons are not few, indicating that studying buildings in the context of their authors' ideas is likely to provide enlightening conclusions. The critics of Duhart's building never addressed the question that *AUCA* rightly asked from the beginning: what was the most appropriate composition to express the essential content of the international community involved in a United Nations building? Duhart arrived at Harvard in 1942, at the beginning of the debate on new monumentality, and later became fully aware of the criticisms of the UN buildings in New York and Paris with regard to their meaning.[42] Duhart's building shows at least five qualities in pursuit of this monumentality. The first is the definition of a plinth formed by a system of bearing walls built traditionally with local stones, which gives strength and corresponds to the dimensions of the geography. The second is the clear exhibition of the structural effort, both by the horizontal definition of the main beams and by the four columns per side that support them, freeing the cantilevered angles of the suspended floor **(fig. 12)**. The third is the diaphanous free plan achieved by suspending the upper floor, which, in the manner of a palace, proposes a modern *salle des pas-perdus* and induces an open spatial conception, reaffirmed by the bridges' centripetal orientation from the core to the edges. The fourth is the system of references to the past, both to the colonial Ibero-American courtyard house typology and to the monumental dimensions of pre-Columbian forms. Finally, the system of cultural and collective representations, such as the integration of art, the bas-reliefs of the history of humanity in the ascending path of the snail, the objects of poetic reaction such as the inverted canopy over the entrance, or the construction team's handprints across the wall of the main facade **(figs. 13-14)**.

The building meets most of the criteria demanded by the new monumentality: the application of new materials and structural conceptions, the care taken in the siting of the building, the relationship with geography and nature in the courtyards and gardens, the integration of art—among others—all satisfying the collective aspirations of "joy, pride, and excitement."[43]

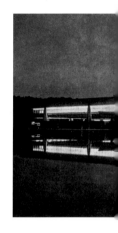

[37] Emilio Duhart, "Discurso al recibir el Premio Nacional de Arquitectura, 1977," in Montealegre, *Emilio Duhart Arquitecto*, 21.
[38] Ingrid Quintana Guerrero, *Filhos da rue de Sèvres: Os colaboradores latino-americanos de Le Corbusier em Paris (1932–1965)* (PhD diss., FAU-USP, 2016), 297–303.
[39] Le Corbusier, *Plans 1951–1952. Echelle-1* (Paris: Fondation Le Corbusier, 2005).
[40] Le Corbusier, *Oeuvre Complete Volume 6: 1952–57* (Berlin: Birkhäuser, 1995), 54–55, 95–101.
[41] Duhart, "Entrevista."
[42] Fabry, "Consonances et affinités," 93–94.

The Duty of Criticism

Criticism is a form of architectural knowledge, and its processes and approaches concern that knowledge. How can countless intelligent and influential critics have fallen for the reproduction of an improbable argument? Here it is not a question of responsibilities but of understanding the acceptance of conjectures that are assumed to be valid interpretative criteria and that reside in considerations of the influence and physiognomy of the building. Anyone who has ever visited the work would certainly not have fallen for the argument of Corbusian influence. There are too many differences for a critical eye; too obvious is the work's true magnitude. Even if a first cursory reading seems to suggest formal influences, careful observation and reliable documentation would allow anyone to affirm a different reading based on the real problem Duhart faced, that of embodying a new monumentality and giving significance to an international building through modern architecture.

    The recurring penchant for seeing resemblances or influences as part of the critical sense is almost as much an initial state of knowledge as any physiognomic pretension. In the repetition of interpretations, a long-term framework is established in which the analyses of buildings can be considered. Criticism also has the duty to reveal its own structures, its objectives built over time, because these enduring dispositions in collective knowledge can become a belief system that is trusted beyond all evidence. In the case of the United Nations building in Santiago, criticism has alas operated by annulling one of the most important problems faced by architectural knowledge, that of the significance of the international community and the monumentalization of its meaning.

fig. 12
Photograph of one of the suspending bridges.
Photo: Fondo Emilio Duhart.
© Archivo de Originales FADEU PUC.

fig. 13
Nighttime photograph of the CEPAL-ECLAC building.
Photo: Fondo Emilio Duhart.
© Archivo de Originales FADEU PUC.

fig. 14
Concrete shingle signaling the main entrance to the building.
Photo: Fondo Emilio Duhart.
© Archivo de Originales FADEU PUC.

[43] Giedion, Sert, and Leger, "Nine Points on Monumentality," 16.

Biography:

Horacio Torrent (Argentina, 1959) has a degree in architecture from the National University at Rosario, Argentina (1985), a master's degree in Architecture PUC (2001), and a PhD UNR (2006). He has developed research on modern architecture at the Canadian Centre for Architecture, the Getty Institute for the Arts and the Humanities, the National Gallery of Arts in Washington, and the Iberoamerikanisches Institut in Berlin. He is the author of publications on the history of modern architecture and the city, on Latin American modern architecture, and on contemporary Chilean architecture. He is president of Docomomo Chile and is currently a professor of architecture at the School of Architecture Pontificia Universidad Católica de Chile.

Critical Influence: The Influence of the Popular Architecture Critic on Architectural Decision-making

Kristen Harrison

fig. 1
Models of the three towers, as initially designed and presented as a part of the first design scheme for Mirvish+Gehry Toronto, at the unveiling of the project on October 1, 2012. Image: Jack Landau.

This paper is an exploration of the influence of the popular architecture critic on architectural decision-making within the context of a democratized media and critical landscape. It examines the established theories of popular criticism by architectural scholars Peter Collins, Wayne Attoe, and Michael Sorkin and overlays them on an analysis of the case study of Mirvish+Gehry Toronto, the critical response it received, and the lack of influence attributed to its critics. It also includes findings from the 2016 POP//CAN//CRIT: Current Conditions in Popular Canadian Architecture Criticism symposium to inform an understanding of the critic's ability to create influence.

Introduction

Writing in his 2014 essay "Critical Measure," architecture critic and scholar Michael Sorkin states, "I don't mean to trivialize either the function or the concept of criticism but—just like architecture—it must also be judged by its effects."[1] This notion of the effect or influence of the popular architecture critic, the critic most synonymous with newspaper critiques and columns, leads to questions about the duty and power of the critic in their role of influencing architectural decision-making and the need to evaluate their effectiveness. Thus, in order to examine the contemporary influence of the critic on the practice and products of architecture within the context of a democratized media and critical landscape, this paper will explore the theoretical groundings of the critic's influence as theorized by Peter Collins, Wayne Attoe, and Michael Sorkin as well as review the failed influence of Toronto's popular critics in the case study of Mirvish+Gehry Toronto to better understand the significance of the popular architecture critic. This includes findings from the 2016 POP//CAN//CRIT: Current Conditions in Popular Canadian Architecture Criticism symposium that included a panel discussion about the project and featured two of the most outspoken critical voices writing in support of it, despite significant criticism from the local municipal government, among others.

Theoretical Groundings: Peter Collins

Most notable in terms of contributions to the study of popular architectural criticism, Peter Collins's *Architectural Judgement* (1971) and Wayne Attoe's *Architecture and Critical Imagination* (1978) are the two most seminal scholarly texts that approach the role of the critic within a theoretical framework. As such, these two theorists and their writings form the academic grounding on which this analysis of the influence of the popular critic is situated; for while the texts explore the topics of architectural criticism and judgment more broadly rather than popular architecture criticism specifically, both express views on the lack of influence that the critic has in regards to architectural decision-making. From these two foundational scholars, architect and critic Michael Sorkin's more recent sentiments on the influential potential of popular criticism will also be explored.

Professor and architectural historian Peter Collins is today considered to be one of the most influential scholars on popular architectural criticism and judgment, and his text, *Architectural Judgement*, is noted to be one of the most important theories on the

keywords:

architectural, architecture, critic, criticism, influence, popular architecture criticism

[1] Michael Sorkin, "Critical Measure," in *Critical Juncture*, ed. Louise Noelle and Sarah Topelson (Mexico City: Docomomo, 2014), 51–52.

fig. 2
Site model of the initial design scheme, as presented at the launch of Mirvish+Gehry Toronto on October 1, 2012. Image: Jack Landau.

forms of architectural criticism that exist outside of academia.[2] Yet while Collins only pays minor attention to the popular critic, whom he refers to as a journalist and believes has little ability to create any form of material impact,[3] the text results in an overarching sense of the architect's obligation to society and the judgment of architecture as a means to help ensure the best possible outcome in this regard.[4]

This results in Collins's attempt to formalize the categories of architectural judgment into: (1) the design process, (2) competitive assessment, (3) control evaluations, and (4) journalism.

It is in this first category that Collins believes architectural decision-making happens, as the architect is continually making decisions as to the direction of the project. As such, for Collins, it is at the exact opposite end of the influence spectrum that architectural journalism acts—or rather does not act but is situated. According to Collins, "At the opposite extreme is architectural criticism in its journalistic sense; an activity which, despite its many merits, may be regarded as the antithesis of design."[5] Collins's disdain for this form of architectural judgment, while only briefly mentioned in the text, is sharply focused on the inability of architectural journalism (popular criticism) to have any influence over the process of architectural design itself. He continues, "Whether enunciated by architects, art historians or laymen, it can have no possible effect on the building under review. It may educate the public. It may publicize the architect, ulcerate the client or help overthrow the municipal government. But its *immediate* influence on the environment is nil."[6]

This perceived lack of ability for popular criticism to impact architecture, and the understanding that "whatever it creates, it creates for the future"[7] rather than effecting change in real time, is then illustrated by a reference to the 1968 cartoon by Alan Dunn. Collins explains, "The most sagacious evaluation of this kind of judgement was probably the cartoon published in a recent issue of the *New Yorker* where a workman, assembling the foundation steelwork of a sky-scraper, remarks laconically to his mate: 'I see in *The Times* that Ada Louise Huxtable already dislikes it.'"[8] This reading of the cartoon that the building will be, and is being, constructed as planned, despite Huxtable's objections, fully emphasizes Collins's view of popular criticism's ineffective nature.

Collins also explores the differences and nuances between professional and public, or lay, criticism, and overlays them to make one more scorching attack on popular criticism

[2] Naomi Stead, "Criticism in/and/of Crisis," in *Critical Architecture*, ed. Jane Rendell, Jonathan Hill, Mark Dorrian, and Murray Fraser (New York: Routledge, 2007), 76.
[3] Peter Collins, *Architectural Judgement* (London: Faber and Faber Limited, 1971), 147.
[4] Collins, *Architectural Judgement*, 169–70.
[5] Ibid., 147.
[6] Ibid.
[7] Ibid.
[8] Ibid.

when he states, "Whatever the cause, . . . it seems doubtful whether acrimonious exchanges in the public press help architects to fulfill their responsibilities to the general public."[9] He then relaxes his approach, however, reiterating: "This is not to deprecate. On the contrary, it has already been emphasized more than once that serious criticism, based on questions of principle, is the indispensable condition of professional progress."[10] Thus the problem for Collins is more the seeming lack of effective criticism than popular criticism itself, as, for him, the fact that it cannot influence active projects remains a significant drawback.

Theoretical Groundings: Wayne Attoe

Following in the legacy of Collins's *Architectural Judgement*, Attoe's text, *Architecture and Critical Imagination* (1978), is today considered to be the most seminal text on popular architecture criticism. This is supported by Dr. Naomi Stead's claim that Attoe's writing is "the most comprehensive and significant text on architectural criticism" and "remains a highly useful . . . reference point."[11]

Writing seven years after Collins, the professor of architecture takes a very different approach to theorizing architectural criticism, moving away from Collins's strict attention to the concept of evidence and verdict and instead focusing on the methods and tools of criticism, coming to the conclusion that criticism should be seen as behavior rather than final judgment.

Attoe first approaches the topic of architecture criticism in his paper "Methods of Criticism and Response to Criticism," published in 1976. In this essay, Attoe outlines his thoughts on the significance of criticism and questions whether criticism could be a "key to excellence in professional work," rather than simply "newspaper filler" or "heady entertainment."[12] This opening question immediately establishes that Attoe places greater focus on more popular forms of architectural criticism than does Collins, in addition to his similar belief that criticism is not effective or influential in its current state. Attoe also echoes Collins in the assertion that criticism, while not necessarily effective at a decision-making level, can be useful in a future sense, working to create change in projects yet to be realized.

To establish this point, Attoe works to distinguish what he refers to as "environmental criticism" (i.e., architectural criticism that considers its larger urban context) from literary and art criticism, due to its ability to be forward-looking. He states, "What is special about environmental criticism is that it can have an effect on the future . . . . To capitalize on this unique feature of environmental criticism, the critic should emphasize what is in the future and should not be satisfied with categorical judgements about the past."[13] This brings Attoe to the notion that the content of a critique should be focused on "how events in the present can teach us better how to handle the future,"[14] with the ultimate aim for criticism being that of "purposeful response."[15]

This short text leads to Attoe's polemic *Architecture and Critical Imagination* in 1978, where he works to categorize the forms, categories, methods, tools, and tactics of criticism in light of his understanding of criticism as both behavior and purposeful response toward the built environment. The text makes the striking claim that architectural criticism has failed in its ability to develop as a "major and widespread endeavour" due to the majority of its efforts being inconsequential, because "critics, in the conventional, narrow use of the term, have made few identifiable contributions to our understanding of the environment and, more importantly, to improving it."[16]

Attoe states that popular architecture criticism has been ineffective due to most critical responses coming after the design phase (and more often construction) of the project. He states, "criticism will always be more useful when it informs the future than when it scores the past," and should therefore "attempt to influence current decisions to affect a more tolerable future."[17] This is significant, as it begins to recognize the potential for popular criticism to become influential at the level of architectural decision-making and pushes the boundaries for the profession past those previously set by Collins. Attoe also sees the exchanges between legislators and the profession, among other relationships, as possible moments of criticality, noting that "architects, planners and policy-makers need to know how successful previous decisions were made so that future decisions might be influenced."[18]

[9] Collins, *Architectural Judgement*, 205-206.
[10] Ibid., 206.
[11] Stead, "Criticism in/and/of Crisis," 77.
[12] Wayne Attoe, "Methods of Criticism and Response to Criticism," *Journal of Architectural Education* 29, no. 4 "Architecture Criticism and Evaluation" (April 1976), 20.
[13] Attoe, "Methods of Criticism," 21.
[14] Ibid.
[15] Ibid.
[16] Wayne Attoe, *Architecture and Critical Imagination* (New Jersey: John Wiley & Sons, Ltd., 1978), xi.
[17] Attoe, *Architecture and Critical Imagination*, xv.
[18] Ibid., 2.

Ultimately for Attoe, popular criticism needs to look forward to become effective, as "the ends of criticism should be beginnings. If criticism does not have a forward-looking bias it will be of little use and in fact of only passing interest. After-the-fact, harangues and gushes of approval mean little if they do not relate to future issues, future problems, and aspirations for the future."[19] As such, recognizing the potential power of popular criticism to influence architectural decision-making works to help establish a new understanding of the critic's own role and influence.

Theoretical Groundings: Michael Sorkin

Writing thirty-six years after Attoe, Michael Sorkin moves the conversation from discussing potential influence to the effects required in order for popular criticism to have any merit. He states in his 2014 article "Critical Measure" that "architecture is never *not* political, given both its economic stakes and its commitment to setting social life."[20] This is due to Sorkin's understanding of architecture as a "service profession," being a profession that should work to better the lives of its users, community, and larger environment, and that its related criticism must therefore be influential in its application to successfully hold the profession to account.[21] As such, Sorkin states: "It is not sufficient for criticism merely to note that things change, our task is to influence the direction of change."[22]

For while Sorkin notes that critics most often "arrive on the scene too late, giving their useless thumbs up or thumbs down to some zillion dollar pile on which their opinions will have not the slightest impact,"[23] he clarifies that this is not meant to trivialize the work of criticism, but that, just as with architecture itself, "it must also be judged by its effects."[24] Sorkin also states that the future of criticism must see the critic's "critical gaze" applied to situations where "the stakes are real," as opposed to only acting as a literary pursuit.[25]

For Sorkin, it is the critic's duty to celebrate the artistic and qualitative merits of architecture while still bringing light to the "nuances and systems" of its context and processes, as formal analysis cannot be separate from these other social, environmental, and/or political concerns.[26] Yet Sorkin's concept of the political nature of architectural criticism goes past the need to simply acknowledge and record the context of architecture, as both Collins and Attoe had previously discussed, and calls for a critical practice that actively involves itself within architectural decision-making, while also suggesting that the very political processes that influence architecture be opened up in order to present real alternatives. Sorkin explains, "While most planning [and] decision-making belongs to the powerful, reacting belongs to the people . . . . Perhaps it is time for a little less management and a little more democracy."[27]

This understanding of architectural criticism's political potential leads to a need to discuss Sorkin's view on the democratization of criticism: a phenomenon often associated with the death of traditional, authoritative, "expert" criticism. For Sorkin, however, this idea that "everybody's a critic"[28] is not novel or of concern, but rather a logical and important step in increasing the critical voices needed to better our built environment. This includes the popular critic and the need for them to play a more active role in architectural decision-making, because, according to Sorkin, "Democracy is not simply a matter of being heard but of having the power to sway the course of events."[29]

This is an important distinction, for while the democratization of criticism has been faulted with weakening the significance and influence of the professional popular critic, Sorkin distinguishes between the ability to have one's voice heard and the ability to create change. He also notes that, while the notion of criticism's democratization has been related to the more general democratization of media as a whole, within architecture everyone is already a critic as we all live and work within the built environment and "cannot escape its influence."[30] Likewise, "You don't need to be an architect to hit your head against the wall. Nor, one might add, to be a critic in order to shout 'ouch!'"[31]

In reference to this, Sorkin remarks that popular critics are always quick to gather and lament over their "meagre reach"; however, he turns this around by suggesting that criticism is in fact "flourishing" and that one simply needs to "identify, channel, and amplify

[19] Ibid., 163.
[20] Sorkin, "Critical Measure," 38.
[21] Ibid., 35.
[22] Ibid., 38.
[23] Ibid., 51.
[24] Ibid., 51–52.
[25] Ibid., 53.
[26] Michael Sorkin, *All Over the Map: Writing on Buildings and Cities* (New York: Verso, 2011), 266.
[27] Sorkin, *All Over the Map*, 32.
[28] Ibid., 263.
[29] Ibid., 69.
[30] Ibid., 263.
[31] Ibid., 264.

fig. 3
Process models of the three towers, as initially designed and presented as a part of the first Mirvish+Gehry Toronto design scheme, at the unveiling of the project on October 1, 2012. Image: Jack Landau.

its manifold messages."[32] As such, for Sorkin, "The task of criticism is surely not to 'resolve' this polyphony in a single approach but to enable more voices to be heard"[33] in order for it to be of positive effect and influence.

Thus, the public's increased critical voice should not be seen as a threat to the professional architecture critic, but rather as another opportunity for the critic to fulfill their duty of sharing the meanings of architecture with their audience and thus to help empower readers by giving them "analytical tool[s] with which to the make the environment more comprehensible and tractable—to make the *public* more critical."[34] Ultimately for Sorkin, as a proponent of the politically active and meaningfully influential critic, "Architectural criticism is obliged to support the primary duty of architecture itself: making life better. This is the lamp that should illumine every building we make and every sentence we write."[35] And it is this statement that fully highlights Sorkin's optimism for the potential of architectural criticism. For while Collins states that criticism's "immediate influence on the environment is nil"[36] and Attoe claims that "architecture criticism . . . . especially within the popular press, has typically failed to look forward, to attempt to influence current decisions,"[37] Sorkin is steadfast in the belief that "it is not sufficient for criticism merely to note that things change, our task [as critics] is to influence the change."[38]

Mirvish+Gehry Toronto
To better understand how these theories apply to the reality of contemporary architectural practice, the case study of Mirvish+Gehry Toronto, currently in development, will be explored in relation to its critical response. The large-scale, mixed-use development, originally owned by David Mirvish, was slated to be the first freestanding project by Toronto-born architect Frank Gehry in the city of his birth, before receiving an unprecedented critical reaction upon its public unveiling in the fall of 2012. The signature Gehry-esque project originally proposed the construction of three 82–86-story residential towers in addition to two podium bases that would include retail, institutional, and art gallery components. To accommodate this density of program within an already established part of the city, however, the initial plan called for the demolition of four recently designated heritage warehouses—as well as the Princess of Wales Theatre, opened in 1992 by Mirvish—to add approximately 2,600 residential units in an area whose city services were already notably strained.

Accordingly, the project raises many issues, from signature architecture, cultural capital, heritage conservation, and urban density to the importance of public space and amenities in the downtown core. Yet despite serious criticism of the project's original scheme from the

[32] Ibid.
[33] Ibid., 265.
[34] Ibid., 267.
[35] Ibid., 272.
[36] Collins, *Architectural Judgement*, 147.
[37] Attoe, *Architecture and Critical Imagination*, xv.
[38] Sorkin, "Critical Measure," 38.

City of Toronto's chief planner, Jennifer Keesmaat, as well as multiple media outlets, online architectural commentators, and members of the public, the three primary architecture critics who responded to the project—Christopher Hume (*Toronto Star*), Lisa Rochon (*Globe and Mail*), and Alex Bozikovic (*Globe and Mail*)—all wrote at least in part in favor of and, in some cases, in defense of the project. This included efforts such as Hume's involvement in multiple events with the project owner to defend its design and his public criticism of Keesmaat in his column. Ultimately, however, and despite the critics' attempts to educate the public and municipal government as to why the project should go ahead as designed by Gehry, the original scheme underwent multiple and extensive revisions before a second, fully redesigned scheme was approved by the city in May 2014. As a result, the critics would publicly prove to lack decisive influence in the architectural and political decision-making related to the design of a significant project for the city.

It will be shown, however, that for at least one of these critics, a deeper review of the project reveals that they failed to be critical enough of the deep-rooted issues in the original design. It is also important to note that Gehry himself would come to deem the redesigned scheme more successful architecturally.[39] Thus the critics not only lacked a criticality needed to influence the work or move it in a more successful direction but also would be placed on the erroneous side of the history of the project, as the critical voices were found to be in favor of a design that largely ignored its historical and urban context.

It is therefore important to note Bozikovic's critical efforts in comparison to those of his colleagues, even if in hindsight they were not as forthright as he would have hoped. As seen in his December 7, 2013, *Globe and Mail* article, "Frank Gehry and David Mirvish's Tall Order in Toronto,"[40] Bozikovic's first piece on the project is balanced in its appraisal. He opens by detailing the project and its program before exploring the numerous city-zoning bylaws it would break, including height and density, heritage conservation, and a lack of public amenities. In doing so, Bozikovic looks beyond the project itself to the wider context of the surrounding area and the concerning precedent it could set, as originally designed, at an urban scale. Bozikovic concludes by stating he hopes to see the project built, but that it would require progress in order to be more "generous to the city."[41]

Bozikovic's second article, "Mirvish-Gehry Vision for King Street is Scaled Down, but There is Nothing Timid about It,"[42] was published in response to the unveiling of the redesigned scheme, which would go on to win city approval. Bozikovic first states that the redesigned scheme "looks great," before sharing that the original scheme was "vague," "never going to happen," had "no chance of winning approval," and had "serious problems."[43] He refers back to his original critique, in which he called the proposal a "bluff," going on to suggest that it was unclear how the design would ever be detailed structurally or built. He then refers to the updated plans as "both realistic and much improved" as well as "compelling,"[44] before detailing the redesign, which included a reduction in the number of towers from three to two and the retaining of the theater and two of the warehouses. Thus, whether consciously or not, Bozikovic suggests that some of his criticism of the original scheme may have been taken into account in the redesign.

As such, a return to an analysis of the critic as an influencer, in light of this case study, shows the current ineffectiveness of the professional popular critic. Speaking at the 2016 POP//CAN//CRIT: Current Conditions in Popular Canadian Architecture Criticism symposium, Rochon states that, while a critic's opinion might influence a developer or the city on occasion, it should not be assumed that it means a project should progress a certain way; it would be naive to think the critic's voice should be held above the others in the complex web of decision-making for projects of this scale.

fig. 4
Process models of the three towers, as initially designed and presented as a part of the first design scheme, at the unveiling of the project on October 1, 2012. Image: Jack Landau.

[39] Katrina Clarke, "David Mirvish to Keep Princess of Wales Theatre in Revised Design for King West Condo Towers," *National Post*, May 27, 2014, https://nationalpost.com/news/toronto/david-mirvish-to-keep-princess-of-wales-theatre-in-revised-plans-for-king-west-condo-towers

[40] Alex Bozikovic, "Frank Gehry and David Mirvish's Tall Order in Toronto," *Globe and Mail*, December 7, 2013, https://www.theglobeandmail.com/news/toronto/frank-gehry-and-david-mirvishs-tall-order-in-toronto/article15809360/

[41] Bozikovic, "Tall Order in Toronto."

[42] Alex Bozikovic, "Mirvish-Gehry Vision for King Street is Scaled Down, but There is Nothing Timid about It," *Globe and Mail*, May 30, 2014, https://www.theglobeandmail.com/news/toronto/mirvish-gehry-vision-for-king-street-is-scaled-down-but-theres-nothing-timid-about-it/article18935131/

[43] Bozikovic, "Mirvish-Gehry Vision for King Street."

[44] Ibid.

For Bozikovic, the rigorous questions the critics should have been asking, and which would have been useful in informing the criticism and its intended audiences, include: what impacts should we care about? What should we want to get out of the project? How will the decision be made? And how should it be made?[45] But, as Bozikovic notes on multiple occasions, the criticism was not critical enough nor did it come soon enough, going so far as to say that "the critics lost."[46]

Rochon has a very different view of the role, however, referring to herself as a *booster*. She states that "I think my role as an architecture critic, in this case, was to provide some energy and fuel and encourage the daring,"[47] despite having some deep reservations about the design. Interestingly, for Bozikovic, however, it was the *boosterism*, a role he disagrees with, of Hume and Rochon that most likely had the biggest impact, despite it being in support of a project that was ultimately revised and scaled down. Bozikovic also indicates that he did not have much of an influence on the project, even though his pieces on the project were widely read, stating, "I am not quite sure that [my columns] had any impact at all. Certainly, I educated people, but I am not quite sure that I changed a lot of minds."[48]

But how, then, does the critic become effective and influential? For Bozikovic, it is the planners, and not the critics, who have influence. He remarks, echoing Sorkin, that in reality all processes are political—despite what the critics write. Bozikovic also notes that this project would therefore have been an excellent opportunity for a critic to have written about the "opaque" planning processes at City Hall for the general public, in order to explain why those processes are working or not working and how they are negotiated, and by whom.

However, where the influence of criticism comes into the political process for Bozikovic is hard to determine. For while he believes there might be a role for criticism to play in the political arena, he notes that it would be very difficult to establish what that is and how it would affect political negotiations, such as the compromise that brought about the approved second scheme. Bozikovic believes it would require an investigation into whether there was any impact from the public discourse on the political outcome, as he knows they are interrelated, just not how or to what degree.[49] He concludes: "It may be true that me articulating some concerns about the project [helped the planning department] in their negotiations to a certain degree or reinforced their resolve to pursue this, but I think fundamentally, I would suggest probably not that much critical influence and that it would be very difficult to measure what that influence would look like on this sort of project."[50]

While Bozikovic may not take credit for his potential impact on the direction of the project or be able to measure the extent of the influence his writing had, it is plausible to suggest that the work of at least one of Toronto's critics helped shape the project to some degree, and for the betterment of the city at an urban scale. And in doing so, Bozikovic begins to move the needle on the work of the critic from the inconsequential position of Collins and Attoe, to the political and persuasive position of Sorkin.

45 Azrieli School of Architecture and Urbanism, "Panel 5: Case Study: Mirvish+Gehry Toronto – The Critical Response," POP//CAN//CRIT: Current Conditions in Popular Canadian Architecture Criticism symposium (Carleton: Carleton University, October 21, 2016), 00:36:38.

46 Azrieli School of Architecture and Urbanism, "Panel 5: Case Study," 00:22:34.

47 Ibid., 00:24:30.

48 Ibid., 00:25:05.

49 Ibid., 00:30:36.

50 Ibid., 00:28:09.

Biography

Kristen Harrison, M.Arch, MRAIC, holds a bachelor of architectural studies and professional master of architecture degree from the Azrieli School of Architecture and Urbanism, Carleton University. While continuing her postgraduate research, she is also the advocacy and engagement manager at the Royal Architectural Institute of Canada and has taught both lecture-based and studio courses at the Azrieli School. Her critical and editorial writing has been published in *Canadian Architect, Canadian Interiors, Building, Spacing,* and *ArchDaily,* among others, and she has presented her research internationally. Harrison is the founding organizer of the award-winning POP//CAN//CRIT architecture symposium series.

In Search of the Latent Kairos of Architectural Form

paolo conrad-bercah

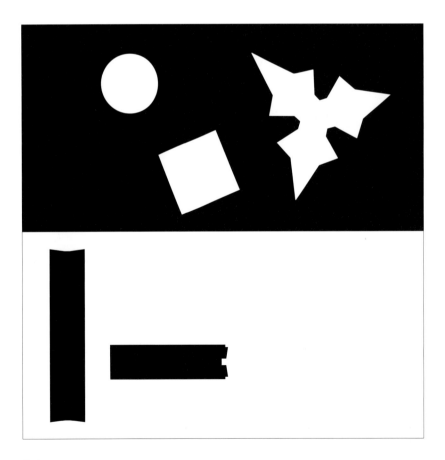

fig. 1
Kuehn Malvezzi, Axel Springer Campus competition entry. General plan.

"True critique," wrote Ludwig Feuerbach, "lies in elaboration itself, because the latter is possible only through the separation of the essential from the accidental, of the necessary from the contingent, of the objective from the subjective."[1] What Feuerbach demonstrates is that reworking another's form is not separate from the creative act but often expands upon it, clarifying its meaning or underscoring its unexpressed potential. This essay elaborates a recent, unbuilt project in Berlin from the point of view of a practicing architect to demonstrate, first and foremost, the practitioner's need for architectural criticism.

Kairos and Stimmung

It is 2021. Eighteen months into a pandemic that forced people to communicate mostly in a remote fashion, the planet has fallen into a sort of Dark Age driven by Instagram values: compulsive posting of visual information sponsoring self-promotion and wild narcissism. The Instagram age leaves very little space for criticisms of any sort. The practicing architect worthy of the name is then left with but one option: to react by offering reflection on the power of images, making sense of the few meaningful pictures circulating in order to grasp the genuine—namely, not doctored—pathos that animates them so they can be used in architectural practice. This should also perhaps try to "evoke" pathos rather than "explaining" it as if were something directly connected to natural or scientific events, like the unrepentant "digital modernists" of Silicon Valley would like one to believe by sponsoring the absurd linear notions of time first introduced by modernism itself.[2]

As a practicing contemporary architect, I find this effort necessary to regenerate today's architectural form through a criticism that "dares" to remain indifferent to the reigning values of Instagram. The intent is not to formulate yet another new, unsustainable architectural language. The language used is mostly existent, analogous, and ready for use. It is devoid of flaccid judgments and moral prejudices. It is a non-apophantic and deliberately anachronistic language, one that is very careful to avoid cheap quotations. It lives on the relationships of its elements, experimenting with them and with aesthetic translations capable of intercepting form's due time—its *kairos*—to release the power latent in the form itself.[3]

Kairos represents the opportune or profoundly particular moment in which an act finds its greatest impact, embodying an understanding of both timeliness and appropriateness. What I want to express, in other words, is an interest in a "kairologic" conception of form that is capable of regenerating form itself through an ineffable *Stimmung*—or Warburgian pathos—in which the term pathos identifies the fundamental nature of the form itself.[4] To be clear and to avoid being misunderstood, the language that I think we should be looking for is a language that dwells in a time populated by a *Nachleben* that continuously shapes language itself,[5] weaving three different but indispensable characteristics into one single tapestry: *mneme, aisthesi, and phantasi*; namely, the preservation of memory, the actuation of sensitivity, and the projection of the faculty of imagination.

keywords:

Berlin, transference, Warburg, *Nachleben, Lebensenergie*

[1] Ludwig Feuerbach, *Esposizione, sviluppo e critica della filosofia di Leibniz* (Naples: La Scuola di Pitagora, 2019).

[2] My remarks reflect the belief expressed by Giacomo Marramao that the contingent is the most useful ontological category in which to talk about the contemporary, because it shows a clear dissatisfaction with the linear notion of temporality expressed by modernism, which aspires precisely to forget the fundamental role that contingency plays in historical evolution. Cf. the inquiry that Giacomo Marramao carried out on the political categories of modernity: *Potere e secolarizzazione. Le categoriedel tempo* (Turin: Editori Riuniti, 1983); *Minima temporalia. Tempo, spazio, esperienza* (Milan: Il Saggiatore, 1990);and *Kairós. Apologia del tempo debito* (Turin: Bollati Boringhieri, 2020). As Marramao himself points out, "Today the future no longer appears, as it did at the time of the industrial revolution, to be a liberating dimension, but an innovative routine removed from the will of individual subjects and delegated to impersonal technological structures." Time, in other words, no longer seems "at our disposal" but appears more and more as an a priori factor that Western rationalism and the logic of the market uses to tyrannize thanks to a "mephistophelian" welding of the technology of "real time" with the incessant and pressing digital needs in which the means have become the ends.

[3] The thesis is based on the ancient Greek conceptions of time. In the *Timeaus*, Plato described *chronos* (chronological time) as an authentic *image of aion* (the suspended time of eternity). Human beings can only

Berlin Transference and Nachleben

A number of projects recently built in Berlin provide immediate evidence to the thesis just mentioned. Berlin is an appropriate place to deal with the topic because it has become one of the most emblematic places in history—as if history has had no other place on the planet in which to rage, releasing unknown violence capable of solidifying a significant part of the contemporary world's "darkness" in built form, which architects have an even greater responsibility than others to take on. Berlin seems in fact to be the place where history has been incarnated architecturally with the most perverse consequences. This is the reverse of what has happened since the fall of the Wall, which released, on the contrary, a strange, uncalled-for *Stimmung,* mixing neglect and the boring feeling of mending a historical picture that never existed except in the very militaresque mind of Senator Stimman who, in hindsight, seems the one who paved the way for a climate that eventually led to mind-boggling episodes like the royal family's residence being extravagantly "reconstructed" with no thought whatsoever given to its final use. [6]

A set of more interesting suggestions are instead delivered by Kuehn Malvezzi's project for the 2013 competition for the expansion of the Axel Springer Campus. [7] The project provides the practicing architect with an intriguing notion: to design an architectural form in which a number of aesthetic ideas are encoded by the *Frühromantik* (the Early German Romanticism of the late 1700s) in order to generate a more interesting *Stimmung,* one that is able to provide a new form-of-life for historical precedents and which has played an important role in German architectural history. [8] In spite of being a simple competition entry, the project houses a number of stimulating hypotheses regarding architectural form that are worthy of elaboration.

The hypothesis one sees in Kuehn Malvezzi's entry is an explicit proposal of historical transference; it promises to give full expression to the potential of an architectural form that shows no fear in employing its anachronism. The project site is bordered to the south by another property on which the two juxtaposed modernist lamellae that have housed the Axel Springer Campus since 1966 still stand. The two areas had been separated by the Berlin Wall but, after its fall, the land to the north was bought for expansion. Kuehn Malvezzi proposed a radical volumetric inversion here. In contrast to the modernist void in the area to the south, an all-encompassing solid space was envisioned that would be punctured by three large courtyards: one reproducing Mies's building for Friedrichstrasse and two "suprematist" courtyards, a square and a circle that allude to two other famous projects by Loos and Schinkel, one never built and one subsequently demolished. The schematic plan duly synthesizes the architects' intention to expand the original lot through a lot which is "inverse" to it. A clean break between the two lots remains. It is as if the Wall that had once separated not only the land but also two opposing worlds were still present *(fig. 1)*.

Inversion is a recurrent theme in Kuehn Malvezzi's work, a choice that is clearly influenced by their collaboration with Michael Riedel, a virtuoso in reproduction who is known for reconfiguring existing material to generate new meaning. The radical inversion in the Axel Springer Campus project—the solid versus the void—is what unleashes an unexpected *Lebensenergie* that echoes Warburg's sensitivity. Before going into greater depth on this, let's focus on some of the project's key characteristics. [9]

First and foremost is the fact that it occupies the entire surface of the lot and its sides correspond to the lot's edges. Indicative then, too, is the language the designers used for the facades of the large block, characterized by a sober, anonymous modernism in which the facades take shape through the stacking of the floors and the use of glass panels. The rhythm of the floors is interrupted, especially at the corners, by the double-heights and the balconies they define on the facade, which seem to be memory-traces providing a new, translated form-of-life to the Loosian *Raumplan* that is now no longer boxed in but exposed in plain sight. The aim is to create a building that serves as a background, one that exhibits the life going on inside. Because of how the designers have avoided a clear distinction between

perceive this image with the help of *chronos,* as if the latter were nothing more than the energy needed to set in motion the frames of the film of the world (which preexist the world, because the film of the world is eternal). Aristotle developed the Platonic concept in his reasoning on time in Book IV of *Physics,* which for many remains the most authoritative confirmation that time is to be considered a field of investigation for physics but not metaphysics. For Aristotle, "time is a number of movements with respect to a before and after," or rather a mathematical act put into play by the human mind to try to find a chronological order in what is devoid of order because it is timeless. Both Plato and Aristotle think of time as a complementary and indissoluble relationship between *aion* and *chronos,* as if it were a fusion that defines the insurmountable enigma of time.

[4] Aby Warburg (1866–1929) was an historian of art and culture. German by birth, he felt at home in Florence whose history became the center of his focus as a scholar with wide-ranging interests that centered on the Renaissance. Warburg understood art as a means of understanding, through works and authors, the civilization that had expressed them. He is widely credited to have enlarged the scope of visual art studies by founding a new method that introduced for the first time psychoanalyses as an investigating tool. *Stimmung* is a typical example of such attitude. It means disposition of mind, mood. It is today a term of frequent use in the language of literature and aesthetic criticism.

[5] *Nachleben* is one of the conceptual pillars of Warburg's work. He used it to emphasize how images, unlike human beings, do not cease to exist after their time is up and continue to live a certain number of lives in different places and forms. *Nachleben* contains a polarity: it can be translated as afterlife (the afterlife, for example, of an author in the sense of their posthumous reputation) or as the act of living one's own life according to the teachings of others. This calls the linearity of time into question inasmuch as the image is characterized as an artifact in which a plurality of times flow.

[6] The Stadtschloss (Royal Palace) was demolished in 1951. The German Democratic Republic (GDR) *Nomenklatura* showed no doubts: "We're done with art historians!" Yet one particular fragment of the building was purposefully preserved: Portal IV, including the balcony from which Karl Liebknecht declared the birth of the Socialist Republic on November 9, 1918. From the moment of that speech on, the building became the "people's palace." By destroying the rest of it, it was as if the GDR leaders had declared that the building's real history, the one that had to be kept alive, was the one that had begun with Liebknecht's speech, later integrating Portal IV into the adjacent GDR Council of State building as a relic in 1964. In 1976 the entire area was occupied by a large new public building, the Palast der Republik—that is, the new GDR parliament building—the real political, economic, and symbolic center of the communist state. After the Wall's demolition, the Palast was found to be thoroughly contaminated with asbestos. In the meantime, in 1999, the parliament of

fig. 2
Kuehn Malvezzi, Axel Springer Campus competition entry. Street elevation.

fig. 3
Kuehn Malvezzi, Axel Springer Campus competition entry. Street plan.

fig. 4
Kuehn Malvezzi, Axel Springer Campus competition entry. Render.

the circulation routes and the workspaces, one can imagine moving fluidly between the floors. The assertiveness and the impact of the building's overall volume are then tempered by a roof garden and a sloping green roof that, in addition to designing a new urban silhouette, create a large open public space more than thirty meters above street level.

Also worth noting is the way in which the designers have resolved the entrance to the large block and its general circulation. The ground floor faces the street, and the sides of the building unfold like a grand linear bazaar accommodating multiple uses that exist alongside coworking spaces: supermarkets, cafés, recreational facilities, and small shops. The bazaar seems to invite passersby toward the building, urging them to live on its edges and then drawing them inside, encouraging them to explore the interior **(figs. 2, 3)**.

The leap in perception between the exterior facade and the inner courtyards elicits the same kind of surprise one can feel, for instance, at the Alhambra in Granada when, suddenly, deep inside the Arab citadel, the Palace of Charles V appears in full mannerist garb, or when one encounters the Christian church inside the Mosque of Cordoba. In Kuehn Malvezzi's building, the facades of the inner courtyard appear to be the building's real elevations: they have their own well-defined character, which is quite different from the anonymity characterizing the block's exterior **(fig. 4)**.

What is most striking, however, is the form of the inner courtyards in which the three modern icons are reproposed and "reappear" as though they were reproductions. Three geometric figures, three icons that have never left the debate on the role of form in architecture history: the square (Karl Friedrich Schinkel's Bauakademie), the tondo (the tower/column in Adolf Loos's project for the Chicago Tribune), and the diamond (Mies van der Rohe's skyscraper for Friedrichstrasse). This is an important *Nachleben*, created by reproposing

the newly united Germany had moved back to the Reichstag, under Foster's well-known dome. It was there, in 2003, that the demolition of the Palast der Republik was approved, and then later, in 2006, it was decided that a replica of the Stadtschloss would be constructed to house a museum. Only afterward was it decided that this generic museum which was housed in a copy of a demolished building would, in turn, display Humboldt's collection of art from outside Europe. This led to a competition for the reconstruction of the building as and where it had been, with the exception of the eastern wing along the river.

[7] Axel Springer was a journalist who became a successful tabloid publisher in 1946. During the time of the Wall he purchased a plot just in front of the Wall itself for 1 euro to build a high-rise structure to house the headquarters of his many companies. The location of the high rise was purposefully chosen to be perceived as a slap in the face to the East Berlin *Nomenklatura* trying to hide the value of entrepreneurship and free enterprise. A new large-scale structure has just been added to the original one by OMA after it was selected to do so by the Axel Springer company.

[8] Form-of-life is a term used according to the philosophical sphere determined by Giorgio Agamben in his published work. In Agamben's philosophical

one form that had been demolished (Schinkel's Bauakademie) and two forms that never came to be (Mies's and Loos's towers). It is as though one is being reintroduced into a time in which past, present, and ideal time are all interwoven.

Reproposing unbuilt modern icons is not a new phenomenon in Berlin's history. Oswald Mathias Ungers and his protégé Rem Koolhaas did it a number of times, starting in 1977 with the manifesto to turn Berlin into a Green Urban Archipelago, *(fig. 6)* which was the first to feature the notion of building the failed icons of modernists with whom Koolhaas was obsessed. In a book called *Das Neue Berlin* (1990), Ungers published many projects done during the Wall time, many of which proposed the building of unrealized architectural icons' (including Loos's tower). It is arguably this attitude of Ungers that would enact Koolhaas's idea for the 1980 IBA West Berlin reconstruction competition, where they had proposed to "retroactively" build three previously rejected projects—Mies's tower, Hilbeseimer's housing blocks, and Mendelsohn's headquarters for the metalworkers' union building (IGMetallHaus)—on the lots along the Friedrichstrasse on which they had originally been planned.[10]

Koolhaas's own proposal for IBA 1980 reads today as a clear criticism of the competition guidelines, which had requested that the buildings be reconstructed with their prewar exterior profiles and that their language show unity and regularity. Koolhaas felt these criteria concealed the municipal authorities' guilty conscience: for him, reproposing what had been would have meant repressing it, removing evidence of the war's destruction as if it had never happened, all in the name of expressing history. In reality, the IBA program expected Berlin to fit into a single, nineteenth-century temporal model, omitting the fact that Berlin is not, and has never been, a unitary, compact city and is, on the contrary, an urban model that juxtaposes and overlaps different lives and eras .

In fact, Berlin was the capital of the German Democratic Republic (GDR), the world capital of *Mietkasermen* (tenements), an instant metropolis, the cradle of modernism, the Nazi capital, and the Cold War's most prominent theater, the only one where the two sides actually confronted each other face-to-face. Berlin, in other words, has lived many different lives hidden under a plurality of masks that have transformed the urban conurbation into a sort of permanent Lazarus in the history of urban planning, or an archive of silent but meaningful testimonies that few seem truly interested in questioning. This character has to be respected and this was Koolhaas's message—one that is still relevant today when considering what has happened since 1980. This makes the fact that Kuehn Malvezzi's project will not be built all the more ironic, because the Axel Springer competition was ultimately won by Koolhaas's firm, OMA, which designed yet another minimal object inflated to the architectural scale almost without giving a second thought to the end result.[11]

As a consequence the soon-to-be-inaugurated built object manages to cast shadows that are at once spectral and cheaply populist. The OMA project really appears to show no interest in engaging with either the immediate, short-term context or the long-term, historic context of Berlin. The object housing the campus has no exterior space of any kind and, on the contrary, has turned its interior into a single over-scaled and enclosed theatrical area where it seems impossible to concentrate on anything other than watching other occupants or taking selfies.

In a document prepared to illustrate the project to the client, Koolhaas wrote that OMA wanted to "propose a building that lavishly broadcasts the work of individuals for shared analysis. . . . The essence of our proposal is a series of terraced floors that together form a digital valley. Each floor contains a covered part as a traditional environment, which is then uncovered on the terraces. Halfway through the building, the valley is mirrored to generate a three-dimensional canopy"[12] *(fig. 5)*. Upon learning about OMA's design intent, no one would be surprised that the structure appears to be a reflection of the bad vibes of such rhetoric. The building comes across as a spectral object that seems to be reiterating OMA's notorious mantra—"fuck the context"—two decades later, and it does this right in front of a glorious street corner of Berlin: the Mossehaus, a building that significantly influenced Streamline

dictionary it means defining a use in itself or thinking about a use of potency that is not a simple passing to the act. Agamben writes that Glenn Gould is "the only one who cannot not-play, and, directing his potentiality not only to the act but to his own impotence, he plays, so to speak, with his potential to not-play." In other words, Gould lives the use of himself as a pianist. This use is not an activity, but a form-of-life, a being that is constant and not alienated from what one knows how to do. Thus being does not appropriate ways of being, it requires them; it unfolds in them, being nothing other than its modification. Life is nothing but its form-of-life, which is generated by living.

9   *Lebensenergie* is life energy or the energy that makes life possible, according to Aby Warburg. This energy is comparable to a *motuspermanentis* that allows timeless returns in a continuous play between memory and oblivion. Everything is like a game of competing forces that go back and forth as if on an unstoppable swing. This implies a life of conflicts between active and reactive forces.

10 Cf Oswald Mathis Ungers, *Das Neue Berlin* (Ungers Archiv für Architektur-wissenschaft, 1990).

11 The attempt to shock people by inflating basic geometry out of proportion to produce forms that are supposed to be interesting (but that the majority find childish) seems to be the hallmark of Koolhaas's design since he attained the so-called star-architect status.

12 Cfr. OMA, Axel Springer Campus, Phase II, 2015.

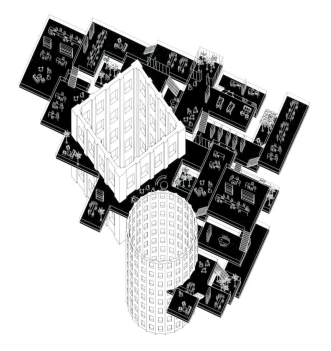 

architecture, thanks to the mastery of the hand of an architect—Erich Mendelsohn—who is worthy of the name. When seen next to the Mendelsohn street corner, the OMA corner seems like a silly joke, one exclusively ruled by the tyranny of Instagram values, promising only to aggressively spread a new virus of images across the world in order to be casually liked by a plethora of followers. In other words, the building seems to be wrapped in a showy mantle, one resulting from a gratuitous spectacularization of engineering that reads almost immediately as tiring: a dark, impenetrable, odd shape that opens up on the southwest corner to reveal, by making a spectacle of it, the very Instagrammable life that is supposed to be taking place inside **(figs. 7, 8)**.

What is interesting about Kuehn Malvezzi's project is the fact that, while it distances itself from Koolhaas's message, it also manages to reinterpret and update it. Their distance defuses the Dutch architect's Calvinist tone, projecting a subtle, sophisticated irony or a reinterpretation of some aesthetic ideas of the Frühromantik. These ideas are the Witz, the arabesque, the fragmented, and what is called the je-ne-sais-quoi or ineffability. By referring to these categories, it may be possible to implement a real cultural transference with the past, so as to reevaluate it and use it as a tool for criticism of contemporary values. Taking leave from the works thus far described, going beyond the implicit or explicit will of their authors who become nothing more than the medium of an extra-temporal message, it may be possible to build a discussion of collective public benefit through this very transference. The limits of the present contribution will allow for the use of only one of these categories: the Witz.[13]

With a certain approximation, the term Witz can be likened to irony. Yet the Witz is a subtler, more elusive and surely blasé irony that is not sardonic at all. The Witz is a form of acute-and-intimate-but-ironic dialogue: a sophisticated flicker of pure cognitive intuition. The Witz is an intuitive act with strong intellectual implications, and one through which the project must be considered. It aims at creating surprise and wonder, and it achieves this with free and, at times, surreal associations of various heterogeneous and distant elements. The Witz plays with the paradoxical, but it does so for purposes other than surrealism (which is aimed at expressing the unconscious), seeking to stimulate the intellect to initiate dialogue.

fig. 5
Kuehn Malvezzi, Axel Springer Campus competition entry. Axonometric view.

fig. 6
Kuehn Malvezzi, Axel Springer Campus competition entry. Interior courtyard render.

[13] The reader interested in the full spectrum of use of such categories is here referred to conrad-bercah, *Berlin Transfert* (Syracuse, Italy: LetteraVentidue Edizioni, 2021).

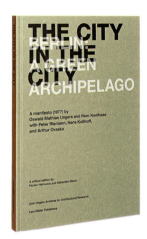

The association between heterogeneous elements cannot be gratuitous; it must make what has remained unexpressed spring forth in the form of recognized expressive means.

In Kuehn Malvezzi's project, Koolhaas's provocative tone disappears, as do the techniques for implementing it, such as "cut and paste." The icons of modern architecture are not just simply reproposed in their project; a true aesthetic transference is achieved through the inversion of the solid areas and the voids, the main interior facades and those of the anonymous exterior, and more. The past they take on becomes an evocation, not a crude slogan; though the icon is physically absent, its presence is perceived.

If we imagine entering the three courtyards, it would be as if we were enveloped by the invisible aesthetic cloak of these three previously unbuilt projects. This would create a sort of perceptive estrangement, in which the time of architectural form, its chronology, would be shaken up and replaced by the time of memory that is always within us. It is an anachronistic Witz, one that has very little to do with the citational and kitschy postmodernism of the 1980s. The citation here is elusive and sophisticated, it is veiled with irony and pervaded by good taste, and it leads to works that, despite their recent construction, appear suspended in time. It is as if they were living outside chronological time in a time devoid of time, a time indifferent to the "real time" that increasingly haunts collective life.

fig. 7
OMA, Axel Springer Campus project render.

fig. 8
Berlin as a Green Archipelago, 1977. Book cover. © Lars Müller Publishers.

fig. 9
Erich Mendelsohn, Mossehaus, 1921–1923. Photo: bpk/Kunstbibliothek, SMB/Arthur Köster © 2022, ProLitteris, Zurich.

fig. 10
OMA, Axel Springer Campus, 2021.

This very quality seems to inform another project by the firm that is currently under construction just a couple of blocks north of the Axel Springer Campus: House of One. This is a project that confirms the seriousness of their stance and the fact that they appear (in their work) to be looking (perhaps unconsciously) for the latent kairos of architectural form referred to at the beginning of the essay. It is a project that dares to tackle head-on the ghastly emptiness of its surroundings (GDR modernism) by rediscovering Berlin's Mediterranean soul[14] *(fig. 9)*. House of One shows in no uncertain terms the courage of presenting itself as an iconic act, as the best of Berlin tradition dictates.

Considered this way, the building appears to be an accusation against the inexpressive banality or cheap spectacularity with which the German conurbation has been designed since 1989. House of One is a particular house of worship that keeps spectacularity at bay and, on the contrary, gives no outward hint of its daring program. Inside, the synagogue, church, and mosque each have unique and specific configurations that reflect their own liturgy. Above these three houses of worship, a sphere appears to float over the dome of the central square where there is a belvedere. The sphere is not perceptible from the street and is housed within a lantern-shaped volume that, with its thin brick partitions, dematerializes the building's incursion in the sky. As a whole, the latter has the appearance of a neutral monolith with one-meter-thick masonry walls: its anonymity was studied in such a way as to conform to the symbolic reasoning of the three creeds and to represent a moment of communion between them. From the outside of the strong-but-not-connotative building, one does not recognize a specific house of worship; one does not see bell towers, minarets, or Hebrew script. The designers sought to create an object whose character was poised between the distinguished and the anonymous—a presence that is at once assertive, laconic, and enigmatic. Therefore House of One opens a much-needed space for an analogical rift that, with due differences, replaces *chronos* with kairos of the necessary form in its intimacy and lyricism.

The Dialectical Image

In his seventh thesis on the philosophy of history, Walter Benjamin argues that the real stake in the conception of history is cultural heritage. History is made by the victors, who are quite frequently disinterested in hearing the stories of the vanquished, and heritage is thus incomplete and artificially reconstructed. A proper reading of cultural heritage should instead be delineated by three other factors: historicism, faith in progress, and the linear (chronological) conception of time. Once precautions have been taken against these three enemies, the historian's task is to "brush history against the grain," deconstructing its long-established automatisms. Benjamin applies this to images as well, asking himself how they are formed. For him, they are nothing more than the result of a dialectic that only emerges after having brushed away the false conceptions of history, destroying and reconstructing history in an increasingly inclusive way. Benjamin defines this as a "dialectical image,"[15] namely an image whose dialectic is revealed through history's *discontinuum* as opposed to its assumed *continuum* and one that takes into account involuntary as well as explicit memory. For Benjamin, as for all the dialectical materialists, history does not have to be confined to its time; it must always have a reverberation in actuality—it has to be actualized to reappropriate the present. This applies to images as well. Reactivating an image of the past means using it tangibly to change, to revolutionize, the present.

If we then, through a sort of transference, apply all of this to architecture, it follows that a building worthy of note is one that comes to terms with a much wider past, a past that embraces all, and one that expresses the presence of this past in current terms. This building will be the bearer of a dialectical image, a glimpse that is caught for a moment and then disappears. The understanding of history and images is thus a fleeting moment of stasis, a momentary illusion, always destined to throw itself back into motion. The time that nourishes Benjamin's theory is clearly not chronological. It is not the time of *chronos* but that

[14] Horst Bredekamp is to be credited for having identified the *longue durée* of the passion for the atmosphere of the Mediterranean world that has been present in Berlin for more than four centuries. The most convincing "interpretation" of this is found in the work of Schinkel, which, taken as a whole, involves the conurbation's entire landscape. Cf. Horst Bredekamp, *Berlin am Mittelmeer. Eine kleine Stadtgeschichte: Kleine Architekturgeschichte der Sehnsucht nach dem Süden* (Berlin: Verlag Klaus Wagenbach, 2018).

[15] In addition to being a sort of spiritual testament, Walter Benjamin's well-known text "Theses on the Philosophy of History" can be seen both as a theory of the dialectical image and as the intellectual arsenal behind his unfinished book on Baudelaire. These theses attempt to formulate a fascinating hypothesis on the formation of images in time (even if they have often been read from other perspectives outside the sphere of the art world, especially in politics and theology). Today's interest in these theses lies more in their *pars destruens* of the demolition of universal history, the distancing from the victors, the brushing against the grain than in the messianism that characterizes the *construens* aspect. Perhaps the theory's main contribution lies in having demonstrated the erratic density of the historical process beyond a reasonable doubt. Cf. Walter Benjamin, *Illuminations: Essays and Reflections*, ed. Hannah Arendt, trans. Harry Zohn (New York: Schocken Books, 1981).

of opportunity; it is kairos, the time caught at the right moment according to the Greeks. This is what one must deal with, forgetting *chronos*, or at least putting it in parenthesis.

What has been said thus far can be summarized as follows. The true image of the past has to be understood as an experience that is the result of a dialectic. This dialectic does not resolve contradiction. It simply comes to be in a present moment that contains a moment of the past, and together they create a third time, the time of Memory. The work of Kuehn Malvezzi can arguably be seen, at least potentially, as an attempt to "brush history against the grain," to develop a dialectic capable of proposing a building that places the question of time at its root and, with it, that of the anachronism of the form. It nobly aspires to establish a dialogue between past and present in a single moment, a single *augenblick*—a single blink of the eye.

The Puff Pastry of Time

Wilfried Kuehn wrote: "The world is full of objects and full of artworks. With all this overcrowding, the challenge seems to be less one of inventing more objects and more one of curatorial design to create new and more intelligent relations between the already existing. In this sense, both art and architecture must be conceptual and act precisely in concrete situations, avoiding all formal narcissism. It means generating new perspectives on what is already there."[16] His words are indebted to Benjamin's and Warburg's work. The latter was built not only on history's refuse but also on the anachronism that constantly jolts human memory. Warburg made the image (*bild*) the hinge around which his research revolved, and he did it at the time when the Bauhaus had just banned words like "images." For Warburg, images can

fig. 11
Kuehn Malvezzi, House of One.
fig. 12
Kuehn Malvezzi, House of One.

[16] Francesca Petretto, "Kuehn-Malvezzi, architetture come construzione intorno all'arte," Il giornale dell'Architettura.com: Magazine Libero e Indipendente Sulle Culture Del Progetto e Della Città, March 5, 2018, https://ilgiornaledellarchitettura.com/web/2018/03/05/kuehn-malvezzi-architetture-come-costruzione-intorno-allarte/.

only be experienced as *Nachleben*, as the manifestation of a new life of something that has remained latent, ultimately as something whose life had not previously been expressed, or at least not fully. From this point of view, the image plays on different tables of history at the same time. This complexity, made up of latencies, crises, survivals, and symptoms, is what the art historian—and the architect—is called upon to consider in relation to the specific time, place, and program in which they are working.

In Kuehn Malvezzi's project, this happens in an explicit way through the visual inversion of the Campus's inner courts. The memory of the projects they cite regenerates the projects themselves, rooting them in Berlin's history and in the unconscious of the city's inhabitants. Regenerated, the pathos remains, amalgamating itself into what Hans Enzensberger calls the "puff pastry of time."[17] The project suggests that architectural form, its temporalities duly kneaded, can generate a collective cultural psychological dimension. Its implicit thesis seems to be this: tradition is a fact, a supra-personal memory, and a language with which successive generations must contend according to the needs of the time in which they operate. To do so adequately, one needs to be able to intercept the latent kairos of architectural form.

[17] Lucid reflections on a conception of time capable of revealing the virulence of the hysterical optimism of modernism can be found in Hans Magnus Enzensberger, "The Puff Pastry of Time," in *Zig-Zag: The Politics of Culture and Vice Versa* (New York: The New Press, 1998).

Biography

paolo conrad-bercah founded c-b a in 2005, an architectural design office that has developed a variety of projects in Europe for public and private clients, including libraries, a museum, a sea port, a hotel, sport facilities, commercial spaces, workplaces, and residential developments. He collaborated in the Milan offices of Aldo Rossi and Ignazio Gardella, and in the New York office of PEI COBB FREED & Partners. He graduated cum laude from the Polytechnic of Turin and Harvard University Design School, where from 1996–2009 he was instructor, fellow, and visiting professor. His professional activity merges with the complementary activities of drawing and writing. He has published numerous texts and seven monographic books: *Berlin Fragments. Heterography of an architectural form* (2019), *Berlin Transfert. An atlas as aesthetic ideas* (2021), and *Berlin Stimmung as an urban concept for the coming urbanization* (2022) form a Berlin aesthetic trilogy on architecture and city. Other texts include *bercahaus* (2020), that documents the construction process of a multi-level timber residential building in Berlin and *Modernism. An American wake* (2002) and *Fogli di Architettura* (2022), which provides aesthetic atlases of ideas revealed by a series of drawings investigating the mysterious relations between time and architectural form. His drawings have been exhibited in Florence (Palazzo Vecchio), Rome (casa dell'architettura, Galleria Embrice), and Milan (Spazio Arena). The architectural drawing series called *the Anticity that is coming* (2020) won the 2021 competition "La città come cultura" held by the Triennale di Milano and the Maxxi museum in Rome.

The Squatting of Technology: A Twofold Continuum

Berna Göl

fig. 1
The view of the Çamlıca TV and Radio Tower from the south of Istanbul.
Credit: Berna Göl.

Architecture and technology have reciprocally amplified meaning in one another for many centuries. In the case of Istanbul's Çamlıca TV and Radio Tower (2011–2021) by Melike Altınışık Architects, the concept of technology and ideas surrounding it distinctly shape the project in terms of function, design, construction, and representation. However, architectural knowledge has been excluded from the public discourse, reducing criticism of the project to criticism of Turkey's governmental policies. Is it possible to formulate an architectural criticism that, by analyzing the concept of technology, unifies discrete aspects of the design? Why does architecture depend on technology? To such questions, architectural criticism must respond.

Sometimes metaphors work both ways. The two parties of a metaphor may mutually feed meaning into each other, just like two parallel mirrors projecting infinity onto one another. In the context of this essay, these two mirrors are architecture and technology, which have depended on each other for centuries in everything from enormous monuments to tiny experiments. Yet what if all technological references of one particular building are brought together to discuss what has been concealed and what has been overtly emphasized within architecture?

This essay applies architectural criticism as a means of insight, centering on the concept of technology, through critique of a dauntlessly visible example of architecture in Istanbul's cityscape. Melike Altınışık Architects' (MAA) Çamlıca TV and Radio Tower (initiated with a design competition entry in 2011 and completed in 2021) is, as stated on the official website, intended to symbolize Istanbul's growth as a megacity. The tower's primary function, the initial design idea, the design process, the materials, and the construction method all rely on ideas associated with technology. It has replaced over a hundred drab structures and transmitters, transforming "the poorly planned squatting of technology," as explained by Altınışık in reference to the previous condition of Istanbul's Çamlıca Hill, into one monumental building emphasizing its innovative engineering techniques.[1] While technology and ideas related to it dominate much of the conversation, many issues regarding architecture remain in the dark. The lack of systematic criticism on any architectural project—but in this case the TV and radio tower—I argue, is not a coincidence, an accident, or an error, but rather the result of a bigger problem that follows the course of, as Reinhold Martin calls it, an "architectural imaginary" that is part of the existing world system.[2] Why would an example of twenty-first-century architecture claim to symbolize a city's growth? Why does architecture insist on the idea of technology as a necessarily beneficial thing? What happens if one of the two mirrors is tilted away slightly, fragmenting the parallel worlds of architecture and technology?

According to Martin Heidegger, technology is neither a mere means to an end nor just about human activity: it is a way of revealing.[3] This revealing may happen, as Heidegger suggests, indirectly, when considering the idea of technology as something separate from its essence. That is to say, while technology is a complex set of contrivances regarding its means and human activities, it itself is another contrivance, an instrument. In the context of this essay, technology as a concept, as an idea, as a topic, or as a mantra, is a dubious one meant to help reveal discourse around architecture. It helps enhance architectural criticism by problematizing what is often taken for granted—and overtly emphasized—while other issues are cast aside.

keywords:

technology, architectural imaginary, cityscape, spectacle

1 Melike Altınışık ile Robot Science Museum, Çamlıca TV, Radyo Kulesi | MASADA #4 [Robot Science Museum and Çamlıca TV, Radio Tower | MASADA #4]

2 Reinhold Martin, "Money and Meaning: The Case of John Portman," Hunch, 12 (2009): 36–51.

3 Martin Heidegger, The Question Concerning Technology and Other Essays, trans. William Lovitt (New York and London: Garland Publishing, Inc, 1977).

The Squatting of Technology: The Story of a TV and Radio on a Hill

The Çamlıca TV and Radio Tower is set on the Küçük Çamlıca Hill at the heart of the megacity of Istanbul. While it is the tallest structure in the contemporary cityscape, it also sits on one of the highest points topographically, making the tower an even more conspicuous character on the skyline *(fig. 1)*. From the day the project was announced to the opening of the tower to visitors, it received opposition from architects, writers, commentators, and many others. However, while the project indeed aims to be a monument and thereby had to be visible, the majority of these reactions did not concern the structure's architectural design, but its economics and politics. Many believed this was a "monument of a splurge,"[4] a significant waste of the state's resources, built for a soon-to-be outdated communications technology. The debate included how this was a strategic decision to make the nearby Çamlıca Mosque, another new project representing the Turkish government's ideals (if not solely its president's), visually and physically more accessible *(fig. 2)*. These discussions predominantly set questions of architecture and architectural knowledge aside, yet both the mosque and the tower were projects selected through architectural design competitions.

The project by MAA came in third place in a 2011 national design competition. The Çamlıca Hill TV and Radio Tower Design Idea Competition called for a project to simultaneously fulfill the specified technological requirements and the need for recreational facilities. Officially, the project site was an area of the hill's nature reserve designated as a recreational zone. Thereby, regardless of the project's primary function (telecommunications) and its inev-

fig. 2
Another new project, Çamlıca Mosque, viewed from the tower. Credit: Berna Göl.

fig. 3
The view from the first entrance of the tower, to be followed by a walking pathway. Credit: Berna Göl.

fig. 4
The former antennas and drab structures that were replaced by the new tower project. Image taken from: https://www.yenisafak.com/gundem/bakan-karaismailoglu-yeni-kulede-calismalar-bitme-asama-sinda-3570526

fig. 5
A typical *gecekondu* settlement from Istanbul. Credit: Paul Ousterlund.

[4] Ege Cansen, "Fırsat Maliyeti" [The cost of opportunity], accessed July 15, 2021, https://www.sozcu.com.tr/2021/yazarlar/ege-cansen/firsat-maliyeti-6514928/.

itable high-tech qualities due to the required height (340 meters), the project had to "blend in" with the site. According to the official design brief, the competing projects had to: (1) replace existing antennas that were causing visual pollution; (2) serve as a viewing tower open to the public; (3) protect the natural landscape; and finally, (4) constitute a new symbol for the city in the form of a tower.[5]

The Istanbul Metropolitan Municipality initiated the competition in 2011; however, only in 2013 was the project personally selected by the prime minister from among the prize winners (bypassing those in first and second place) and commissioned by Turkey's Ministry of Transportation and Communication. The tower's construction took around twice the anticipated time and budget, all of which was funded by the state.[6] Nevertheless, the building was completed in May 2021 *(fig. 3)*. The tower did replace the old antennas *(fig. 4)*; it was indeed open to visitors, but arguably not to the public; the existing vegetation partly remained; and the quest for a new symbol of Istanbul appeared too big a question to be answered. That is to say, the design decisions mainly followed the competition brief.

The architects MAA delivered their take on the state of the hill before construction in a video interview, calling the old, drab structures of antennas *teknolojinin gecekondulaşması*—which translates as a "squatting of technology"—a reference to the decades-long phenomenon called *gecekondu*, the type of informal housing built overnight by newcomers to the city via squatting on part of what is often public urban land *(fig. 5)*. According to Altınışık, the old, drab structures were neither planned nor designed and thereby were lacking the necessary capacity to adapt to new technological requirements, were obstructing the cityscape, and had to be replaced. While the design brief of the competition described the old antennas as "visual pollution," Altınışık referred to them as the "squatting of technology," or to be more specific, the squatting of the cityscape by technological structures. While the history of *gecekondu* in Turkey's cities is beyond the scope of this essay, it should be noted that the history of informal housing in Istanbul is also a history of large urban renewal projects in the context of dominant land speculation and profit-making, amplifying existing socioeconomic asymmetries between its people. If, as stated by Altınışık, the idea of *gecekondu* or the squatting of technology is inarguably bad, it may be necessary to underline how the new project also sits on public land, initiated and constructed by public funds but now run by private capital with an entrance fee for the visiting public. With its telecommunications functions, the new tower project is squatting on Istanbul's Çamlıca Hill overlooking the Bosporus.

The competition brief called for a project that would serve as a viewing tower open to the public. Yet, despite its public functions and inhabitable spaces, visitors have to take a vehicle to reach the site due to its sloped topography, security control, and entrance fee. It is a controlled semipublic space with commercial attributes isolated from the rest of the city, especially in terms of accessibility. The tower serves the visitors as customers and attempts to offer an almost wholly designed experience. Miodrag Mitrasinovic likens such privately owned public spaces to amusement parks: complex artifacts within a reconstructed public realm, specialized in providing their visitors with an experience while shifting the idea of what is public and replacing it with that of the commercial.[7] Here, the technological structure is meant to serve as a space of leisure in which various activities may be held. The first gate marks the beginning of a slight uphill walk under the trees with a view of the city, a recreational experience. The second gate indicates the start of a designed landscape, with the continuing walkway leading visitors to a theater. Viewing platforms surround the tower's base, which has an entrance hall or a public foyer with cafés and a gift shop *(fig. 6)*. Two panoramic elevators overlooking opposite ends of Istanbul take the visitors, or the customers, to the observation terraces and the restaurant located hundreds of meters above sea level. All these leisure-oriented functions of the project are attempts to achieve a sense of community among people by mimicking town squares and streets, as is the case in many commercial spaces such as shopping malls or theme parks.[8] The amphitheater by the tower's entrance, more than any other attribute of the project perhaps, supports this assertion *(fig. 7)*.

5 İstanbul Büyükşehir Belediye Başkanlığı Etüd Ve Projeler Daire Başkanlığı Projeler Müdürlüğü, "Çamlıca Tepesi Tv Radyo Kulesi Fikir Projesi Yarışma Şartnamesi," competition brief and documents, 2011, accessed July 5, 2021, http://docplayer.biz.tr/3071593-Camli-ca-tepesi-tv-radyo-kulesi-fikir-proje-si-yarisma-sartnamesi.html.

6 Kamil Naim Altıntaş, "Çamlıca Kulesi Nerede? Nasıl Gidilir?," Kuponall, accessed July 19, 2021, https://www.kuponall.com/camlica-kulesi/#.~:-text=587%20metre%20y%C3%BCk-seklikte.-,%C3%87aml%C4%B1ca%20Kulesi%20Maliyeti%20Ne%20Kadar%3F,nin%20maliyeti%201%20milyardan%20fazla.

7 Miodrag Mitrasinovic, *Total Landscape, Theme Parks, Public Space* (Hampshire and Burlington: Ashgate Publishing Limited, 2006).

8 Ian Woodward, "The Shopping Mall, Postmodern Space and Architectural Practice: Theorising the Postmodern Spatial Turn through the Planning Discourse of Mall Architects," *Architectural Theory Review* 3, no. 2 (1998), 45–56.

The leisurely functions obscure the primary role of the project as a telecommunications tower. However, the project's relationship to the idea of technology goes beyond that. Architectural design relies heavily on other technological attributes: the form of the structure, its construction method, and the materials and their joints, as well as the structure's maintenance, all involve technical ventures. Technology, at this point, is not only squatting in the cityscape but also beginning to dominate the imaginary in the architectural realm.

Technology Squatting Architecture: The Design of the Tower

Kenneth Frampton describes technology as some kind of maximization of industrial production and its consumption.[9] While technology has designated or amplified megalopolitan growth within the past decades, he claims, architecture has not been able to respond to these changes in any effective way. The disassociation between architecture and urban proliferation likely underlies the belief that technology is ultimately beneficial, as many intend to translate such inadequacy to an advantage. In the case of MAA, this attempt is visible. Altınışık openly claims that architecture is always one step behind technology.[10] This assumption renders technology as something undergoing a constant transformation, something that needs to be caught up with. From such a point of view, architecture must continually adapt itself to the evolution of technology, always investigating new modes of technological engagement or improvement.

Altınışık openly expresses a personal interest in technology and in multidisciplinary practice, particularly with engineering. For her, this is partly about exploring new possibilities by experimenting with new technologies, which is what architecture has been doing for centuries, but, according to Altınışık, this experimentation needs constant updating; technology, she asserts, continues to advance even within the course of a design process. The updates may include anything from building information modeling (BIM), a new kind of material, a new joint technique of that material, and the organization of the workforce within the office to the design of new construction methods. The office's in-house lab is only a part of these explorations, says Altınışık, aiding in further design experimentation.

fig. 6
The tower and the amphitheater in front of it. Credit: Berna Göl.

fig. 7
The amphitheater from the entranceway of the tower.

[9] Kenneth Frampton, *Studies in Tectonic Culture* (Cambridge, Boston, and New York: Harvard University Graduate School of Design, 1985).
[10] Bidebunu Izle, "Kentlere ve Geleceğe Umutlu Bir Bakış | Şehirler / Şekiller," YouTube live stream on January 4, 2021, accessed in June 23, 2021, https://www.youtube.com/watch?v=JrVix_cgGrk.

The tower's structural design consists of a 203-meter-tall central concrete core with an additional steel structure of 145 meters. The first emphasis on technology, therefore, is the wind-testing systems related to the structure's height. The second involves the staging of the construction, which was innovative, if not experimental. As Altınışık explains, the upper steel portion of the tower was first constructed inside this core on the ground level, later to be pulled upward. As Altınışık states in video interviews and as represented in the construction time-lapse video **(fig. 8)**, following the construction of the slip-formed concrete core, the inhabitable floors were initially built on the ground level in groups and later elevated to their final positions. The facade elements such as glass-reinforced concrete (GRC) panels, tested both in the office and in professional laboratories, were installed before the final raising up. The individual panels of the facade were all designed and calculated digitally; it was both the details (in terms of the building envelope) and the form of these panels that had to prove solid against the wind tests.

    Technological concepts that inspired and shaped MAA's tower design vary in scale and detail. However, both the written material and the video interviews about the tower's design predominantly cover technological attributes that align with Andrea Phillips's account on the politics of architectural pavilions.[11] Phillips traces the changes around the making of pavilions over decades to observe that, unlike early design experimentations like those of Aldo van Eyck or the Smithsons, new examples such as the Serpentine Pavilions use technology almost as a mask to conceal existing relationships between architecture and capital. She displays how, in the pavilion projects, the mixing of a public program with privately branded enterprise serves only to fulfill public–private ventures in which existing socioeconomic relations are reproduced: the visitors are encountered with architectural forms disinterested in their ways of inhabiting the space presented and thereby the possibility of a new sociability is eliminated. Whether in the example of the pavilions, which are often regarded as the intersection of experimentation and architecture, or in the Çamlıca TV and Radio Tower, not only is the public realm dominated by business relations and capital circulation, but the experimentation of and within architecture is undermined as it is driven by and restricted to what the reigning capital

fig. 8
Istanbul Çamlica TV and Radio Tower construction time-lapse video shot by Sena Özfiliz.
Credit: Sena Özfiliz.

[11] Andrea Phillips, "Pavilion Politics," *Log* 20 (2010), 104.

interests allow. Furthermore, the lack of critical discussion concerning technology and architecture intensifies such confusion, thereby making the two, architecture and technology, constantly affirm one another. That is to say, while new technologies and their explorations inspire the design of the tower, the concept of technology primarily serves as a commercial spectacle, dominating the architectural imaginary and eliminating any thought for how things could have been different.

Technology as a Spectacle: The Squatting of the Architectural Imaginary

The architectural imaginary, in the context of this essay, is something other than architectural imagination. While imagination concerns an act of picturing and a materialization of thought in itself, architectural imaginary has a social connotation. It corresponds to a patterned set of meanings, ideas, or tendencies that are taken to be self-evident—a set of views that appear absolute as collective "common sense."[12] In the case of the Çamlıca TV and Radio Tower, the sphere of architectural imagination is dominated by technology on many levels that extend beyond the primary architectural program or the design process; it is about making a spectacle out of the technological attributes of the tower. The phenomenon is about capital being condensed into an image, and its representation disguising socioeconomic relations.[13] The goal of this architectural image is to create a narrative that makes systemic monetary relations appear esoteric or inscrutable.[14]

fig. 9
The nighttime tower lighting, which does not comply with the architect Altınışık's design. Credit: Doruk Yurdesin and Berna Göl.

The technological spectacle of the tower is unfolded via two particular statements Altınışık made in interviews. The first one was about the construction of the building and the second about what the tower is meant to symbolize. According to the architect, the technology-inspired design of the tower was a performance on the scale of the city itself; from the beginning, the people of Istanbul were able to clearly observe the different stages of this construction. The height, the location, and the design of the tower indeed contributed to this performance. Altınışık also noted the way many people assumed that the construction was complete before it was halfway done, due to them not knowing how parts of the structure completed on the ground were to be elevated later on to their final position. This surprise within the construction method perhaps strengthened the performative value of such a technological spectacle.

The second statement Altınışık made was about the desire to represent the growth of Istanbul as a megacity. This statement stems from a social imaginary, or rather an architectural imaginary, that assumes the growth of a city as something that needs to be represented. It is possible to draw a parallel between the assurance of this proliferation and the assumption of technological developments as being inherently good; technological advances and the city's growth are two phenomena to be caught up with, to be emulated. This representation of the city's growth is a spectacle that reminds its citizens of something that they already know, assuring them of something they witness every day without suggesting anything else or offering a vision of how things could have been any different. The tower does not offer people anything other than itself, just like the Serpentine Pavilions Phillips mentions.[15]

Just as contemporary architectural pavilions do, the tower displays to its visitors what they already know, proclaiming what is already visible. After obtaining an hourly ticket, visitors are welcome to take the panoramic elevators, carefully placed on opposite sides of the structure for comprehensive views of the city. However, whether the result of an architectural decision or of an administrative intervention, the elevators' interiors contain walls of LED screens that display videos showing scenes from Istanbul. Thus, during the thirty seconds it takes for the

[12] Manfred B. Steger and Paul James, "Levels of Subjective Globalization: Ideologies, Imaginaries, Ontologies," *Perspectives on Global Development and Technology* 12, no. 1/2 (2013), 31.
[13] William S. Saunders, ed., *Commodification and Spectacle in Architecture: A Harvard Design Magazine Reader*, vol. 1 (Minneapolis: University of Minnesota Press, 2005).
[14] Andrzej Piotrowski, "The Spectacle of Architectural Discourses," *Architectural Theory Review*, no. 13:2 (2008), 130–44.
[15] Phillips, "Pavilion Politics," 104.

elevator to arrive at the observation terraces and the restaurant, the visitors are simultaneously exposed to a view from the window overlooking the physical city and a number of digital cities on the LED walls. As the elevator keeps climbing, it gets harder to tell one view from the other.

While it is difficult for an observer to draw the line between the design decisions of an architect and a client's interventions, as in this case of screens inside elevators, there is one point of discontent that the architect Altınışık shared with the public in one of her interviews: the facade lighting of the completed project does not comply with MAA's original design. "When it comes to the lighting design, everyone is a designer," says Altınışık.[16] According to the architect, the current project's facade lighting is very loud, which does not make the project more commercially attractive in any way *(fig. 9)*. This is why, she adds, cities of the future will require lighting codes regulating the nighttime cityscape.

Conclusion

Altınışık's discontent with the tower's facade lighting does not involve a mere design intervention. It is the trespassing of the boundaries of architecture by capital, of the architects by the project's commissioners. It is a story of the production of a spectacle, the abolishing of the sphere of architecture, reminding architects of the global system that they often choose to look away from. This is a new version of the crisis that has been focused on for decades by many architects, including Manfredo Tafuri.[17] Once an architecture practice becomes a part of capital production (and reproduction), it is inevitably compromised, and a purely architectural solution to the problem remains inadequate. In the new version of this crisis, architecture cannot even be commissioned unless it serves the spectacle of the government; furthermore, it no longer tries to solve present problems. The concept of technology serves not as a solution to these problems, but rather as a tool for legitimizing architecture in the context of mega-sized projects. This is not technology's squatting of the cityscape, of architectural design, and of the architectural imaginary, but politics in the disguise of technology.

Whether technology is associated with a function, with exploration of design potentials, or with a project's representation, it may dominate the architectural imaginary. However, technology and the ideas surrounding it may also be used to reveal architecture's potential operation within the world system and its socioeconomic context. It is the duty of architectural criticism to look for ways to uncover what is often concealed; in this case, through stripping away the practice of the systematic dissociation of monetary relations, or through the recognition of the business model in operation as much as through a glimpse of the people truly shaping the public realm. This initiative should stem from the discipline's own sphere, bringing socioeconomic relations into architectural discourse. Only then may architectural criticism allow true articulation of meaning and thereby disrupt the continuum of the presently closed circuit of affirmation between architecture and technology.

[16] Bidebunu Izle, "Kentlere ve Geleceğe."
[17] Manfredo Tafuri, *Architecture and Utopia: Design and Capitalist Development* (Boston and New York: MIT Press, 1976).

Biography

Berna Göl works as an assistant professor at Beykent University, Department of Architecture (Istanbul). She focuses on intersections of architecture, literature, and critical theory. Her research area covers architecture and the city, inadequacies of architectural practices, and discourse in architectural design through changing modes of production and reproduction. Her dissertation "Leisure as Criticism in Architectural Texts" (Istanbul Technical University) was followed by texts such as "Water as Fetish in Architecture" and "Limits and Ruptures: Discussing Criticism in Architecture through Capitalism." She is a member of the music duo kim ki o and a part of Root Radio.

The Architecture of Redemption: A House on the Periphery of the Discipline

Jaime Solares Carmona

fig. 1
Casa da Vila Matilde access, São Paulo, Terra e Tuma Arquitetos Associados, 2016, https://www.archdaily.com.br/br/776950/casa-vila-matilde-terra-e-tuma-arquitetos, accessed July 30, 2021. Photo: Pedro Kok.

Through the analysis of Casa da Vila Matilde, by the São Paulo office Terra e Tuma Arquitetos Associados, I intend to evaluate how our contemporary architectural criticism has discussed, both materially and narratively, the issue of self-construction in Brazilian cities. What I intend to analyze are the reasons, or lack therof, for the exceptionality of the project, which won several awards and was widely publicized; in what ways the discipline has rebranded itself in a populist/reformist image; and this revisioning's relation to the peak and decline of liberal democracy worldwide in the late 2010s.

"Intellectuals are the ones who like misery, poor people actually like luxury!" Forged in the sociology of everyday life and sensitive to the aesthetics of the media and the masses, this quote from the famous samba artist Joãozinho Trinta sheds light on the contradictions of a Brazilian intelligentsia fond of the aestheticization of poverty. The Casa da Vila Matilde seems to belong to the category of objects produced, both materially and narratively, to serve as justification for this type of populist progressivism. Far beyond the classic debate between popular and pop, the work we are going to analyze is a sui generis case of lack of exceptionality.

The production of the house in the year of 2015 is commonplace: Dona Dalva, a client with few resources who lives in an unhealthy and precarious house, decides to remodel it. Seeing that this would not be possible, she decides, together with the architects, to demolish the existing house and build a new one. The whole process takes one year. The lot has the traditional dimensions of the city's peripheral subdivisions: five by twenty-five meters. Long and narrow, it imposes the challenge of guaranteeing good lighting and ventilation to all rooms. To do this, the architects create a central patio that separates the social area from the private area, the two being connected by a functional corridor that shelters a sequence of service spaces: bathroom, kitchen, and laundry. The elegant distribution of the plan allows cross-ventilation in the front portion of the house and insolation in the master bedroom. The intelligent placement of permanent ventilation windows on top of the bathrooms, facing the stairway topped by a zenithal opening, optimizes the air exchange and illumination of these environments. In addition, the upper floor has a terrace that, added to the vertical garden on the first floor, responds to the pleasure that Dona Dalva finds in gardening.

In a country where nine out of ten buildings are built without the involvement of an architect, we must highlight the architectural quality of the project.[1] A simple but efficient design, comprising a built area just under one hundred square meters, the house won the Building of the Year by popular vote on the *ArchDaily* website in 2016, as well as the Azkonobel Award from the Tomie Ohtake Institute, having represented Brazil at international events such as the Venice Architecture Biennale. Furthermore, what can be considered a rare phenomenon in Brazilian architecture occurred: the house appeared in several nonspecialized media outlets, ranging from weekly magazines to television shows and YouTube channels. After being ignored for a period of almost five years, the project was once again in the spotlight when the Argentinean newspaper *La Nación* recently praised it saying, that it stood out for its "innovation and high architectural quality."[2]

keywords:

self-construction, Casa da Vila Matilde, Terra e Tuma Arquitetos Associados, social architecture, contemporary Brazilian architecture

[1] "Pesquisa Inédita: Percepções da sociedade sobre Arquitetura e Urbanismo," Conselho de Arquitetura e Urbanismo do Brasil, October 12, 2012, accessed July 30, 2021, https://www.caubr.gov.br/pesquisa-caubr-datafolha-revela-visoes-da-sociedade-sobre-arquitetura-e-urbanismo.

[2] "Una casa en una favela ganó un premio internacional de arquitectura," *La Nación*, June 24, 2021, accessed July 30, 2021, https://www.lanacion.com.ar/propiedades/construccion-y-diseno/la-casa-de-una-empleada-domestica-gano-un-premio-internacional-de-arquitectura-nid24062021/.

[3] "Casa Vila Matilde/ Terra e Tuma Arquitetos Associados," *ArchDaily*, November 11, 2015, accessed August 6, 2021, https://www.archdaily.com.br/br/776950/casa-vila-matilde-terra-e-tuma-arquitetos.

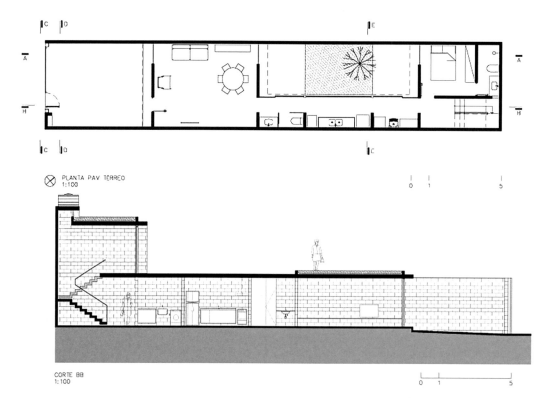

fig. 2
Casa da Vila Matilde footprint, São Paulo, Terra e Tuma Arquitetos Associados, 2016, https://www.archdaily.com.br/br/776950/casa-vila-matilde-terra-e-tuma-arquitetos, accessed July 30, 2021.

fig. 3
Casa da Vila Matilde longitudinal section, São Paulo, Terra e Tuma Arquitetos Associados, 2016, https://www.archdaily.com.br/br/776950/casa-vila-matilde-terra-e-tuma-arquitetos, accessed July 30, 2021.

To understand if the work lives up to the praise, and also to understand the reason for all this visibility, the project will be broken down to its two central aspects: its form (construction, language, typology) and the discourse generated from its construction (disciplinary narratives, the reception policies for such works).

What we will see throughout the formal analysis of the house is that a kind of "typological overlapping" occurs. In other words, we can notice at all times a concurrence of formal solutions, between the vernacular of self-construction, typical of the Brazilian suburbs, and the erudite project of the architects. This overlapping, however, is not even remotely an aesthetic negotiation nor a linguistic or constructive strategy. It is, rather, an opportune coincidence. Two constructive universes that are strangers to each other are simultaneously unified and repelled, generating a fiction that suggests conciliation, but which, as we will see, is rather a negation.

In spite of the restricted budget, and even considering the demolition that was carried out, the amount of 150,000 reais (38,000 US dollars) spent on construction of the house is completely in line with the expected cost for this kind of building. As the authors of the project remind us, the house was not cheap: it cost what it should cost. The main issue was where to invest the money. In this sense, there are two fallacies: the first says that the cement block was the most rational and economical option for the project; the second says that the choice of unfinished surfaces was financial.

The authors inform us that they chose the concrete block, among other reasons, due to previous experiences with the material, notably in an earlier project, known as the Casa Maracanã (2009)[3] **(fig.4)**, authored by one of the associates. In fact, if we compare the two houses they are materially identical. However, we cannot say that the two used concrete blocks for the same budgetary reasons. What is not clearly stated by the architects is that this choice is mainly aesthetic, having deep roots in erudite traditions that flourished locally. The office is part of the third generation of architects inspired by the brutalist modern architecture of the 1950s to the 1970s in São Paulo. The use of exposed concrete, as well as the search

fig. 4
Casa Maracanã living room, São Paulo, Terra e Tuma Arquitetos Associados, 2009, https://www.archdaily.com.br/br/01-87312/casa-maracana-slash-terra-e-tuma-arquitetos-associados, accessed July 30, 2021. Photo: Pedro Kok.

for structural and technical virtuosity, constitutes the primary features of their architectural language. In these houses, instead of concrete cast on-site, they used concrete blocks—also a standard material in the works of, but used less by, local brutalist architects—synthesizing a different tectonic from many of the works that inspired them, such as the FAUUSP building by Vilanova Artigas and Carlos Cascaldi (1969). The block is thus a kind of promise, albeit an old one, that technique itself can be an instrument in our social emancipation. Sufficiently industrial in its production and artisanal in its assembly, this element synthesizes the contradictions of a contemporary Brazilian practice.

But the question still remains whether the block could, in fact, be an interesting structural solution. After all, it is more standardized and robust than the traditional ceramic block (which it denies and alludes to at the same time), allowing a more rationalized construction site. But it is no mere coincidence that Brazilian favelas and periphery houses are red. The ceramic block, both as a seal and as a structural element, costs 30 percent less than the concrete block and is 40 percent lighter, which facilitates its transportation within the construction site. In addition, the ceramic block offers better thermal insulation than its concrete counterpart. In contrast to the traditional column-beam system that we see in those self-constructed houses, the architects used a system that was alien to the project's context; that is, the structuring of the floor slabs on perimeter walls. What we see, therefore, is an exogenous technique—distinct, implanted without the traditional know-how.

Which brings us to another issue. Imbued with a shrewdness typically seen in São Paulo's brutalist movement, the "unfinished" part of the house is, according to the authors, intended as a free space for the owner to personalize and customize. If this were the main motivation for the choice of materials, one would expect the house to be ready to receive such finishes, and this is not the case. Ideally, the burnt cement floor would need to have a subfloor to receive any finished floor, from ceramic tile to wood parquet. The same can be said for the electrical and lighting system. The conduit fixed on the concrete block does not allow a proper finishing with

putty and paint, because, unlike the traditional socket, it has no depth adjustment. The whole system, metallic cases and visible tubes, would have to be uninstalled and then reinstalled on the newly plastered wall. The house was not designed to receive the client's "customization"; that claim is a complete fabrication. It is finished. It was designed and executed with materials that work well as they are, but not so well when other layers are applied.

    Finishes usually account for about one-third of the total value of a house. Since they can be done later, it is actually a good strategy to initially invest more of one's money in the structural elements of the space. However, in this specific case, the gain is quite relative. Besides the reasons presented above, both the concrete block and the precast slab need to be coated with a proper resin for maintenance, the price of which is close to that of economical finishing solutions, such as painting directly on the structure. The burnt cement floor usually costs a little more than leaving the slab exposed, and if it is not done to perfection, it will develop several cracks throughout its useful life. The client herself said in interviews that what bothers her most is the absence of a ceramic floor, which will be her first addition to the house.[4]

    With the relocation of the budget to doors and windows, custom-made and according to a very elegant design, the architects made a choice that is, again, more aesthetic than economical. The doors are made entirely of wood, floor-to-ceiling, pivoted on an asymmetrical axis, and topped by wooden lintels. All the windows are also floor-to-ceiling—tripartite, with the middle module made to be opened—in black aluminum. In other words, the modernist language is starkly contradicted, since the only element that is actually designed is exactly the one that depends on a bespoke system of craft for its production. The promise of industrialization/mas-

fig. 5
Casa da Vila Matilde living room, São Paulo, Terra e Tuma Arquitetos Associados, 2016, https://www.archdaily.com.br/br/776950/casa-vila-matilde-terra-e-tuma-arquitetos, accessed July 30, 2021. Photo: Pedro Kok.

fig. 6
Favela do Sapé, São Paulo. Photo: Rodrigo Villar.

fig. 7
Casa da Vila Matilde yard, São Paulo, Terra e Tuma Arquitetos Associados, 2016, https://www.archdaily.com.br/br/776950/casa-vila-matilde-terra-e-tuma-arquitetos, accessed July 30, 2021. Photo: Pedro Kok.

[4] Gaby Garciia, "Tour Casa Premiada na Vila Matilde—#GabyNaSuaCasa #1—Building of the Year," architectural tour, April 14, 2016, YouTube video, 16:39, accessed July 30, 2021, https://www.youtube.com/watch?v=54832s2zMC4&ab_channel=GabyGarciia.

sification of the modern project is limited to prototypes multiplied ad nauseam, not in any kind of interpretation or negotiation of the architect in the productive cycle of the construction industry.

In this sense, a perfect counterpoint to the Casa da Vila Matilde is the Casa do Caseiro, built four years previously by the firm 24 7 Arquitetura *(fig. 8)*. Also a simple house for residents on a low income, it has a built area of only seventy square meters and cost 50,000 reais (23,000 US dollars). Unlike the Casa da Vila Matilde, however, it has finishing in every room and uses mass-market doors and windows. It is, in many ways, a house more in tune with the social and cultural reality of its clients, and it represents an entirely different set of values regarding what does or does not matter in a low-budget house.

In the end, what distinguishes the two houses is that the Terra e Tuma house seeks distinction: a house made by architects needs to look like it was made by architects. And here we are talking about a distinction very typical of the intellectuality Joãozinho Trinta described. A progressive São Paulo elite that has in austerity—or, if you like, in the "minimalist style"—a strong element of social differentiation. As individuals who carry the bourgeois guilt of possessing resources in a country of astounding social inequality, they opt for a construction devoid of ornament, color, excess, or individuality.

Marcos Napolitano, in analyzing the work of sociologist Marcelo Ridenti,[5] reminds us of the oversizing of the category "people" in the 1960s within this Brazilian intellectuality. That same late romanticism can be seen, in this case, in the reiteration of the use of apparent materials in architecture. What in the 1960s was narratively constituted as "material honesty," capable of bringing class consciousness to poor people, today remains a desire, albeit a decadent one, for the enlightenment of the poor. That is, the materiality of the Casa da Vila Matilde can be read as a will to teach the poor how to build. The question is: what is the point of trying to teach the poor about what they already experience intimately every day? In this sense, there echoes a notion that the architect knows how to build better than the bricklayer,

fig. 8
Casa do Caseiro access, São Paulo, 24 7 Arquitetura, 2012, https://www.archdaily.com.br/br/789570/casa-dos-caseiros-2-arquitetura-design, accessed July 30, 2021.
Photo: Pedro Kok

[5] Marcos Napolitano, "Em busca do tempo perdido: utopia revolucionária e cultura engajada no Brasil," *Revista Sociologia e Política*, no. 16 (2001), 149.

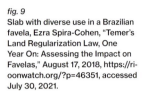

fig. 9
Slab with diverse use in a Brazilian favela, Ezra Spira-Cohen, "Temer's Land Regularization Law, One Year On: Assessing the Impact on Favelas," August 17, 2018, https://rioonwatch.org/?p=46351, accessed July 30, 2021.

and that they need to teach the latter how to do their job correctly. It is like saying: "Concrete blocks are better than ceramic blocks, haven't you got it yet?"

    The same can be said of the upper floor slab designed by the architects. This slab does not have a guardrail on the front, only one at the side overlooking the space that leads to the patio. This decision responds to the architects' desire to not interfere with the facade—a wall at half height, or even the use of the same metal railing as at the back, would impair the sense of continuity between the perimeter wall and the facade in front of the house—resulting in a solution for the residents' safety that is incomplete, to say the least. Furthermore, this slab is not open, free to adapt to any use, but determined, because a box filled with expanded clay, a garden of sorts *(fig. 9)*, was built on top for thermal insulation—which was necessary, after all. In this sense it overwrites the famous "waiting slab" of the slums and peripheral houses, at once the ceiling and the promise of another floor *(fig. 10)* in the never-ending process of house growth. Of course, we can say that this element can very easily be demolished when a new room is built, but it still expresses that the slab is not a space of free use, or constructive power, but rather a sculptural element of completion. Were it not so, the room below would not depend on this clay for adequate thermal insulation rather than the traditional system of concrete beams with ceramic block enclosure that, having a better thermal insulation, would better solve this issue.

    The analyzed elements—such as the concrete block and the burnt cement floor, the lack of finishing and the use of types such as the waiting slab—displaced from their original meaning, generate the effect that may be called "typological overlapping," as they were not able to constitute a field of adherence or opposition to the current building system of the Brazilian peripheries. The unfinished state of the house is showcased as something new, a solution to be followed. The house thus becomes, purely and simply, a strangely familiar body—one which never generates recognition, only strangeness, for the client and the surrounding population. The house has consequently become the symbol of a professional struggle for expansion of the profession's struggle to co-opt the informal self-construction practices used in Brazilian cities.

    In 2016 the representative body of the CAU (the Council of Architecture and Urbanism) launched a nationwide campaign called "Architecture transforming lives," with the Casa da Vila Matilde as their poster child for good, accessible architecture. The website reads:[6] "Before starting a construction, there are always two sides: one of the architect, where there is economy, order, functionality and especially the future. And another where empiricism, reaction

[6] "A Arquitetura transformando vidas," Conselho de Arquitetura e Urbanismo, campaign website, accessed July 30, 2021, https://www.caubr.gov.br/vidas/.

fig. 10
Casa da Vila Matilde slab/roof, São Paulo, Terra e Tuma Arquitetos Associados, 2016, https://www.archdaily.com.br/br/776950/casa-vila-matilde-terra-e-tuma-arquitetos, accessed July 30, 2021. Photo: Pedro Kok.

and improvisation prevail."[6] In spite of the authoritarian positivism of classifying architecture as something that brings order and functionality to one's life—and that this would be the means to achieve a better life—what draws attention is the demeaning of the construction done by the bricklayer. The text goes on to state that "buildings made with the help of architects and urban planners end up costing less than buildings made with bricklayers alone." What we see, therefore, is a class that reproduces the same institutional arrogance that for so long was responsible for its exclusion from any political and social decisions in our country.

    The house functions, thus, not as a prototype or a project of urbanity—like Paulo Mendes da Rocha's Gerassi House, or Le Corbusier's Ville Savoye—and much less as a sign of the struggle for the right to housing, but as an advertisement saying: "you can hire an architect"! It is not intended as a new industrial paradigm to help build the city, but as a one-by-one service. Any ideal of "housing for all," an inalienable right provided for in Brazil's Constitution, is replaced by a timid promise of the "house for all"—as long as everyone pays for it, of course.

    Both the project itself and the disciplinary narrative built around it point to what sociologist Rosana Pinheiro-Machado has called "inclusion through consumption."[7] This concept aims to explain the social ascension that occurred during the Lula era (2002–2011). Through various social funding programs such as ProUni (which allowed access to private education for the poorer section of the population) or the elimination of taxes on home appliances, the government sought to improve the quality of life of a population that finally escaped from poverty. The problem is that this ascent produced citizens who understood themselves as citizens not by fighting and attaining rights, but by consumption.

    The PT (Workers Party), founded in 1980 by trade unionists, local church communities, and leftist intellectuals, is one of the largest labor parties in the world, and in 2002 elected the first president of working-class origin in Brazil, Luiz Inácio Lula da Silva. For more than ten years, and through four mandates (the last one unfinished), the party structured a project for the country: one full of contradictions, it's true, but rooted in values such as national sovereignty, investment in education and technology, and South–South diplomacy. From this period emerged strengthened globalist and regional initiatives such as Mercosur and BRICS (an acronym for the five largest emerging economies of the world at the time: Brazil, Russia, India, China, and South Africa).

    In the early 2010s Brazil saw the PT project derail. In a contradictory way, the June Journeys protests that occurred in the country in 2013, with an anti-party and anti-systemic bias, represented at the same time an organic mass movement that strengthened the sense

[7] Rosana Pinheiro-Machado, *Amanhã vai ser maior* (São Paulo: Planeta do Brasil, 2019).

of democracy in the country but also the risk of a diffused populism. According to political scientists Levitsky and Ziblatt,[8] from 2010 to 2015 the world was experiencing the heyday of liberal democracy. From the Arab Spring of 2011 to the Black Umbrella movements in Hong Kong in 2014, struggles for a more horizontal and participatory system of representation multiplied around the world. Against this democratizing aspiration, which walked side by side with feminist, black, LGBTQIA+, and other identity struggles, we have seen an aggressive backlash. The same movements that in Brazil fought for a high-quality public transportation system were co-opted by the populist right that, years later, would come to impeach the elected president Dilma Rousseff.

The architect as a professional category, bewildered like everyone else at the time, seemed brimming with the will to ascribe social meaning to a practice that had been gradually detaching itself from any cultural relevance it had ever had in the country, especially in the first half of the twentieth century. With the end of the democratic developmentalism from 1930 to 1960, and of the dictatorial developmentalism from 1960 to 1980, we were sinking into a neoliberalism that only aggravated the social inequalities afflicting our communities. The Lula era brought, in this sense, the promise of rescue through a project that would finally distribute the wealth of what was one of the six primary economies in the world.

It would not be absurd, therefore, to associate the yearning of Brazilian architects to participate in the construction of more inclusive cities with this social effervescence. From this perspective we could also understand the 15th Venice Architecture Biennale, whose theme *Reporting from the Front* sought to "foster discussion and reflection around the role of architects in the everyday battle to improve living conditions in a wide variety of political, geographical, social, and economic contexts."[9] Unlike the previous iteration, organized by Rem Koolhaas, a European architect discussing the constitutive elements of architecture, this edition was curated by Latin American Alejandro Aravena, who sought to locate the limits and boundaries of the profession. When he received the Pritzker Prize that same year, Aravena was noted as a socially engaged architect.[10]

In any case, what we see is an exaggerated optimism, based more on voluntarism than on real political engagement. Whether in the Casa da Vila Matilde, the Biennale, or even ELEMENTAL's "half-houses" (which are directly inspired by the 1966 Peruvian PREVI housing projects), despite their differences, one will not find any direct inspiration in the prefigurative, horizontal, and anti-systemic struggle of the popular movements of the early twenty-first century. In none of these cases resides the revolutionary tone of the previous century, but rather the aftermath of a faltering progressivism that appeals to the market dimension of its practice. The democratic regression we would see in the following years, especially Trumpism in the United States and Bolsonarism in Brazil, points to the climax of a now-declining movement: the last gasps of a professional category of architecture that optimistically, but also too naively, bets on a social reform without political ruptures.

The hypertrophy of a situation as ordinary as the construction of a popular house may be an echo of this same optimism, moments before the political collapse that would follow. To again quote Napolitano: "In these terms—a mixture of voluntarist activism and the monolithic and idealized vision of the popular classes —the relationship of the Brazilian left with the masses, the collective actors of the revolution, should be analyzed."[11] In other words, the house is only justified as a cultural artifact because it is presupposed that someone was helped, aided, and led to the path of dignity through architecture. Only an idealized vision of common people as needing to be saved by leftist intellectuals (a vision contrary to the most generous sense of emancipation) could explain the euphoria surrounding the project.

By stating that "architecture does not find in people, in society, an adequate way to work,"[12] the author of the house reveals the only truly exceptional aspect of the project: its client. She was the only unusual element in the whole project cycle. She was the one who, unlike all the poorer people, hired an architect instead of a bricklayer. And yet, she always starred in the official narrative of the work as the great beneficiary, the one blessed by the blessings of architecture.

8 Steven Levitsky and Daniel Ziblatt, *Como as democracias morrem* (Rio de Janeiro: Jorge Zahar Editor, 2018).
9 Romullo Baratto, "Bienal de Veneza 2016 (um panorama preliminar)," ArchDaily, May 24, 2016, accessed July 30, 2021, https://www.archdaily.com.br/br/788091/bienal-de-veneza-2016-um-panorama-preliminar.
10 The Pritzker Architecture Prize, "Alejandro Aravena of Chile Receives the 2016 Pritzker Architecture Prize," January 13, 2016, accessed July 30, 2021, https://www.pritzkerprize.com/laureates/ale-jan-dro-ara-ve-na.
11 Napolitano, "Em busca do tempo perdido," 149.
12 Danilo Terra, "Casa da Vila Matilde," talk at TEDxUSP, April 14, 2017, YouTube video, accessed July 30, 2021, https://www.youtube.com/watch?v=qATMYaQop1c&ab_channel=TEDxTalks.
13 Gaby Garciia, "Tour Casa Premiada na Vila Matilde."

fig. 11
"Architecture transforming lives," Conselho de Arquitetura e Urbanismo, campaign website, https://www.caubr.gov.br/vidas/, accessed August 10, 2021; casa-vila-matilde-terra-e-tuma-arquitetos, accessed July 30, 2021. Photo: Pedro Kok.

From the raison d'être of the thing, it became discourse. Interestingly, in an interview, the client says that the first thing she felt when entering the house was safety.[13] Of course, what led her to build the house in the first place was, primarily, the risk to life that the old house represented (a piece of the roof fell on her bed). Somehow the service provided by the architects did not transcend necessity, for it did not render a home in which Dona Dalva could recognize herself. Therefore, it would not be an exaggeration to assert that, even if it is a competent project, the house does not present anything exceptional in architectural terms. There is no aesthetic renewal in the project. There is no critical reflection on the building site or the issue of peripheric self-construction. There is no destabilization of the concepts of lot and private land ownership. There is nothing really new. The house is, thus, conservative in an inverted sense, because it conserves, deep down, an order of the past, not one for the future—like those who, after years of battle, are more concerned with strengthening their garrisons than creating new fronts for struggle. Suddenly, the progressive camp found itself surrounded by a hollowed-out aesthetic project on one side and the vertiginous growth of an antidemocratic reaction on the other. There is only one guarantee: the old formulas, even if revisited, will not build a new world. They will, at best, build the image of a world that was meant to be built.

In the end, the work's great merit is to be common. Its trump card is to sell itself as something at hand, accessible to everyone. A popular product, not because it responds to the people's desire for luxury or because it reexamines the necessity of yearning for it, but because it is what it can be. An architecture that can redeem us from our idiosyncrasies and finally be accessible to all. Something good, safe, something that "won't fall down." Something that, if you save your meager resources for thirty years, you can one day afford. And, with luck, you will be able to put in the tile floor you've always wanted.

Biography

Jaime Solares Carmona is MSc Architect and Urban Planner (University of São Paulo, 2020). He holds a postdoctoral fellowship in architecture, education, and society at Escola da Cidade. He has been a member of the Critical Thinking and Contemporary City (PC3) research group since 2015, and coordinates the Educational Platform of IABsp. He has worked in several architecture firms, including ELEMENTAL Chile and Estúdio Mariana Wilderom. He has published articles in specialized media such as *ArchDaily* and *Architectural Journal* (China). His research focuses on the theory and critique of issues related to gender, the body, and sexuality in contemporary Brazilian architecture